New Nukes

India, Pakistan and Global
Nuclear Disarmament

D0890543

New Nukes

India, Pakistan and Global Nuclear Disarmament

by Praful Bidwai and Achin Vanaik
introduction by Arundhati Roy

OLIVE
BRANCH
PRESS

An imprint of Interlink Publishing Group, Inc.
NEW YORK

First published 2000 by

INTERLINK BOOKS
An imprint of Interlink Publishing Group, Inc.
99 Seventh Avenue • Brooklyn, New York 11215 and
46 Crosby Street • Northampton, Massachusetts 01060
www.interlinkbooks.com

Library of Congress Cataloging-in-Publication Data

Bidwai, Praful.
  New Nukes : India, Pakistan, and global nuclear disarmament / by
Praful Bidwai and Achin Vanaik ; introduction by Arundhati Roy.
      p.   cm.
  ISBN 1-56656-318-6 (hardback). — ISBN 1-56656-317-8 (pbk.)
  1. Nuclear nonproliferation.   II. Nuclear weapons--India--Testing.
  3. Nuclear weapons--Pakistan--Testing.   I. Vanaik, Achin.
  II. Title.
JZ5675.B53   1999
327 .1'747'0954--dc21   99-23965
                                                                    CIP

Printed and bound in Canada
10 9 8 7 6 5 4 3 2 1

Beg my boy's pardon!
Apologize on your knees
Those who made the atomic bomb!

—*Extracted from the poem, "I Wanted to Live" by the mother*
of Fumiki Nagoya, who died in Hiroshima at age seven.

This book is dedicated to the memory of the victims of Hiroshima and Nagasaki, and to the struggle for the abolition of nuclear weapons worldwide.

Contents

Acknowledgements

We would first and foremost like to thank Phyllis Bennis, of the Institute for Policy Studies and Olive Branch Press, who persuaded us, indeed insisted, that we should write this book now and that we should—and could—meet her extraordinarily demanding deadlines. This is our book, but it has emerged from her pushing, cajoling and encouragement, and hence owes a special and singular debt to her. We have also benefited from her editorial skills. However, she should not be held responsible for any deficiencies for which we alone must plead guilty.

We would also like to thank a number of other people, adult and junior, who have in one way or the other helped and inspired us. Special thanks are due to Zia Mian, Pervez Hoodbhoy and A.H. Nayyar of Pakistan, all of them scientific experts and courageous anti-nuclear activists both in their home country and internationally. We owe much to our discussions with them. Their practical solidarity in the common cause of regional and global nuclear disarmament has always been a source of strength to us, as has been the work and passionate concern of yet another scientist-peace activist, M.V. Ramana. Our gratitude also to Kanti Bajpai for his unstinting support and helpful suggestions.

Those familiar with the path-breaking critiques of political realism by Justin Rosenberg and Fred Halliday, both of the London School of Economics, (International Relations Department), will recognize the measure of our indebtedness to them. Fred Halliday, a former colleague at the Transnational Institute of Amsterdam, of which we are both Fellows, has been a stimulating source of ideas. We cannot fail to mention other TNI colleagues, in particular Fiona Dove, its present director and labor movement fighter against apartheid.

Thanks are also due to the following: To Olle Nordberg of the Dag Hammarskjold Foundation, Uppsala, who has been a great source of encouragement and who earlier published our joint little book, *Testing Times: The Global Stake in a Nuclear Test Ban (1996)*. To Neloufer de Mel, of the University of Colombo, who made several valuable comments on the manuscript. To Ritu Menon of the remarkable publishing venture, Kali for Women, on whose authority of judgment in publishing matters we have relied heavily. And to Krishna Raj, who edits that unique Mumbai-based journal, *Economic and Political Weekly*, where we have had an occasional column, "Nuclear Notebook" for over fifteen years, and who never tires of encouraging worthy causes.

Our friends in MIND (Movement in India for Nuclear Disarmament), of which we are proud activists, deserve a special mention, as do numerous others such as Admiral L. Ramdas, Amartya Sen, and author Arundhati Roy, who showed the courage of their convictions by swimming against the tide when it mattered the most.

Pamela Philipose has given us her moral and practical support, without which we could not so effectively have concentrated on the task at hand. Our thanks to Shri Ram Gupta for invaluable secretarial help; to Anish Vanaik whose computer expertise made him our regular troubleshooter/problem-solver in this regard; and finally to Samar Vanaik who carried out innumerable errands for us, despite occasional murmurs (good-humored we hope) about the use of child labor.

Preface

The South Asian Tinderbox in the Global Nuclear Setting

Less than eighteen months after India and Pakistan dealt the cause of nuclear restaint and disarmament a severe blow, it has suffered yet another jolt with the United States Senate rejecting the Comprehensive Test Ban TReaty (CTBT) in the vote for ratification. This shameful rejection, following systematic scheming and plotting by the Republican Right and a "little-too-late" committment by the Clinton Adminstration, represents a significant setback, itself part of a larger hardcore conservative agenda opposing all arms restraint and control. It weakens the entire post-Cold War global momentum favoring nuclear weapons elimination, and may even unravel existing resraint agreements. There is a real danger that the window of opportunity for a serious advance toward disarmament may slam shut.

In the South Asian region, the setback represented by the nuclear tests stands further enlarged by the outbreak of serious hostilities between India and Pakistan and the military coup in Pakistan, as well as the hardening of India's nuclear stance revealed in its "Draft Nuclear Doctrine" (August 1999). This Draft makes a mockery of the earlier posture of "minimality" by recklessly advocating an open-ended, super-ambitious, nuclear arsenal capable of prompt "punitive retaliation" against any nuclear adversary state or group of states. It signifies the beginning of a new Asian nuclear arms race.

The latest flare-up in the India-Pakistan conflict broke out once again over Kashmir. In the spring of 1999, Muslim guerrillas under Pakistani control, backed by army regulars, attacked across the Line of Control that separates the Indian and Pakistani zones of disputed Kashmir. India fought back, shelling the guerrilla positions. It was soon dubbed the "Kargil Crisis," after the town at the center of the fighting. As the conflict escalated, it brought an ominous turn to the South Asian nuclear crisis as a whole. Domestically, in Pakistan, it accelerated processes that culminated in the overthrow of the Nawaz Sharif government by the military.

Kargil was the first military conflict in nearly thirty years between the two recently nuclearized rivals. It was the only large-scale land-air conventional engagement ever between any two nuclear states. Kargil took a toll of nearly 1,300 lives (according to the Indian government) or over 1,750 (according to Pakistan). And there is a potential for more Kargils. Pakistan's top leaders make no bones about this.

Kargil confirms some of our worst fears and gives rise to new ones. Nuclearization has not only failed to instill greater confidence or maturity in either India or Pakistan or in their mutual relations, but instead has reinforced mutual distrust, fear, suspicion, and paranoia. Conflicts like Kargil, however limited, are militarily and politically destructive because they undermine the potential for improvement in regional security. Worse, they make a nuclear confrontation considerably likelier.

Indian and Pakistani leaders exchanged direct or indirect nuclear threats no less than thirteen times in just five weeks during the Kargil crisis. These varied from warnings that they wouldn't hesitate to use "any weapon," to threatening devastation in answer to the adversary's nuclear "threat."

It would be irresponsible to downplay the significance of such threat-mongering. During the Cold War, nuclear adversaries confronted one another, escalating military preparations and fighting countless proxy battles and full-scale surrogate wars. But since the 1962 Cuban missile crisis, it is hard to think of an instance where the US and the USSR exchanged serious threats of nuclear devastation so casually and cavalierly. It would be even harder to think of Washington and Moscow so easily resorting to purely military exchanges without first exploring diplomatic possibilities.

So what about the much touted summit between the Indian and Pakistani prime ministers, A.B. Vajpayee and Nawaz Sharif? This meeting, on February 20-21, 1999, culminated in the launch of the first-ever direct bus service between Delhi and Lahore and produced the Lahore Declaration that was to inaugurate a new era of *qualitative* improvement in mutual relations. Though all efforts at reducing tensions between the two neighbors are welcome, the fact is, Lahore brought limited results. India, having initiated the nuclear arms race in the region, had a vested interest in appearing moderate and "responsible." It is noteworthy that the summit did not emerge from a unilateral or even bilateral initiative; direct US mediation was crucial, with Deputy Secretary of State Strobe Talbott visiting New Delhi and Islamabad beforehand.

The bomb lobbies of both countries, however, went hyperbolic about the accomplishments of Lahore—the summit, they said, was an example of the security advantages gained by nuclear deterrence. Hawks on both sides claimed that with nuclearization, conventional wars would be averted. The Kargil fighting that broke out scarce weeks later meant that rarely had so many "nuclear experts" suffered so swift, embarrassing, and comprehensive a comeuppance and exposure of the falsity and naivete of their arguments.

The Lahore Declaration contained not one serious measure or even promise of nuclear restraint. Indeed, the agreement reached on extremely limited measures, such as informing each other beforehand of ballistic missile tests, effectively legitimized the very process of both countries' further nuclearization. On future nuclear tests, the moratorium in both countries would continue—unless "national interest" dictated otherwise!

The Kargil fighting, then, was not the total and blatant violation or negation of the "Lahore process" that it was made out to be. India and Pakistan's verbal nuclear war-mongering and one-upmanship during the conflict, and their failure afterwards to undertake any serious soul-searching, are hard to explain solely by the nature of their regimes, the revanchism and bitterness of their hawks, or even the severe crisis of legitimacy facing their rulers. It is crucial to understand that their search for nuclear weapons (especially India's) was not driven primarily by considerations of security and real, felt dangers, and how best to meet them.

That is why it has been so easy for New Delhi and Islamabad to practice a complex and deeply contradictory policy. On the one hand, they claim they need nuclear weapons for their security; on the other, they sever and disconnect nuclear weapons from real security, brandishing dangerous nuclear threats against each other. Had their search for nuclear weapons been organically linked to security, rather than to false notions of prestige, they would not have behaved in such a grossly irresponsible manner.

This is obviously not the place for a lengthy discussion of the genesis of the Kargil crisis, Pakistan's wrongful violation of the Line of Control (LoC) status quo, or the larger Kashmir conflict. But the Kargil confrontation is best understood through the prism of three phenomena. First, it derives from long-term India-Pakistan hostility and what either or both regard as "unresolved" issues, including Kashmir. Thus, sections in India and Pakistan's armed forces and secret services, backed by political leaders, have always wanted to "get even" with one another through covert operations, and low-cost, low-intensity warfare.

Pakistan's army leaders clearly saw the Kargil LoC as India's Achilles' heel, where infiltrating a few hundred troops/guerrillas could destabilize the situation. They were emboldened by New Delhi's failure to anticipate this or to heed intelligence warnings. Even if this misadventure had succeeded, it would not have given Islamabad significant strategic advantage. But the fact it was still launched, at considerable political-diplomatic cost to Pakistan, speaks of the strength of the bitterness among Islamabad's hawks.

Secondly, although its planning may have preceded the Lahore meeting, the Kargil operation must also be seen as an attempt to undermine whatever positive momentum and spirit of conciliation the summit generated. There has been strong resentment against conciliation within the Pakistan military establishment and the political-religious right.

The resentment toward the Lahore process was stronger in Pakistan, where some saw the Declaration as Islamabad's retreat from an aggressive Kashmir agenda. To these hardliners, challenging India by crossing the LoC around Kargil, while masking it as a "spontaneous" act led by the *mujahideen*, or God's soldiers—although this is inconceivable at that altitude without

Pakistani army support—must have seemed a worthwhile low-cost strategy. If it failed, the (military) costs would not be high. If it succeeded, Pakistan would have, in effect, altered the LoC alignment, and internationally highlighted the Kashmir issue as never before. Even former Prime Minister Nawaz Sharif was probably tempted to try this out.

The third and extraordinarily important factor, however, was that South Asia's nuclearization seems to have created a false sense of complacency in India, coupled with greater willingness in Pakistan to embark on military misadventures. As we argue in this book, many political and military leaders and strategic "experts" in the two countries permit themselves the dangerous delusion of invulnerability on account of their bombs. Their sordidly boastful claims of superior military-nuclear prowess reflect a nuclear mindset that tempts them to raise the conventional danger threshold, to see how far they can irritate and harass the adversary at the sub-war level. They believe their opponent will only make a nuclear threat *in extremis*, once many levels of tolerance have been crossed. Ergo, brinkmanship is in order. Besides, they believe in their own deterrent.

As is usual with most such military "plans," this game-theory scenario failed to account for one vital factor—*politics* and the role of the international community. The world was horrified by Kargil's potential for something far more destructive than limited conventional warfare. The Big Powers got active. A three-way "dialogue-facilitation" process began at the initiative of the US, which favored India's stand on the LoC, led to Pakistan's isolation, and finally to the July 4 Clinton meeting with Nawaz Sharif in Washington that resulted in a phased pullout of Pakistan-backed forces.

Both India and Pakistan ended up paying heavily for Kargil. Pakistan was politically weakened, winning little support from its old friend China, let alone the US. Internally, Kargil dealt another blow to democratization, further weakened the crisis-ridden economy, and aggravated the regime's legitimacy crisis. The explosion of religious bigotry and Islamic fanaticism was a severe setback to Pakistan's healthy development.

Kargil greatly sharpened civilian-military differences within Pakistan. The army was bitter at Nawaz Sharif's decision to pull back the mujahideen and Pakistani troops. The decision was widely condemned by the political opposition too as a betrayal of the cause of Kashmir's "liberation." Sharif tried to manipulate and subjugate the army leadership, as he had done with all other institutions. His attempt recoiled.

Thus it was not a total surprise when on October 12, General Pervez Musharraf overthrew Sharif, suspended the constitution and imposed military rule. This was more a counter-coup than a coup since Sharif was himself planning to replace key figures in the armed forces with loyalists, so as to strangthen himself. Nonetheless, the takeover revealed the utter fragility of the Pakistani establishment and rifts within its military leadership, and the great temptation for any Pakistani government to use external tension as both a factor of diversion and domestic "unification." An endemically unstable but nuclearized Pakistan under military rule is obviously far worse for South Asian and global security than a stable Pakistan under civilian rule.

Whereas nowhere as onerous as in Pakistan, the costs that India bore on account of Kargil were not insignificant. India lost hundreds of men—410 according to the government. (This is almost certainly a gross underestimate: the number of wounded was said to be 594, and an injured-to-dead ratio of 4 or 5 to 1 is the accepted Indian norm.) The economic cost for India was over $2.5 billion in direct expenses—all to recover its own territory in "peacetime." The economic toll will mount as the Kargil LoC is patrolled daily, becoming the next Siachen. Since 1984, India and Pakistan have lost over 10,000 lives and spent $10 million a day patrolling this glacier, the highest point of military confrontation anywhere in the world. But even heavier have been the social costs: the outbreaks of jingoism and religious chauvinism; the celebrations of militarism and male-supremacy; the growth of intolerance, media manipulation, and censorship; and the suppression of debate and dissent. These costs are only one component of the social and economic burden that nuclearization will impose on two of the world's poorest societies—a burden that deserves to be more deeply explored than we have been able to do here.

The specifically nuclear lessons of Kargil are also clear. The conflict dramatically highlighted South Asia as *the* most likely place in the world for a nuclear exchange to take place. It is when war-time or near war-time conditions prevail that a nuclear outbreak becomes most likely—whether because brinkmanship goes over the edge, hostile emotions and suspicions get out of hand, or the dynamic of military escalation careens out of control.

Kargil revealed the horrific absurdity of relying on nuclear deterrence. The most faithful Indian adherents of this doctrine repeatedly declared during the conflict that Pakistan is a "rogue state," with leaders who are "irrational," irresponsible and impossible to trust not to use nuclear weapons—so India *had* to be "prepared." Many of them also declared that the US would somehow ensure that Pakistan would not use its nuclear weapons. What then became of the assured efficacy that these same people had attributed to the workings of *mutual* India-Pakistan deterrence?

One of the dangerous outcomes of the Kargil crisis was to increase the influence of the religious fundamentalist forces in both countries. These groups, in their demonizing of the Other, essentialize the mutual hostility, rooting it in the allegedly "incompatible" nature of Islam and Hinduism, leading to the false conclusion that the sources of conflict are permanent and inescapable, and therefore beyond the Kashmir issue alone. This is a recipe for political disaster. Such demonization feeds on itself, reinforcing the tendency in each country to prepare for or even pre-empt the worst expected from the other side—including the use of nuclear weapons.

Frightening as the possibility of a nuclear exchange was during the Kargil crisis, it can only be magnified once India and Pakistan openly deploy nuclear weapons, and their intentional or accidental use becomes even more likely.

Kargil's nuclear warning is clear. India and Pakistan must move firmly toward denuclearization, beginning with an immediate freeze on nuclear and missile development and fissile material production—meaning no further weaponization, no induction, and no deployment. Both countries must accede to the Comprehensive Test Ban Treaty (CTBT), even though the US has refused to ratify it, and be pressed to carry out the actual dismantling of their nuclear-fission assemblies. Nuclear and military tensions between them must be systematically reduced. This is unlikely to happen through bilateral talks alone, which in any case would require, as with Lahore, international pressure to take shape.

There is indeed a strong case for some external encouragement, if not intervention, to defuse the India-Pakistan nuclear rivalry, especially across the LoC, where they confront each other so menacingly. Who, morally or politically, could oppose external, multilateral, intervention to separate Indian and Pakistan forces physically should they move toward nuclear engagement? One positive, if unintended, "gain" from Kargil, then, is that it has focused world attention on the volatility of the India-Pakistan strategic situation and the critical importance of Kashmir. Of course, in order to be fair, equitable, effective and sustainable, such intervention would need to be multilateral, non-manipulative, and strictly neutral.

India and Pakistan have to accept a bitter lesson. India crossed the nuclear threshold largely out of its grandiose ambition to influence world affairs. Neither was Pakistan immune to exaggerated ideas about enhancing its world stature when it decided to go nuclear. Both countries now have to pay a price: the world will now influence *their* affairs. Kargil underscores this, even as it darkens the nuclear shadow over the one-fourth of humanity that lives in South Asia.

But most of the impetus toward denuclearization must come from within. Kargil made many Indians and Pakistanis distinctly uneasy about the existence of nuclear weapons in the armories of two such intensely and openly hostile rivals. Even many who had welcomed the nuclear tests of May 1998 were affected by this unease. But this *unease* has yet to be translated into *active opposition* to nuclear weapons and a practical demand for their non-manufacture, non-deployment, and rapid dismantling.

Indeed, in India, media-cultivated jingoism and false euphoria over "victory" in Kargil threatens these stirrings of discomfort. In Pakistan too, the bomb lobby is trying to provide false assurances that nuclear weapons remain necessary for the country's security. Its weight within the establishment has risen after the major setback to democratization represented by the military coup. And yet, there is anti-nuclear protest in both countries. The protection of this nascent spirit of protest, and its cultivation as a powerful sentiment and force of opposition to nuclearism, is a moral and political imperative. As is the struggle in the older nuclear weapons states to eradicate the nuclear scourge forever. We hope this book can contribute to that goal.

—New Delhi, December 1, 1999

We wrote many articles on the Lahore summit and the Kargil crisis—articles that were critical of both governments' handling of the issue, warned against escalation, and took a strong stand against jingoism and chauvinism. Most of them can be accessed through the website of "South Asians Against Nuclear Weapons" [www.mnet.fr\aiindex\NoNukes.html]. Here is a non-exhaustive list:

Praful Bidwai, "From Pokharan to Kargil: the Nuclear Danger is No Fantasy," The Times of India, (New Delhi) 2 June 1999; "India-Pakistan Hold Reins to World's Nuclear Future," The Daily Star (Dhaka) 1 January 1999; "Bus Diplomacy," Mid-Day (Mumbai) 17 February 1999; "Pakistan-India Ties: Talking Peace but far from Detente," Dawn (Karachi) 25 February 1999; "Indo-Pak Conciliation: The Nuclear Shadow Must Go," The Times of India (New Delhi) 20 March 1999; "Voices for Peace," Frontline (Chennai) 26 March 1999; "Can There Ever Be Peace between India and Pakistan?" The Sunday Times of India (New Delhi) 2 June 1999; "Sack George," Mid-Day (Mumbai) 6 June 1999; "Information War," Mid-Day (Mumbai) 16 June 1999; "Playing with Fire in Kargil," Frontline (Chennai) 18 June 1999; "Kosovo, Kargil, Kashmir: towards South Asia's Denuclearisation," The Times of India (New Delhi) 19 June 1999; "Border Situation Becomes more Dangerous," Inter-Press Service, 30 June 1999; "And Now, Information Warfare," Frontline (Chennai) 2 July 1999; "Between Two Stools: BJP's Flawed Kargil Strategy," The Kashmir Times (Jammu) 4 July 1999; "No Place for Triumphalism: don't Demonise Pakistan," The Kashmir Times (Jammu) 12 July 1999; "Voice of Reason," Mid-Day (Mumbai) 14 July 1999; "The Charade over Kargil: no "Secret Deal," Mr Vajpayee?," The Kashmir Times, (Jammu) 19 July 1999; "The Mind War," Mid-Day (Mumbai) 21 July 1999; "Kargil Raised Risk of Nuclear Confrontation," Inter-Press Service, 27 July 1999; "Misplaced Triumphalism," Frontline (Chennai) 30 July 1999; "A Kargil Post-Mortem: Now Comes the Hefty Bill," The Kashmir Times (Jammu) 26 July 1999; "What a Waste!," Mid-Day (Mumbai) 28 July 1999.

Achin Vanaik, "The Politics of Symbolism," The Hindu (New Delhi) March 18, 1999; "Mediation is the Message," The Telegraph (Calcutta) 26 July 1999; "No Paradigm Shift," The Hindu (New Delhi) 23 July 1999.

For a longer discussion of the Kashmir issue, see Achin Vanaik, India in a Changing World, Orient Longman, Delhi, 1994, chapter 5; and Praful Bidwai, "Face to Face with Janus?: Kashmir's Challenge to Nationalism," Frontline (Chennai) 3 December 1993; "Narasimha Rao's Kashmir Gambit: A Recipe for Trouble," Frontline (Chennai) 1 December 1995; "New Opening in J&K: The Art. 370 plus Solution," Newstime (Hyderabad) 7 October 1996.

Introduction

The End of Imagination

The desert shook, the Government of India informed us (its people).

The whole mountain turned white, the Government of Pakistan replied.

By afternoon the wind had fallen silent over Pokhran. At 3:45 P.M., the timer detonated the three devices. Around 200 to 300 meters deep in the earth, the heat generated was equivalent to a million degrees centigrade—as hot as temperatures on the sun. Instantly, rocks weighing around a thousand tons, a mini mountain underground, vaporized... shockwaves from the blast began to lift a mound of earth the size of a football field by several meters. One scientist on seeing it said, "I can now believe stories of Lord Krishna lifting a hill."
—India Today

MAY 1998. It'll go down in history books, provided of course we have history books to go down in. Provided, of course, we have a future.

There's nothing new or original left to be said about nuclear weapons. There can be nothing more humiliating for a writer of fiction to have to do than restate a case that has, over the years, already been made by other people in other parts of the world, and made passionately, eloquently, and knowledgeably.

I am prepared to grovel. To humiliate myself abjectly, because, in the circumstances, silence would be indefensible. So those of you who are willing: let's pick our parts, put on these discarded costumes and speak our second-hand lines in this sad second-hand play. But let's not forget that the stakes we're playing for are huge. Our fatigue and our shame could mean the end of us. The end of our children and our children's children. Of everything we love. We have to reach within ourselves and find the strength to think. To fight.

Once again we are pitifully behind the times—not just scientifically and technologically (ignore the hollow claims) but more pertinently in our ability to grasp the true nature of nuclear weapons. Our Comprehension of the Horror Department is hopelessly obsolete. Here we are, all of us in India and in Pakistan, discussing the finer points of politics and foreign policy, behaving for all the world as though our governments have just devised a newer, bigger bomb, a sort of immense hand grenade with which they will annihilate the enemy (each other) and protect us from all harm.

How desperately we want to believe that. What wonderful, willing, well-behaved, gullible subjects we have turned out to be. The rest of humanity may not forgive us, but then the rest of the rest of humanity, depending on who fashions its views, may not know what a tired, dejected, heart-broken people we are. Perhaps it doesn't realize how urgently we need a miracle. How deeply we yearn for magic.

If only, if *only* nuclear war was just another kind of war. If only it was about the usual things—nations and territories, gods and histories. If only those of us who dread it are worthless moral cowards who are not prepared to die in defense of our beliefs. If only nuclear war was the kind of war in which countries battle countries, and men battle men. But it isn't. If there is a nuclear war, our foes will not be China or America or even each other. Our foe will be the earth herself. Our cities and forests, our fields and villages will burn for days. Rivers will turn to poison. The air will become fire. The wind will spread the flames. When everything there is to burn has burned and the fires die, smoke will rise and shut out the sun. The earth will be enveloped in darkness. There will be no day—only interminable night.

What shall we do then, those of us who are still alive? Burned and blind and bald and ill, carrying the cancerous carcasses of our children in our arms, where shall we go? What shall we eat? What shall we drink? What shall we breathe?

The Head of the Health, Environment and Safety Group of the Bhabha Atomic Research Center in Bombay has a plan. He declared that India could survive nuclear war. His advice is that in the event of nuclear war we take the same safety measures as the ones that scientists have recommended in the event of accidents at nuclear plants.

Take iodine pills, he suggests. And other steps such as remaining indoors, consuming only stored water and food and avoiding milk. Infants should be given powdered milk. "People in the danger zone should immediately go to the ground floor and if possible to the basement."

What do you do with these levels of lunacy? What do you do if you're trapped in an asylum and the doctors are all dangerously deranged?

Ignore it, it's just a novelist's naiveté, they'll tell you, Doomsday Prophet hyperbole. It'll never come to that. There will be no war. Nuclear weapons are about peace, not war. "Deterrence" is the buzz word of the people who like to think of themselves as hawks. (Nice birds, those. Cool. Stylish. Predatory. Pity there won't be many of them around after the war. Extinction is a word we must try to get used to.) Deterrence is an old thesis that has been resurrected and is being recycled with added local flavor. The Theory of Deterrence cornered the credit for having prevented the cold war from turning into a third world war. The only immutable fact about the third world war is that, if there's going to be one, it will be fought after the second world war. In other words, there's no fixed schedule.

The Theory of Deterrence has some fundamental flaws. Flaw Number One is that it presumes a complete, sophisticated understanding of the psychology of your enemy. It assumes that what deters you (the fear of annihilation) will deter them. What about those who are not deterred by that? The suicide bomber psyche—the "We'll take you with us" school—is that an outlandish thought? How did Rajiv Gandhi die?

In any case who's the "you" and who's the "enemy"? Both are only governments. Governments change. They wear masks within masks. They molt and re-invent themselves all the time. The one we have at the moment, for instance, does not even have enough seats to last a full term in office, but demands that we trust it to do pirouettes and party tricks with nuclear bombs even as it scrabbles around for a foothold to maintain a simple majority in Parliament.

Flaw Number Two is that deterrence is premised on fear. But fear is premised on knowledge. On an understanding of the true extent and scale of the devastation that nuclear war will wreak. It is not some inherent, mystical attribute of nuclear bombs that they automatically inspire thoughts of peace. On the contrary, it is the endless, tireless, confrontational work of people who have had the courage to openly denounce them, the marches, the demonstrations, the films, the outrage—*that* is what has averted, or perhaps only postponed, nuclear war. Deterrence will not and cannot work given the levels of ignorance and illiteracy that hang over our two countries like dense, impenetrable veils.

India and Pakistan have nuclear bombs now and feel entirely justified in having them. Soon others will too. Israel, Iran, Iraq, Saudi Arabia, Norway, Nepal (I'm trying to be eclectic here), Denmark, Germany, Bhutan, Mexico, Lebanon, Sri Lanka, Burma, Bosnia, Singapore, North Korea, Sweden, South Korea, Vietnam, Cuba, Afghanistan, Uzbekistan... and why not? Every country in the world has a special case to make. Everybody has borders and beliefs.

And when all our larders are bursting with shiny bombs and our bellies are empty (deterrence is an exorbitant beast), we can trade bombs for food. And when nuclear technology goes on the market, when it gets truly competitive and prices fall, not just governments but anybody who can afford it can have their own private arsenal—businessmen, terrorists, perhaps even the occasional rich writer (like me). Our planet will bristle with beautiful missiles. There will be a new world order. The dictatorship of the pro-nuke elite.

But let us pause to give credit where it's due. Who must we thank for all this? The men who made it happen. The Masters of the Universe. Ladies and gentlemen, the United States of America! Come on up here folks, stand up and take a bow. Thank you for doing this to the world. Thank you for making a difference. Thank you for showing us the way. Thank you for altering the very meaning of life.

From now on it is not dying we must fear, but living.

All I can say to every man, woman and sentient child in India, and over there, just a little way away in Pakistan, is: take it personally. Whoever you are—Hindu, Muslim, urban, agrarian—it doesn't matter. The only good thing about nuclear war is that it is the single most egalitarian idea that man has ever had. On the day of reckoning, you will not be asked to present your credentials. The devastation will be indiscriminate. The bomb isn't in your backyard. It's in your body. And mine. *Nobody*, no nation, no government, no man, no god has the right to put it there. We're radioactive already, and the war hasn't even begun. So stand up and say something. Never mind if it's been said before. Speak up on your own behalf. Take it very personally.

The Bomb and I

In early May (before the bomb), I left home for three weeks. I thought I would return. I had every intention of returning. Of course things haven't worked out quite the way I had planned. While I was away, I met a friend whom I have always loved for, among other things, her ability to combine deep affection with a frankness that borders on savagery. "I've been thinking about you," she said, "about *The God of Small Things*—what's in it, what's over it, under it, around it, above it..."

She fell silent for a while. I was uneasy and not at all sure that I wanted to hear the rest of what she had to say. She, however, was sure that she was going to say it. "In this last year—less than a year actually—you've had too much of everything—fame, money, prizes, adulation, criticism, condemnation, ridicule, love, hate, anger, envy, generosity—everything. In some ways it's a perfect story. Perfectly baroque in its excess. The trouble is that it has, or can have, only one perfect ending."

Her eyes were on me, bright with a slanting, probing brilliance. She knew that I knew what she was going to say. She was insane. She was going to say that nothing that happened to me in the future could ever match the buzz of this. That the whole of the rest of my life was going to be vaguely unsatisfying. And, therefore, the only perfect ending to the story would be death. My death.

The thought had occurred to me too. Of course it had. The fact that all this, this global dazzle—these lights in my eyes, the applause, the flowers, the photographers, the journalists feigning a deep interest in my life (yet struggling to get a single fact straight), the men in suits fawning over me, the shiny hotel bathrooms with endless towels—none of it was likely to happen again. Would I miss it? Had I grown to need it? Was I a fame-junkie? Would I have withdrawal symptoms?

The more I thought about it, the clearer it became to me that if fame was going to be my permanent condition it would kill me. Club me to death with its good manners and hygiene. I'll admit that I've enjoyed my own five minutes of it immensely, but primarily *because* it was just five minutes. Because I knew (or thought I knew) that I could go home when I was bored and giggle about it. Grow old and irresponsible. Eat mangoes in the moonlight. Maybe write a couple of failed books—worst sellers—to see what it felt like. For a whole year I've cartwheeled across the world, anchored always to thoughts of home and the life I would go back to.

Contrary to all the inquiries and predictions about my impending emigration, that was the well I dipped into. That was my sustenance. My strength. I told my friend there was no such thing as a perfect story. I said that in any case hers was an external view of things, this assumption that the trajectory of a person's happiness, or let's say fulfillment, had peaked (and now must trough) because she had accidentally stumbled upon "success." It was premised on the unimaginative belief that wealth and fame were the mandatory stuff of everybody's dreams.

You've lived too long in New York, I told her. There are other worlds. Other kinds of dreams. Dreams in which failure is feasible, honorable, sometimes even worth striving for. Worlds in which recognition is not the only barometer of brilliance or human worth. There are plenty of warriors I know and love, people far more valuable than myself, who go to war each day, knowing in advance that they will fail. True, they are less "successful" in the most vulgar sense of the word, but by no means less fulfilled.

The only dream worth having, I told her, is to dream that you will live while you're alive and die only when you're dead. (Prescience? Perhaps.)

"Which means exactly what?" (Arched eyebrows, a little annoyed.)

I tried to explain, but didn't do a very good job of it. Sometimes I need to write to think. So I wrote it down for her on a paper napkin. This is what I wrote: *To love. To be loved. To never forget your own insignificance. To never get used to the unspeakable violence and the vulgar disparity of life around you. To seek joy in the saddest places. To pursue beauty to its lair. To never simplify what is complicated or complicate what is simple. To respect strength, never power. Above all, to watch. To try and understand. To never look away. And never, never to forget.*

I've known her for many years, this friend of mine. She's an architect too. She looked dubious, somewhat unconvinced by my paper napkin speech. I could tell that structurally, just in terms of the sleek, narrative symmetry of things, and because she loves me, her thrill at my "success" was so keen, so generous, that it weighed in evenly with her (anticipated) horror at the idea of my death. I understood that it was nothing personal... Just a design thing.

Anyhow, two weeks after that conversation, I returned to India. To what I think/thought of as home. Something had died but it wasn't me. It was infinitely more precious. It was a world that has been ailing for a while, and has finally breathed its last. It's been cremated now. The air is thick with ugliness and there's the unmistakable stench of fascism on the breeze.

Day after day, in newspaper editorials, on the radio, on TV chat shows, on MTV for heaven's sake, people whose instincts one thought one could trust—writers, painters, journalists—make the crossing. The chill seeps into my bones as it becomes painfully apparent from the lessons of everyday life that what you read in history books is true. That fascism is indeed as much about people as about governments. That it begins at home. In drawing rooms. In bedrooms. In beds. "Explosion of self-esteem," "Road to Resurgence," "A Moment of Pride," these were headlines in the papers in the days following the nuclear tests. "We have proved that we are not eunuchs any more," said Mr. Thackeray of the *Shiv Sena* (Whoever said we were? True, a good number of us are women, but that, as far as I know, isn't the same thing.) Reading the papers, it was often hard to tell when people were referring to Viagra (which was competing for second place on the front pages) and when they were talking about the bomb: "We have superior strength and potency." (This was our Minister for Defense after Pakistan completed its tests.)

"These are not just nuclear tests, they are nationalism tests," we were repeatedly told.

This has been hammered home, over and over again. The bomb is India. India is the bomb. Not just India, Hindu India. Therefore, be warned, any criticism of it is not just anti-national but anti-Hindu. (Of course in Pakistan the bomb is Islamic. Other than that, politically, the same physics applies.) This is one of the unexpected perks of having a nuclear bomb. Not only can the government use it to threaten the Enemy, they can use it to declare war on their own people. Us. When I told my friends that I was writing this piece, they cautioned me. "Go ahead," they said, "but first make sure you're not vulnerable. Make sure your papers are in order. Make sure your taxes are paid."

My papers are in order. My taxes are paid. But how can one not be vulnerable in a climate like this? Everyone is vulnerable. Accidents happen. There's safety only in acquiescence. As I write, I am filled with foreboding. In this country, I have truly known what it means for a writer to feel loved (and, to some degree, hated too). Last year I was one of the items being paraded in the media's end-of-the-year National Pride Parade. Among the others, much to my mortification, were a bomb-maker and an international beauty queen. Each time a beaming person stopped me on the street and said "You have made India proud" (referring to the prize I won, not the book I wrote), I felt a little uneasy. It frightened me then and it terrifies me now, because I know how easily that swell, that tide of emotion, can turn against me. Perhaps the time for that has come. I'm going to step out from under the fairy lights and say what's on my mind.

It's this:

If protesting against having a nuclear bomb implanted in my brain is anti-Hindu and anti-national, then I secede. I hereby declare myself an independent, mobile republic. I am a citizen of the earth. I own no territory. I have no flag. I'm female, but have nothing against eunuchs. My policies are simple. I'm willing to sign any nuclear non-proliferation treaty or nuclear test ban treaty that's going. Immigrants are welcome. You can help me design our flag. My world has died. And I write to mourn its passing.

India's nuclear tests, the manner in which they were conducted, the euphoria with which they have been greeted (by us) is indefensible. To me, it signifies dreadful things. The end of imagination.

On the 15th of August last year we celebrated the 50th anniversary of India's independence. Next May we can mark our first anniversary in nuclear bondage.

Why did they do it? Political expediency is the obvious, cynical answer, except that it only raises another, more basic question: Why should it have been politically expedient? The three Official Reasons given are: China, Pakistan and Exposing Western Hypocrisy.

Taken at face value, and examined individually, they're somewhat baffling. I'm not for a moment suggesting that these are not real issues. Merely that they aren't new. The only new thing on the old horizon is the Indian government. In his appallingly cavalier letter to the US president our prime minister says India's decision to go ahead with the nuclear tests was due to a "deteriorating security environment." He goes on to mention the war with China in 1962 and the "three aggressions we have suffered in the last fifty years [from Pakistan]. And for the last ten years we have been the victim of unremitting terrorism and militancy sponsored by it... especially in Jammu and Kashmir."

The war with China is thirty-five years old. Unless there's some vital state secret that we don't know about, it certainly seemed as though matters had improved slightly between us. The most recent war with Pakistan was fought twenty-seven years ago. Admittedly Kashmir continues to be a deeply troubled region and no doubt Pakistan is gleefully fanning the flames. But surely there must be flames to fan in the first place?

As for the third Official Reason: Exposing Western Hypocrisy—how much more exposed can they be? Which decent human being on earth harbors any illusions about it? These are people whose histories are spongy with the blood of others. Colonialism, apartheid, slavery, ethnic cleansing, germ warfare, chemical weapons, they virtually invented it all. They have plundered nations, snuffed out civilizations, exterminated entire populations. They stand on the world's stage stark naked but entirely unembarrassed, because they know that they have more money, more food, and bigger bombs than anybody else. They know they can wipe us out in the course of an ordinary working day. Personally, I'd say it is arrogance more than hypocrisy.

We have less money, less food, and smaller bombs. However, we have, or had, all kinds of other wealth. Delightful, unquantifiable. What we've done with it is the opposite of what we think we've done. We've pawned it all. We've traded it in. For what? In order to enter into a contract with the very people we claim to despise.

All in all, I think it is fair to say that we're the hypocrites. We're the ones who've abandoned what was arguably a moral position—i.e., *We have the technology, we can make bombs if we want to, but we won't. We don't believe in them.*

We're the ones who have now set up this craven clamoring to be admitted into the club of superpowers. For India to demand the status of a superpower is as ridiculous as demanding to play in the World Cup finals simply because we have a ball. Never mind that we haven't qualified, or that we don't play much soccer and haven't got a team.

We are a nation of nearly a billion people. In development terms we rank number 138 out of the 175 countries listed in the UNDP's Human Development Index (even Ghana and Sri Lanka rank above us). More than 400 million of our people are illiterate and live in absolute poverty, more than 600 million lack even basic sanitation, and more than 200 million have no safe drinking water.

The nuclear bomb and the demolition of the Babri Masjid in Ayodhya are both part of the same political process. They are hideous byproducts of a nation's search for herself. Of India's efforts to forge a national identity. The poorer the nation, the larger the numbers of illiterate people and the more morally bankrupt her leaders, the cruder and more dangerous the notion of what that identity is or should be.

The jeering, hooting young men who battered down the Barbi Masjid are the same ones whose pictures appeared in the papers in the days that followed the nuclear tests. They were on the streets, celebrating India's nuclear bomb and simultaneously "condemning Western Culture" by emptying crates of Coke and Pepsi into public drains. I'm a little baffled by their logic: Coke is Western Culture, but the nuclear bomb is an old Indian tradition?

Yes, I've heard—the bomb is in the Vedas. It might be, but if you look hard enough you'll find Coke in the Vedas too. That's the great thing about all religious texts. You can find anything you want in them—as long as you know what you're looking for.

But returning to the subject of the non-vedic 1990s: we storm the heart of whiteness, we embrace the most diabolical creation of western science and call it our own. But we protest against their music, their food, their clothes, their cinema and their literature. That's not hypocrisy. That's humor.

It's funny enough to make a skull smile.

We're back on the old ship. The SS Authenticity & Indianness.

If there is going to be a pro-authenticity/anti-national drive, perhaps the government ought to get its history straight and its facts right. If they're going to do it, they may as well do it properly. First of all, the original inhabitants of this land were not Hindu. Ancient though it is, there were human beings on earth before there was Hinduism. India's tribal people have a greater claim to being indigenous to this land than anybody else, and how are they treated by the state and its minions? Oppressed, cheated, robbed of their lands, shunted around like surplus goods. Perhaps a good place to start would be to restore to them the dignity that was once theirs. Perhaps the government could make a public undertaking that more dams of this kind will not be built, that more people will not be displaced.

But of course that would be inconceivable, wouldn't it? Why? Because it's impractical. Because tribal people don't really matter. Their histories, their customs, their deities are dispensable. They must learn to sacrifice these things for the greater good of the Nation (that has snatched from them everything they ever had).

Okay, so that's out.

For the rest, I could compile a practical list of things to ban and buildings to break. It'll need some research, but off the top of my head here are a few suggestions.

They could begin by banning a number of ingredients from our cuisine: chilies (Mexico), tomatoes (Peru), potatoes (Bolivia), coffee (Morocco), tea, white sugar, cinnamon (China)... they could then move into recipes. Tea with milk and sugar, for instance (Britain). Smoking will be out of the question. Tobacco came from North America. Cricket, English and Democracy should be forbidden. Either *kabaddi* or *kho-kho* could replace cricket. I don't want to start a riot, so I hesitate to suggest a replacement for English. (Italian? It has found its way to us via a kinder route: marriage, not imperialism.)

All hospitals in which western medicine is practiced or prescribed should be shut down. All national newspapers discontinued. The railways dismantled. Airports closed. And what about our newest toy—the mobile phone? Can we live without it, or shall I suggest that they make an exception there? They could put it down in the column marked "Universal?" (Only essential commodities will be included here. No music, art or literature.)

Needless to say, sending your children to university in the US, and rushing there yourself to have your prostate operated upon will be a cognizable offense.

It will be a long, long list. It would take years of work. I could not use a computer because that wouldn't be very authentic of me, would it?

I don't mean to be facetious, merely to point out that this is surely the shortcut to hell. There's no such thing as an Authentic India or a Real Indian. There is no Divine Committee that has the right to sanction one single, authorized version of what India is or should be.

Railing against the past will not heal us. History has *happened*. It's over and done with. All we can do is to change its course by encouraging what we love instead of destroying what we don't. There is beauty yet in this brutal, damaged world of ours. Hidden, fierce, immense. Beauty that is uniquely ours and beauty that we have received with grace from others, enhanced, re-invented and made our own. We have to seek it out, nurture it, love it. Making bombs will only destroy us. It doesn't *matter* whether we use them or not. They will destroy us either way.

India's nuclear bomb is the final act of betrayal by a ruling class that has failed its people. However many garlands we heap on our scientists, however many medals we pin to their chests, the truth is that it's far easier to make a bomb than to educate four hundred million people. According to opinion polls, we're expected to believe that there's a national consensus on the issue. It's official now. Everybody loves the bomb. (Therefore the bomb is good.)

Is it possible for a man who cannot write his own name to understand even the basic, elementary facts about the nature of nuclear weapons? Has anybody told him that nuclear war has nothing at all to do with his received notions of war? Nothing to do with honor, nothing to do with pride. Has anybody bothered to explain to him about thermal blasts, radioactive fallout and the nuclear winter? Are there even words in his language to describe the concepts of enriched uranium, fissile material and critical mass? Or has his language itself become obsolete? Is he trapped in a time capsule, watching the world pass him by, unable to understand or communicate with it because his language never took into account the horrors that the human race would dream up? Does he not matter at all, this man?

I'm not talking about one man, of course, I'm talking about millions and millions of people who live in this country. This is their land too, you know. They have the right to make an informed decision about its fate and, as far as I can tell, nobody has informed them about anything. The tragedy is that nobody could, even if they wanted to. Truly, literally, there's no language to do it in. This is the real horror of India. The orbits of the powerful and the powerless spinning further and further apart from each other, never intersecting, sharing nothing. Not a language. Not even a country.

Who the hell conducted those opinion polls? Who the hell is the prime minister to decide whose finger will be on the nuclear button that could turn everything we love—our earth, our skies, our mountains, our plains, our rivers, our cities and villages—to ash in an instant? Who the hell is he to reassure us that there will be no accidents? How does he know? Why should we trust him? What has he ever done to make us trust him? What have any of them ever done to make us trust them?

The nuclear bomb is the most anti-democratic, anti-national, anti-human, outright evil thing that man has ever made. If you are religious, then remember that this bomb is Man's challenge to God. It's worded quite simply: *We have the power to destroy everything that You have created.* If you're not religious, then look at it this way. This world of ours is four billion, six hundred million years old.

It could end in an afternoon.

—Arundhati Roy

This article originally appeared in the The Guardian (UK) August 1, 1998. Another version of this article was published in Frontline (India) August 1–14, 1998. Reprinted by permission.

Chapter 1

The Top Story of the Century

The nuclear bombing of Hiroshima and Nagasaki remains the top news story of all of the twentieth century. That is the conclusion of a February 1999 survey of opinion of top US journalists and scholars, conducted by "Newseum," an archive on news gathering.

Hiroshima was the Number One choice, well ahead in salience of Astronaut Neil Armstrong's walk on the moon, Japan's bombing of Pearl Harbor, and President Kennedy's assassination. It scored several ranks higher than Watergate, the invention of penicillin, or the making of the microchip-based personal computer, and at another remove, above the extension of the franchise to women and racial desegregation of schools in the US.[1]

No doubt Hiroshima and Nagasaki would be regarded as the top news stories of the century in many other countries of the world as well.

Nuclearism: Sanctification or Popularization?

The shattering impression on the public mind of those climactic moments of twentieth century history came from the revelation of the two inextricable dimensions of nuclear weapons—first, their incredible power and second, the epochal destruction and unimaginable suffering that they can cause. Embodying and symbolizing both these dimensions, nuclear weapons have evoked awe and revulsion, wonder and horror from their first use. They have continued to do so ever since.

The most ardent advocates of nuclear weapons have constantly sought to invest these weapons with a religious-like authority and importance—to emphasize the awe and wonder rather than the revulsion and horror—and to give them an accepted and respectable place in the mass popular culture of our times. What better way to legitimize their existence than to do both?

If nuclear weapons can come to acquire the same "profound value" as the sacred symbols that condense the meaning and purpose of a religion, and if the discourse surrounding them can seem as arcane and complex as the higher reaches of religious philosophizing can be for the ordinary believer or the uninitiated, then one has surely succeeded in making the politics and ideology of nuclear weapons possession virtually incontestable. After all, to sacralize something is precisely to remove it from

1

the domain of normal contestation into the realm of the "qualified" few.

The other approach to making the presence of nuclear weapons and the discourse that justifies it incontestable is to immerse nuclear weapons in the web of everyday life until their presence is "normalized" and considered unexceptional and unobjectionable. These two approaches, the religious and the cultural-popular, may seem to work at cross-purposes. But they do not. In fact, the greatest success is achieved when the two can be fused— when the religious-sacred is both revered *and* seen as an unproblematic and normal part of everyday life.

The great dilemma for the advocates of nuclear weapons and the great hope for those who unreservedly oppose them is that, despite all efforts to either sanctify or popularize these armaments, the nuclear protagonists have never been able to gain anywhere near as much ground as they wished. This has certainly not been for want of trying. Ever since such weapons were invented, pro-nuclearists have been trying to make them into desirable icons, to build glorious myths and weave attractive images around them, to routinize and domesticate their meanings. Yet there is a *relative failure*.

We need both to look at the reasons for failure and to remind ourselves that the failure is only relative. It is relative to the much greater success in implantation that genuine religious systems achieve, and to the much stronger successes that other forms of militarism have secured in the general culture of a mass society. Militarism is an ideology that sustains and promotes the values associated with it: violence, aggression, coercion, survival of the fittest, etc. Militarism promotes sexism and sexist stereotypes because it portrays such values as part of a supposedly natural and desirable masculinity. It is hardly surprising, then, that the discourse justifying nuclear weapons production and deployment should also be deeply sexist and macho in the most blatant and obvious ways—from the loaded, sexual symbolism of "penetration" of enemy spaces, to the "mating" or "coupling" of warheads with missiles and other delivery vehicles, to the depiction of the nuclear-tipped missile as a phallic symbol of national power and virility.

Militarism also invades the various forms and practices of mass popular culture—books, comics, music, films, toys, TV programs, etc. Again, this paves the way for the more specific discourse surrounding nuclear weapons to make its way into all kinds of areas. When a society is not just steeped in the ideology of militarism but also in that of commercialism, then the consumerist-advertising world of concocted symbolisms, artificial demand-stimulation, and market strategies will not remain immune. Throughout the '50s, advertising and marketing professionals in the United States used nuclear and atomic icons and symbols to great effect.[2]

True, the discourse justifying, prettifying, and normalizing nuclear weapons has never extended its tentacles into the mass societies of today to anywhere near the same extent as the more standard non-nuclear forms and motifs of militarism. But what has been achieved is disturbing enough. Anti-nuclearists must be constantly on guard to recognize where and how these efforts are made, then to repeatedly contest them.

So why the relative failure? The two intertwined dimensions of nuclear weapons stimulate two different kinds of discourses. The first is one of power, dominance, and impact as the derivative properties of nuclear weapons and with them, the alluring promise of *control*. The glorification of such attributes (and the promise that they embody) can find a place in a range of activities, from strategic studies speculating about pre-emptive use and deterrence efficacy to cigarette advertising, and from James Bond stories to graphically sexist and masculinist representations in the construction of popular images.

The second kind of discourse emerges from the recognition of the overwhelming destructive power, and therefore, the *uncontrollability* and irredeemable evil of nuclear weapons. This is a discourse not of acceptance or glorification, but of opposition to the horrific properties and attributes of nuclear weapons. It therefore defends human dignity, decency, and the values of community, caring and sharing. This is a discourse not of power or strategy, vicarious thrill, or consumer manipulation, but of ethics and respect for life, peace, harmony, and hope—hope in a humane future for the whole world. Arundhati Roy's powerful essay introducing this book is an expression of the endurance and importance of just this kind of discourse.

The problem for pro-nuclearists is the indissoluble tension between the two discourses: in fact, the second implicitly or explicitly, openly or in subterranean ways, contests and rejects the first kind of discourse. This tension cannot be resolved because it is not possible to fully separate the awe-inspiring dimension of nuclear weapons from its destructive-repulsive aspect. But all efforts to sanctify and popularize the properties of nuclear weapons aim *precisely* to carry out this separation and are always only partially successful.

The intrinsic "power" of nuclear weapons gives them an attribute similar to religion—the capacity to evoke awe—making nuclear weapons suitable candidates for worship. Religious systems use rituals to organize collective forms of worship around the symbol or object that is invested with sacredness. In doing so, they make religious power quotidian: The transcendental is connected to the everyday and the ordinary. Religious belief and practice is thus both normalized and institutionalized through these rituals, which help cement a wider community of believers. But because sacred power is necessarily nebulous and polysemous, religious elites (those who most strongly control the organization, infrastructure, and interpretation of rituals) can never come near to monopolizing the meaning, purpose, and role of worship. This flexibility and diversity, this possibility for ordinary people to invest sacred power with benign properties appropriate to addressing in a positive way their actual human conditions, gives religion a popularity and meaningfulness that the worship of nuclear weapons, or nuclearism (to give it its more sophisticated label), can never have.[3]

The inevitable connection between the two dimensions of nuclear weapons means that they cannot have the "natural" or popular appeal to which genuine religions can, at least, aspire. To preserve a system of nuclear weapons worship, a much greater burden of responsibility has to fall on a powerful but also relatively more isolated nuclear-religious elite. It is the ways in which this elite, its apprentices and allies, its acolytes and admirers, organize and control the production, dissemination, and consolidation of the discourse of nuclearism that enables it to have the degree of popular support it has. The nuclear elite comprises people who fulfill two sometimes overlapping functions—shaping and making decisions, or shaping and making opinions that endorse the possession, production, or deployment of nuclear weapons.

There are no everyday or truly popular rituals of nuclearism. If the nuclear elite and its supporters are to sanctify nuclearism (a matter to be entrusted to the special priesthood of strategic and security experts) and to popularize it (via the domain of culture), then this elite must rely on two key structures of mass communications. The first is the print media of mass-produced journalism—newspapers and wide-circulation magazines. The second is the audio-visual media of TV news broadcasting and programming, and popular films.

Cutting across this technical divide, however, is the more important contrast between non-fictional and fictional forms of representation in the discourse and imagery of nuclearism. Non-fictional forms of discourse are deadly serious and quite transparent. Here the nuclear elite has been like the fairy-tale Emperor without clothes, who, even when he discovers the truth of his nakedness, must pretend he is clothed. Indeed nuclearism is, intellectually and politically, the *haven of mediocrity*. The chapter in this book on deterrence and the more general style of strategic thinking that lies behind it explains why. In few other professions or areas of so-called expertise is it possible for so many to become so prominent or to get away with so much while knowing and understanding so little! Problems of global and national security and power in today's era of modernity (or "late" modernity as some would say) are, by their very nature, so incredibly complex and dynamic in their character that they are not amenable to easy solutions or to the pretensions of those who would provide easy solutions.

Nuclear elites resemble nothing more than an esoteric, quasi-religious cult who have long convinced themselves that they have the right to "play God," to gamble with the dice of unimaginable destruction in the name of national security, with themselves as its self-appointed interpreters and guardians. They pretend to know best and most about matters of security and power when they actually know so little, and because they know so little, search most desperately for the "strategic easy-fix"—that symbol of incontestable power that they believe all should acknowledge and worship as they themselves do. Nuclear elites have sought to make nuclearism's vileness and irrationality publicly palatable precisely through legitimizing discourses in print and TV, especially in the nuclear weapons states (NWSs) themselves.

Hollywood and the Bomb

The fictional world of popular movies is somewhat different. Here, the United States and Hollywood occupy a distinctive place. No other country has had anywhere near the same resources, the same degree of national self-confidence, or as strong a belief in its universal mission. *What is good for America is good for the world.* Hollywood has always reflected this real, albeit always contested, common sense. But here there are important differences from the world of non-fictional representation of nuclearism. Driven by commercial and entertainment considerations more than strictly ideological ones, pro-nuclear films from the US have generally indirectly defended the dominant elite ethos regarding nuclear weapons. And when these elite values have changed over time, the change too has been reflected. Thus nuclear weapons have usually figured as a vital backdrop to the more up-front story of heroic endeavor by American men or governments, especially in the genre of Cold War and post-Cold War spy-thrillers and dramas.

When films have focused explicitly and centrally on nuclear weapons, they have often provided an anti-nuclear message. Such has been the case with films like *Dr. Strangelove, The Day After, Failsafe,* and the films and sequels of the *Planet of the Apes* and *Mad Max.* To swim against the tide represented by the dominant elite ethos has always required a strong conviction, found only among the more politically committed filmmakers. To swim with the tide on the issue of nuclear weapons can take many more, and a wider variety of, indirect forms of cinematic and thematic representation.

Naturally, the production and popularity of both kinds of films—explicitly anti-nuclear, implicitly pro-nuclear—is affected by the changing rhythms of popular concern with the issue of nuclear weapons and its associated politics. What is particularly disturbing in this regard is not just the fact that there have always been far too many pro-nuclear films and messages emanating from Hollywood, but that the situation has not changed with the end of the Cold War. Indeed, now that the American nuclear elite must find new rationales for the retention of nuclear weapons, fresher and stronger life has been given in Hollywood to a genre seeking to resolve just this problem. Since even the "nasty" Arab or Iranian or Islamic "fanatic" (common enough hate-figures in recent Hollywood productions) is too weak in real life to warrant a nuclear riposte, the burden of justification for the presence of nuclear weapons has to fall on the genre of movies concerning alien invasion or cosmic threat, which is then resolved through their judicious use. Recent films like *Independence Day, Deep Impact,* and *Armageddon* have all carried the message that America can save the world—with its nuclear weapons.

To leave all this uncontested or uncriticized would be a mistake. Wherever the ugly messages of nuclearism surface, in fictional as well as non-fictional forms, they must be opposed. Indeed, if the battle for the hearts and minds of people is to be consciously fought and fully won then it must be waged as determinedly, consistently, and strongly as possible on the terrain that the most popular forms of print and audio-visual media provide. In the national societies of the NWSs, where the battle must be most strongly joined, the achievements on behalf of the anti-nuclear cause have hardly been dramatic. It is in spite of the weaknesses of anti-nuclearists on this score, not because of their successes, that progress has nonetheless been made.

We can be thankful that, whatever the predilections of Hollywood filmmakers in the post-Cold War era, the discourse of ethics has nevertheless gained ground over the discourse of power, even in the United States. Ordinary people have become more aware of the unacceptably dangerous nature and epochal futility of nuclear weapons as a means of security. A clear transition is in evidence: at the end of the century, and at the threshold of a new millennium, the prospect for nuclear abolition appears brighter than at any time since 1945. But there is no guarantee that the second discourse will continue to overshadow the first. Much of humanity has overcome in large measure its long-standing fascination with raw power, power divorced from its purposes and freed of limits. But if significant numbers of people still hesitate to go all the way to demand unconditional, rapid nuclear disarmament, it is because they have not committed themselves fully to the second discourse.

What This Book Is About

The central argument of this book is that nuclear disarmament is an absolute imperative. It is eminently desirable and feasible. A transition to the second, ethical discourse is an overwhelming necessity for all of us. The crossing of the nuclear threshold by India and Pakistan further reinforces, rather than weakens or renders less feasible, this proposition.

And yet, there is a paradox here. People the world over have rarely been horrified by an evil as strongly as they are by nuclear weapons, with their overwhelming power of destruction. Many have opposed such weapons, regardless of their general political innocence and inactivity. This evil is not ubiquitous in the ordinary sense of the term: only about half a dozen states concentrate the world's nuclear weapons in their possession; nevertheless, the danger is, and is considered, universal and global. But despite this, the nuclear obsession of the ruling elites in a handful of states has proved thoroughly addictive and almost irresistible to change. It is only recently that the obsession has begun to weaken or loosen.

In effect, nuclear weapons have proved far more durable and difficult to eradicate than just about any other kind of evil—at least in relation to the sentiment against them and popular mobilization against them.[4]

The contentious terrain of debate over nuclear disarmament has not permitted the free and full expression of popular sentiments. Nuclear elites, comprising experts, strategists, and specialists of various kinds, most of them not really accountable to the public, still tend to dominate and try to hijack discussions of the feasibility and desirability of nuclear weapons abolition.

This book is a critique of the nuclear elite's mindset and debased sensibilities. It questions the main premises underlying nuclearism. It polemicizes against the principal arguments the NWSs advance for developing, manufacturing, inducting, stockpiling, refining, deploying, using or threatening to use, such weapons, and criticizes their reluctance to move rapidly toward the total abolition of nuclear weapons. It is equally critical of states (and their apologists) who wish to emulate the nuclear weapons powers, and deals with some of the artifices they use to delay or obstruct progress toward nuclear abolition.

We as authors have tried to address different kinds of audiences simultaneously—always a hazardous endeavor! We hope, therefore, that both informed insiders such as long-time anti-nuclear activists, NGOs, the more open-minded members of decision-making and decision-shaping national elites, and the general public, will find much of value in these pages. The book has been laid out in such a way as to try to take the reader on a particular journey. We start with a wide historical overview of the Nuclear Age until the present, aiming to situate the more specific politics of nuclearism within the wider framework of Cold War and post-Cold War international politics. It is systemic rivalry between East and West that dominated nuclear politics in the first period, although the real threat of the actual use of nuclear weapons emerged mostly in the context of the North-South conflict, which was, of course, also connected to the East-West rivalry. In the second post-Cold War period, new rationales are being found to justify the retention of nuclear weapons. If the West is trying to give new meaning to NATO to justify its nuclear activities, Russia sees the possession of such armaments as almost the sole mechanism for retrieving something of its former "superpower" status, whose loss its political elite laments.

Having brought matters up to date, as it were, the focus shifts to the more specific story of how and why India and Pakistan treaded the path of nuclearization until the recent denouement of May of 1998. The justifications given for going nuclear are exposed. We describe the official positions and explanations and the ways in which even these violate the earlier stated official doctrines, certainly in the case of India. Through rebuttal and critique, the real reasons for the tests are highlighted along with a comprehensive survey of the various negative consequences of the Indian and Pakistani actions. These range from the diplomatic-political (e.g. Kashmir) to the security-related (the nuclearization of tensions in the India-Pakistan face-off, complications vis-à-vis China) to the domestic (advancement of the Hindu communal and Islamic fundamentalist agendas, the socio-economic wastefulness and burden imposed by the costs of maintaining nuclear weapons systems in both countries) to the international (the damage done to the global momentum for disarmament).

Two central chapters then take up, respectively, the unique evil of nuclear weapons and their unique danger. The purpose of doing the first is to stress the centrality of having a controlled moral anger if the effort to bring about a world forever free of nuclear weapons is to ever succeed. Colonialism would not have been overthrown without generating and politically harnessing such moral opposition. The same holds true of bringing a permanent end to nuclearism. We also seek to attack the nuclear mindset, not just at its weakest point (its immorality), but also at its supposedly strongest point—its claim to promoting strategic security through reliance on nuclear deterrence. The illogicality and fallacies of nuclear deterrence-based thinking and practice are highlighted. The historical record shows that, far from endorsing the claims of deterrence, reliance upon it led to behavior such as the arms race, which promoted greater nuclear insecurity and danger. Readers must judge for themselves how successful we are in these twin endeavors, just as they should ask what is left of a pro-nuclear case, which cannot adequately or satisfactorily answer criticisms at either or both these levels.

The subsequent chapters look more closely at the combination of intrinsic and extrinsic factors that have shaped the political context in which India and Pakistan made their decisions and the implications this has for the wider gamut of inter-state relations in which the two countries are embedded. We also explore the implications of Pokharan and Chagai on the general character of the post-Cold War nuclear order. The penultimate chapter in particular asks and then addresses the question of how badly or how little damaged (if at all) is the existing global nuclear order by the efforts of India and Pakistan to join the nuclear club. Here the central conclusion is that it is not the non-proliferation order, but the struggle for disarmament that has been most seriously damaged—not just by what India and Pakistan have done but by the continuing behavior of the other existing NWSs.

Finally, we look at the lessons of the past, from which we must draw to best arm ourselves for rapidly bringing about a nuclear-weapons-free world. We trace the obstacles to this, the most promising lines of pursuit, and a combination of comprehensive and partial disarmament perspectives. Here many issues arise. We explore the question of how to set up a genuine multilateral body empowered to negotiate full and final global nuclear disarmament. We investigate matters like the Comprehensive Test Ban Treaty (CTBT) and the Fissile Material Cutoff Treaty (FMCT). There is a survey of the strengths and weaknesses, the relevance and value of extending the spread of nuclear-weapons-free zones. We discuss at some length how transitional measures like de-alerting and No First Use pledges can help lead to more comprehensive reductions, and ultimately, to the abolition of nuclear weapons. We believe that it is crucial not just to prepare a desirable wish list, but to show how to make it achievable in the real world.

The General Perspective

We should clarify our general stand and disposition. We have long been connected with the international peace movement and nuclear disarmament campaigns. We are aware of, and participants in, the debates and arguments that are part of these campaigns' lives. At the same time, we are firmly rooted in the realities of South Asia, and are an integral, activist part of the movement for nuclear restraint and disarmament in that part of the world. We have been witnesses to, and critics of, the growing phenomenon in South Asia of a coarsening of the ruling elite's political sensibilities and its moral degradation over the past thirty years, especially in India. This is the period that saw India shift from nuclear abstinence to nuclear ambiguity, and then on to the wholesale embrace of nuclearism with the crossing of the nuclear Rubicon. As witnesses, analysts, and activists, we believe the process must be and can be reversed. This book explores ways in which that could be done.

There are no easy solutions to the problem of how states can be impelled to move away from a pathological and misguided reliance on weapons of mass destruction in their search for security. Two things, however, should be evident. One is that the primary impetus toward nuclear weapons abolition cannot simply come from state-level actors and governments. The very nature of the present global nuclear regime is such that those who possess nuclear weapons have no real or immediate stake in getting rid of them. And those who do not possess them lack the leverage and the will necessary to achieve that objective by effectively persuading or compelling the NWSs to undertake qualitative nuclear disarmament.

The Nuclear Non-Proliferation Treaty (NPT) is indeed a poor and rusty instrument in this regard, separating as it does the non-proliferation regime from the goal of disarmament. That this should be the case even a decade after the Cold War ended, undermining NATO's fundamental stated rationale of massive military-nuclear preparations, is both a tragic reality and a deeply unflattering comment on the quality of leadership in some of the most powerful and prosperous nations on earth.

Secondly, no one today has, or can have, a fully worked-out blueprint or road map of how to reach the goal of elimination of nuclear weapons from the present starting point. This is quintessentially a case of learning by doing, where the process of progressing toward and realizing the final goal will itself illuminate how we are to sustain that desired end-state permanently. This creates, on the one hand, a huge conceptual obstacle, and makes the task of potential agents for disarmament extraordinarily difficult. How indeed can they generate the necessary energies and gather the numbers without a well-defined road map? On the other hand, it presents a truly exciting opportunity for them to bring to their task an amazing range of ideas and imaginative schemes, to be creative in a foundational sense: to produce something, as it were, out of nothing.

We see ourselves as just two participants in this process, as learners along the road to the final destination. We envision our role not just as chroniclers and analysts, nor as publicists and evangelists. Above all, we are concerned scholar-activists, or activist-scholars, who reject the status quo and who are committed to altering it through conscious public action. Our basic stance is that of *independent* analysts and campaigners, who believe it is important to integrate into the core of our analytical work our moral concerns and our commitment to universal objectives such as nuclear disarmament, peace, defense of human rights, pluralism, social justice, and equality.

We lay claim to another distinctive characteristic as regards our perspective and work. We are from, and belong to, the global South. We believe that it is vital to have a strong Southern input into the global struggle for nuclear disarmament. So far, not just state-level activities and negotiations on the nuclear weapons issue, but even the international peace movement and nuclear disarmament campaigns, have borne a strongly Northern stamp. Many of the perspectives, ideas, and debates in that movement have tended to reflect the concerns and predilections of activists from the industrially developed states. This is also true of their methods of organization, of campaigning, of public education, advocacy, and lobbying.[5]

All these need to be enriched with strong input from the South, rooted in different sensibilities, experiences, and methods. Such pluralism is not just intrinsically worthy and desirable. It is indispensable to the construction and advancement of a truly global momentum and an authentically international movement for nuclear disarmament. Such a movement cannot be a mere aggregate of different national campaigns with their discrete, domestically driven, agendas. It must be truly internationalist in outlook, concerns, reach and representation. The regrettable fact that the world's Nuclear Club now features two Southern members should only further underscore the importance of this proposition.

The recent Indian and Pakistani nuclear tests have spurred the urgency of this book. We have been campaigners against nuclear weapons for many years, and we would have preferred to write a book that might have helped *prevent* the nuclear tests in South Asia. It is a pity that the world has begun to recognize the full salience of South Asia's silent race toward nuclearization only because the tests made it unavoidably clear.

This long non-recognition, or slippage from global consciousness, is undoubtedly related to the structure of power distribution in the world and its reflection in the media and hence in the shaping of global public awareness. In some ways, this is a reminder, even if a grim one, that the struggle to abolish nuclear weapons is integrally connected to the larger agenda to change the world, to alter the distribution of power, to re-evaluate the content, purpose, and meaning of power. This calls for a broad campaigning front and a holistic, inclusive agenda. The fight for nuclear disarmament is thus a fight for more than disarmament alone, although its specific focus must of necessity be narrowed if it is to be sharp.

Such a struggle, we believe, cannot be left to political leaders, military experts, disarmament and arms control negotiators, diplomats, and other state-level actors, however competent, sincere, and well-meaning they might be. It must at its center involve social movements, non-governmental organizations, and activists—the broadest coalition of civil society groups. It is these collective resources that can generate the moral commitment, the political conviction, the imaginative and practical forms of dissemination of information, coupled with the expertise and technical competence that are necessary for the task.

Perhaps never before has global society been called upon to intervene so centrally, so universally, and with such commitment, as it is in this instance. This challenge is part of the broader democratic agenda before humanity: to bring under public scrutiny plans and programs conceived, designed, and operated by experts and strategic specialists, which claim to guard the public interest and generate security for the people. If the process of democratization involves detaching expertise and specialized knowledge from vast bureaucracies and military machines, and putting it into the public domain, then nothing could serve its aims and objectives better than the rightful appropriation of the supposedly specialized sphere of defense and security by the public, whom it is meant to secure, and in whose name it is created and run at a massive expense.

Denuclearization and democratization of the world are inseparable processes. As the peace movement has always argued, issues such as security, war and peace, nuclear weapons, and their elimination, are too important to be left to experts and specialists alone. The people of the world must appropriate, or rather recover, these agendas. We can only hope this book contributes in a modest way to that recovery.

NOTES

[1] Results of the "Newseum" survey, sponsored by Freedom House in the US were released on February 23, 1999. Published in "Hiroshima comes first, then the moonwalk," *The Pioneer* (New Delhi) February 25, 1999.

[2] Half a century later, the image of the mushroom cloud and the icons of Pokharan and Chagai are being turned into the brands and logos of products in India and Pakistan as well as finding their way into the materials used for partisan political propaganda by the Bharatiya Janata Party (BJP) and its cohort organizations in the Sangh Combine.

[3] This term *nuclearism* features in Robert Jay Lifton and Richard Falk, *Indefensible Weapons* (New York: Basic Books, 1982), where it is defined as "the ideology and doctrines of extreme, pathological dependence on nuclear weapons for a range of goals and objectives, among them security.

[4] Recent polls show that 84 percent of Americans and over 60 percent of the British population want nuclear disarmament. 73 percent of Indians are against the use of nuclear weapons. "72.8% opposes use of N-weapons, says survey," *The Economic Times* (New Delhi) June 24, 1998.

[5] Thus in his fine book, *The Gift of Time* (New York: Henry Holt and Company, 1998), Jonathan Schell does not even mention, let alone interview, a single person from the South. All those who figure in it are from the United States and Europe, barring the one half-exception of Merav Datan, an Israeli-American. The book is strong, often excellent, when it deals with the deficiencies of nuclear deterrence and related security perceptions. However, in no way does it challenge standard US liberal assumptions about the general political nature of the Cold War era in which role the US and Western imperialism is effectively disguised. This could be excused on the grounds that for the most part it is not the voice of Schell that we are hearing but of his interviewees. These are for the most part either prominent liberals or former Cold Warriors who have had some change of heart on the nuclear issue.

But Schell himself adds no corrective of his own. Indeed, he persistently uses the ideologically loaded and conceptually bankrupt term of "Totalitarianism" to describe the formerly Communist societies of the East. However, the very manner of Communist collapse was itself the most striking confirmation of the theoretical incoherence of the concept which had its origins in right-wing Western Cold War hisoriography before becoming widely dispersed in liberal mainstream discourse.

For an alternative framework and a different discussion of the politics of the Cold War era, see the following chapters.

Chapter 2

Bloc Rivalry and the High Noon of Nuclearism

What happened to the nuclear arms race when the Cold War ended definitively answered a debate that had raged within the Western anti-nuclear peace movement during the '80s.[1] For despite its horror and terror, its inertial continuity and irrationality, that arms race did not command or control the politics of the Cold War. On the contrary, the politics of nuclearism was firmly embedded within the wider-ranging politics of general Cold War rivalry and subordinated to it. The distinctive self-reinforcing dynamic of the nuclear arms race emerged out of the degenerative logic of deterrence and from the politics of nuclearism. But it did not have an independent "life of its own."

Any survey of the era (1945–87) of strong nuclear rivalry and arms racing thus has to situate itself in an understanding of the Cold War's beginning, its subsequent course, and the manner of its ending. This is a prerequisite for understanding the politics of nuclearism of that period, which in turn sheds invaluable light on the current politics of nuclearism in the post-Cold War era. In the latter half of the '80s, there emerged for the first time since the nuclear age began in 1945, a new and real momentum of actual disarmament and not just arms control. It is this precious outcome that we seek to preserve and strengthen. But we cannot adequately grasp the deficiencies of this momentum if we do not first understand the end of the Cold War and its negative consequences.

The General Politics of the Cold War Era

The Cold War confrontation was many things, but above everything else it represented a political-ideological systemic rivalry between two blocs led, respectively, by the US and USSR. This was a conflict between two different social orders. It was not simply a conventional Great Power conflict of the kind that "balance of power" theorists belonging to the realist school of international relations love to discuss. On one side was a set of nationally-structured, advanced capitalisms usually taking the political form of perverse democracies. In their internal make-up these countries were, and are, liberal democratic and thus justifiably attractive to those living under more authoritarian regimes. But they were (and are) perverse democracies because

13

most such governments repeatedly supported foreign policy positions or carried out practices that were anything but democratic—the pursuit of economic and political imperialism. On the other side were perverse socialisms. Despite often significant national variations in the distribution of popular rights, the countries of what was called the Communist bloc rested on a common foundation of authoritarian-bureaucratic structures denying basic political and civic liberties to their respective populations.

This systemic rivalry was also significantly fed and shaped by intra-bloc and inter-state rivalries and conflicts of various kinds that did not themselves have the same character as the conflict represented by the central fault-line of the overarching Cold War system. Thus, even within the advanced capitalist world or between the poorer South and the richer North there were a range of inter-state tensions. Similarly, within the Communist world there were also inter-state and intra-state tensions of various kinds, among which the most notable in the post-World War Two period were the Sino-Soviet and China-Vietnam conflicts, the intra-Indochinese wars, and the political eruptions in the Eastern European bloc of countries dominated for decades by Soviet military might. In this last case, the conflicts were not of an inter-state character, but were related much more strongly to popular resentments against both Soviet overlordship and the authoritarian internal practices of what were perceived as client regimes of the USSR.

While responsibility for the perpetuation of the Cold War was shared between both sides, it was not equally distributed. The US emerged from World War Two as the only major participant whose territory was physically unscathed, whose material losses were the least, and whose economy was booming as a result of wartime preparations and activity. The USSR, by contrast, was devastated, with between 20 to 25 million dead and its industrial structure severely damaged. Its foreign policy perspectives had to be, and were, of a deeply defensive nature and concerned above all with retrenchment, not expansionism. This did not preclude belligerence on its part, nor a fierce determination to hold onto what it had—that is, control over an East European buffer zone. Nor does it mean the USSR did not have some responsibility for the creation of Cold War tensions and hostilities, especially through its behavior in Eastern Europe over subsequent years and decades.

But the West, and the US, in particular, bore greater responsibility for it. The US more strongly shaped the general pattern, pace and course of the Cold War. This simple truth is likely to be increasingly obscured in contemporary and future histories of this period because of the victory of the West in this historic confrontation. The *systemic* character of this conflict was revealed, not just by the political collapse of the Soviet bloc, but by its acceptance of the fundamental anti-Communist ideological precepts of the winning side and by its determination to establish a capitalist economic system in place of what it earlier had. All this will undoubtedly promote those evaluations most strongly associated with Cold War right-wing Western historiographies. These kinds of history writing have portrayed Western behavior as a legitimate moral-political response against Communist evil and expansionism, itself seen as the principal source of Cold War tensions and problems. The West, led by the US, has been portrayed as largely the reactor and defender in this stand-off between the "Free" and the "Communist" worlds. Moreover, the final outcome of this confrontation is widely perceived as providing powerful validation for Western practices and behavior during that period, thereby disguising the objective realities of that time.

With the benefit of hindsight we can see that some kind of Cold War was probably unavoidable, even though the weaker side (the East and the USSR) was always more willing to accommodate to, and compromise in search of, some kind of global status quo arrangement. The inability to arrive at such a *modus vivendi* was due, not so much to a subjective failure, that is, a misperception on the Western side of Soviet intentions or ambitions, but to an objectively rooted one. Though over time the West came to accept the reality of Europe's division and the satellite status of Eastern Europe, it could never reconcile itself to the challenges to US imperial power, in particular, thrown up by decolonization, national liberation struggles, and anti-capitalist revolutions in the third world. From today's vantage point of comprehensive victory in this historic bloc confrontation, it is easy for many in the West to forget that between 1945 to 1979 there was, on average, one successful anti-capitalist revolution every four years, which shifted one country or the other from the capitalist to the non-capitalist, so-called socialist sector.

These victories were not the handiwork of the USSR, but for the overwhelming part had independent sources indigenous to the countries concerned. But the objective fact was that they strengthened one side of the systemic divide at the expense of the other. Any successful long-lasting compromise between the US and USSR that could have avoided the Cold War required what the latter could never have delivered, even if it had wanted to—the elimination of such third world challenges to the US and to Western imperialist power. Furthermore, Cold War hostilities between the two leading countries meant the USSR could not but seek to exploit, however half-heartedly or hesitantly or in however contradictory a fashion, the opportunities that thereby emerged in the third world for weakening the US's global authority, thus adding further fuel to this systemic face-off. Soviet support to third world challenges to US power was uneven, cautious, and uncertain, but rarely absent.

Throughout, the central arena in which the Cold War was fought was not Europe but the third world.[2] To be sure, Europe was an enduring terrain of tension and the most *explicit* site of the politics of nuclearism associated with Cold War hostilities. But it was in the third world and over third world issues that nuclear weapons came closest to actually being used. Apart from the definitive moment of the Cuban missile crisis in 1962, the use of nuclear weapons was contemplated on several occasions, ranging from the 1948 Soviet-Iranian Azerbaijan crisis, to the 1950 retreat from Chosin reservoir in Korea, to the last days of French control in Vietnam (Dien Bien Phu in 1954) to the Formosa Straits crisis of 1959, to the siege of Khe Sanh in Vietnam in 1968, to the 1973 war in the Middle East between Israel and Egypt/Syria.[3]

It was, of course, mostly the US that was tempted to use nuclear weapons on these and other occasions. Though Krushchev did publicly threaten such use of these weapons against Israel/UK/France expeditionary forces in the 1956 Suez crisis, he was careful to do so only after the US had come out against the Israel/UK/France combine, and when it was clear that the real crisis was over and the latter would have to retreat. The one occasion when the Soviets most seriously contemplated use of their arsenal was in 1969 against China. The 1948 Berlin Airlift crisis was the one exception when the US considered the use of nuclear weapons against the USSR over a European-related issue.

Yet sizeable popular movements against nuclear weapons were always limited to Western Europe and the US. Their absence in the USSR and China can safely be attributed to the absence of a democratic civil society. But in Eastern Europe, during the '80s there was widespread and growing public sympathy with the anti-nuclear cause, even if this could not be openly expressed in the form of public demonstrations. It was here in Europe and the US that the possibility of a nuclear outbreak was a *popularly felt* danger. This was because it was in Europe and the US that a *constantly looming overhang* of nuclear weapons prevailed as a persistent reminder in public imagination of the reality of the nuclear threat.

In contrast, the stronger likelihood of the use of nuclear weapons in the third world was only sporadically expressed and, except in the case of the Cuban missile crisis, did not directly portend a US-Soviet nuclear exchange as distinct from a (usually) US threat against a non-nuclear regime. Such possible use did, of course, indirectly raise the prospect of escalating into an eventual US-Soviet exchange, but not as an immediate, direct, or "impossible to avoid" outcome. Moreover, most such threats in the third world were not publicly or widely known at the time and have been confirmed *post facto*, often only by the release in later years of official documents. That the US government was repeatedly tempted to use nuclear weapons in third world conflicts is undeniable. But despite strong pressures on each such occasion, their use was not ultimately sanctioned. This is not because of any so-called efficacy of deterrence, i.e. the fear of possible Soviet retaliation. It is difficult to seriously believe that the US, or the USSR, or any NWS, would be prepared to risk nuclear suicide by going into a nuclear war for the sake of some third world ally, no matter how supposedly close.

The decisive reasons for the US ultimately deciding not to resort to nuclear arms had to do with (1) the peculiarly *astrategic* character of nuclear weapons as a means of providing general foreign policy support, and (2) fear of domestic and international public horror, opprobrium, and anger. It is not the case that general public opinion in the US was, or is, unequivocally anti-nuclear in all circumstances. But recent surveys show that about eighty-four percent want the complete elimination of such weapons as rapidly as possible.[4] Also, after Hiroshima and Nagasaki and increasingly over time, public opinion has become more and more unwilling to endorse the use of nuclear weapons, except in the case of extreme self-defense when territorial US is itself seriously threatened. Throughout the Cold War period, no third world-related conflict has ever possessed any such logic or threat for the US.

In fact, so many decades have now passed, that despite innumerable political crises, an ever stronger, even if not always explicit, public resistance has built up against any "casual" or "easy" use of nuclear weapons "merely" for general foreign policy or so-called strategic purposes and gains. Of course, this is not a guarantee that nuclear elites will never use such arms in the pursuit of their foreign policy ambitions. As long as nuclear weapons and nuclear elites exist, the possibility of their use exists. But the strongest obstacle to their actual use is not the mindset of deterrence or the fear that such weapons inspire, but the wide and deep public consciousness, in the NWSs themselves, that opposes their use in any circumstances, barring the most extreme.

This sentiment was no doubt widespread in the USSR and China, as well, and therefore acted as a powerful barrier. Soviet and Chinese rulers could hardly be unaware of it. But the existence of an authoritarian political set up in the two countries meant that this public sentiment could not exercise the kind of institutionalized pressure that could be expected to operate in the more internally democratic system of the US. In one sense, this left the Soviet and Chinese rulers "freer" than otherwise to use nuclear weapons if they so desired. Thus the Soviet regime, as pointed out earlier, considered a nuclear strike on China in 1969. It tentatively explored the prospect of a joint US-USSR strike, but was rebuffed by the US.

Similarly, only one like Mao Zedong, the leader of an undemocratically controlled society, could speculate with callous equanimity about China's ability to "absorb" a nuclear attack that might kill tens or even hundreds of millions, but according to him would still leave tens or hundreds of millions as "survivors." This was the partial basis for his famous claim that nuclear weapons were a "paper tiger." The other more sensible assumption of the paper tiger claim—that such weapons were strategically useless—was not seriously held by Mao and was effectively belied by Mao's leading China into the development and deployment of such weapons.

If overall, during the Cold War, the US leadership behaved with greater nuclear irresponsibility than its Soviet and Chinese counterparts, this is because the greater virtue provided by its internal democratic system was outweighed by the vice of its much stronger imperialist ambition. But the importance of the general lesson to be learned is undiminished. It is one that is confirmed by the history of the Cold War period. The existence of a democratic polity and of strong popular sentiment *does* constitute a vital bulwark against any "easy" use of nuclear weapons.

The Politics of Nuclearism in the Cold War Era

The dropping of the bombs over Hiroshima and Nagasaki was also the first act in the nuclearization of post-World War Two politics. It was clearly directed as a symbolic-political warning to the USSR. The bombing was not an act of deterrence—Japan had no warning and the USSR no nuclear weapons then—but a conscious attempt to harness nuclear weapons for general political and foreign policy purposes in the post-War era.

The early efforts to internationalize control over nuclear weapons—the Baruch Plan and the Soviet counter-proposal—were, in retrospect, clearly doomed to fail.[5] The general political circumstances of mutual suspicion more or less ensured this. Time and again, this pattern affecting possible arms restraint measures was to be revealed. Not only the prospects for arms restraint, but the specific character of arms control/management perspectives would invariably reflect the general character of US-USSR political relations at the time. Shifts in the character of that relationship—what would come to be called the alternating phases of thaw and freeze or detente and deterioration—would witness similar shifts in the nature of arms racing and arms control. Arms control, throughout the Cold War era, should not be seen as something counterposed to arms racing and the ongoing politics of nuclearism, but as an integral part of both. Arms control perspectives did not emerge, however, until the '60s when Soviet nuclear strength reached the point where the US and Western Europe had to recognize its potential for devastation of their territories in a second strike. Arms control measures became an ever more important part of the general dynamic of arms racing as the USSR reached a rough nuclear parity with the US in the '70s and early '80s.[6]

Every country that went openly nuclear and improved this capacity in the Cold War era did so because it was motivated by a politics of nuclearism that went beyond the issue of nuclear deterrence itself. This is obvious enough in the case of the US, which exploded the bombs and produced warheads and delivery systems for reasons intimately related to its general foreign policy ambitions and perspectives. Certainly, once the USSR developed its own nuclear arsenal, then deterrence arguments became an additional and ever more important rationale for both countries in justifying their possession and further development of such weapons.

If, for the USSR, the initial spur to developing such weapons was US possession and deployment of them, this was not the only purpose behind its subsequent investment in the perpetuation and modernization of a nuclear weapons system. Indeed, the effort and resources the USSR devoted to making their weapons system ever more sophisticated, diverse, and larger, went well beyond the needs of any notion of a sensible, let alone minimal, deterrence posture.

For the UK and France, matters of national pride and a desire to maintain a supposedly global status, partly to compensate for their unavoidable decline as major colonial powers, were absolutely crucial factors in their decisions to go nuclear. China, too, sought nuclear status not only for deterrent purposes, but as a perceived currency of power for foreign policy and diplomatic projection.

But the central axis of Cold War nuclearism was always the US-USSR relationship and dynamic, of which the former has been the principal shaper and initiator. This is why it is legitimate to treat a taxonomy of the different phases of Cold War nuclearist politics as effectively synonymous with the different phases of US nuclear politics. There were four such phases: (1) 1945 to about 1960—massive retaliation; (2) early '60s to the beginning of the '70s—flexible response; (3) from the early '70s to the end of that decade—detente and the acceptance of a rough nuclear strategic parity; (4) 1980 to 1987—the search by the US for nuclear superiority and winnable nuclear wars.

None of these phases should be seen as sharply exclusive of the preceding one. Within the US nuclear establishment, different currents have continuously vied for dominant influence, and the frequent interchange of personnel between these currents has meant that the same people have had different views at different times. If these categorizations have a meaning, it is as a rough description of the dominant policy-shaping trend at the time. The shifts from one phase to the other were decisively determined by two things. The first was the change in general political relations between the US and USSR as systemic and global rivals, a relationship that was itself always subject to changes in a host of factors, both external to, and domestic in, each country and bloc. The emergence of many such factors, and the kind of impact they had, was effectively out of control of either government.

The second was related to the more narrow assessment of comparable nuclear capabilities between the two countries. It was here also that the degenerative logic of deterrence and arms racing operated. It was here that the problem of limited nuclear war most strongly asserted itself. No matter if the USSR from the '60s to the end of the Cold War period said it only believed in massive nuclear retaliation. Should deterrence break down and a nuclear exchange be initiated, it remained in both countries' interests to restrict the outbreak as much as possible, that is, to be able to fight a limited nuclear war and to make their respective nuclear preparations accordingly. But to carry out such preparations, thereby making a limited war more feasible, further undermined the credibility of the concept of deterrence. What emerged was an arms race that fed on and generated insecurity, a spiral with quantitative and qualitative increases at all levels, whether in regard to tactical or strategic weapons/delivery systems.

"Massive Retaliation" to "Flexible Response"

Thus the first two phases of US nuclear politics were never counterposed to each other. From the early '50s, Washington was clear about the need to have tactical weapons in Europe, not only to counter a possible Soviet conventional threat on that continent, but to separate the European battleground from a transcontinental Soviet-US one. Nonetheless, given the great imbalance between the US and Soviet arsenals even after the latter developed the bomb in 1949, the US's early nuclear posture was about (1) maintaining an overwhelming nuclear superiority, both in numbers of warheads, and in the range, extent and spread of delivery systems, that is, reaching the USSR with air bases from Iceland to Italy to Turkey to Japan and places in-between; and (2) translating this superiority into tangible political gains. It was only around 1960 that the USSR developed the capacity to threaten the US mainland through land-based intercontinental ballistic missiles, and really only in the mid-'60s that it had such missiles in sufficient numbers that they could constitute an assured second strike capacity.

Massive retaliation in Europe meant deterring any Soviet "adventurism" of even a conventional kind by creating a fear of the disastrous consequences for the USSR of making any such decision. Of course, from the Soviet side, interpretation of US and NATO designs was very different. In any event, once the USSR had equipped itself with a sufficiently large, diverse, and sophisticated arsenal to not only threaten the US mainland but also to wreak nuclear damage on Western Europe roughly equivalent to what NATO could do to it, whatever "political advantages" the US and the West thought it had obtained from the nuclear imbalance in its favor had disappeared, even by the peculiar and distinctive logic of nuclearism subscribed to by the Western nuclear establishment.

Flexible response was the reaction to the changed nuclear equation in a larger political context marked by a general and continuing Western confidence in its ability to contain Communism worldwide, despite increasing unease about growing Soviet influence in the third world and revolutionary successes in certain regions. Krushchev may have talked of the need for "peaceful coexistence" from the mid-'50s onward and suggested long-term compromise with the US and the West. But this was still, in Western eyes, the era of "containment" and "possible roll-back." The German question lying at the heart of European politics was still perceived in terms faithful to the immediate post-World War Two period. The West was still a decade away from *Ostpolitik* and the definitive recognition this would embody of the permanency of the "post-War settlement" in Europe.

Flexible response was a new way of pursuing an older US aim. Earlier, the nuclear battleground of Europe and Russia was separated from the US mainland by virtue of the sheer inability of Soviet nuclear forces to reach the North American continent in sufficient numbers. In the new situation, flexible response was a way for NATO and the US to pursue three aims. First, such a policy practice would presumably retain some credibility for the NATO trip-wire principle, i.e., deterring a Soviet conventional attack across NATO lines through the threat of a nuclear retaliation. By introducing gradations and new possibilities in the form that such a nuclear response by a US-led NATO might take, the West no longer had to hang on to the supposedly implausible and less credible option of an all-out nuclear response.

Second, for the same reason that nuclear responses could now be more measured and "limited," there were more chances of it not leading to a direct exchange between the US mainland and the USSR. That is to say, if nuclear war did break out, it could more likely be confined to the European battleground. Third, by introducing more gradations and therefore more and newer levels of sophisticated tactical weaponry, one was creating more rungs in the ladder of possible escalation. If NATO then possessed nuclear superiority at all or most of these rungs, this would be yet another way of achieving political gains through the application of perceived "nuclear superiority." This time superiority would not be of the old kind. It could not come from the threat of massive retaliation by the West, combining with the inability of the USSR to adequately target the US mainland. It would now come about because the West could now better control the "ladder of escalation." At the maximum limit (something that would obsess the Reaganite war-fighting hawks of the '80s) NATO might possess, not merely "escalation control," but "escalation dominance"—that is, "superiority" at each and every rung of the ladder of escalation.

The political purpose of the new flexible response strategy was the same as that of the earlier phase—to somehow harness a perceived or hoped for "nuclear weapons superiority" to the pursuit of general foreign policy and political ambitions. But two developments forced the West to shift from flexible response to acceptance of arms control and acknowledgement of "strategic parity" between the US and USSR. By the late '60s, Washington was mired down in Vietnam, losing not just the political war but international prestige and its own self-confidence as a global power and policeman. Furthermore, the USSR had by the end of the '60s acquired the capacity to threaten second-strike devastation on the US mainland. As both arsenals proceeded to gross and multiple overkill levels (and formal disparities in numbers were also declining considerably), a strategic parity of sorts became an obvious fact of life. If a world order amenable to Western interests was still to be maintained, it now seemed to require the establishment of "responsible" regional powers, that is, pro-Western surrogates, as well as a greater degree of compromise with the USSR, with the aim of enlisting its support in containing third world revolutions.

In recognition of the Soviet nuclear advancement, a new era of arms control activity was inaugurated. But it is important to note that this arms control regime was only initiated because of a relative shift in the overall political relationship of forces between the USSR and the US against the latter, caused by accumulating Western defeats in the third world. The future course of the arms control regime and of this period of detente politics would also remain hostage to the larger political-global ambitions and perceptions of the West and the US. Detente would not inaugurate, as the Soviets may have hoped, a new era of global political equality between itself and the US or between East and West.

It was seen from one side as a deal to sustain (under pressure) the existing status quo of Western dominance of the global order, albeit a dominance less prominent than in the past. The USSR would be offered a more honorable status as a Great Power, but it had to play its part in stemming the tide of challenges emanating mostly from the third world. In return, the West made a concession that represented little more than making a virtue out of necessity—it prepared itself to formally acknowledge the permanency of the post-War European settlement. In August 1968 during the crushing of the Prague Spring, the West had by its reaction acknowledged its impotence in this regard. Except as fodder for ideological-moral rhetoric by the West, Soviet control of Eastern Europe was neither on the agenda of serious disputation between the two sides nor something that the West was much interested in challenging. Willy Brandt's *Ostpolitik* was largely the formal endorsement of this reality, a carrot offered to the USSR in return for its upholding of detente. Detente, however, was bound to fail—as it eventually did—because what each side understood as its rationale and purpose was different and did not coincide. The crucial condition for its sustenance—the absence of further third world challenges to Western power—simply could not be ensured, even if the USSR had wanted to.

On the arms control front during the period of detente, though such negotiations only sought to manage the race, not put an end to it, there did emerge the second great gain in the effort to bring about some restraint. This was the 1972 Anti-Ballistic Missile Defense (ABM) Treaty. The first important breakthrough in arms restraint measures, which was also in a way a deep disappointment, was the 1963 Partial Test Ban Treaty, or PTBT. This became possible because of the Cuban missile crisis of October 1962 and the fright it caused in government circles in both the US and USSR, as it brought them to a literal hair's breadth from an actual exchange.[7] Furthermore, throughout the '50s and early '60s, significant public hostility to the environmental effects of atmospheric testing was gathering. The final draft of the PTBT emerged from side negotiations between Moscow, London, and Washington and disappointed the other countries that subsequently became signatories. The widespread expectation then was that a comprehensive test ban treaty was in the offing. The non-nuclear weapons states (NNWSs) were putting pressure for this and anticipating this as the final outcome. Instead, what finally emerged, a PTBT, was therefore also seen as a betrayal of universal hopes and an indication of how these three NWSs wanted to contain arms restraint measures within the wider framework of continued arms racing and further development of their arsenals. France and China rejected the PTBT and continued to test in the atmosphere until the early '80s, only then shifting to purely underground testing.

The manner in which the 1972 ABM treaty emerged reflected various pressures. Domestic factors in the US were as important as external ones, even as they were influenced by the latter. The success of the Soviet nuclear expansion in the '60s and the emergence of China as a nuclear weapons power after 1964 increased the pressure within the US to construct a nationwide ABM system. On the one hand, growing Soviet might suggested the need for strategic stability and compromise, but on the other hand, the standard US reflex of wanting to maintain a strong lead over the USSR was also in play. In 1967, US Secretary of State Robert McNamara inaugurated the debate about a possible ABM system by stressing the need for strategic stability and hence the dangers represented by an ABM system. But he simultaneously attempted to rationalize the construction of a "light" nation-wide ABM system, both to shield the US from a future Chinese arsenal and as a counter to a Soviet strike.[8]

In short, McNamara was mired in a contradiction forced upon him by fealty to the traditional US desire for one-upmanship over the Soviets (embodied in flexible response doctrines) and growing awareness of the need to promote strategic stability. The Soviets had begun developing an ABM system around Moscow, thus pushing many lobbies in the US to pursue a "keep-ahead-of-the-Russians" approach. The US thus began developing a Sentinel system of fifteen ABM sites near major cities. What was unexpected was the sudden public eruption of concern and debate, which between 1967 and 1970 involved scientists and Congressmen in a way that no nuclear weapons-related issue had ever done before. First, the very siting of such proposed systems highlighted the vulnerability of city populations as never before. Second, even according to the logic of "security through deterrence," the instability generated by defense systems created further public fears. The Nixon administration sought to reorient the ABM toward a Safeguard system aiming to protect not cities, but the newly developing Minuteman missile fields. But by now a sophisticated technical opposition had emerged to such attempts to "destabilize" the terror logic of Mutual Assured Destruction (MAD).

Such domestic opposition and the Nixon administration's general political weakness, caused by a wealth of domestic and external factors, pushed the government toward the idea of using the ABM as a bargaining chip within the framework of the first Strategic Arms Limitation Talks (SALT I). At the same time, the US view was that it needed to build multiple warhead missile systems or multiple independently targeted re-entry vehicles (MIRVs) to overcome a Soviet ABM system and that it needed to have an ABM system of its own to protect against Soviet developments of their own MIRVed missiles. The overall result was the enshrinement of the principle that the best way to control arms was also through threatening to build more arms, hence the importance of the ABM as a bargaining counter.

Nonetheless, though the ABM Treaty did not halt MIRVing on both sides nor the development of mobile delivery systems on land, it did stop for some time the search for constructing ballistic missile defense (BMD) systems, until the Reagan administration changed track. The Reagan administration put forward a radical reinterpretation of the ABM Treaty's provisions that effectively nullified it. It claimed that the Treaty did not explicitly prevent research, testing, development, and deployment of space-based systems or those involving exotic new technologies. Reagan's Strategic Defense Initiative (SDI), better known as the "Star Wars" project, would have effectively rendered irrelevant the 1972 ABM Treaty. But the latter secured a reprieve because of the demise of the Star Wars project through the ending of the Cold War. But new pressures have emerged in the current phase of the post-Cold War period that once again threaten the gains of the ABM in the name of constructing theater (as supposedly opposed to strategic) BMD systems.[9]

Arms Race Management to the Second Cold War

If the '70s, through treaties like SALT I and SALT II, marked an effort at managing the arms race, albeit in modest and insufficient fashion, why was this breakdown to be followed by a period of greater nuclear belligerence from roughly 1979 on? Why was detente followed by what came to be called the "Second Cold War"? The basic explanation was not difficult to find. The MPLA (Popular Movement for the Liberation of Angola) triumph in Angola (1975), the victory of the Sandinistas in Nicaragua (1978), the fall of the Shah in Iran (1979), and the emergence of a succession of pro-Soviet regimes in Afghanistan eventually backed by direct Soviet invasion (1978–80) sounded the death knell of detente. Neither the overall political strategy of the US and the West, nor the nuclear arms control regime as a component in that wider scheme, had succeeded in their larger purpose. Both the general politics of Cold War conflict and the more specific politics of nuclearism entered a new phase.

Its essential direction was again set by the US and the Reagan administration, though the previous Carter administration had already begun moving in this direction. Well before the Soviet invasion of Afghanistan and the fall of the Shah, the Carter government called for escalating arms spending, deploying intermediate range Cruise and Pershing-2 missiles in Europe, and proclaimed the need to set up a Rapid Deployment Force in the Gulf, while SALT II was stymied in Congress. Indeed, Presidential Directive (PD) 59 on July 25, 1980, which raised the idea of nuclear warfighting as an official doctrine, was promulgated under Carter.

While the strategic goal—reversing the global weakening of US-led Western dominance in its systemic rivalry with the USSR and the Socialist bloc—remained the same, the means now changed. Given the failure of détente, this was inevitable. The specific politics of nuclearism to which this gave rise was embodied in the new Reagan doctrine of preparing to fight and win nuclear wars. In this regard, two key initiatives were pursued—NATO's placement of Pershing-2 and Cruise missiles (or Euromissiles) in Europe for targeting the USSR; and the 1983 Strategic Defense Initiative or Star Wars program, whose first concrete fruits were anticipated to emerge in the mid-'90s. The first initiative had a history preceding Reagan. The second, although it had a continuity with fears and desires expressed earlier by significant lobbies in the US, was the Reagan government's own decision. Star Wars sought to destroy the spirit, intent, and purpose of the 1972 ABM Treaty and thus introduce a dangerously destabilizing new dimension into the arms race.

Both initiatives were part of a new nuclear warfighting perspective.

In the '60s and '70s, NATO reduced the vulnerability of its theater nuclear missiles by making them sea-based (fitted onto Polaris submarines), and made them more devastating by MIRVing them. NATO removed land-based missiles by choice. And by the calculus of nuclear accounting, it had an advantage over the USSR in this field of intermediate range missiles. The main point at issue in the SALT II negotiations from 1972 to 1979 was this imbalance in theater nuclear forces between the two sides. The USSR repeatedly sought to get the issue into the negotiations, but was constantly opposed. After 1976 it sought to redress this imbalance somewhat by producing and deploying SS-20s, which were mobile and MIRVed but still markedly inferior to NATO's weapons systems, which were far less vulnerable and had a longer range.

The SS-20s were not seen as a problem by the US and Western Europe at the time (and consequently were left out of the SALT II negotiations) but their deployment later became the publicly declared justification for deploying their own Pershing-2 and Cruise missiles. In actual fact, a complex of factors led to the decision to deploy the Euromissiles. These included West Germany's (headed by Chancellor Helmut Schmidt) desire to have a strong symbolic expression of continuing US commitment to NATO and the defense of Western Europe against the USSR. The eruption of the Euromissile controversy, which then rocked the West German government and stimulated an unprecedented, huge anti-nuclear peace movement was not expected. It was the nature of these missiles, their relation to a new warfighting strategy, and the growing technical expertise available to anti-nuclear activists and groups that ensured the subsequent political turmoil.

NATO was now reintroducing, after a prolonged stretch of over a decade, land-based weapons and siting them in densely populated Western Europe near major cities, making them in effect more attractive targets. Worse still, the Pershing-2's were far and away the most accurate missiles yet produced. They represented a qualitative leap in this respect, with the capability of hitting a target within a radius of a 100 feet. Their proposed deployment fitted into a new strategy different in one decisive respect from flexible response or earlier strategies for fighting limited or protracted nuclear wars. These were consciously perceived as first strike weapons par excellence. Cruise missiles (fitted either with conventional or nuclear warheads) undetectable by existing radar facilities or by satellites represented the first breakthrough in stealth technology and delivery systems. They were ideal tools for waging a limited nuclear war and thus powerful complements of the Pershing-2 missiles. What the latter provided the US and NATO with was the new ability to "decapitate" the political-military leadership of the Soviet weapons system.

Coming on top of the already imposing arsenal of the West, imposing both in quantity and quality, their introduction made no sense except to provide a much more refined ability than ever before to carry out the decapitation option.

Insofar as five or ten percent of Soviet warheads (400 to 800) might still survive such a decapitating first strike, these were to be taken care of by the development of a Star Wars system covering the US mainland. Thus, Euromissiles and SDI were complementary and integrated parts of a new politics of nuclearism aiming to set the pattern for the next decade and more. Of course, the SDI project was ridden with enormous difficulties. Building a near impenetrable shield was always something of a chimera, but what is important here, and disturbing, is that large and very influential sections of the US nuclear elite believed in the efficacy and feasibility of SDI and in nuclear warfighting generally and were preparing accordingly.

The new political and nuclear belligerence brought about by Reagan's doctrines and nuclear preparations was not only deeply provocative to the USSR, but obviously raised fears of a pre-emptive strike by the Soviet Union (before such preparations could come into effect) and led to a dramatic increase in nuclear tensions and arms racing. The Euromissiles made Europe particularly vulnerable. Here the peace movement reached hitherto undreamed of heights and led to much more radical demands. By contrast, in the US the central unifying demand of the growing anti-nuclear peace movement was not for dramatic reductions in arms or an end to the Cold War or for growing European neutrality across its East-West divide, both of which surfaced strongly in the European peace movement. It was simply for a nuclear freeze. But this movement was also bigger and wider than anything in the US since 1945, far eclipsing the 1967–70 opposition to the Sentinel and Safeguard ABM systems. This movement of the late '70s and '80s had significant influence on the US's political institutions from the local to the Congressional level.

Because, despite massive and unprecedented popular mobilization, the two major peace movements never succeeded in achieving their central demands, it is easy to dismiss them as of no ultimate consequence in weakening or halting the arms race. But to do this would be to make a fundamental error regarding the overall impact and relevance of these movements, which was very considerable indeed. They helped produce and disseminate a radical and powerful critique of nuclearism. They paved the way for future mobilizations and activities, thereby clearing the ground for sustained NGO interventions in later years. This has now become an institutionalized and important part of the general political scene concerning disarmament negotiations. Governments and officials became accessible and "answerable" to non-official sources in ways quite different from the pre-peace movement era. A proper evaluation of these peace movement will be taken up in a later chapter. For the moment it will suffice to point out that apart from raising and changing consciousness on a mass scale, they decisively influenced the terms of nuclear discourse and debate.

Advocates of continued arms racing and, worse, of preparing for limited nuclear wars, were pushed onto the defensive, having to rely ultimately on their rock-bottom "trump-card" claim that the Cold War necessitated such measures.

Thus, when the Cold War began to unwind it was no longer possible for decision-shaping and decision-making elites to avoid the new path of actual nuclear restraint and reductions. This shift toward greater sanity would neither have been so easy or so rapid or so widely endorsed without the prior impact of these peace movements. Furthermore, Gorbachev's own efforts to progressively denuclearize East-West relations through his specific proposals banked heavily on the influence on policy making exerted by a public made more responsive precisely by these peace movements in the US and Western Europe.

NOTES

[1] This was a debate about the meaning of the nuclear arms race and the nature of its relationship to Cold War structures. It was sparked off by E. P. Thompson, perhaps the single most representative figure on both sides of the Atlantic of the peace movement of the '80s. His powerful essay, "Notes on Exterminism, the Last Stage of Civilization," postulated an "exterminist logic" out of superpower control that overrode the Cold War face-off and subsumed it, thereby posing an even more acute danger than thought. Thompson sought to uncover the "distinctive" sources (beyond recognized Cold War theorizing of the time) of this terrible logic. For all his many insights, Thompson's basic argument was flawed. For a comprehensive survey of various arguments for and against Thompson's thesis at the time, see *Exterminism and the Cold War*, edited by New Left Review (London: Verso, 1982).

[2] See in particular the essays by Mike Davis, "Nuclear Imperialism and Extended Deterrence," Roy and Zhores Medvedev, "The USSR and the Arms Race," and Fred Halliday, "The Sources of the New Cold War" in the above collection.

Between 1948 and the present time, Russia directly invaded three countries, all of which were on its borders—Hungary (1956), Czechoslovakia (1968), and Afghanistan (1979). Over the same period, the US sent troops and bombers to many more countries far from its borders: Korea (1950–53), Iran (1953), Guatemala (1954), Lebanon (1958 and 1984), Vietnam (1960–75), the Congo (1960), Cuba (1961), the Dominican Republic (1965), Laos (1960, 1970s), Kampuchea (1970–75), Grenada (1983), Honduras (1985 onward), Panama (1989), Iraq (1991), Somalia (1993), Haiti (1995) and Kosovo: Serbia (1999).

[3] See M. Kaku & D. Axelrod, *To Win a Nuclear War* (London: Zed Books, 1987) Chapters 1, 2, 3 & 7.

[4] See results of a poll conducted by Lake Sosin Snell & Associates which asked the question, "Do you feel safer knowing that the US and other countries have nuclear weapons, or would you feel safer if you knew for sure that no country including the US had nuclear weapons?" Appeared in a leaflet issued by the Global Resource Action Center for the Environment (GRACE), New York, April 1997. Information also available at aslater@igc.apc.org.

[5] The Baruch Plan (named after a Wall Street financier, Bernard Baruch) called for the creation of an International Atomic Development Authority that would take control of "all phases of the development and use of atomic energy." Three aspects of the Plan doomed it in Soviet eyes. This Authority, though under the UN, would not be subject to the Security Council or otherwise be subjected to a national veto. The

USSR, not unreasonably, felt this would ensure US domination. The Plan also threatened "condign punishment" for violators. In this case the only potential violator was the USSR and the US the only country in a position to impose punishment. The Plan also assigned vague obligations to the US and clear and harsh ones to the USSR. The US would have retained a knowledge monopoly on how to make the bomb.

The Soviet counter proposal insisted on the retention of national sovereignty but called for an international convention "prohibiting the production and employment of weapons based on the use of atomic energy." All stocks would be destroyed within three months of the convention coming into force. Two other committees would respectively ensure circulation of relevant information so as to eliminate a knowledge monopoly, and devise a system of safeguards against violation. This would emerge in full and institutionalized form only after the stocks were destroyed. The US viewed this Soviet proposal with deep suspicion as aiming to eliminate the US "advantage" without a prior Soviet sacrifice, while not trusting that the Soviets would not hide their capabilities afterward.

6

Perceived nuclear balance in 1963

	US	USSR
ICBM launchers	229	44
SLBM launchers	144	97
IRBM launchers	105	20–40 in Cuba (before removal)
Strategic bombers	1,300	155+

By 1970

	US	USSR
ICBMs	1,054	1,300
SLBMs	656	240
Strategic bombers	520	140
Total warheads	4,000	1,800
Megatonnage	4,300	3,100

By 1980

	US	USSR
ICBMs	1,050	1,398
SLBMs	544	920
Strategic bombers	375	150
Warheads	9,900	7,800

For the US, submarines carried 57% of total warhead strength, land-based ICBMs carried 22%, and bombers carried 21%. For the USSR, land-based ICBMs carried 68% of warhead strength, submarines carried 23%, and bombers 9%.

By 1988

	US	USSR
ICBMs	1,000	1,382
SLBMs	640	922
Strategic bombers	396	155

The US had a total of 23,400 warheads, of which 13,012 were strategically deployed; the USSR had 20,600 warheads, of which 11,450 were strategically deployed.

Sources: Harvard Nuclear Study Group, *Living with Nuclear Weapons* (Cambridge, Massachusetts: Harvard University Press, 1983) 87, 90, & 120. *SIPRI Yearbook 1988*

(Oxford: Oxford University Press, 1988) Tables 2.1, 2.2, 2.4 & 2.5; pp. 36, 37, 39 &40.

7 Information released in 1995 and 1996 revealed that there were three occasions during the three-week Cuban missile crisis when either side could have launched a strike because of system failures and miscalculation compounded by fear. There was a routine missile test flight by the US Navy from Florida into the Atlantic that was not immediately identified. The US thought it might be a launch from Cuba at them; the Soviets thought it might be a launch by the US against Cuba. Ten minutes of high tension passed before the character of the incident became clear. From a secret airbase in North Dakota a false alert was triggered, leading to nuclearly equipped planes already instructed to hit targets in Russia almost taking off before being stopped at literally the last minute. From Alaska, a US plane mistakenly intruded deep into Soviet airspace and two Soviet planes equipped with air-to-air missiles were sent to knock it down. Before this could happen, two US planes went after the plane because tower signals were not reaching it. Fortunately, these US planes reached the offending pilot first and radioed him to turn back and get out of Soviet airspace before the Soviet planes could reach him. But it was a close call.

All this was quite apart from the pressure put on Kennedy by military and civilian leaders to launch a first strike. In this regard, see the book transcript of *The Kennedy Tapes* by E. R. May and P. D. Zelikow (Cambridge, Massachusetts: Belknap Press of Harvard University, 1997); and *One Hell of a Gamble: Krushchev, Castro, and Kennedy 1958-64* by A. Fursenko and T. Naftali (New York: W. W. Norton, 1997).

8 See J. Finney, "A Historical Perspective" in *The ABM Treaty: To Defend Or Not To Defend*, ed. by W. Stutzle, B. Jasani and R. Cowen (Oxford: SIPRI publications, Oxford University Press, 1987).

9 The ABM Treaty allows theater missile defenses (TMDs) but places two limits on them. TMDs cannot be given "capabilities to counter strategic missiles" nor can they be "tested in an ABM mode," i.e., against targets with the characteristics of strategic missiles. But since the ABM Treaty does not clearly define the difference between theater and strategic missiles nor the meaning of "capabilities to counter," this gray area is currently being exploited by the US through the development and testing of two high altitude wide-area TMD systems—the Army's Theater High Altitude Area Defense (THAAD) system and the Navy's Upper Tier System.

Both intend to make intercepts above the atmosphere and appear to have intrinsic strategic capabilities. They raise serious compliance problems with the ABM Treaty. The US is currently seeking modifications in the ABM Treaty through negotiations with Russia in favor of these TMDs. The key issue is to fill the lacuna in regard to TMD demarcation.

Chapter 3

Hesitant and New: Disarmament Momentum after the Cold War

Ultimately, the single most important reason why the Cold War began to unwind and then ended was that the Gorbachev leadership of the USSR decided to end it by offering, in effect, what can be called a "global historic compromise."[1] This was a deeply contradictory political phenomenon with both negative and positive consequences. Its negative aspect was most clearly visible in the third world, where the USSR then effectively abandoned all efforts to provide a counterweight to Western and US power. Third world challengers to any Western-approved form of the status quo could no longer count on the existence of a systemic rivalry to mean even cautious Soviet support for themselves. From Namibia to Cuba to Somalia to Panama to the anti-Iraq Gulf War, since 1987 the USSR (and its successor Russian state) has silently acquiesced, explicitly endorsed, or even sought to partner, US initiatives. Insofar as Russia today has expressed unease and opposition to US and Western political initiatives, these have to do with its concerns in the regions of the former USSR and in Europe, but not in regard to US and Western behavior in the third world, except in those parts of Asia closer to home, such as Afghanistan, where Russia has been somewhat more critical.

Global historic compromise was a Soviet attempt to rewrite the rules of systemic incommensurability in a way whereby rivalry would be replaced by a longer term acceptance of systemic difference and a more determined search than ever before for strategic cooperation, if not quite strategic partnership. Gorbachev did not envisage a systemic convergence of the two different social orders. He pursued the chimera of an enduring and stable compatibility between two different social systems to be brought about by changes on both sides. On the Western side it should rest on (1) the emergence of a new non-antagonistic foreign policy toward the USSR and the Soviet bloc of countries; (2) political approval of, and non-interference with, the domestic changes he was preparing to make; (3) material and economic-financial help. On his side it would rest on wider popular legitimacy for the "socialist system" to be brought about by internal democratization in the USSR and guided, steady democratization in the Eastern European countries, and Soviet economic reorganization in the direction of establishing a vaguely-understood and vaguely-defined form of market socialism.

Six Renunciations

The ending of the Cold War had its most positive impact in two areas. The first involved the freeing of Eastern Europe from decades of Soviet domination, even if its systemic collapse was not foreseen. There was also the reunification of Germany. This was a positive step because it was ultimately desired by the overwhelming majority of Germans on both sides of the former divide. But there was also an unfortunate dimension to this historic event because what actually took place was not reunification but the effective annexation by West Germany of the eastern part. Second, the end of the Cold War completely derailed the politics of nuclearism pursued by the US under Reagan. But any hopes (between 1986 and 1989) that the dismantling of the various structures of the Cold War would be effected somewhat symmetrically and that the decline of Soviet hegemony would be paralleled by a broadly commensurate decline in US-led Western imperialism, would be dashed by the cataclysmic and revolutionary events of 1989 and after.

The systemic collapse of Soviet Socialism, its own political, territorial, economic and ideological breakdown as a result of the general dynamic let loose (but not controlled) by the specific pattern and pace of the Gorbachev reforms, led to a "victory" for the other side. This was a victory utterly unexpected both in its comprehensiveness and in the speed with which it came about. This had to have significant consequences for the new politics of nuclearism that was, and is, slowly emerging after the end of the Cold War. Not all of these consequences have been positive.

The end of the Cold War and the initiation of a process of arms reduction effectively extinguished the felt danger of a nuclear exchange, which had been the vital emotional foundation for the existence of an active, anti-nuclear mass movement in Europe and the US. After all, the political basis for fearing an exchange was no longer present and a momentum of sorts involving genuine and substantial arms reductions much beyond the scope of earlier arms management exercises, had been well and truly established. From the 1987 Intermediate Nuclear Forces (INF) Treaty eliminating all land-based theater missiles, to the removal (not formalized by treaties) of tactical missiles from all surface ships of the US and Russia (this began from 1991 on), to the negotiation of the Strategic Arms Reduction Treaties (START I and START II), which cut strategic warheads by more than half, much was seemingly being accomplished and more promised.

So far as things go this judgment was not incorrect. Other restraint and disarmament measures also got a fillip. Three actual NWSs—Belarus, Kazakhstan and Ukraine—all gave up their NWS status. The first two countries (had they wanted to) would have found it difficult to buck Russian objections to their retaining this status, since Moscow claimed their missiles as its own. But they didn't want to keep the weapons systems even though they had the sovereign right to do so. Ukraine, with the third largest arsenal in the world, could have done so much more easily, if it had wanted to, overriding any Russian objections. Again, it chose to trade in its nuclear arsenal to Russia for financial rewards from the West. All three joined the Non-Proliferation Treaty (NPT). Three nuclear capable states—South Africa, Argentina, and Brazil—gave up nuclear threshold status, motivated at least in part by the emergence of a new climate of global disarmament and restraint in nuclear matters. Certainly, the white de Klerk regime had begun to dismantle the nuclear arsenal because the end of apartheid and the accession of a black majority government was near. To put it bluntly, neither they nor their Western protectors wanted a black government to have the bomb. But it is necessary to note that the African National Congress (ANC), even during the period of racist rule, had always opposed nuclear status for South Africa. When apartheid was overthrown and the Mandela government took over, South Africa also became (under majority rule) one of the most active governments anywhere in regard to issues of general and global disarmament.

All the NWSs joined and ratified the South Pacific Nuclear Weapons Free Zone (NWFZ) agreement called the Treaty of Rarotonga. Two new NWFZ treaties were drawn up—the African NWFZ, or Treaty of Pelindaba, and the Southeast Asian NWFZ, or Bangkok Treaty. For the latter to come into formal existence, it had to be ratified by the Philippines; this has now happened. The US and China, however, still have reservations about recognizing this Southeast Asian NWFZ because of their objections to its insistence that there be no transit of nuclear weapons in sea areas the US and China deem should lie outside the Treaty's purview. Moreover, the Treaty of Pelindaba did not demand a real sacrifice on the part of the existing NWFZs, especially as the nuclear munitions base of Diego Garcia was excluded from the Treaty. Nevertheless, these NWFZs were valued gains in themselves as well as in their creation of the possibility of more NWFZs—some which would, if established, require the dismantling of existing nuclear placements. In general, the overall disarmament momentum was being strengthened by such developments, even though more sacrifices on the part of the NWSs had to be demanded. But to be accurate, the overall assessment of post-Cold War disarmament possibilities has to consider more than just these treaties, which alone encourage excessive optimism.

The weaknesses inherent in the way in which the Cold War ended were beginning to surface more clearly. Since West and East shared the blame (albeit unevenly—the West was more responsible) for initiating and perpetuating the Cold War, its long anticipated ending was expected to bring about more changes and improvements than it actually did. Many, if not most, opponents of the Cold War who also did not align themselves with either side, expected both military-nuclear blocs in Europe to be dismantled more or less completely. The drift that had emerged during the

'80s toward greater European independence from, and neutrality in, bloc politics was expected to be reinforced by the ending of this bloc conflict. Instead, what emerged was the complete collapse of the Warsaw Pact, but not of NATO.

Not only was US ascendancy in Europe retained, but strengthened. The earlier pressures for the establishment of a series of European NWFZs, such as in the Baltic-Nordic region, the Balkans, and in Central Europe, were actually weakened. The way in which Germany was unified deprived the former Soviet Union of any bargaining power whatsoever. So, while the eastern part of Germany would, in deference to Soviet wishes, be kept nuclear-free, the same would not apply to the western part, where US-controlled NATO missiles would remain. The presumed East-West imbalance of the past would now be reversed. Earlier it had been claimed that the Warsaw Pact countries enjoyed a conventional superiority over their NATO counterparts, which had to be countered by NATO's nuclear arsenal. Now the Soviets felt the need to rely more strongly than before on their nuclear might in order to compensate for their conventional inferiority vis-a-vis NATO forces. As it was, the massive collapse of the ex-USSR reinforced the views of those Russians who now felt that a strong nuclear weapons system was the one symbol of Great Power status that Russia still possessed and should retain. In a striking reflection of its new strategic reliance on a nuclear (albeit much reduced) arsenal, Russia retracted its decades long commitment to No First Use of nuclear weapons. Of the five first NWSs, only China still continues to adhere to this posture.

Many of the former members of the East European socialist bloc, in the face of their own crises of transition to capitalist democracies, had no other strategic vision beyond a desperate desire to join the European community as quickly as possible. Insofar as joining NATO could be paraded as an expression of their determined loyalty to the European Union (EU) and to its related Atlantic Alliance, the new East European leaderships had no qualms whatsoever about joining NATO on whatever terms it or the US might propose. Such is the alacrity of countries like Poland, Hungary, and Czechia in this regard that they unilaterally declared themselves willing to accept NATO nuclear emplacements on their territories without this even being stipulated as a requirement for their membership.

With the end of the Cold War, the earlier rationale for the existence of NATO had greatly weakened. But only one bloc was demilitarized. The other military-nuclear bloc continued, indeed was strengthened politically and territorially, and was under no serious public pressure from any direction to dismantle itself. Russian desires in this respect were impotent and incapable of being fulfilled. What NATO had to do was to find a newer rationale as well as clothe an older one (keeping Russia out, Germany down, and the US in) in an outward public garb different from that of the past, which had simply been to protect Europe against the Soviet threat. Only a small dissident minority in the US strategic establishment has rightly seen the historic opportunity arising after the end of the Cold War to completely reorganize US-Soviet and European-Soviet relations on a dramatically newer basis of a "common" European security, in which Russia would be invited to play an honorable and welcome part. This would imply taking rapid and very significant steps toward the steady de-militarization and de-nuclearization of NATO, as well as a much more dramatic withdrawal of the US military-political presence in Europe.[2] The much larger majority within this establishment has been happier promoting an *expanded* political-military role for NATO, and they have won out.

NATO Enlargement and Stockpile Stewardship

NATO enlargement as a now approved and established policy perspective represents a dangerous continuity with previous policy aspirations. It indicates that the US still seeks to use its "victory" in the Cold War to institutionalize and consolidate its relative political gains vis-a-vis Russia in a global game the latter is no longer able to play. This policy is dangerous because it continues to treat Russia as a strategic opponent (no matter what other public rationale for NATO expansion is given) and in doing so has all the makings in a worst-case scenario of becoming a self-fulfilling prophecy. Even if the worst does not happen, it will still certainly create and sustain avoidable tensions whose outcome is deeply unpredictable in the longer term. NATO expansion in Europe is also a way for the US to maintain political-strategic-military dominance over a potential capitalist rival—a German-centered Europe, should that emerge as a likely possibility in the future.

The specifically nuclear consequences of NATO enlargement are two-fold. It virtually guarantees that there will be stronger limits on further Russian de-nuclearization. It is also one of the two most serious blows that have been inflicted on the new global disarmament momentum that emerged after 1987. Thus this momentum had slowed and become more tenuous and uneven well before the Indian and Pakistani tests of May 1998 added their own body blows.

Another consequence of the particular manner in which the Cold War ended was that it effectively left a much freer hand for the US to pursue its imperialist ambitions in the third world. On the level of nuclear politics this means the emergence of a peculiar contradiction. On the one hand, third world challenges no longer imply by proxy a Russian or systemic conflict against the US or West. Therefore, the astrategic irrelevance of the nuclear threat for coping with such challenges is reinforced. The US might feel freer to indulge in such threats without fear of this escalating into a Great Power nuclear exchange. But it also has much less reason than ever to engage in, or carry out, such threats. On the other hand, this situation of greater flexibility and freedom for US power also reinforces the non-proliferation dimension of US strategic-nuclear thinking and its approach to post-Cold War arms restraint and disarmament proposals and measures. Hence "counter-proliferation"—not disarmament—has become the new code word for a developing policy of preventing at all costs potential opponents in the third world from getting such weapons or otherwise trying to pose any kind of strategic threat to the US.

To be sure, after the end of the Cold War there was in the US a definite shift in the relationship of forces between arm reducers/moderators and arms racers in favor of the former. But the other side of the picture is not so positive. While there is a growing lobby in the opinion-shaping elite that genuinely wants to move toward complete arms elimination, it remains so small as to be literally dwarfed by arms retainers, whether of the more moderate or extreme kind. The earlier autonomy of the Arms Control and Disarmament Agency (ACDA) has ended; it is being merged into the State Department. In both houses of Congress, Republican domination has created another major obstacle to pressing the scope and pace, and sometimes even the fact of arms reductions.

In the US, the basic direction of the new politics of nuclearism is revealed by two important strategic documents—the Nuclear Posture Review, or NPR (September 1994), and the Presidential Decision Directive, or PDD-60 (November 1997). Recognizing a new post-Cold War reality in which the overall trend will be toward further reductions in the arsenals of the US and Russia, the crucial aim of these documents is to provide a new strategic rationale for the enduring *retention* of nuclear weapons. Thus even though the US establishment is not in its decisive majority willing to buck the current trend of qualitative restraint and quantitative decline in nuclear weapons (unless there is some dramatic change in global politics or a sharp reversal in the existing disarmament momentum) it is determined not to allow that momentum to gather such force that the US is no longer able to partly control, direct, and factor this momentum into its overall nuclear strategy.

Thus NPR and PDD-60 try to make a smaller number of nuclear weapons do newer and more things. Newer, yet-to-be-fully-articulated, strategic tasks for these weapons have to be established and newer enemies—"rogue states"—have to be discovered to justify their retention. With the end of the Cold War, these "rogue states" are to be found in the third world, especially in places of continuing strategic importance like the Middle East—but not only there. The countries the US has in mind as actual or potential rogue states are Iraq, Libya, Iran, and North Korea. But, of course, the label can fit any other possible challenger to future US interests. The formulation of a new nuclear-strategic doctrine is obviously connected to the need to formulate a new general ideology of justification for continued US efforts to dominate the world order. Thus the peregrinations of a Samuel Huntington is also part of this same process of wider and newer ideological and strategic rethinking in the post-Cold War era. His thesis about the "clash of civilizations" obviously aims to highlight the possible new challenges to US political dominance by, on one hand, the "Islamic" states of the Middle East, and on the other hand, to US and Western economic eminence by the "Confucian" countries of the Far East, that is, China and other rapid industrializers in that region.

Since a smaller arsenal must do more things, it must last longer: hence the US's Science-based Stockpile Stewardship and Management Program (SBSS & MP). Ostensibly directed at assuring the "safety and reliability" of an aging stockpile, it is a much more comprehensive program, which, when allied to ongoing sub-critical experiments, computer simulation activities, and R&D of direct fusion weapons, clearly aims to continue developing new applications of existing weapons designs and designing new weapons to the degree possible within the limits imposed by the ban on explosive testing. The US has already carried out a first series of six sub-critical tests, with more such tests contemplated. Russia has also carried out (up to February 1999) five sub-critical tests. Research into direct fusion is, of course, a leap into the unknown. But it is continuing. The point is that there exists a strong pro-nuclear lobby with particularly strong roots in sections of the defense services and especially in the weapons laboratories and its associated bodies and personnel. If these groups are not decisively weakened, their activities will continue.

True, a Comprehensive Test Ban Treaty (CTBT) imposes powerful limits on what can be achieved in qualitative advance through all such activities. Nonetheless, the SBSS & MP violates the general intent and spirit of the CTBT, which aims to put an end to such efforts at qualitative advancement regardless of how successful or unsuccessful they might turn out to be. Even if they fail to achieve their desired ends, such activities preserve much of the software and prepare much of the hardware for rapidly getting back on to the track of major qualitative advances in nuclear weaponry should the US ever break out of the CTBT.

All this, then, is part of the continuing project of ensuring US global political-military dominance. While there has been (since 1987) a significant relative decline in nuclear arsenals and preparations when compared to what was taking place during the Cold War period, it is noteworthy that in regard to conventional weapons preparations and expenditures by the US, there is no such comparative decline over a similar period![3] The post-Cold War era, then, has seen a distinctive mix of the positive and the negative in its ongoing and contested politics of nuclearism. Unlike during the 1945–87 period when the negative outweighed the positive—despite the PTBT and the ABM Treaty, the overall trajectory of the arms race was upward—today the positive has so far outweighed the negative.

But even positive measures of significant import like the CTBT and the "Advisory Opinion" against the legality of nuclear weapons issued by the International Court of Justice (ICJ) or World Court in July 1996 have had their effects weakened by the continued perfidy and hypocrisies of the existing NWSs, most notably, but not solely, the US. The one country that is today uniquely placed to lead the world rapidly to complete or near-complete nuclear disarmament is the country most determined still to use the possession of nuclear weapons for the pursuit of general political and foreign policy objectives.

Indefinite Extension of the NPT

If NATO consolidation and expansion was one major assault on the post-Cold War disarmament momentum, the other big blow was given by the permanent and indefinite extension of the NPT in April 1995. This showed as nothing else did the determination of the existing NWSs to maintain their exclusive club and to completely distort the original purpose of the NPT. Through its permanent and indefinite extension, this one living institutionalized commitment of the NWSs to carry out their own eventual disarmament has been finally and fully transformed into nothing more than the central institutionalized mechanism for ensuring the enduring exclusivity of the nuclear club.

The fact that France and China finally joined the NPT regime in the post-Cold War period did not reflect a newfound commitment on their part to obey Article VI, which calls on the NWSs that are signatories to the treaty to pursue negotiations for complete disarmament "in good faith." Nor did it mean a newfound enthusiasm on their part for promoting global disarmament. Both countries had earlier repeatedly committed themselves to joining disarmament negotiations if the US and Russia reduced their arsenals by fifty percent. Once this became feasible and certain in the post-Cold War era, both quite shamelessly drew back from their promises in this regard. France and China (along with the UK) now declared that they would only enter such negotiations when the US and Russia had reduced their arsenals by ninety-five percent. It is in keeping with this cynical mentality that China and France joined the NPT. That is to say, they joined the NPT when they correctly perceived it to have been reduced to nothing more than a collective mechanism for ensuring non-proliferation outside the ranks of the NWSs, while also legitimizing their own "formal" entry and status into the nuclear club.

How did this betrayal of earlier hopes in the NPT entertained by the NNWSs come about? It was due to a combination of factors. At the heart of the NPT lay a bargain—renunciation of the nuclear option by NNWSs in return for a commitment by NWSs who were members of the treaty to move toward complete global disarmament. The NPT still contains the only legal commitment made by the NWSs to carry out total disarmament, hence its enduring attraction to many NNWSs and anti-nuclear activists and groups who see in this fact the existence of some minimal point of international diplomatic leverage vis-a-vis the NWSs. Even the World Court ruling took strength from Article VI and the legal commitment it embodied.

So disillusioned, however, had the NNWSs become with the perfidious behavior of the NWSs in not obeying this Article that by the time the treaty's life was ending (twenty-five years after 1970, when it came into force) and the issue of its possible extension came up, the precise fate of the NPT was quite uncertain. It was by no means self-evident that the NPT would survive. Certainly, its permanent and indefinite extension was widely considered to be among the less likely outcomes. The most widespread view was that the NPT would be extended, but not indefinitely, and that most bargaining would be around the length of time for which it should be extended. The NWSs would want as long a time period as possible, while NNWSs would have to arrive at agreement about what would be a reasonable time period. It was obvious to all that as long as the extension was limited, the NNWSs would possess stronger leverage on the NWSs, since the NPT's future life could again be made more easily conditional on future behavior by the NWSs.

Yet the unexpected happened: the NPT was permanently and indefinitely extended, thereby depriving the NNWSs of the earlier leverage they had and could have maintained. Three factors best account for this denouement. First, the NWSs were broadly united in expressing and pressing for this common aim. The US, in particular, carefully played the numbers game, exercising enormous behind-the-scenes arm-twisting pressure to get the maximum number of NNWSs lined up in support of its own position. Second, while the NPT was not itself in any way responsible for the reductions in arms that took place after 1987 between the US and Russia, the fact of such reductions and the existence of a new more positive climate of restraint and disarmament in its own way also gave something of a reprieve, a new infusion of life, into the NPT regime. A number of NNWSs were more inclined to believe that in the new improved political context maybe the NPT could be made to function as it was earlier expected to, with Article VI being taken more seriously. The fact that certain key NNWSs, such as South Africa, who were among the most pro-active on disarmament, were inclined to support permanent extension also helped to swing matters that way. But the single most important factor was almost certainly the time-bound commitment made by the NWSs (for the first time) to conclude a Comprehensive Test Ban Treaty, or CTBT, before the end of 1996. This commitment was legally enshrined in the new "Principles and Objectives" drawn up and appended to the newly extended NPT. Without this commitment to the CTBT, the whole NPT regime risked unraveling. The CTBT, then, was a vital concession, one which the NWSs had to make in order to preserve the NPT as the central pillar in its non-proliferation regime.

The final passage of the CTBT, despite Indian opposition to it, marked one of the more significant gains in the effort to promote arms restraint and a cap to the qualitative nuclear arms race. The political-psychological, health, and environmental effects of a world permanently free of further testing should not be underestimated. Apart from this, the CTBT had other distinctive strengths. Unlike the PTBT or even the NPT (where the penultimate draft was drawn up behind closed doors by the US, USSR and

UK and passed with only minor revisions), the CTBT was the first ever genuinely multilaterally negotiated nuclear arms related treaty. As such, it set a crucial precedent—that global disarmament and restraint measures are too important to be simply left to the NWSs alone. Furthermore, after entering into force, the CTBT would for the first time set up a genuinely international monitoring system of structures, institutions, and powers that in key respects would override national authority and sovereignty. Insofar as a world free of nuclear weapons necessarily requires a mindset that transcends both nationalism and its actual institutions, and structures that override national sovereignty, all in the interests of a universal humanity, the CTBT in this regard too, sets a vital practical-institutional precedent.

But the CTBT in its final form also suffers from two serious weaknesses. The first pertains to the manner prescribed for its coming into force. This requires states like India and Pakistan, which at the time of writing have not done so, to sign the treaty before it can enter into force. Not only is this undemocratic and unfair to the countries concerned, who have the right (howsoever mistaken it might be to exercise it) to refuse their assent, but more importantly it is unfair to the treaty, which should enter into force as quickly as possible and apply to all those countries that have agreed to come under its aegis.

The second major flaw is that the CTBT is important not just in itself but as a step that further strengthens the momentum to more restraint and disarmament measures. Here the linkage of the CTBT to this general process is significant. In order to promote the multilateralization of disarmament negotiations, the CTBT should have been linked to the setting up of an Ad Hoc Committee on global nuclear disarmament in the Conference on Disarmament (CD) with at least a discussion mandate to begin with, striving for a negotiating mandate later. It is an Ad Hoc Committee because the mandate for it has to be renewed each year in accordance with the CD's special procedures. Achieving this would have constituted a major breakthrough, and endorsing the setting up of such an Ad Hoc Committee could have been embodied in the preamble of the treaty.

This is absent from the final treaty but could have emerged as a very real likelihood if India had been prepared to lead many other NNWSs in fulfilling this demand, for which they were already pressing hard. Since India's accession to the CTBT was greatly valued by the NWSs, it could have bargained for this as the price for its assent. But New Delhi was never serious about wanting a better or stronger CTBT. It was primarily concerned with justifying its rejection of the CTBT not just on "national security" grounds but on moral grounds, calling it deceptive, flawed, discriminatory, manipulative, etc.[4] Thus an opportunity to strengthen the link between the CTBT and the wider process of disarmament was lost.

A Spate of New Initiatives and the World Court Verdict

If the various treaties embodying arms reductions, the establishment of more NWFZs, the CTBT, and a possible fissiles materials cut-off treaty (FMCT), can all be said to represent the "hardware" of the new global restraint and disarmament process, then there is also the matter of generating new "software" products. Changing the "software" means, above all, attacking the moral legitimacy of nuclear weapons possession, undermining its strategic-political claims, and eroding the appeal and hold of the deterrence mindset. The credibility and authority of nuclear elites—their "security managers" and their pro-nuclear opinion-shapers—has to be progressively weakened. In the post-Cold War era, among the most important initiatives in this regard have been the Canberra Commission Report, the public statement against nuclear weapons by over sixty retired admirals and generals from seventeen countries, and the spate of new UN resolutions by NNWSs—for example, Malaysia— newly motivated to activate themselves and others on the disarmament issue.

On December 4, 1996, the former head of the US Strategic Air Command, George "Lee" Butler, and former NATO Commander, Andrew J. Goodpaster, issued a statement calling for the ultimate elimination of nuclear weapons from the world's arsenals. They were joined by sixty others the next day. It has since become a very important point of reference precisely because so many of its signatories were former advocates of deterrence and have now turned opponents of this doctrine. One of its leading figures, General Butler, has repeatedly declared that, far from nuclear deterrence providing security during the Cold War era, the truth was that for the decision-making elite of which he was so important a part, it did *not* provide such security; this elite never felt the US was safe during the whole period of arms racing.[5]

On November 26, 1995, the Australian Premier, Paul Keating, announced the formation of a fifteen-member Canberra Commission to outline "practical steps toward a nuclear weapons-free world including the related problems of maintaining stability and security during the transitional period and after this goal is accomplished." Members of the Commission included General George Butler, Field Marshall Lord Carver (UK), Robert McNamara (former President of the World Bank and ex-US Secretary of State), Professor Joseph Rotblat (Nobel Prize Winner), and Michel Rocard (former Premier of France). The Commission submitted its report on August 14, 1996 outlining a phased program for total disarmament.

The following year, the Malaysian-sponsored UN Resolution (A/C.1/51/L.37) of November 6, 1996 called for the "commencement of negotiations leading to the conclusion of a Nuclear Weapons Convention..." It declared that the

> time has now come for the issue of the elimination of nuclear weapons, which is an equally important, indeed integral, part of the NPT process, to be

addressed... by the international community. Unless this issue is addressed, and addressed promptly... the entire trade-off would be questioned by many a non-nuclear weapons States Parties... if this trend were to continue, it could only undermine... the prospects of its attaining universality.

The Resolution called for sponsorship and support

> of all delegations who share these sentiments and are opposed to the threat or use of nuclear weapons and who would like to ensure that concrete and effective steps are taken now to pave the way for their total elimination within a realistic time frame, in the interest of ensuring the well-being and survival of humanity.

On December 10, 1996, there was a landmark vote in the UN General Assembly, with over two-thirds of the 169 voting states supporting the resolution for an NWC.

In late 1998, after an SPD-Greens coalition government was formed in Germany, the new government publicly called for a re-evaluation of NATO's nuclear doctrines. Specifically, Germany called for NATO to reconsider its first-use trip-wire perspective and to consider the adoption of a No First Use of nuclear weapons pledge. This badly shocked the US, France, and the UK. Under pressure, the new German government reiterated that it was not questioning the general rationale for NATO's nuclear arsenal but still did not budge on the issue of re-evaluating existing first use doctrine. Belgium and Canada, also NATO members, did the same. For the first time, some NATO members called for the strategic re-evaluation of NATO nuclear doctrines in the post-Cold War era. In December 1998, seven countries (Sweden, Ireland, Egypt, Mexico, Brazil, New Zealand, and South Africa) in what is called the New Agenda Coalition, pushed an anti-nuclear resolution at the UN that got overwhelming support, including abstentions from twelve out of sixteen NATO countries who defied great pressure from the US, UK and France to vote against the resolution. The US, UK, France, Russia, India, and Pakistan voted against this resolution. The new political cracks in NATO regarding the doctrinal basis for the Alliance's retention of nuclear weapons are real and will not go away.

But perhaps the single most significant event was the historic ruling on July 8, 1996, by the World Court at The Hague. The UN General Assembly had put the following question to the World Court: "Is the threat or use of nuclear weapons in any circumstances permitted under international law?" Through its verdict, the ICJ (considered the highest tribunal in the world on matters of international law) provided the first ever legal determination on the issue. It held that "the threat or use of nuclear weapons would generally be contrary to the rules of international law applicable in armed conflict, and in particular the principles and rules of humanitarian law." The ICJ also unanimously affirmed that Article VI of the NPT obligated the NWSs to move toward rapid disarmament, and called upon them to do so.

The verdict vindicated the principles of international humanitarian law, judging not just the use, but the existence and possession of, and the preparations for developing, nuclear weapons a violation in this regard. The phrase "general incompatibility" indicated both the minimum basis of agreement on the unethicality and the indefensibility of nuclear weapons and of nuclear deterrence thinking. It also revealed that there was no collective agreement or ruling among all fourteen judges on the narrower and legally problematic issue (which some judges held invalid to start with) as to whether the use of nuclear weapons may be justified in extreme and exceptional circumstances such as threats to "the very survival of a state."

The whole case was considered so weighty that all fourteen judges passed separate opinions, some of outstanding quality like the eighty-seven-page document of the Sri Lankan judge, Weeramantry, which declared that "the use or threat of use of nuclear weapons is absolutely prohibited by existing law—in all circumstances and without reservation." Though the appointments to the ICJ are political choices, and judges usually vocalize and defend the views of the nominating states, this did not prevent an overall verdict that deeply dismayed the NWSs, despite the presence of judges from Germany and Britain who were expected to be more favorable to their nuclear concerns. The ICJ verdict did not fully delegitimize nuclear weapons possession but it was an historic step forward in the effort to do so. It was an example of what NGOs and other actors in international civil society can do to strengthen the general disarmament process. It was, after all, a coalition of peace groups that took the initiative known as the World Court Project, got it adopted by the UN system, and referred to the ICJ for a ruling.

If we were to sum up the overall trajectory and character of the post-Cold War disarmament momentum up to the middle of 1998, we could in a single sentence say that it was hesitant, uneven, frequently faltering, and fully capable of being reversed, but nonetheless, new, genuine, alive, and significant. It was in this context that the Indian and Pakistani tests erupted in May 1998. That they severely damaged this momentum is beyond doubt. That they might lead to its reversal has yet to be seen or determined. The final outcome depends on what can be done from now on to salvage what has been gained, to preserve and strengthen this momentum through other positive steps. This is the central task of our times.

NOTES

[1] *Compromesso Storico* or "Historic Compromise" was a term first coined in the '70s by Enrico Berlinguer, then leader of the Italian Communist Party (PCI), to justify his new strategy of calling for a new partnership to replace the longstanding and deep-seated historical rivalry between the two major forces in domestic Italian politics—the PCI and the Christian Democrats. This seemingly bold venture did not impress the CD and did not provide the hoped for political breakthrough to the PCI. It was part of a developing Eurocommunist strategy in Western Europe. However,

Eurocommunism merely paved the way for the rise of Eurosocialism (the eclipse of mass Communist parties in Western Europe by their social democratic rivals), which in turn swung to the right and thereby paved the way for the dominance of a hard right neo-liberalism among its liberal and conservative opposition.

2 A German "non-paper" was apparently submitted before the election of the new coalition government of the Social Democratic Party and the Greens that reportedly called for substantial denuclearization of NATO. This report gained credence from the fact that after the elections the new government publicly called for re-evaluating NATO's traditional nuclear doctrines and effectively scrapping its first use of nuclear weapons policy.

3	US	Russia	UK	France	China
Total operational	8,420	10,240	160	449	400
Awaiting dismantling	1,350	12,000	220	50	50
Reserve		2,300			
Total	**12,070**	**22,500**	**380**	**500**	**450**

Source: W. M. Arkin, R. S. Norris, J. Handler, *Taking Stock: Worldwide Nuclear Deployments, 1998* (Washington, DC: Natural Resources Defense Council, March 1998).

4 For a detailed refutation of the criticisms of the CTBT by the Indian government and its supporters, see P. Bidwai and A. Vanaik, "Why India Should Sign the CTBT: Returning to Our Own Agenda," *Economic and Political Weekly* (Mumbai)   19–25   Sept.   1998.

5 The Statement called for the following steps to be taken.

"First, present and planned stockpiles of nuclear weapons are exceedingly large and should now be greatly cut back;

Second, remaining nuclear weapons should be gradually and transparently taken off alert, and their readiness substantially reduced both in nuclear weapons states and in de facto nuclear weapons states;

Third, long-term international nuclear policy must be based on the declared principle of continuous, complete, and irrevocable elimination of nuclear weapons."

Chapter 4

The Road to Pokharan II and Chagai

The Fateful Days of May 1998

When the Prime Minister's Office (PMO) in New Delhi announced in the early afternoon of May 11, 1998 that Atal Behari Vajpayee, then having completed only seven weeks in office, would hold a press conference at 5:30 P.M. Indian Standard Time (12 noon GMT that day), only a few journalists in India could have guessed that he would make the fateful declaration about Indian nuclear test explosions that shocked the world. At that hour, barely 8 A.M. in Washington, the junior officer at the Defense Intelligence Agency monitoring images from satellites that periodically fly over northwestern India had yet to notice that a series of three explosions had actually taken place just two hours earlier at Pokharan, in the desert state of Rajasthan, where India first tested a nuclear explosive device in May 1974, and which had long been suspected to be the site of further nuclear preparations.[1]

It took the world some hours before responding, with a mixture of astonishment, shock, anger, disbelief, and disgust, to India's announcement. Many Indians were stunned. Some were impressed at what they thought was an act of defiance directed at the world's nuclear hegemons. Some were persuaded that the explosions were a political stunt. And a few (especially supporters of the Hindu-chauvinist Bharatiya Janata Party (BJP), which led the rickety coalition in New Delhi) were overjoyed at this technological "feat."

Meanwhile, India's media managers—guided by the handful of journalists and spin-doctors who were privy to the information, or at least some of it, of a likely test or some such event at Pokharan—got busy writing, rewriting and displaying the story, hyping the "achievement," getting selective accolades and favorable comments from self-styled "experts," crafting captions and slogans for adulatory editorials and catchy lines: "Explosion of Self-Esteem," "Megatons of Prestige," an "India That Can Say No," etc.

In the offices of India's major political parties, utter confusion prevailed, amid stunned silences and resentment that the BJP had successfully pulled off what might be a populist trick, which could win it some support and help it outmaneuver the alliance partners with whom it had been having serious trouble ever since the coalition was sworn in on March 19, 1998. The resentment was soon overpowered by the impulse to give out what many politicians thought to be the standard but safe reaction: congratulate the scientists and engineers responsible for the tests, but remain silent on the politicians who directed them and mandated the tests in the first place.

44

In the heart of New Delhi, where Sonia Gandhi, president of the Indian National Congress, the country's oldest and largest political party, lives, a debate broke out between those who thought the party should strongly condemn the tests as adventurist and unrelated to India's security, and those who believed it would be more expedient not to criticize the tests since the popular mood was pro-nuclear. Gandhi was inclined to be critical. She was soon persuaded to issue a statement questioning the tests' rationale and reiterating India's commitment to global nuclear disarmament, reaffirmed by Rajiv Gandhi in a well-drafted three-stage plan submitted to the United Nations General Assembly's Special Session on Disarmament in 1988.[2] Just as the statement was about to be released, news came from Madras that Sharad Pawar, former defense minister and a senior Congress leader, had congratulated the scientists responsible for the tests, but expressed reservations about the government's intentions. In particular, he also criticized the BJP for not taking the Congress into confidence over so important a matter as crossing the nuclear threshold. Sonia Gandhi decided to withhold her own statement.

The Congress's intervention was widely taken to mean it had signaled its approval and gone along with "the current." But the "current" was now being defined by the media. Instant television soundbites were manufactured and recorded, *ex post* justifications were proffered by India's nuclear "paid priesthood" (from the state-funded Institute for Defense Studies and Analyses in the capital). Statistically meaningless and fraudulent telephone interviews were broadcast as the unalloyed truth—this in a country where fewer than a tenth of all households have a telephone connection! The cameras selectively focused on BJP supporters bursting firecrackers and dancing with joy in the streets. Much of this contrived scenario in favor of the tests would soon unravel.

The element of surprise in the tests was undeniable, despite the February 1998 BJP election manifesto's statement that, if elected, the party's government would "review India's nuclear policy and exercise the option to induct nuclear weapons," and the common program of the BJP-led coalition called "National Agenda for Governance," which, in March, also reiterated that formulation—among the few phrases transported verbatim from the party's manifesto. Many saw nothing new in the formulation. The BJP—beginning with its earlier avatar, the Bharatiya Jana Sangh—had been demanding the bomb since the early '50s. And it had stepped up the hawkish rhetoric during the Comprehensive Test Ban Treaty (CTBT) debate of 1994–96. Nevertheless, a majority of India's strategic "experts" did not expect the party to do something so irreversible and controversial within only a few weeks of coming to power.

The BJP also consciously tried to mislead the public on the issue. When asked in April what the phrase "exercise the option to induct nuclear weapons" meant, Vajpayee said India would cross the threshold only if it was considered absolutely necessary, and hinted at a strategic review prior to such a decision.[3] Defense Minister George Fernandes was explicit on this: There would be no major change in India's nuclear posture before a proper strategic review and evaluation of the country's security needs.[4] And, citing these very statements, an editorialist in *The Times of India* dismissed all talk of a shift in India's defense and nuclear policy as irresponsible and alarmist.[5]

Washington Misjudges

The new government managed to disguise its real intentions and plans from its international interlocutors, too. Specifically, it misled Bill Richardson, whom President Clinton sent as a special envoy to talk to the new government in April. Richardson came with an entourage consisting of officials from the state department, including its newly established South Asia desk, and the US Arms Control and Disarmament Agency (ACDA). After several rounds of discussions with Indian ministers, diplomats and bureaucrats on a range of issues, the delegation went back convinced that the BJP-led coalition would maintain a high degree of continuity with the core policies of its predecessor regimes. It would do so on the economy, on foreign and security policies, cooperation with the West, on domestic matters such as attitudes toward the religious minorities, especially Muslims (which the BJP has long regarded with suspicion and hostility, and which it, along with its cohorts, explicitly confronted by demolishing a sixteenth-century mosque at Ayodhya in Uttar Pradesh in December 1992).

"No, we don't expect a major shift; we are convinced that the Vajpayee government is not about to do anything dramatic and alarming," a state department official told one of us. "The South Asia desk line is, 'expect continuity, and a friendly stance toward the US and Washington's concerns.'"[6] He accepted distinctions between three different possible postures on the part of the US toward the Vajpayee government. First, in view of the BJP's history of extreme positions on some issues and its right-wing religious-chauvinist character, the US would seek definite proof of "normal" behavior before endorsing the Indian government and accepting it as friendly and legitimate. Second, Washington would wait and watch, while maintaining an open and friendly stand, but not rush into giving the government its approval. Third, the US would proceed on the assumption that the BJP had already "reformed" and "normalized" itself, and that the experience of actually wielding power—with all its presumed responsibilities—would further sober and moderate the party's policies and actions.

"We are clearly inclined to the third," the official emphasized. "We don't believe the BJP is about to do anything radical—like nationalize foreign capital, start a war over Kashmir, or conduct a nuclear blast. We expect them to be sensitive to US concerns; we appreciate the fact that the BJP was among the few parties in India that during the Cold war were strongly anti-Soviet and largely supportive of the US." Adding to the complacency were the signals that intelligence personnel read from satellites monitoring activity in and around Pokharan. According to *Newsweek*, they found nothing "unusual" in the desultory movements at the site that had witnessed a flurry of activity late in 1995.[7] Satellite pictures in 1995 had clearly pointed to the drilling of a hole in the Pokharan test range, similar to the one drilled for India's first nuclear test in 1974.[8] In December 1995, intelligence sources leaked the story to *The New York Times*. India first denied the story as "baseless" and "speculative." But when US Ambassador Frank Wisner confronted Indian Foreign Minister Pranab Mukherjee with satellite photographs, the government, then led by the Indian National Congress, sheepishly confirmed that there was activity at the site. For Wisner, this was not enough. He asked Mukherjee to declare that New Delhi would not, and was not about to, conduct a test. Mukherjee did.

Later, imagery from commercial satellites too confirmed preparations for a test in late 1995. Analyzing the data, US nuclear weapons laboratories were satisfied that such imagery would provide fairly reliable verification of nuclear test preparation and would be a very useful tool in the CTBT verification process in the long run.[9] But this was wisdom in retrospect—verification after the event. No analyst even suspected anything much before May 4. Yes, there was some activity at Pokharan range, but the site had been downgraded in the DIA's list of priorities. Other sites, in Bosnia, Afghanistan, Sudan, and in Russia, were far more important. A junior officer had been put in charge of looking at the Rajasthan desert in northwestern India, where Pokharan is situated.[10] The intensity of monitoring had been reduced, too—only casually scanning images, instead of high-alert frequent monitoring, was recommended for sites. Fairly crude camouflage methods—such as nets and meshes—further obscured the reality at Pokharan—hectic activity, visits from the top brass of the Department of Atomic Energy (DAE), Defense Research and Development Organization (DRDO) and the Indian military, actual transportation of explosive assemblies, wiring up of detonation devices, the triple fence with high security erected around the blast site, etc.[11]

It is possible that the level of activity in the weeks preceding May 11 was far lower than in late 1995, and that the preparations made then were never fully dismantled. This time around, the DRDO-DAE-military personnel were of course not starting from scratch. It is also possible that sandstorms in the Rajasthan desert, which are routine, and acquire greater frequency in the hot months of April to July, further complicated the picture, reducing the accuracy of satellite imagery. But the general complacency in the US administration about the BJP's intentions and the downgrading of the monitoring level were clearly far more important factors.

"Safe" Tests and Popular Doubts

Official Claims and People's Experience Don't Match.

One of the biggest myths propagated by a section of the Indian media was that the Pokharan tests were greatly popular in the vicinity of the test site in Western Rajasthan. There too, villagers, charged with patriotic fervor, enthusiastically welcomed the explosion of national "self-esteem." This was held out as proof that the bomb had found acceptance even in this extremely poor, inhospitable part of Rajasthan, essentially a desert, the best of whose land grows shrubbery and a few hardy millets. Similar claims have been made about the Baluch tribes that live close to Chagai Hills in Pakistan. Nothing could be further from the truth.

For the inhabitants of Khetolai, the village closest to the Pokharan Firing Range, May 11, 1998 was a black day. At about 1 P.M., soldiers of the Indian Army rudely herded out of their houses Khetolai's 1,500 residents and told them that there was "going to be a big explosion, a big bomb." The residents could not leave the village. Nor could they stay indoors or seek the shade of trees to escape the scorching sun. (The temperature in the shade that day was 47°C/117°F).

They were made to stand out in the open for four hours. (The three simultaneous explosions occurred at 3:45 P.M.). And then they were told they could safely go home. When they entered their homes, they found there were huge cracks in the mud walls, and the water had drained out of a number of village wells, whose walls too had cracked.[1]

The people of Khetolai were livid. On May 20, the day Vajpayee visited the Pokharan test site, they decided to stage a protest against the treatment meted out to them, and more important, against the refusal of their demand for an independent investigation into the health and environmental effects of the tests. Vajpayee originally intended to stop at Khetolai. On reports of the protest plan, he changed his itinerary.

The people in villages close to Pokharan, including Khetolai, have had grievances against the setting up of the range since 1967. They have registered their protest in a variety of ways. In June 1998, they welcomed a Japanese peace delegation, including a *hibakusha* from Hiroshima, and passed a resolution condemning all nuclear test explosions and calling for a permanent ban. In November, they voted overwhelmingly against the BJP in elections to the Rajasthan legislature. In Khetolai, the turnout was a record high of 93 percent; it is believed everyone cast their vote against the BJP.

The government maintains that the "perfect tests" posed no risk to the people or to the environment.[2] No radioactivity was discharged. The government refused, however, to divulge details of background radiation, concentration of long-lived radionuclides such as Strontium-90, Cesium-137, or Plutonium-239 in the soil, air, water, and vegetation close to the site. It had made a similar claim in the first test of 1974 too.

The residents of villages in the vicinity, such as Khetolai, Loharki, Bhadariya, Mava and Dhauliya, have a different story to tell. They say that the rate of incidence of cancer and numerous physical deformities rose significantly some years after 1974. For instance, the village headman in Khetolai says that there have been eighteen deaths from cancer between the mid-'80s and 1998—indisputably high for a population of 1,500.[3]

It is known that the fence erected around the test's explosion site in 1974 rotted and disintegrated soon after security forces abandoned the site in the late '70s. Cattle, sheep, and goats belonging to the villagers, many of whom are shepherds, routinely strayed into the test range area.

How could dangerous radionuclides in the shrubbery and grass the animals browsed in not contaminate the food chain? But the government did not bother to monitor the health of the surrounding population. Nor did it regularly check the environment for radioactivity and the presence of products of fission and other matter released during the 1974 test.

Some of the suspicions and claims of the villages are corroborated by a group of doctors from S.N. Medical College in Jodhpur, Rajasthan, the nearest teaching hospital. Drs. R.G. Sharma, M.S. Maheshwari and S.C. Lodha, writing in *The Indian Journal of Cancer*,[4] analyzed cancer data collected from the records of government hospitals and private clinics in Jodhpur in 1984–1988—that is, beginning ten years after Pokharan-I. Since the findings are from non-exhaustive sources and take no account of precisely where the patients came from or who they were demographically, the data cannot be interpreted to say anything about the absolute incidence of cancer. And since no pre-1974 data are available for comparison in the Jodhpur region, in which Pokharan is located, all conclusions must be extremely tentative.

Nevertheless, some results are noteworthy. The Jodhpur region shows a high frequency of cancers of the mouth and throat (in relation to the rest of India and also to the WHO numbers for developing countries). There was also a higher incidence of ovarian cancer, lymphomas, and leukemias. Ovarian cancers were more frequent by 50 percent, compared to the average figures for either developed or developing countries. Lymphomas in men and leukemias in both men and women were more frequent by 50 to 80 percent.

Again, a comparison of the Jodhpur region with the incidences reported to the National Cancer Registry in 1983 from various cities of India shows a high frequency of cancer of the urinary bladder. Leukemias are higher by a factor of 50 to 150 percent. Bone and skin tumors are more frequent by a factor of 40 to 300 percent.

Even in the absence of base-line data, comparison with which alone can permit decisive conclusions, these results constitute a sufficient and strong reason for an *independent* epidemiological survey of the region. Similarly, there is a powerful case for an independent survey and monitoring of the environment for radiation, radionuclides, and other harmful substances.

Much less information is available from near the Chagai site in Pakistan's Baluchistan province. Moreover, since the 1998 tests were the first, it is not yet possible to determine their related health effects. But there was a strong popular protest against Pakistan's tests from that province, which in turn prompted its chief minister to complain to the federal government. In Pakistan too, there is a powerful case for an independent health and environment survey and continuous monitoring.

NOTES

[1] Personal interview with the authors, June 1998.

[2] This claim has been repeated, parrot-like, by the local administration, the Atomic Energy Commission and other agencies. On February 3, 1999, AEC chairman R. Chidambaram said the tests were "perfect" and no radioactivity was released. [See Note 2 in "Mine is Bigger than Yours" on pg. 99) Such claims about the "safety" of nuclear testing have been routinely made by governments all over the world. The truth is radically different, especially as it is recorded in testimonies of victims of nuclear testing, whether in the South Pacific, in Nevada or in Kazakhstan. See International Physicians for the Prevention of Nuclear War, *Radioactive Heaven and Earth*(London: Zed Books, 1991).

[3] Personal interview, June 1998.

[4] *The Indian Journal of Cancer* 29 (September 1992): 126–35.

By conducting the tests on May 11 and then again on May 13, New Delhi shocked not just the rest of the world, but some of its own policy-makers, past and present. Vajpayee chose to first explain the rationale of the tests not to the Indian public, but to President Clinton. On May 11, in New Delhi, he only issued a bland technical statement announcing the tests and their purpose—developing nuclear weapons of a diverse range and capabilities, their explosive yield varying from a few hundred tons (equivalent of TNT) to a claimed forty-five kilotons, and encompassing what India claimed was a thermonuclear bomb as well as first-generation fission weapons. India had suddenly crossed the threshold and plunged headlong into weaponization.

Although there was a gradual degeneration in India's nuclear policy and practice, especially after the first May 1974 test, there was a far higher measure of continuity at the doctrinal level. Going by its stated policy, until May 11 New Delhi never accepted the view that nuclear weapons are legitimate, strategically rational, or essential to security, whether of a nation or of the world. It had always forcefully rejected the doctrine of nuclear deterrence as "repugnant" and unworthy. For years, it demanded that the manufacture and possession, and use or threat of use of nuclear weapons be declared "a crime against humanity." It rightly argued that one great lesson of the Cold War is that reliance on nuclear deterrence can lead to a runaway nuclear arms race, with strategically disastrous and economically ruinous consequences.

True, New Delhi repeatedly and sharply criticized the unequal global nuclear order dominated by the Big Five. And it saw its own established nuclear capability as a form of defiance of that order. But until May, that was only a capability, a technological prowess to make nuclear weapons. That is one thing. Actually making weapons, with a finite possibility that they will be used—a possibility always bound up with their existence—is another thing altogether. India executed that doctrinal rupture—suddenly, swiftly, without as much as the pretense of a policy review, an analysis of the strategic environment and of new security "threats," or of the best ways of meeting them. According to highly placed sources, the order to conduct these tests was issued well before Vajpayee's government won the vote of confidence in the lower house of India's Parliament. Interestingly, a leader of the Rashtriya Swayamsevak Sangh (RSS) confirmed that the BJP, which formed a minority government that lasted a mere thirteen days in 1996, had ordered a nuclear test, although there was virtually no chance of the government's surviving: the test was planned for the day of the vote of confidence![12]

Clearly, the BJP was bent on crossing the nuclear threshold, regardless of India's strategic environment. It conducted the tests simply when it could— that is, when it came to power. The real rationale for the decision had to do with its long-standing nuclear obsession, not India's security or foreign policy goals. Two consequences followed. One, the BJP had to invent a plausible-sounding rationale for the doctrinal breach it had effected. And two, it had to create a *post facto* regional rationalization for its own tests by goading Pakistan to follow in its own footsteps. On the second count, it was successful: Pakistan followed on May 28 and 30 with its own explosions, discussed below. On the first count, New Delhi was more than just a little ham-handed.

Vajpayee Rationalizes

In his May 11 letter to Clinton, soon leaked to *The New York Times*, Prime Minister Vajpayee cited clandestine nuclear collaboration between China and Pakistan, India's old adversaries, as the principal justification for crossing the nuclear threshold. So preoccupied was Vajpayee with naming the two neighbors, and so keen to curry favor with the US, that he even offered "cooperation" with Washington in its efforts to promote nuclear non-proliferation and "disarmament." When this did not wash, and Pakistan accused India of having created a new threat to its security via nuclearization, New Delhi changed its tune and said its nuclear decision was not "Pakistan-specific" and that it went beyond South Asia or regional considerations. Meanwhile, by the end of the week after the tests, Home Minister Lal Krishan Advani had launched a fiercely militant rhetorical attack on Pakistan, linking the new nuclear equation with the Kashmir dispute.[13]

When China reacted with strong words and anger at having been named specifically as a "threat"—a term Fernandes had repeatedly used in April, without provocation, let alone reason, even accusing China of having built a helicopter landing-pad on its territory—the Indian government hastened to "clarify" that China was not really a threat. Vajpayee's powerful principal secretary, Brajesh Mishra, (a former diplomat known for his hardline views) was roped into mollifying Beijing.[14]

As soon as Pakistan conducted its tests—an outcome for which Indian leaders devoutly prayed—Vajpayee announced that India's stand was "vindicated." The tests only confirmed Pakistan had a hidden bomb as well as every intention to detonate it. New Delhi once again got busy citing the Pakistan "factor" or "threat" as a justification for its own nuclearization. By late June/early July, India had again returned to the old, familiar theme of attacking the nuclear "hegemons" and their refusal to undertake nuclear disarmament.

Ironically, this happened after India had colluded and collaborated with these very powers in effectively smashing the unity of the non-aligned Group of 21 (G-21) at the Conference on Disarmament in Geneva (CD) on the conditions under which they would agree to begin negotiations on a Fissile Material Cutoff Treaty (FMCT), on which there had been an impasse for several months. The principal condition was that the nuclear weapons-states must agree either to negotiate a Nuclear Weapons (Abolition) Convention or to set up in the CD a formal committee on the subject of nuclear disarmament—a proposal they have vetoed for years.

The mutually inconsistent and contradictory explanations and rationalizations at the official level were supplemented outside the government by hawkish nuclear lobbies, often inspired by clandestine official briefings, offering expedient apologia wherever possible for India's nuclearization. The rationalizations varied: India had done nothing new, dramatic or unexpected on May 11 and 13. It was long known that we had bombs in the basement; we only put them out. What was covert became overt. India's "compulsions" arose from reliable information that Pakistan was about to conduct its tests. It had to be pre-empted (why?). India lost its patience with the P-5 when the NPT was extended and it became apparent that the prospect for disarmament had receded. (But this happened in 1995, three years before the tests). China may not have been an immediate threat, but it is a long-term threat: did it not go to war with India in 1962? And did it not covertly aid Pakistan (probably even gifted it a fully made nuclear bomb in 1989)? Sooner or later, India would have to have a credible deterrent against China as well as Pakistan. The BJP only created it sooner, rather than later.

Wild imagination, flights of fancy, semi-literacy in strategic affairs, pure prejudice, misinformation, inaccuracies, half-truths, and outright lies were mixed in varying proportions to churn out this smorgasbord of apologia to suit different hawkish tasks and cater to various notions of national "pride" and hubris. In all this, it is impossible to separate fiction from fact, or to find a thread of consistency in the logic proffered in explanations of India's violent departure from its own stated doctrines and positions.

The Indian attempt to goad Pakistan into testing was equally deplorable. It was probably the first instance of an NWS actually instigating its own rival to go nuclear. Islamabad's first reaction to the Indian tests was a mixture of shock and anger. But Nawaz Sharif, despite severe domestic political pressure, did not rush into conducting a test in retaliation. Indeed, he carefully weighed his options during the week of May 11, reckoning that the economic consequences of crossing the nuclear threshold would be almost unbearable. There was advantage to be reaped from showing restraint: not only would Pakistan escape attracting opprobrium, it would occupy the moral high ground as a responsible, peace-loving state. This would help it overcome to some extent the stigma of its involvement with the Taliban and support to Kashmiri secessionists in India, as well as the links of Pakistani military agencies with narcotics smuggling. Besides, the US was offering it a $5 billion package of economic aid and military assistance in special negotiations opened by the deputy secretary of state, Strobe Talbott.

The BJP, however, had already decided that the road to Chagai (the nuclear test-site in the Baluchistan mountain ranges) must traverse through Kashmir. Beginning on May 18, the home minister, Advani, consciously started linking India's newly acquired nuclear weapons status to Kashmir. He announced that in the now-changed "geostrategic" environment, which had rendered Pakistan much weaker in relation to India, New Delhi would follow a "pro-active" policy on Kashmir, resorting to "hot pursuit" into Pakistan territory of the militants, whom it claims Pakistan infiltrates into the Kashmir Valley to foment trouble there.

Advani, and following him, Fernandes, issued statement after militant statement chiding Pakistan, and threatening military action in Kashmir. BJP party functionaries went even one step further. They demanded that Proud New Nuclear India must "recapture" the part of Kashmir that Pakistan illegitimately annexed in 1948–49—although this would violate the 1972 Shimla Agreement, which prohibits either state from unilaterally altering the status quo and mandates that all differences be resolved through bilateral negotiations alone.

Teased, chided, insulted, threatened, Sharif in the last week of May finally asked Army Chief General Jehangir Karamat to evaluate the Kashmir situation and the impact of India's bellicose rhetoric on the Pakistan army. Karamat was clear: the troops' morale would collapse unless Pakistan conducted retaliatory tests and equalized with India. On May 27, Pakistan suddenly announced it had definite intelligence that India was about to launch an armed incursion into its territory. The next day, five claimed nuclear explosions followed at Chagai. On May 30, Pakistan announced yet one more test—a total of six to get even with India's five earlier that month, in addition to the very first test of 1974.

There was some confusion over the number of tests. On May 30, Pakistan's foreign secretary was first quoted as saying that two more tests had taken place that day. This was later "corrected" to one. The claimed yields have also been open to question [See "Mine is Bigger than Yours," page 99]. India's assertion that it conducted a successful "thermonuclear" explosion (with a yield of forty-five kilotons) on May 11 has been challenged by a number of scientists, both at home and abroad. And there are reasons to doubt the veracity of the Pakistani claim of as many as six fission tests. The two have long engaged in competitive boasts about their scientific and technological prowess, of having mastered complex and difficult processes, and they have rarely missed a chance to denigrate and run down each other's nuclear and science and technology establishments.

Whatever the truth about the nature and number of the nuclear explosions and their yields, without a doubt the two subcontinental rivals now possess not just a well-established nuclear capability, but the wherewithal to manufacture at least first-generation fission weapons (if not higher yield boosted-fission or fusion weapons), which can be delivered by various means, including short-range missiles, to large population centers— to devastating effect. In May 1998, the world added two more overt nuclear weapons-states to its tally of five, increasing the global nuclear danger.

India and Pakistan under Flak

The crossing of the nuclear Rubicon by India and Pakistan was bound to shock, revolt, and anger the rest of the world. And it did—all the more strongly because their action had no clear, obvious security rationale, and because it seemed to be such a terrible perversion of what should be the real priorities before the two countries, which have among the lowest ranks in human development in the world (between 134 and 140 among the 174 covered by the UN Development Program's "Human Development Report"), and which together are home to the largest number of poor and destitute people in the world: nearly one-half of their over one billion people live in want and suffer from all manner of deprivation.

Following the tests, the US, Japan, and some other states in the industrially developed world imposed sanctions and cut off aid, loans, and credit guarantees to India and Pakistan. The European Union did not. Nor did major European individual states such as Russia, Germany, France and Britain. The G-8, however, met to pass a tough resolution reprimanding India and Pakistan, calling upon them to sign nuclear restraint agreements such as the NPT, as well as the CTBT—that is, effectively to give up their nuclear capability.

The UN Security Council met in June and unanimously passed Resolution 1172 reprimanding India and Pakistan and urging them to exercise restraint; a number of international/multilateral forums—from the Conference on Disarmament to the European Union, and from the Non-Aligned Movement (NAM) to the Association of Southeast Asian Nations (ASEAN) Regional Forum—sharply criticized the two.[15] In November, by a vote of 98 to 6, the First Committee of the United Nations General Assembly passed a resolution reprimanding India and Pakistan for their tests and asking them to sign the CTBT. By 68 to 44 votes, India moved a resolution in the General Assembly calling for the de-alerting of nuclear weapons. This was India's new diplomatic gambit: appear to be responsible in advocating nuclear restraint, but only to the point that India and Pakistan do not explicitly deploy ready-to-use nuclear weapons—with delivery vehicles on hair-trigger alert. The move might be seen to be making a virtue out of necessity—given the relatively low level of India and Pakistani nuclear preparations and the alarm that an eyeball-to-eyeball nuclear confrontation would generate. But it can hardly be regarded as constituting adequate restraint or as reversing the negative consequences of the May 1998 tests that shattered the global nuclear status quo.

By June, the sanctions had begun to bite. In the three weeks after the tests, the Pakistani currency plunged from forty to fifty-six rupees to the US dollar. The Indian rupee lost fifteen percent of its value. The effects were compounded by the unfolding of the Asian meltdown. Foreign investment began to dry up, and withdrawal of state credit for US and Japanese exports and infrastructure projects meant that their costs rose sharply. The cost of borrowing for Indian industry in international markets rose significantly. Most important, the drying up of aid from Japan—the largest donor to India—seriously affected social sector spending, including drinking water supply and rural sanitation projects, as well as literacy and health programs, in which the poor have the highest stake.

In October 1998, the US Congress gave to Clinton a special one-year authorization to lift sanctions selectively. In November, many prohibitions on multilateral loans and export credit and guarantees were removed. But forty Indian "entities" (companies, laboratories, and institutions) with 200 affiliates or subsidiaries were placed on the US blacklist for trade. Pakistan, virtually on the brink of economic collapse, got a breather in the form of an assurance that Washington would not veto an urgently, desperately, needed IMF loan. By this time, it was plain that the sanctions deeply affected both countries, and that their costs would prove onerous if the sanctions were to continue, although it was unlikely that would happen. Indeed, sanctions were subsequently further eased.

There have been differences among India and Pakistan policymakers over the likely effects of the sanctions and the best ways of coping with them. What is incontrovertible and beyond doubt is that nuclearization has led to India's and Pakistan's isolation in the international community and to a considerable lowering of their stature, not only in the eyes of the Global North, but of the Global South. The vast majority of the world's nations and peoples see India and Pakistan in a negative light after May 1998. Few believe they have challenged the unequal global nuclear by trying to transform it radically. Rather, they have joined it on the side of the discriminators.

The Evolution of India's Nuclear Policy

Supporters of nuclear weapons and the May 11 and 13 tests argue that India's decision under the BJP-led coalition to cross the nuclear threshold was essentially continuous with New Delhi's past policies: to the extent there was any change, it happened only in response to the altered situation on the ground, especially in India's neighborhood.

This is misleading and false. At the doctrinal level, May 1998 marks a violent break with India's past postures and policies. The decision to acquire, and plan to deploy, nuclear weapons is a betrayal of India's past commitments to nuclear disarmament and its repeated promises never to use nuclear energy for military purposes.

This does not mean that India's nuclear weapons policy has been constant and unchanging for the fifty-one years since Independence. It has gone through four distinct phases, culminating in the disastrous decision to test and acquire these weapons of mass destruction.

Phase I: 1947 to the Mid-'60s—Abstinence in the Nehru Era

This might be termed the period of voluntary nuclear abstinence. Nehru was not only deeply committed to the complete elimination of all nuclear weapons, but also opposed to their manufacture and possession by any state, including India. He was opposed to nuclear weapons on moral, political, and strategic grounds, and demanded that their possession be declared a "crime against humanity." He integrated this opposition into India's foreign policy, giving it an activist edge. He was the first world leader to call for an end to all nuclear testing, in 1954, following US hydrogen bomb tests in the Pacific, and their disastrous radioactive fallout. India's civilian nuclear energy program, however, had a "dual-use" or military capacity, of which other major figures like Homi Bhabha (the first chairman of the Atomic Energy Commission) were fully aware, and which they wanted to develop. Bhabha himself was not as categorically opposed to a possible future bomb as was Nehru.

On July 24, 1957, Nehru said in the Lok Sabha, "We have declared quite clearly that we are not interested in making atom bombs, even if we have the capacity to do so, and that in no event will we use nuclear energy for destructive purposes... I hope that will be the policy of all future governments."

Just months before his death, when reports were pouring in of

China's nuclear preparations, Nehru rejected the suggestion that India should follow China and acquire nuclear weapons for "deterrence."

A top secret US government document of 1961, declassified in 1995, contains valuable material on the American assessment of Nehru's commitment to opposing nuclear weapons even in the face of Chinese preparations to acquire and detonate such weapons, preparations and plans that were detected by Western intelligence agencies.[16] The State Department document deals with "anticipatory action pending Chinese communist demonstration of a nuclear capability" and considers providing active assistance in nuclear weapons technology to India as a counterweight to a nuclear China. It notes that in US Ambassador John Kenneth Galbraith's assessment, Nehru would reject the idea with a probability of ninety percent, and, therefore concludes that other methods, including influencing Homi Bhabha and launching a "covertly mounted informational campaign," are necessary.

The document is devoted to a discussion of the "early action we might take to minimize the impact on US and free world security interests of a first Chinese Communist explosion of a nuclear device." It locates the need for such action in the following way:

> If Communist China could detonate a nuclear device as early as 1962, as has been estimated, we should consider now what actions should be taken in anticipation of the event, instead of later in reaction to it. The initial impact will be primarily psychological, with secondary political and military effects deriving from it. This establishes the psychological field as one deserving immediate attention.

China, it argues,

> is likely to get at least two types of psychological dividends from its explosion: (1) Many Asians are likely to raise their estimate of Communist China's present and future total military power relative to that of their own countries and the capabilities in the area of the US; and (2) they are likely to see the accomplishment as vindicating claims that the Communist method of organizing a backward state's resources is demonstrably superior. Both reactions are likely to contribute to feelings that communism is the wave of the future and that Communist China is, or soon will become, too powerful to resist... It will not be possible to prevent the accrual to Communist China of such dividends, but it may be possible by advance action to reduce them.

The argument goes on to say, however:

> If another, but non-Communist Asian state detonated a nuclear device first, a subsequent and consequently a somewhat anticlimactic Chinese Communist explosion would not carry a comparable implication of Communist superiority, or make quite as much impact on those who fear China's growing power.

The document holds that India is the best candidate for this:

> According to one estimate, India's atomic program is sufficiently advanced so that it could, not many months hence, have accumulated enough fissionable material to produce a nuclear explosion. While we would like to limit the number of nuclear powers, so long as we lack the capability to do so we ought to prefer that the first Asian one be India and not China.

But there was a catch. Nehru, the document admits, was not willing to play ball:

> Nehru was quoted as saying, upon his arrival in Belgrade on August 31 [1961] and in the context of the Soviet decision to resume weapons tests, "I am against nuclear tests at any time in any place." The same day, an official spokesman in Delhi was quoted as making the less categorical statement: "We are against all tests and explosions of nuclear material except for peaceful purposes under controlled conditions..." Given the context and taken together, these statements suggest that it would be difficult to get Nehru to agree to any proposal for an Indian nuclear test in the near future, and that the chances of its acceptance would depend upon the extent to which it met rather narrow criteria.

> Galbraith confirmed this: "The idea has also been discussed with Ambassador Galbraith, who is strongly opposed to any US approach to Nehru. He thinks the chances are roughly only one out of fifty that Nehru's reaction would not be the negative one that we are seeking India as an atomic ally.

The document then goes on to evaluate the reservations raised by officers in different sections of the State Department, although "preliminary exploration within the Department has elicited concurrence with the idea, per se, that it would be desirable if a friendly Asian power beat Communist China to the punch, and it has turned up no likelier candidate than India."

These reservations and doubts are listed:

> (1) India might require considerable technical assistance in order to explode a nuclear device before Communist China does; (2) there appear to be legal obstacles to the supplying of such assistance by either the British or ourselves; (3) we are not good at keeping such things covert, whereas the explosion could be expected to have utility only in proportion as it appeared to be an Indian accomplishment; (4) there probably would be considerable difficulty in finding a practical peaceful use for such an explosion, and fall-out from it would be open to the usual and valid objections, including ones related to the fears which could arise or be created among an ill-informed and partly superstitious populace; (5) alternately meeting the requirement of 'controlled conditions' for an experimental explosion might present problems;

(6) Pakistan could be expected to react most adversely to an Indian explosion which might subsequently be exploited against it, and to be highly resentful of any outside instigation and assistance, known or surmised; (7) an Indian explosion would provide the Chinese Communists basis for urging that the USSR increase its assistance to the Chinese Communist nuclear program.

Nevertheless, it concludes that an approach should be made to Bhabha (although not to Nehru). Galbraith took a dim view of raising the issue with Nehru: not only did he think the chances of Nehru rejecting a US offer of assistance were forty-nine out of fifty, but he saw "the calculus of prospective benefit inherent in the one chance as outweighed by the harm implicit in the other forty-nine." He believed his British and Canadian colleagues would also be unwilling to make such an approach to Nehru.

The most that Galbraith was prepared to do was allow a US nuclear energy official, Dr. Wiesner, on a possible future visit to India, to raise in the course of conversations with Dr. Bhabha the matter

of the prospective Chinese Communist nuclear explosion and ask what effect if any it will have on India's program in the atomic field. Presumably any further initiatives in the matter, if the idea germinated in Dr. Bhabha's mind and bore fruit, would have to come from the Government of India, when we could decide what the US response should be within the framework of something more concrete than we now have to work with.

The document then concludes:

While nothing else would have so much prophylactic value as a prior atomic explosion by a free-world Asian state, a covertly-conducted information program might achieve some effect in reducing the psychological impact of the first Chinese Communist nuclear explosion. Assuming as we do that the Chinese Communists are fully committed to acquiring nuclear capabilities, publicity about their program probably would not have important effect on their determination or rate of progress. It might provide them with an argument with which to press their Soviet ally to give increased assistance, but this would seem unlikely to weigh heavily among the factors considered by the Soviets in determining where their own interests in the matter lay.

And it recommends a "covertly-mounted informational program" to drive home some illustrative points:

(a) India (and perhaps Japan) have nuclear-development programs sufficiently advanced so that they could by now have produced a nuclear explosion; their programs, however, have been directed rather at peaceful uses of atomic energy (b) Observers are puzzled by the failure of the Chinese Communists, who have been engaged in an effort which started in 1950, thus far to explode a nuclear device of their own. Since several other powers pioneered the way, the technological requirements for producing such an explosion have become widely known. Communist China has scientists, including ones trained abroad, of requisite capability; the essential raw materials; and suitable testing areas. (c) It accordingly can only be speculated that Communist China either has organized its effort poorly, or realizes that nuclear weapons are not ones which will contribute to realization of its expansive aims— sincere world opinion, which will condemn all aggression in proportion as it can be identified as such, will tolerate aggression with nuclear weapons even less than aggression by conventional armed forces.

This was also a period during which the idea of a Western "nuclear umbrella" for India was aired. The idea acquired some force especially because of India's defeat in the China War of 1962. The proposal did not, however, fructify. India continued to fight in international forums for nuclear weapons elimination.

Phase II: Mid-'60s to 1974—Preparations for the 1974 Test

The mid-'60s began the period of New Delhi's disenchantment with the prospect for global nuclear disarmament, and its own quiet preparations to acquire a nuclear weapons capability, while retaining a strong opposition to deterrence and weaponization. India's nuclear program under Homi Bhabha underwent a significant shift at the ground level. In 1964, Bhabha commissioned a plant to reprocess spent fuel from the CIRUS "research" reactor built in 1960.

CIRUS (Canada-India Research Reactor, US—standing for the United States, which donated the heavy water to start this Canadian-designed forty MW-thermal reactor) was meant to be operated for "peaceful" purposes only. But there were no formal "safeguards" to ensure this. Exploiting this loophole, Bhabha started reprocessing spent fuel from CIRUS to extract plutonium. This was used in the 1974 test.

Evidence suggests that Bhabha shifted toward active acquisition of a weapons capability after India's defeat in the China war of 1962. In his speech in October 1964, following China's first nuclear test, he said India, too, could conduct a test in eighteen months. But such changes were not articulated at the policy or doctrinal level.

Thus, in October 1965, Prime Minister Lal Bahadur Shastri told Parliament: "Despite the continued threat of aggression from China, which has developed nuclear weapons, the government has continued to adhere to decisions not to go in for nuclear weapons but to work for their elimination instead."

In April, 1968 Prime Minister Indira Gandhi said in Parliament that India's nuclear

> policy is framed after due consideration of the national interest, specifically with regard to national security... we do feel that the events of the last twenty years clearly show that the possession of nuclear weapons have not given any military advantage in situations of bitter armed conflict...The choices before us involve... engaging in an arms race with sophisticated nuclear warheads and an effective missile delivery system. Such a course, I do not think would strengthen national security... it may well endanger our internal security by imposing a very heavy economic burden...

Indian policy pronouncements in the post-Nehru period underwent a subtle shift best described as one from a categorical opposition to nuclear weapons, to a "No Bombs Now" orientation. New uncertainties were reflected in India's role and attitude to the NPT negotiations where it had played a significant role initially. The final draft of the treaty watered down what India and other NNWS wanted, namely a better balance between the differential obligations of the NWS signatories and the NNWSs. Despite this watering down, the other NNWSs went along with the treaty, but India did not sign.

The major reasons for India's non-signature were China's decision not to sign the NPT and India's new reluctance to commit itself to complete or permanent future abstinence. Subsequently, however, India's refusal to sign the NPT was invariably and repeatedly stated in terms of "principled" opposition to the "discriminatory" character of the NPT—that is, the way in which it enshrines different obligations for the nuclear weapons-states and the non-nuclear weapons-states.

The NPT became an exemplar, not just of an unequal global nuclear order, but of unequal, hegemonic distribution of power in the world. Behind the curtain of criticism of the NPT from the moral high ground, however, India intensified nuclear preparations at the ground level.

The ground-level preparations, and accumulation of unsafeguarded plutonium from CIRUS, gave Indira Gandhi an opportunity to conduct Pokharan-I in May 1974—a test which Department of Atomic Energy (DAE) scientists had long been demanding. The test, purportedly for "peaceful" civilian purposes, itself termed a "peaceful nuclear explosion (PNE)," was carried out for primarily domestic political reasons. The Indian media, briefed by the government, announced the test as signifying the country's entry into the "Select" Group of "Technologically Advanced Nations" or the "Nuclear Club." Yet India continued to strongly reject nuclear deterrence or grant any kind of legitimacy to nuclear weapons.

On May 22, 1974, four days after Pokharan-I, Indira Gandhi wrote to Bhutto to assure him:

> I am aware that in popular parlance a nuclear explosion evokes an awesome and horrifying picture. However, this is because our minds have been conditioned by the misuse of nuclear energy for the development of weapons and by the use of these weapons in Hiroshima and Nagasaki. We in India have condemned and will continue to condemn military uses of nuclear energy as a threat to humanity.

She emphasized that "it is strictly in this context that our scientists have launched on this experiment... There are no political or foreign policy implications of this test."

Phase III: 1974 to 1996 — Ambiguity and its Degradation

Further work on India's nuclear weapons capability was suspended after the adverse fallout of the 1974 PNE, and immediate withdrawal of Canadian assistance, and protests from several other powers the world over, including the India-friendly USSR. New Delhi adopted a conscious policy of nuclear ambiguity, which consisted in both affirming and denying that India had/could have a nuclear weapons capability. In effect, India became a Nuclear Threshold State.

In 1978, under the non-Congress Prime Minister, Morarji Desai, the Indian government distanced itself from the 1974 PNE. Desai emphasized distrust of and opposition to nuclear weapons within a framework of ambiguity, all while expressing misgivings about the safety of nuclear power. The DAE's importance within the government was downgraded.

After the mid-'80s, hawkish pressure mounted on New Delhi to respond to Pakistan's reported nuclear preparations by going overtly nuclear itself. During the period 1983–93, India rejected a total of seven proposals by Pakistan for nuclear restraint and regional disarmament. India opposed all regional approaches, saying it would only discuss nuclear disarmament in "global," "multilateral" forums, and in a "non-discriminatory" framework. To contain what was claimed to be the "Pakistani threat," India entreated the US to put pressure on Islamabad, through the Pressler Amendment to the omnibus US Trade Act, which made armaments sales to Pakistan contingent upon annual certification by the US President that Pakistan does not possess, and is not about to make, nuclear weapons. Meanwhile, India's own stockpiling of high-grade plutonium continued, with an estimated 300 to 450 kilograms accumulated by the mid-'90s—enough for sixty to ninety fission bombs.

India did, however, join the Five-Continent Six-Nation Initiative for Nuclear Disarmament in 1986, sign the important "Delhi Declaration" for a nuclear weapons-free world with Gorbachev in the same year, and put forward the Rajiv Gandhi Plan for the total elimination of nuclear weapons in the UN General Assembly's Fourth Special Session on Disarmament (SSOD-IV) in 1988. This involved a step-by-step process including restraint at an early stage by the threshold states, including India. Although a serious, well-conceived plan, it was not energetically pursued after its presentation.

India rejected a number of proposals put forward in the late '80s and early '90s for regional nuclear restraint, or for a nuclear dialogue involving either the P-5 and India and Pakistan, or the US, Russia, China, Germany, Japan, and the two South Asian states. But in 1992, India agreed to start a bilateral dialogue on nuclear weapons with the US. Four rounds of talks at the topmost diplomatic (not ministerial) level were held, but to no avail.

In 1993, India and the US co-sponsored a resolution in the UN calling for the early completion of the CTBT in the Conference on Disarmament. As the negotiations for a CTBT, which India had pioneered, entered their final phase, New Delhi began to stall. In 1995, it made its signature of the CTBT conditional upon a commitment to disarmament within a "time-bound" framework by the P-5. It tried to hedge the treaty in with clauses that appeared radical, but were meant to delay negotiations and prepare the ground for non-accession and opposition to any test ban agreement that might develop.

During this period, there was an operational reorganization of the process of making nuclear weapons and articulating India's policy on them. Foreign Secretary (chief of diplomatic service) J.N. Dixit created new structures of policy consultation and formulation, directly involving the hands-on scientists and bureaucrats of the DAE and the Defense Research Development Organization (DRDO), who had been working on nuclear weapons and missiles development programs. The Indian foreign ministry no longer made nuclear policy and determined the strategy and tactics to be adopted in international forums and bilateral talks. Rather, it asked the DAE and DRDO what their needs were, and how they might best be articulated and satisfied at the diplomatic level through strategic and tactical maneuvers.

Domestically, New Delhi came under growing pressure to oppose the CTBT and then "logically" proceed to conduct test explosions: Why reject the CTBT as a "trap" and "conspiracy" and then behave as if it were still in place? Why bear the costs of opposition to the treaty without reaping the "benefits" of nuclearization?

In late 1995, before the CTBT acquired its penultimate form, the Narasimha Rao government launched preparations for a test at Pokharan. The Cabinet was divided, and US military satellites detected preparations for a test in the Rajasthan desert. Publicity, as well as fear of economic sanctions, deterred India from testing. But a big shift occurred at the ground level in India's nuclear preparations and upgrading of its nuclear weapons option.

Yet, at the stated doctrinal level, there was no change. India passionately argued in 1995 before the International Court of Justice that the

> use of nuclear weapons in any armed conflict... even by way of reprisal or retaliation... is unlawful... Since the production and manufacture of nuclear weapons can only be with the objective of their use, it must follow that... their production and manufacture cannot under any circumstances be considered as permitted... The threat of use of nuclear weapons in any circumstance, whether as a means or method of warfare or otherwise, is illegal and unlawful under international law.

India's foreign secretary Salman Haidar made a special appearance before the Conference on Disarmament (CD) in March 1996, at the height of the CTBT debate, to say:

> We do not believe that the acquisition of nuclear weapons is essential for national security, and we have followed a conscious decision in this regard. We are also convinced that the existence of nuclear weapons diminishes international security. We, therefore, seek their complete elimination. These are fundamental precepts that have been an integral basis of India's foreign and national security policy.

Slippages, however, were already evident from India's professed commitment to nuclear restraint and global nuclear disarmament. Indian "ambiguity" got even more degraded. For instance, policymakers hinted that they would oppose other restraint measures too, besides the CTBT, such as a Fissile Material Cutoff Treaty.

On June 20, 1996, New Delhi formally announced that it would not sign the CTBT. Soon thereafter, Arundhati Ghose, India's ambassador at the CD, announced that New Delhi would not sign the CTBT—"not now, not ever." India blocked the CTBT's passage at the CD, but in an unprecedented (and legally questionable) move, the text was taken to the UN General Assembly and signed. Hawks both within and outside the government raised the level of rhetoric in favor of India crossing the threshold, as if in "retaliation" to this maneuver. The BJP and right-wing commentators in the media seized on the anti-CTBT rhetoric, to which there was little organized resistance from the political left or center.

Phase IV: 1996 to May 1998—Collapse of Ambiguity, Slippage into Nuclear Deterrence

Having thus yielded much ground to hawkish positions and stoked jingoistic nationalism over resisting the "trap" that is the CTBT, New

Delhi now became a prisoner of its own devious maneuvers. The nuclear and defense establishments got hyperactive in lobbying for a policy break that would permit full weaponization of the Indian nuclear option through test explosions.

The BJP articulated this point of view most vociferously at the political level. By 1997, it started getting insistent in asking for overt nuclearization. Its manifesto for the February 1998 national Parliament elections promised that the party, if voted to power, would "re-evaluate the country's nuclear policy and exercise the option to induct nuclear weapons."

Until March 1998, the BJP was the sole Indian party to advocate nuclearization. But the situation changed with the BJP-led coalition's "National Agenda for Governance," which repeated the precise formulation of the BJP manifesto on this issue. The BJP issued orders to the DAE, Defense Research & Development Organization, and the armed forces to prepare for and conduct tests—without consulting its coalition allies. But the RSS was privy to the decision.

Vajpayee offered the first statement of the strategic rationale of the tests not to the people of India, but to the President of the United States, on May 11, the first day of the tests. This statement made no reference whatever to the "unequal global nuclear order," "nuclear apartheid," and the failure or reluctance of the P-5 to disarm, which the Bomb's apologists cite as rationale for crossing the threshold. Instead, Vajpayee offered "close cooperation" with Washington to jointly promote "the cause of nuclear disarmament," thus wrongly conceding that the US has such a commitment in the first place. Vajpayee located the tests' rationale in the so-called threat from China and Pakistan, heightened by alleged Sino-Pakistani strategic-level nuclear and missile collaboration.

On May 27, the government made a feeble but devious attempt to rationalize its reversal of earlier nuclear policies through a paper, entitled "Evolution of India's Nuclear Policy," presented in the Lok Sabha. This strings together half-truths and distortions to claim continuity in the evolution of India's policy. Other ex post facto rationalizations will undoubtedly follow.

NOTES

[1] "Why Only a Bomb Would Do," Newsweek (Asian Edition) 19 October 1998: 15.

[2] Interview by Praful Bidwai with Mani Shankar Aiyar, a Congress party functionary, December 1998.

[3] Vajpayee held out that assurance to Clinton's emissary and former US Ambassador to the United Nations Bill Richardson, during his visit to India

soon after the new government was sworn in. See *Newsweek*: 13–14.

4 Fernandes said at his first press conference after taking ministerial charge: "We did not say that we are going in for nuclear weapons... We will re-evaluate policy and ensure security... In the light of that, we will decide on the nuclear option. We will not fight shy of induction if that becomes necessary." Quoted in "N-option put on hold: Fernandes," *The Hindu* (New Delhi) 21 March 1998.

On March 18, after releasing the "National Agenda" document of the BJP-led coalition, Vajpayee said that India "will induct nuclear weapons only if necessary." Answering questions, he said that there was "no time-frame" to induct atomic weapons. "The option (to induct nuclear weapons) will be exercised if need be." Earlier, releasing the BJP's manifesto in February, the party president L.K. Advani had refrained from unqualified advocacy of a nuclear test, saying: "Nuclear tests may not be necessary for India to induct nuclear weapons." Quoted in "N-weapon induction, if necessary," *The Hindu* (New Delhi) 19 March 1998.

5 "Nuclear Hype," *The Times of India* (New Delhi) 1 April 1998. The editorial not only lambasted Pakistan, but also deplored "the politicization of the issue by the Indian Opposition, especially after both the Prime Minister and the defense minister have clarified that the option would be considered only if necessary. Whether the BJP could have expressed itself in more sophisticated terms is a different matter. Even if the BJP had opted to abjure nuclear weapons, Islamabad would have denounced it as a cunning plot to disarm Pakistan, take away its nuclear deterrent and assert Indian supremacy in conventional armaments." It also said: "Ironically, the chorus against nuclearization is being led by those who have held office in the past and have themselves contributed to building up India's capabilities."

6 Interview by Praful Bidwai with an official of the South Asia desk who preferred anonymity.

7 *Newsweek*: 15.

8 Chidanand Rajghatta, "It walks, squawks like a duck, so it's a duck," *Indian Express* (New Delhi) 21 December 1995. This article quoted a US intelligence officer commenting on satellite pictures of drilling in progress at Pokharan in December 1995.

9 Vipin Gupta and Frank Pabian, "Investigating the Allegations of Indian Nuclear Test Preparations in the Rajasthan Desert," in *Science & Global Security* 6 (Amsterdam: Overseas Publishers Association, 1996).

10 *Newsweek*: 15.

11 See Raj Chengappa's adulatory cover story, "The Bomb Makers," *India Today* (New Delhi) 22 June 1998.

12 K.S. Sudarshan of the RSS, quoted in "PM goes to Opposition for Support," *Indian Express* (New Delhi) 15 May 1998.

13 Advani demanded that Pakistan "roll back its anti-India policy with regard to Kashmir." Proceeding on the assumption that India's "decisive step to become a nuclear weapon state has brought about a qualitatively new stage in Indo-Pak relations, particularly in finding a lasting solution to the Kashmir problem," Home Minister L.K. Advani has called upon "Islamabad to realize the change in the geo-strategic situation in the region and the world." See "Pak told

to roll back proxy war," *The Hindu* (New Delhi) 19 May 1998.

So alarming was this bellicose statement that the US state department commented sharply on it, accusing India of "foolishly and dangerously increasing tensions with its neighbors and being indifferent to world opinion..." See "US takes strong exception to Advani's warning on J-K," *The Hindustan Times* (New Delhi) 21 May 1998.

14 "Pak told...," *The Hindu.*

15 Nelson Mandela, long considered India's friend, delivered India a strong rebuke at the NAM summit in Durban, and said all non-aligned countries remained concerned over the problem in Jammu and Kashmir and "should be willing to lend all our strength for the peaceful solution of this problem."

Vajpayee took strong exception to this and India later claimed that South African Deputy President Thabo Mbeki apologized to India for the remark. This was promptly denied by South Africa. "See South Africa offers an apology to India," *The Asian Age* (New Delhi) 5 September 1998 and "SA apologizes for J&K remark," *The Pioneer* (New Delhi) 5 September 1998.

16 "Top Secret" Note from George C. McChee on "Anticipatory Action Pending Chinese Communist Demonstration of a Nuclear Capability," Declassified Authority: NND 959001, of 17 February 1995. (Washington, DC: National Security Archive).

Chapter 5

South Asia in the Nuclear Trap: The Causes and Consequences of India and Pakistan Going Nuclear

When India crossed the nuclear Rubicon on May 11, 1998, the country embarked on a journey that can only bring more insecurity, tension, and maldevelopment, even as it represents another crucial phase in the ongoing efforts of the Sangh Combine to totally transform the character of Indian society and to impose its version of what constitutes the Indian nation.[1] What is at stake for the Sangh is not simply institutionalizing their version of the cultural essence of India, but imposing their versions of nationalism and what constitutes Indian greatness, national security, national interests, and so on. Overnight, a ruthless political force of great evil and determination changed completely the parameters of debate and struggle on so vital an issue as nuclear security and insecurity, as well as on related concerns such as India's relationship to its neighbors and to the world. The horror and strategic stupidity, the political danger of allowing the Sangh to get away with what it has done, will hopefully sink in to an ever widening public, Indian and international. For only then can one hope to successfully reverse the journey on which India has now embarked.

False Explanations

Three kinds of arguments can be put forward to explain why the Indian government set out on this course. The first has to do with supposed changes in the external security environment, or perceptions about such changes: that is, Pakistan and/or China have become more nuclearly threatening and belligerent. The second argument claims that the nuclear hypocrisies of existing NWSs and their reluctance to move rapidly to full nuclear disarmament have finally "driven" India to try to crash their club. The third set of arguments focuses on changed self-perceptions and the domestic factors behind such changes. Such an understanding must focus on the changing character of elite Indian nationalism and the role of the Sangh Combine in bringing about such changes as well as in pushing its own distinctive agenda.

Those who support the tests and the logic of weaponization the tests unveil, distribute their explanations for the testing between the first two kinds of arguments. To some extent, anti-nuclearists in the other NWSs, notably in the West, have done the same—as a result of their anger against the enduring hypocrisies of their own governments, their lack of knowledge or interest in Indian domestic matters, and the moral capital built on India's past record of serious commitment to global disarmament. But it should be obvious to anyone situated in India today and prepared to think objectively, that neither the changing perceptions of an external threat nor the enduring hypocrisies of the existing NWSs explains the Indian decision. Decisive weight must be given to the third factor of changed elite self-perceptions and the role of the Sangh Combine in bringing this about.

The external threats India's pro-nuclearists most commonly cite to justify the Pokharan-II tests have been Pakistan and China, both separately and in presumed concert. The citation of the Pakistan nuclear threat has always had the great advantage of being publicly highly saleable. But its great disadvantage has been that in more informed circles the argument has had little weight, for the simple and powerful reason that Pakistan's nuclear diplomacy (though not its nuclear preparations) have always been strongly *reactive* to India's. It would never be the first to test, nor the first to go openly nuclear, but would follow an Indian decision in both cases, as eventually proved to be the case.[2]

Indeed, although Pakistan has always had a small, but significant, lobby arguing for it to go nuclear, in order to compensate for the imbalance in conventional forces in favor of India, this group has always been outweighed by those in Pakistan who believed that non-nuclear parity between the two countries was to be greatly preferred. Thus throughout the last decade and a half the Pakistani government has repeatedly put forward a variety of proposals for the denuclearization of the South Asian region. Of seven such proposals, the three most important and comprehensive were the following: Islamabad repeatedly offered joint and simultaneous signature by both countries of the NPT; bilateral renunciation of nuclear weapons; or the establishment of a South Asian NWFZ. In each and every case, on each and every occasion, India and its supporters provided no serious counter-proposals but rejected these initiatives, invariably citing the Chinese nuclear threat to India as well as claiming that these selective, regional measures were inappropriate and a diversion from the task of securing global disarmament. But this argument has not prevented India from supporting, or at least not opposing, NWFZs proposed, or set up, elsewhere in the world.

The reference to an utterly abstract, never exercised or articulated, "Chinese threat," then, has been quite central to the Indian armory of justifications—for first maintaining its position of ambiguity, and now for having gone openly nuclear. The meaning of the Sino-Indian border conflict has therefore been asymmetrically interpreted. For China, this has always been (especially since it got the territory it more or less wanted during the 1962 war) a distant and minor affair. For India, militarily humiliated during that war, the border defeat has always been something of a political open wound, which many in the foreign policy establishment have found useful to scratch and revive from time to time.

Yet, there has also been a widespread recognition within the same establishment that, despite, and regardless of, this border dispute, India-China relations have always been characterized by a basic open-endedness, with room for flexibility. India's casualties in the border conflict were less than half of those suffered during its 1987 military intervention in Sri Lanka. China returned all Indian POWs and imposed no punitive measures, despite its victory. Indeed, although the Indian army was utterly routed, the Chinese unilaterally withdrew to the present Line of Actual Control to indicate that they had no other designs beyond the border dispute. That is to say, Sino-Indian relations have always hitherto (before the Pokharan-II tests) lain between the two poles of strategic friendship and strategic hostility, comfortably distant from either. And although some Indian strategists have repeatedly talked of an inevitable strategic rivalry between the two, this too has always been much more a matter of occasional speculation than of concrete reality.

Thus, India's mainstream terms of discourse on China are quite different from those on Pakistan, with whom strategic hostility has been the defining fulcrum. For the most part, Indian foreign policy and nuclear strategists have never been quite able to define a consistent or strongly felt position on China. On the one hand, to justify their nuclear posture, India's leaders have needed to cite the "Chinese threat" and treat China as at least a nuclear-strategic rival of sorts. On the other hand, some uneasily wonder if doing so risks making relations with China worse than they need be, given the more open-ended character of relational possibilities between the two. Both stances were visible in the aftermath of the Indian tests. Indian Defense Minister George Fernandes, a longstanding and notorious China-baiter, waxed eloquent about the Chinese threat just before the tests, a ploy used by the BJP-led government to subsequently rationalize the tests. After the tests, Prime Minister Vajpayee explicitly referred to the Chinese threat in his first public explanation of the tests, the letter to US President Clinton.[3] To compound matters, letters were sent to all other NWSs except China. Subsequently, however, not only did a very large number of pro-nuclearists from the unofficial sector of the nuclear-strategic establishment criticize the unnecessary provocation to China, but the government officially announced repeatedly that the tests were not directed against China ("not country-specific" has been the official term used) and that it did not consider China to be a strategic opponent.

This was not simple dissimulation. Rather, it reflected the long ongoing difficulty and uncertainty that the "China question" has posed for India's pro-nuclearists. The idea that the "Chinese threat" necessitated the May tests was always false. Over the last two decades, especially since the end of the Cold War, relations between India and China have improved steadily, so much so that on his visit to Islamabad in 1996, Chinese President Jiang Zemin shocked his Pakistani hosts by publicly stating that Kashmir should be bilaterally resolved between Pakistan and India. This was correctly perceived (in Islamabad) as a revision of earlier Chinese policy, indicating a shift away from Pakistan and toward an exploration of better ties with India.

This was not surprising. Sino-Pakistan and Sino-Indian ties were always situated in the wider context of Cold War relationships, more specifically, Sino-Soviet, Sino-US and US-Soviet ties. Here the crucial axis for most of the '60s, '70s and '80s was Sino-Soviet hostility. At the turn of the '70s, not only was Pakistan a crucial conduit for forging a Sino-US entente directed against the USSR, but the Soviets clearly attempted to bring India into an alliance (the Asian Collective Security System) directed against China. For its part, India valued Soviet diplomatic support on Kashmir, military supplies, and economic help, and in the context of the 1971 Bangladesh War for independence, the strategic counterweight the Indo-Soviet Treaty of that year provided against the emerging Sino-Pakistan-US axis. The US and China were both opposed to the dismemberment of Pakistan, although the cause of Bangladeshi independence was entirely justified.

But most noteworthy, then and after, was the refusal of China to provide anything more than rhetorical political support for Pakistan against India, even when it was literally being dismembered, and the parallel refusal of India to allow the Indo-Soviet Treaty to be interpreted as an expression of its strategic opposition to China. Where the Soviets saw the treaty as a part of its China containment strategy, India saw it as a one-time treaty necessitated by the political exigencies of the time. Both China and India were determined not to allow either Pakistani or Soviet concerns to decisively determine their postures vis-à-vis each other. By the late '70s, the Chinese ended their support to rebel insurgents against Indian rule in the northeastern states of the country. The Sino-Pakistan relation has always meant much more to Pakistan than to China. By the end of the Cold War and after the cessation of Sino-Soviet hostilities, the Sino-Pakistan connection simply could not carry the same (limited) strategic-political weight that it had in the past. For the fifteen years leading up to Pokharan II, Sino-Indian relations on the political, diplomatic, military (border dispositions and atmospherics), cultural, and trade fronts were steadily improving. There was simply no way that anyone could logically or convincingly argue that the "strategic situation" between India and China (nuclear or otherwise) had worsened in the last few years, thereby necessitating a change in India's strategic posture—let alone in its nuclear response.

A Sino-Pakistan Axis?

And yet some such claim about some form of Chinese and/or Pakistani "culpability" had to be found to justify Indian behavior! It is in this respect that the Sino-Pakistan nuclear-related connection served an important purpose. This was (and continues to be) played up for much more than it was, or is, worth. That such a connection has existed is undeniable. But in the weight of its contribution to Pakistan's development of a nuclear capability, this connection has been very much a secondary factor in comparison to Islambad's own clandestine efforts at equipping itself with the necessary hardware and software. Building a simple atomic bomb is really no big deal. Purely through purchases on the private markets of the West (especially in Germany), Iraq made, despite the bombing of the Osirak reactor in 1981, very significant advances in its efforts to build the bomb.[4] Pakistan developed its capacity sometime in the early- or mid-'80s.

Perhaps the best way to situate the Sino-Pakistan relationship is to recognize that there have been basically three kinds of nuclear-related relationships between countries. The first can be called a nuclear alliance or near-alliance. The closest historical approximations to this kind of relationship have been the US-UK connection and the Sino-Soviet connection of the '50s. Of course, the US-UK relationship was of a closer and stronger order than the Sino-Soviet one. But in neither case did the senior partner give its most advanced secrets to the other. In fact, Soviet refusal to ultimately divulge the secret of the bomb was one of the key reasons for the Sino-Soviet break up that began in the late '50s. The second kind of relationship can be called a patron-client nuclear relationship. The closest historical approximation here is the relationship between the US and Israel. The third, and far and away the most common form, is that of co-operation in nuclear-related and dual-use materials for mutual political, economic, technological, and commercial purposes. This has characterized (in milder or stronger versions) not only Sino-Pakistan nuclear ties, but the kind of support in nuclear and dual-use technologies and equipment that China has given Algeria and Libya; Germany to Argentina; France to Brazil. France even wanted to supply a plutonium reprocessing plant to Pakistan in 1974—something China has never sought to do—but was prevented from doing so by the US. Russia has given missiles to Cyprus, Iran, and even to China; China to Iran and Saudi Arabia, etc. And, of course, the US has supplied dual-use materials to a number of countries.

In the '90s, Russia has supplied SS-20s, SS-18s, and Cruise missiles to China, but to read into this some "strategic relationship" directed against a third country would be utterly mistaken. China and Russia have been particularly keen in recent years to maximize the commercial benefits of arms and technology sales of various kinds, even while claiming to be adhering to international norms regarding such transfers. China may or may not be violating such norms, but the important point to note is that these transfers do not necessarily constitute a strategic alliance. Insofar as the Sino-Pakistan connection has had a political dimension, the political import of such cooperation should be seen as obeying the general rhythms of their political ties, which were more important during the Cold War and far less so after its ending.

To further put Indian objections on this count into a proper perspective, one only needs to ask what the Indian reaction would be if China were to announce that it was supplying two full nuclear reactors to Pakistan, its most advanced fighter aircraft, and the signing of a ten-year military supply commitment to be known as a "Strategic Accord?" It is hardly difficult to imagine what the reaction would be—an uproar! And yet this is exactly what the Russians have committed themselves to doing with India. Nevertheless, the Pakistani hawk who sees in this connection a strategic alliance of sorts (nuclear-related or otherwise) between Russia and India against Pakistan is as seriously mistaken as any Indian hawk who sees in the Sino-Pakistan nuclear connection today a similar alliance or threat against India.

In 1995, at a meeting with their Chinese counterparts, an official Indian delegation headed by then Indian Defense Minister Sharad Pawar, of the then ruling Congress party, officially raised this issue. The Chinese reply was striking. The Indian side was politely informed that China was in the business of making commercial transactions and would be willing to supply on Indian request each and every item they believed China had supplied to Pakistan! These matters are not unknown to many a pro-nuclearist inside or outside the Indian government. If, in spite of this, so much has been made out of the Sino-Pakistan nuclear-related connection, then it is essentially because of the need to rationalize the May tests of 1998.

Hypocrisy and the Bomb

In this regard, Indian anti-nuclearists have to be somewhat disappointed with those Western anti-nuclearists who have given so much credence to the "China threat" as a factor supposedly provoking India to go nuclear. Or indeed to the claim that the hypocrisies of the existing NWSs "finally drove" India to take this route. Location matters. Anti-nuclearists in the West have a constant responsibility to remind the world that the existing NWSs and the biggest among them, most notably the US, are the biggest culprits. But India was not driven by "frustration" or the hypocrisies of the NWSs to do what it did. After all, what is new about such hypocrisies? In fact, these have more recently operated within a context of greater hope and optimism about the prospects of global nuclear disarmament precisely because of the existence of a new disarmament momentum. India's decision and its excuses for it reflected utter contempt even for the existence of such a momentum. The fact that its past record on disarmament issues has (justifiably) found some considerable sympathy and support from Western anti-nuclear advocates should not be allowed to obscure the reality that the India of the '90s and of May 1998 is a much more cynical India than that of the past.

Hypocrisy never drove any country to go for the bomb. The argument by its very nature does not describe an objective cause for proliferation but justifies a decision to proliferate that has been motivated by other more fundamental reasons. Hypocrisy arguments are to be tackled at the level of ideology and ideological rationales offered and resisted, not at the level of "real" or "true" causes or explanations of causes for going nuclear. It is one thing for anti-nuclear activists and others to resent the hypocrisies of NWSs and to sympathize with the resentment of NNWSs. It is another thing altogether to believe that such resentments serve as major, let alone crucial, motivations for other countries to actually go nuclear. Between 1964 and 1987, despite the persistence of such hypocrisies at a stronger, deeper, and wider scale, there was no addition to the ranks of the nuclear club.

In a post-Cold War context, when a more positive situation emerges and when these hypocritical NWSs make some positive movement of a kind that they did not make before, are the opponents of nuclear weapons suddenly to give more credence to India's self-serving claim that it was motivated to act as it did because of the hypocrisy of the NWSs? There is every reason, in fact, to appreciate that the overwhelming number of not just NNWSs, but of nuclear capable NNWSs are sensible enough to keep the hypocrisy issue in proper perspective and not to let its persistence or even its institutionalization "lead" them to break out into open nuclear status. What this persistent hypocrisy can more strongly, and likely, lead to is a break-out from the NPT and to greater suspicion of disarmament and restraint measures endorsed by the NWSs. It can also lead to a more despairing "well what did you expect" attitude if some newer countries do go nuclear—not, of course, because of "frustration" with hypocrisy, but for other more basic reasons, related to deterrence or the currency of power perceptions.

That is to say, countries go nuclear either because of changes in the perception of external threats or in the self-perception of the elite. In fact, NWSs realize that their hypocrisies are not the reason for proliferation, and this makes it more difficult to get them to renounce hypocritical nuclear behavior precisely because it doesn't cost them so much. Ironically, anti-nuclearists, justly angered by such hypocrisy tend to wish that the culprits were in some way "paid back" for continuing to be hypocritical, and so look for self-confirmation of their righteous anger and of the validity of their implicit or explicit belief/claim/hope that such persistent hypocrisy poses a "danger" and hence will elicit some kind of an eventual "comeuppance" or "lesson" even to the NWSs. Unfortunately, this is not the way the world is, nor is it the way to understand the processes of proliferation and non-proliferation, nuclear armament, or disarmament.

Comeuppance for their hypocrisies can come to the NWSs in one way only—if those who are against nuclear weapons harness the reality of the existence of such hypocrisies to mobilize emotional and intellectual anger and opposition by ever wider sections of society who, being ordinarily moral, may be nauseated by double standards. Such moral anger can generate changes in mass consciousness and practical forms of resistance against the NWSs.

Western anti-nuclear advocates willing to take the hypocrisy or the "China threat" arguments seriously as explanations for Indian behavior make a mistake. They are tempted to "respect" the China factor argument much more than they should because of a number of reasons. Most anti-nuclearists are not anti-realists. As a general rule, they tend to give more serious weight to realist arguments about "external security threats" motivating countries to go nuclear. This tendency is reinforced by the fact that in the cases of the USSR and China, external threats were certainly a very important (though not the sole) motivating factor. It is not so in the case of India, but is obviously so for Pakistan. Moreover, the implicit realism of so much of anti-nuclear thinking about global politics also reinforces the tendency to separate the domestic from the external as explanatory factors and to concentrate on the latter. It is also convenient to do so because it obviates the need then to become seriously familiar with the complexities of domestic politics in a country like India. Most anti-nuclear champions in the West and outside India, for understandable and not unworthy reasons, have neither the time nor the inclination to develop such a familiarization. But it is here, on the domestic terrain of Indian politics, general and nuclear, that the crucial explanations for India's going nuclear must be sought.

Nuclear Nationalism: The Sangh Factor

To understand the fundamental reason why India went nuclear when it did, it is necessary to recognize that, for at least fifteen years, there has been an ongoing battle for the "soul of Indian nationalism." One side—the Sangh—has been imposing its version of what this must mean, internally and externally, with ruthless determination, belligerence, and deceit. It has advanced its cause considerably, winning major support within the Indian elite and so-called middle classes. In a context where this elite's sense of nationalism is frustrated, tension-filled, and insecure, the Sangh's message of an aggressive, belligerent and essentialist-exclusivist nationalism of "blaming the others" (be they Muslims, China, Western hypocrisy, or whatever) has found powerful resonance. The very fact that the RSS (Rashtriya Swayamsevak Sangh, or National Volunteer Corps) was clearly privy to the knowledge of these blasts, while the BJP's coalition partners in the government were not, should indicate not only how deeply authoritarian and contemptuous of democracy the Sangh Combine is, but also how determined it is to carry out a total transformation of Indian society toward the establishment of a *Hindu rashtra*.[5]

The Sangh meant what it said (deliberately contradictory signals and all) about the mosque in Ayodhya and it meant what it said on the bomb.[6] The BJP, including its earlier incarnation, it should be remembered, is the only political party that officially said it wanted India to be an open nuclear weapons power; it has been saying this since the early '50s, well before there was any issue of the Pakistan and Chinese bombs! To be sure, non-BJP governments in the '90s toyed with the possibility of testing, but eventually drew back from such a decision, at least in part because it would (unlike for the BJP) have been such a sharp break from their own declared party positions that they would have had to make great public and private preparation for such a turnaround. The fact that this became a serious possibility only in the last few years itself reflects precisely the point we want to make about the change in the elite's nationalist self-perceptions and how this process of change is linked to what has been happening to India internally ever since the rise of *Hindutva*.[7]

Of course, we cannot provide here a disquisition on the transformation of Indian society in the last fifteen or so years. We will attempt only a very brief survey. From the early '70s onward, in most countries of the third world (partially excepting east and southeast Asia whose plunge into economic crisis is of more recent '90s vintage) capitalist developmentalism met with a deepening crisis—the failure of the post-independence promise. In most countries, this crisis has been a many-sided failure of growing socio-economic inadequacy, serious political-democratic limitations and weaknesses, ideological disarray, and confusion. One consequence has been the dramatic rise of culturally exclusivist political movements, currents, forces, and parties everywhere in the third world. These invariably pivot around issues of ethnicity, religion, and nation, either singly or in some combination. When the latter, the nation, has had the capacity to subsume the other two themes in a way that cannot be reciprocated on their parts, an exclusivist (often viciously so) form of nationalism has emerged and gathered strength. One has in mind here not merely Islamic nationalisms of various kinds, which are usually misleadingly placed for convenience under the single rubric of Islamic fundamentalism, but also Hindu nationalism, Buddhist revanchisms and nationalisms, and irredentist nationalisms of other kinds, especially those in the former USSR and former Yugoslavia.

India has not escaped this trend. Its crisis of capitalist developmentalism has meant the collapse of what was called the Nehruvian Model or Consensus, itself the legacy of the National Movement for independence before 1947. This had four central components, all of which have come under assault—socialism (a Fabian-influenced, social democratic notion of welfarism and social justice within the framework of a capitalist economy), democracy, secularism, and non-alignment. Whatever the deficiencies in the particular understandings and elaborations of these four basic principles, for the twenty-five years following 1947, they provided a relatively humane notion of Indian domestic development as well as its external behavior and ambitions. What is now under attack is not the failure of these principles to be realized or institutionalized effectively, *but the very principles themselves*.

For decades, the incredible plurality and diversity of Indian society, its enormous cross-cutting of communities of all kinds, its great social disparities between richer and poorer, literate and illiterate, meant that its integrating form of nationalism was a centrist, secular-populist one with progressivist pretensions to securing greater prosperity and social justice for the majority, namely those oppressed and exploited in one way or the other.

The failure to make enough such progress, symbolized by the political failure and historical decline of the Congress Party, coupled with the dramatic increase in social polarization between the well-off and the rest, the greater hedonism and arrogant insularity of an elite which in numbers is very big (ten percent of 950 million) and misleadingly calls itself a middle class, has created both a political-ideological vacuum and a shift in the character of elite nationalist inclinations. It is into this vacuum that the forces of Hindu communalism and nationalism, relatively marginal throughout the National Movement and for decades after independence, have stepped with alarming consequences. The basis for an explicitly right-wing party of mass proportions now exists—and has been taken advantage of as never before in India's political past.

What the Sangh Combine has to say is not new. Far from it. The Sangh has been saying the same thing for decades, but before the '80s, no one, including the elite, seriously listened. What is new is the much greater elite *receptivity* to their old message, if only because it seems to promise a way out of the current morass. Though this escape is a fiction, and the way disastrous for the preservation of democracy and decency in the country, the Sangh nevertheless offers a coherent perspective of sorts in a context where opposing forces and ideologies are in some disarray. The central motif of this *Hindutva* ideology is the idea of a "strong India." To become so, India must be united culturally and politically. This in turn requires recognition and acceptance of its cultural foundation, supposedly unambiguously Hindu, and the complete social transformation of society. The construction of this new social anatomy is to be carried out on the basis of the existing skeleton established by the RSS's three million odd dedicated activists, its 50,000 plus branches, and their associated structures of operation. The practices of the government and state apparatuses must also express a new determination and "virility," for India can only secure its proper civilizational role as a major world power if it follows the prescription of the Sangh. The classic statement of *Hindutva* since the 1925 birth of the RSS has been "Unite Hindus and Militarize Hinduism."

No one should underestimate the extent to which the Sangh Combine has extended its influence, especially among the elite and "middle classes" of cities and towns. Over the last decade, the center of gravity of Indian politics has swung sharply to the right in three areas. A right-wing neo-liberalism holds sway over the economy. Both secularism and democracy have been reinterpreted to mean something other than they should mean, or once meant. So, whereas once secularism meant at least a wide public commitment to the maintenance of a non-denominationalist state independent of religious affiliations, it has now come to mean, in many more eyes, a religiously tolerant state where the false self-image of Hinduism as uniquely tolerant becomes the implicit justification for having a Hindu state as the correct or best embodiment of "true" secularism. Democracy has come to be seen as majoritarianism wherein the "majority" who are Hindus should have their voices and interests preferred.

Finally, in the domain of world politics, with the collapse of the Cold War and the growing irrelevance of non-alignment, India must now ruthlessly pursue its global ambitions to become a Great Power, breaking away from a past marred by a namby-pamby third worldism and excessive moral posturing, especially on the nuclear issue. It should come as no surprise that among the great admirers of Samuel Huntington's thesis of the "clash of civilizations" (where civilizations are understood as cultural-religious entities of a sort) are a number of top leaders of the Sangh Combine. For them, the identification of a supposedly unified "Islamic civilization" is vital, not only as a counterpoint for the purposes of identifying a unified "Hindu community" in opposition to Islam and Muslims, but also to promote a perspective that might be attractive to Western right-wingers—of a possible civilizational alliance between strong Hindu and Christian worlds, against Islam certainly, and the Sinic world possibly.[8]

On the specifically nuclear front, this is tantamount to suggesting to the US that it see merit in a potential Indian nuclear ally against its other civilizational rivals. That Indian Prime Minister Vajpayee should therefore send feelers of this kind need not surprise anyone familiar with the Sangh's fundamental ideology. Thus, Vajpayee not only sent the letter to President Clinton immediately after the May tests hinting at such a China-directed alliance, but again sent a feeler in his speech to the Asia Society in New York during his Autumn 1998 UN visit. In an astonishing display of outrageously grandiose ambition, Vajpayee declared, in effect, that not only were the US and India "natural allies," but that this alliance would be the cornerstone of a new and better twenty-first century.[9]

To sum up the basic argument: it was not changes in the "external security environment" or even changes in threat perceptions that was the principal cause of India's decision to go nuclear. It was changes in elite self-perceptions and the fact that the Sangh was in power, albeit in a coalition government. Self-perceptions, unlike threat perceptions, are far more susceptible to alteration as a result of significant changes in domestic politics and dominant ideologies. Elite frustrations have risen in tandem with external ambitions and also have been fed by the lack of adequate fulfillment of these aspirations. Things have not turned out the way this elite expected or hoped. If at the time of independence, India held an easy self-confidence that it would in time "naturally" take its place at the high table of the great nations, or at least become a great Asian power, this has clearly not happened. India's own search for regional eminence has been so uneven and the outcome so uncertain that this too has left its mark on the frustrated ambitions of this more callous and self-serving elite. If the 1987 Indo-Sri Lanka Accord was the high water mark of India's post-independence foreign policy ambitions, its collapse the next year revealed how difficult it was to realize these aspirations in a more complex world.[10]

Unequivocating anti-nuclear advocates in India have for years said that not only is nuclear ambiguity unstable, but that of the three states practicing such ambiguity—Pakistan, Israel and India—it was always India that would go publicly nuclear first, if any of them did. It is important to understand why this prediction was made and why it proved correct.[11] In the cases of both Pakistan and Israel, their retention of nuclear weapons capability was always much more strongly linked to an identifiable and explicit externally perceived threat. It was India for Pakistan, and, for Israel, nearby Arab states. India, on the other hand, could not seriously point to Pakistan, whose policies were reactive, nor with much conviction or consistency to China (though, of course, India repeatedly played on both these themes).

Thus, both Pakistan and Israel pursued a coherent nuclear diplomacy, which India never could. Having clearly identified their external threats, Pakistan and Israel could also clearly spell out the conditions under which they would be willing to give up ambiguity for non-nuclear status, as well as establish the conditions under which they would *not* end their ambiguity— that is, clarify what made their ambiguity more stable. Israel would give up ambiguity for non-nuclear status in the framework of an overall and permanent Middle Eastern settlement extending to acceptance by countries like Iran and Iraq as well as other Arab states. Certainly, it would be better for Israel not to have insisted on an overall political settlement as the precondition for giving up its nuclear option and to have instead endorsed the idea of a Middle Eastern NWFZ or WMDFZ (weapons of mass destruction free zone). But at least its diplomatic posture was clear. Similarly, Pakistan could spell out the conditions under which it would give up its option and those under which it would not break with ambiguity. Pakistan would give up the option if India did so, and it would not break with ambiguity unless India did so first. Of these three countries, India was most likely to end ambiguity in favor of the exercise of the nuclear option, because it alone had a posture that could be swayed more easily by the domestic scene, especially by the changing self-perceptions of the elite.

Hardliners' Muscle-Flexing

It is in this general context that the more proximate causes for the Indian tests should be situated. Here the three most important factors were: the pressures imposed by the nuclear scientific community, the consolidation over the last decade of an unofficial lobby of hardline strategic hawks positioned in various think tanks, in influential academic institutions and in the national print media, and, of course, the impact of the CTBT debate between 1994 and 1996. Headed by key scientocrats in the Atomic Energy Department, the upper echelons of the nuclear scientific establishment have always been inclined to preserve the nuclear option, and then later on, to exercise it. They have seen their own professional prestige, importance, and bureaucratic power as connected to this. The Indian civilian energy program is almost certainly the most inefficient in the world. It is a standing disgrace by all indices, whether of production or safety. Of the nine worst performing reactors in the world, four are in India. Nine out of India's ten power reactors figure in the world's list of the fifty worst. After more than fifty years, India's atomic energy establishment, one of the earliest and largest programs to be initiated in the third world, is working at roughly half its installed capacity and contributes 1 to 1.5 percent of total electricity generation. At full capacity, its share would be just 2.5 to 3 percent. Its safety record is also shameful.[12]

By maintaining the military dimension of the program, and even more by extending it, this scientific establishment is able to hold its position of self-importance and to sustain some credibility for itself. For some years now, its top scientocrats have been pressing for the carrying out of tests. But it was the CTBT issue that really brought things to a head. The decades-long posture of ambiguity obviously raised the question of what to do about the technological upgradation of this option. Since 1974 and the first Pokharan test, all Indian governments made the policy decision that while ambiguity would not be broken, technological upgradation should continue so that if the option were ever to be exercised in the future, it could be at an appropriately higher level than in the past. As a part of this policy, delivery systems potentially capable of being nuclearly-fitted were also continuously upgraded.

As long as the prospect of a CTBT was something distant, various Indian governments could take the moral high ground and endorse it. But the moment that it became an imminent and real possibility, the CTBT raised a decisive problem and dilemma for India that had to be addressed. If India acceded to such a treaty, it would effectively end its capacity to upgrade, thereby putting severe limits on any future nuclear arsenal it might have, if it decided subsequently to go nuclear. Thus, the CTBT issue focused attention as never before on the peculiar incoherence that always underlay Indian ambiguity. Should India give up forever the option of testing? Should it test and then sign the CTBT? That may well have been the purpose when, in April 1995, while CTBT negotiations were going on, India began initial military logistical preparations to carry out a possible test in December 1995. That the US detected them and put pressure on New Delhi not to do so partly accounted for the then Congress government's decision to deny that it had any such intention.

In 1996 when the government finally decided that it would not go along with a CTBT, officials cited "national security" considerations for keeping the bomb option. They spoke, also, of the relevance of "deterrence," something that India had never done before. Indeed, India had always hitherto officially held that nuclear deterrence was "abhorrent." But this was not all. Indian rejection of the CTBT was couched not only in terms of national interest and security, but also as a morally grand posture in support of "genuine" disarmament and in defiance of nuclear hegemony, especially by the US. That many an anti-nuclear activist in the West was taken in by this posturing by the Indian government and the wider strategic establishment in the country was a real disappointment. A new, cynical India was able to pull off something of a stall, due, in large part, to the moral capital that India had built up in the past on global disarmament issues.

The very terms of the Indian debate on the CTBT were so shameful, dishonest, and deceitful that they were even more dangerous than the Indian rejection of the treaty itself. In the generation and sustenance of this discourse, the unofficial lobby of strategic hardliners played a particularly significant role. All political parties, including those of the left, and virtually the whole of the electronic and print media bought into the claims that India must not sign the CTBT, not only to protect its national interest but to avoid the "trap" that the treaty represented for countries like India in particular. The CTBT, it was claimed to virtually total elite agreement, was utterly flawed because it allowed sub-critical tests and computer simulation. It was no check on the US, but was aimed at restraining India. This then raised an obvious question. What then was the point of India formally avoiding the "trap" by not signing the CTBT, but afterwards acting as though it had? Perhaps India *should* test. Thus a powerful logic was created by the distortion of the whole terms of debate on the CTBT issue. Moreover, such had been the (albeit manipulated) public acclaim and approval of India's stand on the CTBT that any future government deciding to test could, with a great deal of confidence, expect widespread public approval for that decision.

When, in the election manifesto of the BJP in 1998, the party promised to "exercise the option to induct nuclear weapons," the writing was clearly on the wall for all who cared to see it. When it came to power, the Sangh destroyed overnight the dominant position, which was still to maintain the option but not exercise it. In effect, the Sangh carried out a dramatic, undemocratic, sudden, political coup, decisively shifting the direction of India on the nuclear question in actual defiance of what until then still remained the dominant perspective. The Sangh had done the same on the issue of secularism when on December 6, 1992, it defied the Indian Constitution and calculatedly and deliberately destroyed the Babri Masjid at Ayodhya. In India's last decade, secularism has become an increasingly dirty word and the bomb an increasingly glorious one.

Nuclearization's Horrendous Costs

Among the various ill effects of this decision to go nuclear, we will highlight five. One of these, the internal social and economic opportunity costs of nuclearization-weaponization, will be taken up separately, because such a form of argument is not in principle a critique of nuclearization *per se* but a critique of any form of wasteful military or militaristic expenditure. This is also the case with concerns about the negative effects of militarization (in any form, nuclear or otherwise) on the ideologies and practices of everyday life. Both are very powerful forms of argument against going nuclear and must, of course, be a major part of the brief of those opposing nuclearism. But it is those effects caused by the specificity of nuclearization and not by the more general issue of militarization that we will concentrate upon here.

Also, we will not address the question of economic sanctions and India's global political isolation, because it is a consequence that is both the most immediate and obvious, and the one most likely to prove ephemeral in a longer time span. Pakistan, too, faces such sanctions and isolation, but as the reactor to India, it does not share anywhere near the same opprobrium. Both the sanctions and the isolation are likely to end if India (followed or even preceded by Pakistan) signs the CTBT. It is clear that this is the minimum price India will have to pay to overcome sanctions, end isolation internationally, and pose semi-successfully as a "responsible" nuclear power concerned about strengthening international arms control regimes. Signing the CTBT would not prevent India's further weaponization and deployment of nuclearized delivery systems. Certainly, a growing lobby within the government, and among the opinion-shaping elite and media, now wants India to do this for precisely the reasons just specified.

But to do so the government has to overcome significant domestic opposition from various quarters. These range from opposition parties out to embarrass the present government, especially in view of the earlier elite consensus against the treaty; from super-hawks whose conception of a "minimum deterrent capability" requires more advanced weaponry, which a CTBT would prevent; and from those who continue to believe that the CTBT is a worthless restraint measure on the NWSs, particularly the US, and therefore is nothing more than an instrument of "nuclear hegemony." Large sections of the Indian left continue to hold this last position. The government is also looking for some kind of behind-the-scenes deal with the US regarding future supplies of dual-use technologies, as well as some form of *de facto* acceptance of India's new nuclear status if it cannot bring itself around to formal acknowledgement of this. The US Senate's rejection of the CTBT has also greatly eased the pressure on New Delhi to sign and ratify the treaty.

In any case, the four main effects that are to be elaborated below are all of a more enduring and serious nature.

The Kashmir Question

The Kashmir question has now been nuclearized and therefore internationalized. For some three decades India had more or less successfully established Kashmir as a bilateral issue.[13] In winter 1996, when Chinese President Jiang Zemin visited Islamabad after his trip to New Delhi, he shook his hosts badly when he declared that Kashmir was a bilateral issue to be sorted out between India and Pakistan. This was a major shift away from China's earlier, more supportive, stand for Islamabad. All this is now over. It is a new ball game. It is one thing to claim that non-nuclear tensions, or even a conventional conflict, are purely bilateral or South Asian issues. It is absurd and laughable to claim that the possibility of a nuclear exchange is purely a bilateral or South Asian affair!

From now on, the discourse over Kashmir will be internationalized and it will be a question of how best to intervene in this internationalized discourse, not how to insist that it remain enclosed within a purely bilateral framework. The nuclearists of India will, of course, argue that India and Pakistan must now establish proper mechanisms of political and military control so that the Kashmir dispute is never allowed to escalate to the nuclear level, so that the conflict can remain bilateral in character. It is characteristic of the casualness of most supposedly strategic thinking by pro-nuclearists that this effect was not foreseen by the Indian hawks. The political-diplomatic defeat for India over the Kashmir issue was as decisive as it was unexpected.

But efforts to keep the conflict bilateral, with the two countries establishing the proper political and military controls, will fail completely. First of all, Pakistan has no reason to let it remain confined to a bilateral framework, but will make every effort, now more legitimate and convincing than ever before, to internationalize the issue. Furthermore, establishing control mechanisms, which will reduce the danger of escalation to a possible nuclear level, is certainly desirable and to be sought after, if further weaponization/deployment by either or both sides can no longer be prevented. But the danger of such escalation cannot be eliminated. Whatever the confidence-building measures or procedures to prevent such a nuclear outbreak, they cannot be a guarantee against such escalation because the political foundations for the persistence of mutual suspicion and hostility remain intact, and such hostilities and suspicions have themselves been deepened by the nuclearization of the Kashmir issue. Putting into place a stable and enduring "firebreak" between conventional hostilities over Kashmir and the possible use of nuclear weapons is not possible when Pakistan has officially rejected India's proposal of both sides agreeing to a No First Use of nuclear weapons.

Before becoming overly critical of Pakistan's stand on this issue, one needs to investigate the Indian motivations. India has taken a unilateral position of No First Use against any NWS and of No Use against any NNWS. This is similar to China's No First Use and No Use declarations. But it is important to understand that so far, India has not deployed or significantly "hardwired" its planes to carry simple gravity nuclear bombs. Thus its declaration of No First Use when it doesn't yet have the capacity to use a weapons system, whether first or second, is really a clever, pre-emptive diplomatic ploy on its part to indirectly *legitimize* going in the direction of having a properly fitted and deployed weapons system. Therefore, it would be a disastrous political mistake for anti-nuclearists opposed to India proceeding in this direction to endorse such a declaration, *at this juncture*. India has so far only tested and declared itself to be a nuclear weapons power. It does not have a viable nuclear weapons system yet and it will take some time for it to establish this and put it into place. Therefore, the opportunity to endorse or applaud its pledge of No First Use really does not exist. Indeed, the pledge must be exposed and attacked for what it is—a clever ploy at pre-emptive justification for going along a path it should abhor! It is only if (and after) anti-nuclear opposition fails to stop India from establishing a viable nuclear weapons system or a meaningful capacity to actually launch a first strike (which, of course, in time is quite possible) that the question of endorsing such an Indian pledge arises.

A crucial distinction must be made here. The importance of continuing to press for a No First Use pledge by all five recognized NWSs is undeniable. This is a vital step that will significantly strengthen the disarmament momentum. But this position should not be confused with the stand that India has currently taken of a unilateral pledge about its own nuclear behavior. Its unilateral pledge must *not* be endorsed by disarmament and peace activists now, even as they continue to press for a similar promise by the five NWSs. The Indian No First Use proposal and pledge is part of its ongoing efforts to construct itself as a "moderate" and "responsible" power after it has shamelessly behaved in the most immoderate and irresponsible manner. The pledge is also a cover for India to put a nuclear weapons system in place. At this point of time, those opposed to nuclear weapons must pursue all efforts to stop further weaponization by India, including the induction of nuclear weapons, their deployment, the building of a command, control, communications, and intelligence infrastructure—that is, the building of all the components that together make up a viable nuclear weapons system. To endorse India's unilateral pledge now is to fall into a major political trap.

China

The relationships of India and Pakistan to China have also been adversely affected by India's and Pakistan's nuclearization. Can anyone doubt that matters here have taken a qualitative turn for the worse, and that once again it is an entirely new ballgame? Yes, the pro-nuclearists will claim that India-Pakistan and India-China relations will improve sooner or later, and become better than they were in the pre-nuclear period. Never underestimate either the arrogance or stupidity of the nuclear elite, whether of India or of other NWSs. For the first time ever, a qualitatively new dimension has been added to the pre-existing level of tensions between India and Pakistan. The pro-nuclearists who say that nuclearization will actually improve relations between the countries have an inverted logic. The causes of the underlying hostility are political, not military or nuclear. Military and nuclear preparations express—and add to—the existing political hostility. They can never be the methods or mechanisms for the resolution of such political tensions. To put it in the form of an historical analogy—the Cold War arms race between two politically hostile countries, the US and USSR, was not reversed because of nuclear weapons. Nuclear weapons preparations did not lead to a reduction, but an increase, in Cold War political tensions. It was only Gorbachev's determination and effort to end the political Cold War that led to reductions in nuclear arms and a reversal of that arms race. South Asia is the only region in the world that has had a continuous hot-cold war for fifty years. Only by first shifting the political foundations of this situation can we hope to decrease nuclear tensions, not the other way around.

As for the India-China relationship, this has now embarked on a different trajectory. From now on, no matter what the fluctuations in China's official declarations and statements on India-China relationships, if India further weaponizes and deploys, as is most likely, (unless somehow prevented by domestic opposition), China must factor India in as a nuclear-political rival and make its nuclear preparations accordingly. The more India tries to establish what it believes will be a minimum credible deterrent against China, the more China must go along this route, too. Defense Minister George Fernandes called China a potential rival and threat; now India's actions have gone a long way toward making China not a potential, but an actual, nuclear threat and political rival to India. This need not ever have been the case. In short, the spectrum within which India-China relations will now operate has, after Pokharan II, decisively narrowed. Its two poles are no longer strategic hostility and strategic friendship, but strategic hostility and, at the other end, something close to strategic rivalry. That India's pro-nuclearists should not have perceived this outcome once again testifies to their strategic bankruptcy.

When China went nuclear, it did so substantially because of its perceived fears regarding the US and USSR, in a context which everyone recognized was one of clear strategic hostility between China and the other two. China explicitly stated as much. It did not have to try to make a case that there was such a hostility, let alone rivalry. This was obvious. Or that the USSR and US were potential strategic opponents to guard against in the future. They were actual opponents, not potential ones, although the later entente between China and the US changed this picture, at least for these two countries. In the case of India, there has never been such clarity or obviousness characterizing the nature of the India-China political relationship—hence the constant need to make out a case that there is (or might be in the future) such a situation of strategic rivalry or hostility. Moreover, China never cited India as the reason for going nuclear or perpetuating its nuclear status, for the simple reason that India has never been, nor ever perceived to be, the threat. To put it another way, the larger web of hostile relationships in which China decided to go nuclear is not comparable to the political context in which India has decided to go nuclear.

That is why the constant harping on China as a nuclear threat to India has been so dangerous. It has now led to a denouement that is a classic case of a self-fulfilling prophecy. China has now become, or is very close to becoming, (once India weaponizes and openly deploys) a nuclear opponent and threat with actual, as distinct from conceivable, nuclear targeting and preparations vis-à-vis India.

But what about the Sino-Pakistan link? Not only was the nature of the Sino-Pakistan nuclear link misrepresented, but now the loosening of these ties in favor of a Chinese exploration of a better relationship with India has now stopped. Chinese pragmatism means that it is not axiomatic that Beijing will want a closer relationship with Islamabad against New Delhi. But, reversing the Chinese trajectory of over a decade, this has now become more rather than less likely. Certainly, the more India regards the Chinese arsenal as a threat and prepares accordingly, the more likely a closer Chinese-Pakistani nuclear relationship will become. No matter how much India talks about its nuclear preparations not being aimed at China (interspersed, of course, with statements about China's more strategic and longer-term threat), the Chinese must be much more inclined than ever before to operate on the opposite premise. But India's community of strategic experts who supported the tests and going nuclear tell us that our security will be greatly enhanced by what has happened!

The Domestic Fallout

In some ways, the domestic effects of India's nuclearization are the most dangerous. The Sangh Combine has moved a decisive step forward in its overall program to transform India and to fulfill its overall project of defining the nature of India and Indian nationalism. Unless this force's general ideological and political vision of nationalism is effectively confronted at the level of nationalist discourse itself, the fight to prevent them from destroying the democratic and tolerant, civilized and humane fabric of India may be lost. In fact, when the RSS-BJP decided to go nuclear they made much more careful calculations about the likely internal consequences than they ever did about the external repercussions. That much should be obvious now. It is also indicative of how much more important to them is their longer-term domestic agenda and of this decision's place within that domestic agenda. The Parliamentary elections of 1999 showed that the BJP lost votes despite nuclearization, but that is to miss the issue. The fact is, that once again, the BJP decisively determined the direction that India is taking and organized to its overall advantage the parameters of future discourse on the issue of national security.

It is truly extraordinary how swiftly and comprehensively the Sangh Combine has destroyed the "middle ground" on the nuclear issue. That was, as pointed out earlier, the posture of nuclear ambiguity, which until May 1998 was still the position of all the other parties and of the overwhelming bulk of the "strategic community" of opinion shapers, and of the leaders of the civilian and military bureaucracies. The Sangh did not seek to adjust its perspectives to suit this community of so-called experts. On the contrary, it accurately assessed the specific moral-political character of this important section of the Indian elite and recognized that it had nothing to worry about from them. They would adjust their perspectives to suit the Sangh's politics! That is exactly what happened. Overnight, the middle ground was destroyed, leaving the opposition parties and members of the "security establishment" with either the option of directly or indirectly endorsing the crossing of the nuclear Rubicon, or of opposing it.

Of the political parties, only the left came out (after initial hesitation and confusion) against the tests. All other mainstream parties, regional and national, took no such unambiguous stand. Some Congress leaders tried to make political capital by questioning the timing of the tests. Some, like the Janata Dal (a key component in the United Front government prior to the BJP-led coalition government), sought to take credit by claiming that they had made the first preparations for the tests and were themselves contemplating them. Most political parties are reluctant to reverse the trajectory now set, though the pace and manner in which it is followed will certainly be influenced by which parties are in power at the center. Only the left parties, the Communist Party of India (CPI) and the Communist Party of India-Marxist (CPM), can be expected to reverse this trajectory. But not only is there no chance of their heading a central government and being powerful enough to do this in the near future, but they also continue to pursue the chimera of restoring ambiguity rather than committing themselves to the complete denuclearization of India or of South Asia, regardless of what the five other NWSs do.

As for the "strategic experts," their *volte face* was almost total. Most (whether active or retired) are drawn from the bureaucratic, military, and diplomatic services, journalism, think tanks concerned with security matters, and academic disciplines like international relations and area studies. They busied themselves trying to justify the Indian decision and explain why the tests were inevitable. In a display that would be laughable if it were not so ironically tragic, the *very same people* who had for years used arguments to explain why India must hold onto the nuclear option yet not exercise it openly, now used the *very same arguments* to explain why India had to go openly nuclear! Interestingly, it was only among academics of the social sciences other than international relations that a much larger proportion of former ambiguists came out clearly against the tests. No doubt, their greater sensitivity than conventional realists' to the moral dimensions of human affairs must have been part of the reason for this.

Global Nuclear Disarmament

The fourth effect is on the general momentum toward global nuclear restraint and disarmament that has existed ever since the decline and end of the Cold War. This momentum, whose existence is testified to in so many ways, may be halting, hesitant, and uneven, but it is nonetheless real and new, and its overall direction has been positive. Now it has been severely damaged by what happened in South Asia. The damage is indeed grave, with the chances of other countries following suit having become greater. If other countries, particularly what the US likes to call "rogue states" (when it is itself the biggest and most dangerous nuclear "rogue state"), get the bomb or start preparing for it, that will not impel the US (and other NWSs) to move more seriously toward denuclearization. The opposite will be the case, and those within these NWSs pushing for meaningful reductions, restraint, and eventually total disarmament will not be politically strengthened, but weakened, by such developments.

Concomitant with this adverse impact on the global disarmament process is the great damage done to India's standing in the world. India's diplomatic stature stands greatly diminished. The decision to go nuclear was the search for a political "easy fix." In truth, even within the nuclear club, membership is graded: India and Pakistan are third class members, with the UK, France, and China occupying the second rung. The so-called diplomatic or "prestige" benefits that India's nuclear hawks have assumed would fall to the country are not just ephemeral, but mostly non-existent. Thus, India's chances of getting a Security Council seat in the UN have greatly diminished, not increased. Neither India nor Pakistan will be "rewarded" in this way for going nuclear, for that would set a terrible precedent. (Of course, the very existence of a Security Council of "special nations," which is not democratically subordinated to the General Assembly, is itself an affront to the struggle to democratize international diplomatic institutions. But that is a separate issue.)

In general, most NNWSs will come to realize that this new India is more cynical, and now talks for the most part—like all the other NWSs—with a forked tongue. As such India's capacity to play a valued world role in pushing for global disarmament has lessened greatly. New Delhi will find that junior and very subordinate status in the nuclear club, accompanied by the ongoing reality of being a poverty-stricken country whose internal "successes" are few and unimpressive beyond the preservation of a vibrant democracy (now itself under threat as never before), will be no diplomatic compensation for what it has now squandered, namely its decades-long legacy of being an important moral-political actor in the pursuit of global nuclear disarmament.

No Peace in the "Land of the Buddha?"

The stereotypical impression worldwide of the "popular" or "mass" reaction to the nuclear blasts in India and Pakistan is the initial "CNN image": groups of young men dancing with joy in Delhi's streets, waving saffron flags to congratulate the Hindu-nationalist Bharatiya Janata Party. Pakistan was presented as the exact, symmetrical, obverse: they celebrated "standing up to" and "getting even with" India.

In reality, such currents of strongly pro-bomb opinion, while telegenic, only represented a small, urban, vocal minority in India. Opinion within the urban majority was sharply divided. Many tentatively supported, without enthusiastically welcoming, the tests, because they saw them as acts of defiance against the nuclear hegemony of the P-5, not because they believe that nuclear weapons are necessary for India's security, or have enhanced her prestige.

The enthusiastic support of the minority soon ran out: the Pakistani tests that followed, India's diplomatic isolation, sanctions, and the growing realization that nuclearization has done little for India's security while diverting scarce resources away from real priorities, all wrought a major shift in public opinion. Within two months of the tests, a clear majority of people polled spoke against the bomb. As many as *72.8 percent* said India must not make, deploy, or use nuclear weapons.[1]

In Pakistan, there was a stronger link in the popular mind between a possible threat from an "inimical" and now-nuclearized India, and Pakistan's own tests. But there, too, opinion was divided. The bomb did not shore up Nawaz Sharif's sinking credibility or create a consensus.

It must be admitted, however, that popular opposition to the tests was at first relatively weak. The anti-nuclear current was a minority. It has since expanded manifold. One of the most significant effects of the tests was to *ignite* a peace and nuclear disarmament movement in India and Pakistan.

Prior to May 1998, the peace and nuclear disarmament movement in India and Pakistan was relatively weak and scattered. It did not have a major political impact in shaping policies or party agendas, although it had strong and organic roots in the environmental, human rights, civil liberties, and women's movements and in a range of non-governmental organizations (NGOs).

One reason for this was the pursuit of nuclear ambiguity in both countries for a decade or more. This bred complacency about the viability of "non-weaponized" or "recessed" deterrence. Since nuclear weapons did not actually exist, and their existence was not admitted, they did not represent a *felt danger*.

Two deeper reasons explain the relative weakness of the peace movement in the subcontinent. The first is the strength of third world anti-colonial or post-colonial nationalism in both India and Pakistan. At least in the public discourse of the two states, which gained independence in 1947, such nationalism made it hard for political leaders, intellectuals, and ordinary citizens to advocate the narrowing or closing of the nuclear weapons option, which was wrongly seen as an instrument of national sovereignty and a repository of pride.

Such is the strength of this nationalism, particularly in the more belligerent and aggressive form it has taken in the past decade or so, that even the parties of the left have succumbed to it, often by pleading that for "tactical" reasons it would be dangerous to allow the right to monopolize the nationalist space. In a situation where globalization and pursuit of neo-liberal policies are seen to be eroding the space for indigenous paths to development, the defense of national sovereignty acquires some legitimacy.

The second factor at work in the pre-May 1998 period was public disillusionment with the prospect for rapid movement toward global nuclear disarmament. Although it would be ludicrous, and utterly dishonest, to make this an excuse for crossing the nuclear threshold as New Delhi did, large numbers of people in India and Pakistan saw few signs of willingness on the part of the NWSs—themselves seen as pushy powers—to do anything to reduce the nuclear danger, and delegitimize and marginalize their dependence on nuclear weapons, let alone abolish them. Had the NWSs "led by example," the case for India and Pakistan also to move in the direction of closing the nuclear option would have become persuasive, if not pressing.

In India, an additional factor has been at work. That is the steady erosion and collapse of one significant current of pacifism in the region—the Gandhian movement, which espoused non-violence, universal brotherhood, and peace. The bulk of Mahatma Gandhi's spiritual disciples who did not join the Congress Party regrouped themselves into the Sarvodaya movement.

Sarvodaya (literally, rise, upliftment, and progress for all) too preached non-violence. But it did not concern itself specifically with nuclear issues, or with other contemporary questions of war, peace, and social strife. It was content to advocate non-violence and peace in the abstract, as spiritual values, not political goals seen as worthy by citizens who relate them to their own priorities.[2]

The task of building public opinion in favor of peace and nuclear disarmament has now been taken up by relatively young people, drawn from varied backgrounds, who see the struggle for nuclear disarmament as being related to the defense of decency, humanity, and democracy, and espousal of the cause of peaceful resolution of conflicts. These people see nuclearism as a perversion bound up with aggressive militarism and religion-based nationalism in South Asia. They are in the process of constructing a campaign for nuclear disarmament, peace, and conciliation with India's neighbors.

Especially noteworthy here is the support that nuclear disarmament groups in both countries have received for a number of initiatives in favor of friendly and improved relations between India and Pakistan, with a special emphasis on people-to-people contacts and exchanges. Many such initiatives were set up and have grown in both countries since the mid-'90s.

Three aspects of the growing nuclear disarmament and peace movements in both countries, especially India, are noteworthy. First, they have strong links with NGOs and "people's movements" structures active in a number of areas. Thus, their "natural" or "organic" constituencies include activists fighting for the right to livelihood, for rehabilitation (of project-displaced people), for equal access to environmental resources, and defense of the natural environment. Equally important are those fighting for empowerment of the underprivileged, for secularism, against religious fanaticism and intolerance, and against child labor.

Second, there is strong and spontaneous participation of women in the peace movement. This link has been established in India and Pakistan—and indeed in the rest of South Asia—at an early stage of evolution of the struggle for nuclear disarmament. Feminists in India and Pakistan have a strong awareness of the connections between nuclearism and patriarchy, and between militarism and suppression of women's rights. (See "Toys for Boys" page 133).

Feminists were among the first group of movement-rooted activists to condemn the nuclear tests. They held an impressive march in Pune in western India in late May 1998 to coincide with the Indian Women's Studies Conference, which had participants from the South Asian region as a whole.

Third, the sub-continent's peace and disarmament movement has a remarkably holistic and comprehensive perspective. Its activists relate their objectives and methods to the larger struggle for a humane, egalitarian, gender-just, ecologically sound, non-hierarchical, free, and open society. They are broad-minded and internationalist in outlook, and acutely aware that the arena of activism must be at once national, Asian, and international. The nuclear disarmament agenda by its very nature has to be addressed nationally, regionally, and above all, globally.

Several groups, networks, and organizations dedicated to nuclear disarmament have sprung up in Indian and Pakistani cities, although their activity in villages is feeble. They made their presence felt through the impressive number of marches, meetings, and cultural events that they organized on August 6, Hiroshima Day, in 1998 and 1999. This was a large and energetic mobilization of people on a non-party-political issue, comparable in strength, for instance, to the pro-secular and anti-sectarian initiatives witnessed on the Ayodhya mosque demolition issue, or on the harassment of Christians.

A sign of the growing strength and moral force of the Indian and Pakistani nuclear disarmament movements is the support they have won from several highly regarded former generals, admirals, and air marshals, from senior diplomats and civil servants, as well as from eminent intellectuals and artists. Despite its late start, and its weaknesses, the peace movement has become an inalienable component of grassroots civil society organizations in India and Pakistan. Its fate is inextricable from the future of the broader agenda of democratization and popular empowerment.

NOTES

[1] Press Trust of India, the country's principal news agency, reported, quoting an opinion poll, "72.8% opposes use of N-weapons, says survey," *The Economic Times* 24 June 1998.

Most opinion polls, especially the early ones, were limited to the urban areas, and thus tended to exaggerate the popular support for the tests. The more systematic broad-sample polls done later suggest that large numbers of rural Indians were not even aware of the tests. According to an *India Today*-MARG poll, published in that magazine on 25 December 1998, 47 percent of people had not even heard of the May tests.

[2] Soon after the initial burst of enthusiasm, and the setting up of a number of spartan ashrams in rural areas in the early '50s, the Sarvodaya movement turned conservative. It became increasingly oblivious of social reality, dominated by intense inequalities in wealth, income, access to land, and entitlements to public goods, in rural India, where it primarily worked. Instead of taking the side of the landless, the poor, and women in their struggle for justice, it advocated that the landed rich generously donate a part of their land to the landless—*Bhoodan. Bhoodan* will go down as one of the greatest hypocrisies and frauds in twentieth century India. It did not, predictably, result in land reform or redistribution. Minuscule quantities of arid and degraded land were all that was donated by the rich.

Failure to engage with social reality was to marginalize Sarvodaya. But its worst degeneration came in the '70s, when its most prominent leader, Vinoba Bhave, became an apologist for Indira Gandhi's Emergency regime, rationalizing it as the Era of Discipline. Since then, most old Sarvodayis have individually strayed into various irrelevant or trivial pursuits, some even joining forces with the BJP and its cohorts in attacking Christians in Gujarat.

There are exceptions, such as Narayan Desai, Thakurdas Bang, and Nirmala Deshpande. But as a group, the Gandhians have totally failed to build public opinion in favor of peace and nuclear disarmament.

Pakistan in Imitation Mode

An earlier single-line summary of Pakistan's decades-long nuclear policy bears repetition. Islamabad's nuclear preparations have been carried out independently of New Delhi, but as soon as Pakistan came close to achieving nuclear weapons capability, successive governments uniformly shaped their nuclear diplomacy with India as their central point of reference. In this sense, Pakistan's nuclear policy has been strongly reactive to India's. Despite internal pressures from sections of the "nuclear establishment," Islamabad has never seriously wavered from the policy of not going openly nuclear first. Indeed, Islamabad has always shown willingness to abandon the carefully constructed nuclear option if New Delhi were prepared to do the same.

The earliest speculations about a possible Pakistani nuclear bomb appear to have surfaced around 1960, when the US was pushing its "Atoms for Peace" program worldwide.[14] Pakistan was then a faithful ally, keen to ingratiate itself with the US. The idea of a possible Pakistani nuclear deterrent against, ironically enough, China (a US bugbear at the time) was then mooted. At this initial stage, developing a minimal level of theoretical expertise and some basic understanding of how to run a (dual-use) program of power and research reactors was essential for laying down the minimal foundations, upon which serious thinking could then be devoted to whether or not a nuclear weapons capability should be sought and constructed. Through the '60s and '70s, the US trained at its various institutions over a thousand Pakistani, and over a hundred Indian, scientists and technicians in nuclear physics, chemistry, and engineering, and their practical applications.

In both countries, the scientists' lobby has ever since been a significant pressure group urging further upward movement on the ladder of nuclear weapons preparations. In Pakistan, the actual decision to go ahead with building a weapons capability, even though no civilian nuclear energy infrastructure of serious note existed, came after the defeat and dismemberment of Pakistan in 1971–72, when Bangladesh was formed. Bomb designing, though, may well have been explored as early as the late '60s. After the second (1965) and third (1971–72) Indo-Pakistan wars, with their continuing tensions throughout the '70s, the Sino-Indian border conflict of 1962, and the secret preparations at the end of the '60s for entente between US and China (via the good offices of Islamabad), the political rationale for a Pakistan bomb was obviously the India threat, and that alone. Indeed, China had come to be seen as a Pakistani political ally (especially after its strongly pro-Islamabad and anti-liberation stand during the Bangladesh war) and a source of possible support in the development of such a nuclear weapons capability.

At the famous Spring 1972 meeting in the northern city of Multan, then Prime Minister Zulfikar Ali Bhutto and a gathering of the country's top nuclear scientists and bureaucrats made the formal decision to prepare a weapons capability. This was two years before Pokharan I in India, although that event clearly stimulated Pakistan to press more aggressively than ever for such a bomb-making capacity. Over the next decade, Pakistan clandestinely acquired the necessary supplies and equipment to build a gas centrifuge uranium enrichment facility at Kahuta. The key figure in organizing this effort was Abdul Qadir Khan, a metallurgist by profession, who has been called in many circles, the father of the Pakistan bomb. It was he who copied the all-important list of private suppliers of crucial components for building a gas centrifuge plant when working at the centrifuge enrichment plant operated by Urenco at Almelo in The Netherlands.[15] He was made head of the Kahuta project, which, in a clear indication of its secrecy and urgency, was separated from the Pakistan Atomic Energy Commission.

Pakistan most likely developed its capacity sometime in the early to mid-'80s. In 1987, Abdul Qadir Khan, in his famous interview with Indian journalist, Kuldip Nayar, publicly declared that Pakistan had the bomb, or to be more precise, could assemble it immediately if required. That is to say, by the mid-'80s, both India and Pakistan could be said to have secured "bombs in the basement with the last wires unconnected."[16] Between then and May 28, 1998, when Pakistan first tested, the government in Islamabad consciously played the ambiguist card of sending mixed signals. Pakistan had the capacity, but no current intention to build the bomb, leaders would hint—but that might or might not change in the future.

In fact, Islamabad was always careful never to formally or officially assert in any written statement or declaration that it had this capacity. Thus it rejected all Indian diplomatic overtures in the '90s for a bilateral declaration on non-use of each country's nuclear weapons capability. It was one thing for different officials, even very senior leaders, to verbally assert that Pakistan had this capacity. But given the various Congressional laws and amendments in the US forbidding military help, and indeed calling for US sanctions against countries pushing nuclear weaponization, Islamabad was always careful never to acknowledge in the form of any treaty or written statement that it had such a capacity. That would have been to greatly complicate and worsen its relationship with the US.

Given that Pakistan secured its capacity through the clandestine route, relying for the most part on private suppliers, how important was Chinese help? Before the early '80s, and not afterwards, Chinese help was clearly at its greatest. Certain kinds of speculation can be safely discarded. No evidence proves that Pakistan ever tested a bomb of its making at China's Lop Nor test site. Similarly, for all the talk of an "Islamic Bomb," no evidence suggests that other states in West Asia or northern Africa (e.g. Libya, Iran, or Iraq) secured significant, let alone decisive, Pakistani support of any kind in this regard. Although the US-Israel relationship is a partial exception, in general, NWSs have imposed strong self-limits on the extent to which they would go beyond provision of certain dual-use technologies, certain forms of information exchange, to help another country secure such capabilities. Perhaps the best way to sum up the level of Chinese help to Pakistan is to point out that: (a) it was more important in the '70s and early '80s than in the late '80s and '90s, (b) its major contribution was more at the level of information (much of which was available in the public domain) than at the level of technology or equipment supplies, and (c) such help was significant but not decisive for Pakistan's quest. At most, it accelerated the pace at which Pakistan reached its goal.[17]

Islamabad's Search for Parity

From the mid-'80s on, the community of nuclear scientists exerted continuous pressure on the government to go ahead and test, citing the first Indian test of 1974 as the political justification. They were joined by a small section of so-called strategic and military experts who repeatedly argued that Pakistan needed the bomb to compensate for the claimed 2:1 or 3:1 imbalance in conventional military forces between itself and India. But despite such constant pressure, there was never any sign or fear that Pakistan would be the first to cross the threshold in South Asia. The nuclear hawks were always considerably outweighed by others within the national security establishment who clearly and sensibly recognized that the negative consequences of precipitating a nuclear arms race with India were much greater than any presumed benefits. The socio-economic burden of carrying on a continuous nuclear arms race with India would be much greater for Pakistan. Being much smaller in size, Pakistan lacked strategic depth of the kind that might lead some Indians to think they could "absorb" a small nuclear exchange.

Thus the search for non-nuclear parity between Pakistan and India always made much more political and diplomatic sense and remained the pivotal basis of Islamabad's nuclear diplomacy. Pakistan was never seriously tempted to even "match" India's first test in 1974 by carrying out its own test for fear that this would be read as a provocation and excuse for India to break out into open nuclear status. Even for Pakistani hawks, whose first preference was for a Pakistan openly equipped with nuclear weapons, the search for a non-nuclear parity made sense as a "second-best option." Thus Pakistan repeatedly proposed to India a variety of measures for bilateral or regional renunciation of such weapons. These were not in the nature of a "bluff" as falsely made out by Indians embarrassed by these proposals. They were seriously meant, though Islamabad was aware that India would be very unlikely to give up its option. In which case, at least Pakistan would gain in terms of diplomatic one-upmanship. Even on the CTBT, Pakistan's position during the 1994–96 negotiations was pegged to Indian behavior. If the latter would sign the CTBT, so too would Pakistan.

Once Pakistan carried out the tests, however, the position and influence of its hawks has become much stronger. Pakistan will continue to endorse and be open to proposals for regional and bilateral denuclearization, but this seems even further away and more unrealistic now than it did before. Thus, the new "common sense" that prevails is that Pakistan, having become a nuclear weapons power, must now keep these weapons to compensate for the conventional military disadvantage it has with respect to India. To be sure, Islamabad continues to say (and there is no good reason to doubt it) that it will not be the first to deploy such weapons, but will only do so after India first deploys its arsenal. But a form of justification for possessing nuclear weapons that did not enjoy much public (or even elite) resonance earlier has now gathered stronger support and will influence in dangerous ways Pakistan's future nuclear-strategic thinking and practice.

Was it inevitable that once India tested and went openly nuclear, Pakistan would have to do the same? The answer would seem to be no. Pakistan waited for two weeks before responding with its own tests, although Abdul Qadir Khan informed the top civilian and military leadership that Pakistan needed at most three days to carry out its own tests. In between, especially during the first week, the government did not state that it would definitely respond in kind, but sought both strong political reassurances as well as significant material help from outside countries, particularly from the US. There were sound reasons for Islamabad's being cautious. Clearly, Pakistan would be subject to economic sanctions (as were imposed on India after its tests) by some important countries and international institutions, and the Pakistan economy was in far more parlous and externally dependent a state than India's at the time. In fact, Pakistan was in a serious economic crisis from mid-1997 on, and to date has remained immersed in it.

Furthermore, something was to be gained in terms of international prestige and political sympathy by not following India. Pakistan could hope to more successfully than ever mount a collective diplomatic campaign against India and thus broaden its own international support base on the Kashmir issue, as well as in regard to its own demands for security, now newly imperiled by the Indian action. In short, there was something to be said for Pakistan's refraining from testing and milking the international community, particularly the US, for what it could get on the economic, military, and political-diplomatic levels. Thus the Pakistan government did seek to bargain with the US for compensatory support. A combination of external and internal factors determined Pakistan's eventual decision to duplicate the Indian behavior.

On the external front, Pakistan was disappointed that the opposition to the Indian action was not as sharp as it had hoped. Even the NWSs did not unite to impose sanctions on India, as Russia and France explicitly refused to do so. Pakistan was further disappointed that the US did not declare its willingness to provide it with a nuclear umbrella. Nor did the US offer a financial-economic-military package up to Pakistan's expectations. But more significant in shaping the final decision were the country's domestic factors. Two considerations were particularly crucial—one political and the other more directly military.

The position of Prime Minister Nawaz Sharif was unenviable. His political support had been steadily diminishing. His party, the Pakistan Muslim League (PML), was under pressure not only from the opposition Pakistan's People's Party headed by Benazir Bhutto, daughter of former premier Zulfikar Ali Bhutto, but also, more seriously, from an array of explicitly fundamentalist, right-wing Islamic forces, which had been immeasurably strengthened by the recent successes of the Taliban in Aghanistan. Since the early '80s, the nexus between Afghanistan and Pakistan had become very strong, as events in the former country had a major impact on Pakistan's social and military life, as well as exacting heavy domestic sacrifices as the price to be paid for sustained Pakistani support to the Taliban militias. Without sufficiently powerful incentives or strong, visible benefits to justify a Pakistani refusal to emulate Indian action, the Sharif government found it very difficult to confront such internal pressures, which had secured majority public support for carrying out retaliatory tests.

The second factor was the sentiment within the armed forces, especially within officer ranks. The military services, dominated by the army, have always exercised enormous influence in Pakistan's polity, despite the steps made in recent years toward stabilizing a civilian regime of "controlled democracy." To begin with, for all the reasons outlined earlier, the head of the army, General Jehangir Karamat, was not inclined to endorse retaliatory tests. It was only after visiting the Pakistan-controlled part of Kashmir to assess military morale that he was persuaded to change his mind. He discovered not only that morale was low after the Indian tests, but that sentiment among the officer corps was strongly in favor of an equivalent Pakistani response to the Indian action. He then advised the Sharif government accordingly.

Precisely in order to create widespread popular opinion that Pakistan could "match" India's nuclear capabilities, Islamabad carried out its own tests on May 28 and 30, claiming six tests in all, so as to balance the six that India had undertaken—one in 1974 and five in 1998. But both the technical data released by both countries and evidence from monitoring stations in other countries, do not substantiate either Pakistan's claim to have carried out six tests or India's claim to have carried out a thermonuclear explosion or hydrogen bomb test.

Mine is Bigger than Yours:
The Indian and Pakistani Test Yields

The overt nuclearization of India and Pakistan is inseparable from fierce mutual rivalry and muscle-flexing over assumed technological prowess and claims of military superiority, as well as of greater valor and virility. Nothing illustrates this better than official statements about the character and number of nuclear test explosions carried out in May 1998 and their yields, as well as competitive claims about each other's missile capabilities.

These "my-bomb-is-bigger" statements have been questioned by independent experts both internationally and in India and Pakistan. It seems highly likely that New Delhi and Islamabad grossly exaggerated their tests' yields. In all probability, India's claimed May 11 "thermonuclear" explosion, by means of which it was supposed to have established decisive nuclear superiority over Pakistan, was a dud. The "secondary" of this "hydrogen bomb" probably did not go off.

India's hawkish publicists and strategic analysts have repeatedly asserted that India has unassailable dominance over Pakistan in missile technology too. India only denies this when it suits them to make the opposite, perhaps equally poorly-substantiable, claim, that India is inferior and needs to sink more investment into its "indigenous" missile program to compete better with Pakistan's "import-based" program.

Pakistan's claims of superiority in missile technology come from the very top. In January 1999, Abdul Qadir Khan, the father of the country's nuclear program and the *Ghauri* missile, asserted that Pakistan's missiles are "far superior to what India had in its arsenal...New Delhi would have to think twice before daring to attack Pakistan." He said, "Our missiles can hit any Indian city within ten to fifteen minutes at a speed of three kilometers per second... Pakistan's missiles [are] far better than the *Prithvi* and *Agni*...[1]

These boastful assertions have little to do with hard facts. Rather, they are an integral part of the exchange of bellicose rhetoric that has become a sub-continental routine. India claimed to have simultaneously exploded three nuclear devices: On May 11, 1998, a fission device with a yield of twelve kilotons (a kiloton is the equivalent of 1,000 tons of TNT), a thermonuclear device, *Shakti-I*, with a yield of forty-three kilotons, and a third device of less than a kiloton. The last was reported to have a yield of 0.2 kilotons. The combined total yield was said to be fifty kilotons. (This was revised upward to sixty kilotons in February 1999, according to Rajagopala Chidambaram, chairman of the Atomic Energy Commission.[2]

As for India's two May 13 tests, these were claimed to be of low-yield devices, with yields between 0.2 and 0.6 kilotons. It is not clear if these involved developing battlefield-usable "tactical" nuclear weapons (some writers have even suggested that these may be adapted into artillery shells), or if they were "boosted primaries" (extremely light devices with yields usually in excess of ten kilotons, which are particularly useful in setting off high-yield "secondary" explosion assemblies in a thermonuclear bomb).

The twelve-kiloton device tested on May 11 (Chidambaram later said it had a yield of fifteen kilotons) was reported to have been a lighter, more compact version of the kind of device India tested in 1974. India's claim about the forty-three-kiloton *Shakti-I* and the May 13 "low-yield" tests soon came under serious questioning from scientists. Some suggested that *Shakti-I* was a "boosted fission" weapon, not a thermonuclear one. Thermonuclear weapons usually have an explosive yield in the megaton (1,000 kiloton) range, while boosted fission devices yield something of the order of thirty to one hundred kilotons.

But Atomic Energy Commission (AEC) chairman Chidambaram insisted at a press conference on May 17 that it was a thermonuclear device. Its yield, he claimed, was kept deliberately low in view of the risk of seismic damage to villages in the vicinity of the site.[3]

Officials of the AEC and the Defense Research & Development Organization (DRDO) were categorical that "weaponization is now complete. We have tested the size, weight, performance, and vibrations for nuclear warheads designed to go on *Prithvi* and *Agni* missiles." They also claimed that

> the tests provided critical data for the validation of our capability in the design of nuclear weapons of different yields for different applications and different delivery systems and significantly enhanced our capability in computer simulations of new designs and taken us to the stage of sub-critical experiments in the future, if considered necessary.

Since then, a number of independent scientists and engineers, including seismologists, nuclear physicists, and weapons designers, have collected and analyzed data from both AEC sources and seismographs at different locations in the world. (The AEC's disclosures about the measurements of the yields in question have all been based on seismic data; data relevant to other methods, such as assays of radionuclides from the explosion tunnel/hole, have not been released at the time of writing).

Terry Wallace, a University of Arizona seismologist, concluded that the total yield of the three May 11 explosions was only ten to twenty-five kilotons, not fifty kilotons.[4] This is similar to other estimates. For instance, according to data compiled by the Natural Resources Defense Council (NRDC), the expected mid-point of a range of probable yields for all three tests on May 11 was only about twelve kilotons.[5]

Seven months after the tests, however, Chidambaram described the Pokharan II series as "the perfect tests." He reiterated that India had conducted its full complement of tests and had "obtained three robust bomb designs" from the Pokharan explosions. He dismissed all doubts raised by independent experts about the AEC's claims, by saying he was not surprised by their reaction. "This was expected," he said, pointing out that "though the Indian side had presented the yield data along with corroborative proof, the credibility of Indian figures continued to be doubted." He described the doubts as "baseless":

> Though the US had conducted 1,030 tests and China 45, India's tests should be considered equivalent to the several which other nuclear weapon states had conducted because the Pokharan tests were undertaken from a higher technological threshold.[6]

There are several internal inconsistencies and contradictions in the official claims. For instance, the claimed yield projections for the 1998 tests are based on the assumption that the May 1974 test at the same Pokharan site had a yield of twelve to fourteen kilotons (and there was no significant change in the geology of the area). But independent estimates of the 1974 yield, confirmed by some Indian officials, are as low as two to four kilotons.[7] If the lower numbers are used, the combined total yield of the May 11 tests only works out to ten to twenty kilotons, not the claimed forty-five to sixty.

P.K. Iyengar, former AEC chairman and the principal physicist involved in the 1974 test, once said its yield was about eight kilotons. But in a recent interview, he said that, based on radiochemical analysis of samples of bomb debris, the yield of the 1974 blast was closer to ten kilotons.[8] While higher than the two to four kiloton estimate, this is still below the originally claimed twelve to fourteen kilotons.

In November 1998, *Nucleonics Week*, the international nuclear industry's trade journal, reported that

> analysts at the Z Division of the Lawrence Livermore National Laboratory, responsible for making estimates of progress in foreign nuclear weapons programs based on classified data, have now concluded that the second stage of a two-stage Indian hydrogen bomb device failed to ignite as planned.[9]

A hydrogen or thermonuclear bomb is a two-stage weapon in which the main contribution to the explosive energy results from the fusion of light nuclei, such as deuterium and tritium. The high temperatures required for that reaction, produced in the secondary stage of the device, are initially generated by fission at the primary stage. *Nucleonics Week* quoted US analysts as saying they "strongly believe that, on May 11, the primary stage of an Indian H-bomb detonated, but its heat failed to ignite the secondary stage."

One US official commented, "If India really wants a thermonuclear capability, they will have to test again and hope they get it right." As a result of the apparent failure, US official sources said,

> the Indian government is under pressure by the Department of Atomic Energy (DAE)... to test the H-bomb again, in the face of ongoing bilateral talks in which the US seeks to persuade India to agree to a global nuclear test ban.[10]

(If the "pressure" did exist, it appeared to have eased off by the end of 1998: India in early 1999 seemed all set to move toward signing the CTBT.)

Chidambaram, however, once again contended that India had indeed tested a thermonuclear bomb. He claimed that this was of a "fusion-fission-fusion" type. A boosted fission device was part of this explosion, he said, "making its separate testing redundant." He added that India "was working on powerful lasers for 'inertial confinement' to produce fusion energy and uranium enrichment."[11]

He also said that Indian scientists had reason to feel proud since they achieved a "perfect three" with the tests—mastering the optimum emplacement design for the nuclear device, getting specific yield calculations, and ensuring zero radioactive contamination.[12] (The optimum emplacement design technology determines how far down to place the nuclear device: deep enough to ensure that there is no nuclear venting and yet not so deep as to incur needless expenditure.)

Another boastful AEC claim is that "India has achieved a world record by conducting five nuclear tests in a span of forty-eight hours." But in the former USSR alone, there is recorded and published data

> on twenty-five different tests where each test comprised four to eight near-simultaneous explosions. In fact, the USSR conducted a test way back on August 23, 1975... consisting of eight near-simultaneous explosions within several seconds, leave alone forty-eight hours.[13]

As for Pakistan, the first tests on May 28, 1998, involved the claimed detonation of five devices, the largest of them yielding, according to A.Q. Khan, thirty to thirty-five kilotons. The other four tests were of small, low-yield weapons ideal for missile attack against troops. But the independently estimated total yield of the five explosions was nine to twelve kilotons.

On May 30, Pakistan first claimed to have detonated two nuclear explosions—Foreign Minister Gohar Ayub Khan was on record as saying so. But later, it was "clarified" that there was only one that took place. "Khan explained the next day that two tests were originally planned, but after the results of the first day's tests were evaluated, it was decided to conduct only one test."[14] Pakistani officials claimed that the yield of that test was fifteen to eighteen kilotons. Some western seismologists insisted it was only two kilotons. (Wallace put it at four to six kilotons).

There are other discrepancies, too. For instance, the Pakistan Atomic Energy Commission said that Pakistan tested only fission weapons and categorically stated that "Pakistan tested no thermonuclear or tactical nuclear device." But A.Q. Khan held that there were five tests: "one was a big bomb... of about thirty to thirty-five kilotons... the other four were small tactical weapons of low yield."[15]

The term "big" bomb was first used by India's Prime Minister on May 15, 1998, although it was quickly withdrawn.[16]

The discrepancies, dissonances, and contradictions highlight divisions within the decision-making establishments and a proclivity to make extravagant claims about scientific and technological "achievements." They also raise questions about the authenticity and reliability of official stands and doctrines, and create doubts about India's and Pakistan's real capabilities.

Quite simply, even the basic assumption underlying deterrence—secure knowledge and understanding of each other's capabilities, security doctrines, military strengths and weaknesses, as well as full appreciation of the adversary's ability to cause "unacceptable damage"—do not obtain in the Indian sub-continent. Such uncertainty degrades stability and greatly enlarges the scope for strategic miscalculation. It also encourages knee-jerk or panic responses in situations of crisis.

Given that weapons of mass destruction are involved, this has potentially devastating consequences. This phenomenon of dubious claims and uncertainty is not confined to nuclear test explosions or weapons alone, but extends to missiles, too. India and Pakistan have both challenged, or mocked, each other's claims about the origins, character, and range of their missiles. Both contend that their missile development programs are basically, if not fully, indigenous and self-reliant, although the truth appears to be more complex.

India obtained some rocketry technology from France and the former USSR, and various components for its *Prithvi* and *Agni* missile series from these and other sources as well. And Pakistan is believed to have obtained M-11 (*Hatf-3*) missiles and other missile technology components/sub-assemblies from China and North Korea.[17]

Few Indian or Pakistani leaders, however, hesitate to point fingers at one another. For instance, India Defense Minister George Fernandes, in April 1998 named China as "the mother of the *Ghauri*." Many independent researchers, on the other hand, believe that the *Ghauri*'s source is North Korea. (Among the more prominent of them is S. Chandrasekhar, formerly with the Indian Space Research Organization, who holds, on the basis of published information and images of the *Ghauri*, that it is a single-stage liquid-fueled vehicle like North Korea's *Nodong* missile.[18]

Tall claims that have little to do with reality have been made about conventional weaponry and the domestic arms industries of India and Pakistan too. For instance, the output of India's military industry has dropped by fifty-seven percent since 1990–91. And Pakistan's military production fell by thirty-three percent between 1973 and 1997.[19]

India's Defense Research and Development Organization (DRDO) claims a budget equivalent to about 6.5 percent of total military expenditure (a proportion exceeded only by Britain, France, Sweden, and the United States). But its biggest projects are in extremely poor shape. The worst examples are the Main Battle Tank (MBT), a plan to develop a nuclear power plant for a submarine, codenamed "Advanced Technology Vessel," and the Light Combat Aircraft (LCA).

For instance, the *Arjun* tank has repeatedly failed to meet service requirement tests. The MBT-*Arjun* project was launched in 1974 and the first prototype planned for 1980. "The design, however, was finalized only in July 1996 and the earliest the MBT can enter service is 2002."[20] The *Arjun* engine has failed to come up to the mark. Strangely enough, the *Arjun* was accepted by the army for limited duty on condition that it would be allowed to purchase more Russian tanks. (A controversy now rages over the T-90 Russian tank, with former Prime Minister H.D. Deve Gowda pleading against its procurement.)[21]

The nuclear submarine-ATV project, launched in 1975, has claimed an R&D expenditure the equivalent in rupees of $600 million—without solid results. The project may not be viable, according to Buddhi Kota Subba Rao, a former Navy captain who worked on the project in the '70s—and was victimized by the DAE for having criticized its functioning, even falsely charged and detained for "espionage." The project's basic pressurized-water reactor design is badly flawed.[22]

The LCA project, launched in 1983, with a view to replacing the MiG-21 fleet by the mid-'90s, is in the doldrums. Its first flight has been repeatedly postponed, "and the most optimistic date for its entry into service is between 2005 and 2007."[23] After its indigenous *Kaveri* engine repeatedly failed tests, India decided to have Lockheed Martin redesign it, but the deal fell through after the nuclear tests. The job is now being contracted out to a Russian company.

In Pakistan's case, the military R&D infrastructure is far weaker and the planning less ambitious. For instance, Pakistan's military R&D claims only 130 million rupees (less than one percent of India's).[24]

Given their budgetary constraints, the ambitious miltary programs in both India and Pakistan often compromise on quality, reliability, and safety. This adds further to uncertainties and raises the probability of conflicts getting out of hand, and military leaders making disastrous miscalculations, triggering accidental wars.

NOTES

[1] "Pak claims nuclear superiority over India," *The Telegraph* (Calcutta) 1 February 1999.

2 R. Chidambaram, during a two hour-long briefing for the Indian Science Writers' Association on February 3, 1999, made a series of claims about the "perfect" character of India's tests and the country's "high technological threshold." Cited in "Further nuclear tests unnecessary," *The Hindu* (Delhi) 4 February 1999 and "No more N-tests needed: AEC," *Indian Express* (New Delhi) 4 February 1999.

3 Joint Press Note issued by the DAE and DRDO (New Delhi) 17 May 1998: 3.

4 T. Wallace, *Seismological Research Letters*, September-October 1998 and B. Barker, et.al. *Science* 25 September 1998, both estimate the yields at nine to sixteen kilotons.

5 Cited in David Albright, "The Shots Heard 'Round The World," *Bulletin of the Atomic Scientists* July/August 1998: 21–25.

6 *The Hindu* 4 February 1999.

7 September 1987 interview by the authors with P.N. Haksar, former principal secretary to the prime minister in 1974. Also confirmed by George Perkovich, cited in *The New York Times* 18 May 1998.

8 Albright 22.

9 Mark Hibbs, "India May Test Again Because H-Bomb Failed, US Believes," *Nucleonics Week* 26 November 1998.

10 Hibbs.

11 *The Hindu.*

12 *Indian Express.*

13 A. Gopalakrishnan, "Margins of Error: Verifying Claims on Nuclear Tests," *The Times of India* (New Delhi) 20 November 1998. Gopalakrishnan is former chairman of India's Atomic Energy Regulatory Board.

14 Albright 22.

15 Cited in Zia Mian, "Pakistan's Nuclear Descent," *INESAP Bulletin,* (Darmstadt) November 1998: 11.

16 "We have the capacity for a big bomb now for which the necessary command and control system is also in place." "India is now a N-weapons state: PM," *The Times of India* (New Delhi) 16 May 1998. Also in "Nuclear weapons only for self-defense, says PM," *The Hindu* (New Delhi) 16 May 1998: "India is now a nuclear weapons state, and... India has a big bomb."

17 For detailed accounts, see W. Potter, H. Jencks (Eds.), *The International Missile Bazaar: The New Supplier Network* (Boulder, CO: Westview Press, 1994) 201–33. Also Andrew Koch, W.P.S. Sidhu, "South Asia goes ballistic, then nuclear," in *Jane's Intelligence Review* June 1998: 19.

18 See excerpts from Ashutosh Misra, "The Pakistani Ghauri Missile," *INESAP Bulletin* (Darmstadt) November 1998: 14.

19 Eric Arnett, "Big Science, Small Results," *Bulletin of the Atomic Scientists* July/August 1998: 46–47.

20 Sidhu.

21 See Kanwar Sandhu, "Virtues of the indigenous tank," *Indian Express* (New Delhi) 26 January 1999.

22 Interview with Subba Rao, 5 February 1999.

23 Sidhu.

24 Arnett.

Inviting Ruin

Because Pakistan was near-universally seen as being "forced" to follow India, political opprobrium internationally was never as great. A reluctant Pakistan was seen as having been pressured to follow an adamant and belligerent India. Nonetheless, it too, had to face economic sanctions, which affected it much more adversely than was the case for India. Its foreign debt is over $30 billion and the country is effectively in default. Such was the extent of its immediate balance of payments crisis that, recognizing the possibility of internal chaos and the fillip this might give to pro-Taliban and anti-US Islamic forces, the US decided in November 1998 to ease the sanctions it had earlier imposed. These had to do largely with agriculture- and aid-related activities, but restrictions on trade related to high technology acquisitions remained. Since it had to appear even-handed, sanctions on India were also eased. But the primary motivation was alleviating the desperate plight of Pakistan.

Nor is it at all a coincidence that toward the end of 1998, when Pakistan had to make a major repayment on its external debt and was simply unable to find the wherewithal to do so, the US finally decided (after more than a year's delay) to release the monies Pakistan had earlier paid for F-16 fighter planes, whose shipment had subsequently been cancelled by Congressional rejection of the deal. But quite apart from the immediate debt and financial crisis, the general state of the Pakistan economy is such that the actual costs of building an "adequate" nuclear weapons system will impose an enormous burden. Only if the current firebreak between testing and not yet deploying is maintained can Pakistan hope to avoid paying this huge price. For an economy and civil society already devastated by the effects of the Afghan imbroglio, further nuclearization and the initiation of an arms race with India will only plunge the economy and civil society into deeper crisis.

In no way can it be argued that Indo-Pakistan security has been enhanced; this was discussed earlier. But a specifically Pakistani perspective would recognize that Pakistan is well behind India in the size of its stockpile of weapons producing fissile material as well as in the range, numbers, and types of delivery vehicles (missiles, submarines as platforms) that it can deploy. It has a real problem in coping with the possibility of a decapitating first strike; that is, one that would target and destroy the headquarters, as it were, from which command, control, communications, and intelligence functions ultimately flow. Moreover, unlike the US or USSR in their nuclear face-off, neither India nor Pakistan has the capacity to establish a highly sophisticated and expensive "early warning system"—however useful such a system could ever be, when missile flight time between the two countries is as little as three to four minutes.

Possessing neither the geographical depth nor the numbers of bombs nor a meaningful warning system to be able to cope with this problem, Pakistan will be under great pressure to disperse its nuclear missiles and planes and to decentralize their command and control. For only then can they hope to "credibly deter" India from a decisive and debilitating first strike. Whether India ever has or does not have such intentions is beside the point. Once the logic of nuclear deterrence operates, Pakistani nuclearists have to prepare for such contingencies. Once such dispersal and decentralization of command and control takes place, the chances of launching or using nuclear weapons through miscalculation or accident become considerably higher. Thus, for systemic reasons, the likelihood of a pre-emptive use is greater on the Pakistani side, not because of a greater belligerence on Islamabad's part, but simply because of the inescapable problems posed by asymmetry between the two countries and their respective nuclear weapons systems.

Pakistan's rejection of the No First Use proposal of India might seem to make sense because a missile flight time of three to four minutes does not give much technical-practical value to such an assurance. Moreover, keeping things uncertain by refusing adherence to the No First Use principle maintains Kashmir as a nuclear flashpoint that could erupt by an escalation of conventional military conflict. This suits Pakistani diplomatic efforts to internationalize the Kashmir issue. Nevertheless, a major reason (and stated as such) Islamabad decided to reject the No First Use proposal of India is that it wants its future nuclear arsenal to compensate for the imbalance between the conventional military strengths between the two countries. That is to say, the last thing Pakistan wants to do is to introduce any kind of firebreak between conventional conflict and its possible escalation into a nuclear exchange.[18]

Such an approach is not only dangerous and irresponsible in itself. It is also based on yet another false premise—that Pakistan can use nuclear deterrence not only to avoid a nuclear conflict, but also to deter or control a conventional outbreak to its advantage. The logic of pursuing such an approach must be the retention of the willingness to use nuclear weapons first if the conventional conflict on the ground is somehow "perceived" to be reaching some point of supposedly decisive disadvantage to Pakistan. Not a few Pakistani anti-nuclear activists have serious reservations about the sense of maturity and responsibility that some Pakistani hawks possess when they are willing to entertain such a logic. Rejection of the principle of No First Use is here linked to a conscious perspective (in at least some Pakistani leading circles) of possible pre-emptive use of nuclear weapons against the "enemy."

Of course, Pakistani hawks can also see value in having some bilaterally agreed restraint measures to reduce the risk of accidental or miscalculated use by either side of their respective arsenals. There will be no surprise, therefore, if once they have openly deployed, both countries were to arrive at limited bilateral confidence-building measures (CBMs) and mechanisms—hot lines, regular high-level meetings of senior military personnel, etc. But the basic factors that ensure the sustenance of political distrust and differences in nuclear doctrines/strategies/perspectives, will remain.

The internationalization of the Kashmir issue has been a diplomatic gain for Pakistan. But its value should not be exaggerated. The very fact of such internationalization is a setback for India. But for this to be a *lasting* gain for

Pakistan, the issue has to be not merely internationalized, but done so in such a way as to bring Pakistani aspirations closer to fulfillment. This is in no way assured. It can only be a matter of time before the Indian government, recognizing that earlier forms of diplomacy are now untenable, adjusts to the new circumstances and itself begins to intervene in an internationalized framework of diplomatic activity in ways that suit its own interests. The future of such Indian and Pakistani interventions in the now wider arena is an open question.

Finally, what are the likely domestic political consequences of Pakistan's going nuclear? In historical retrospect, this might well be seen as the final act that precipitated an historic transformation of the Pakistan polity, dramatically reversing for a long time to come the difficult process of democratic consolidation. One hopes this will not be the case, but the latest coup suggests it could be. Over the last fifteen years, there has been a striking contrast in the general political trajectories of India and Pakistan. Whatever the ups and downs and its enduring strengths, India's polity has drifted in an anti-democratic and authoritarian direction. For Pakistan, whatever its ups and downs over the same period, the direction of its polity, at least until October 1999, was toward a less authoritarian structure. The Musharraf coup may well reverse this.

Whereas the Indian state is officially secular, with secularism its legitimizing ideology, religio-political forces of a very negative and dangerous kind, or what are called communal organizations and parties, have made dramatic inroads into the Indian polity. At the national electoral level, such communal forces have acquired twenty-five percent of the popular vote. In Pakistan, the state is not secular, but confessional, and its legitimizing ideology is Islam. As such, it is not a liberal democratic state, nor does it preside over a properly democratic society with a minimum of constitutionally guaranteed freedoms. But the national electoral vote of all the explicitly Islamic and fundamentalist parties combined has for almost five decades never crossed seven percent, and was as low as three percent in the '90s.

In India, where matters have been worsening over the years, a decisive transformation of the character of the whole country has been a growing and looming threat. The threat has come from Hindu communal forces. Advances for the cause of Hindu nationalism strengthen the cause of Islamic nationalism, and vice versa. Yet something of an equilibrium between state and civil society has so far been preserved. India has not yet tilted beyond the critical point at which a weakened democratic polity becomes a qualitatively different entity, with some form of authoritarian political rule, however mild or strong.

In Pakistan, where over recent years matters had seemed to be getting better, the threat posed by Islamic fundamentalist forces has nonetheless been constant and steady. Here, too, an equilibrium of a different sort has remained; communal forces have not yet been able to come to state power and more actively try to suborn their apparatuses to carry out the wholesale transformation of Pakistan polity and society. But this equilibrium is now threatened. Islamic fundamentalist forces are currently poised to make the kind of dramatic political breakthrough hitherto denied to them for decades. The scale of this threat can be gauged by the extent to which the Sharif government *after the nuclear tests* had to go along with their agenda. The 15th Amendment of the Constitution was a major effort at Islamization of the polity. The Lower House of Parliament passed the Shariat bill, which would change the character of state jurisprudence. A majority in the Upper House, the Senate, fortunately opposes it. But the fact that a beleaguered and desperate government sought to steal the fundamentalist thunder in this way testified to its plight. What Musharraf does on this issue remains to be seen.

A deeper pathology is at work here, one centered on a grim, systemically rooted crisis of legitimacy facing the Pakistan state. This crisis, which has deepened, especially since the mid-'90s, was further aggravated by the post-1997 economic recession, with its growing state fiscal crisis and its declining production and economic malfunctioning, as well as the disintegration of a number of institutions of the state under the impact of corruption, cronyism, Machiavellian political maneuvers, and the exacerbation of ethnic tensions and breakdown of law and order in city after city—all of which, its main commercial-industrial center, Karachi, now epitomizes. Thus, analysts and even some foreign diplomats started in 1996–97 to describe Pakistan as a "failing" or "failed state." The systemic crisis of legitimacy, the increasing loss of the state's moral purpose, and the inability of Islam to provide the foundations of a viable modern state, have all contributed to the growing failure of the Pakistani political system.

Overt nuclearization, which invited sanctions, further aggravated the crisis. If Pakistan proceeds to manufacture and deploy nuclear weapons and missiles, the economic consequences could become unbearable. The state could literally disintegrate and Pakistan become what some commentators have described as a "nuclear Somalia." The Sharif government tried to use Pakistan's newly acquired weapons status to bargain for help from the US to help stave off this possibility, but had only limited success. If the Pakistan People's Party (PPP) of Benazir Bhutto were a united and respected force, then as the major opposition party it would have benefited most from the deep public disillusionment with the Sharif government. But after its two recent stints in power, the PPP has a serious credibility problem of its own. Indeed, it is in great disarray. Thus, the real beneficiaries of governmental unpopularity are a variety of Islamic groups, which can play the card of being an untested alternative that should now be given the chance to rule. Though the nuclear tests were popular, they also had been strongly demanded by both the PPP and the Islamic opposition to the Sharif government. When the government finally decided to carry out the tests, this did not provide any distinctive dividends to the government, but simply reinforced the growing swell of sympathy for the Islamic opposition.

Had the Sharif government not tested, it would in effect have directly challenged these most dangerous internal forces. Sharif could hardly have hoped to defeat these forces simply by accommodating to their pressures. Admittedly, given the Indian action, it would have been very difficult for any Pakistan government to resist emulation. But decisive political conjunctures always call for statesmanship of the highest order, if the threatened negative momentum is to be stemmed and reversed. In May 1998 and after, neither the Indian nor the Pakistani governments nor their respective national security establishments have shown that they possess such qualities of statesmanship. This judgment was only confirmed by the symbolically much-touted, but practically quite pedestrian and empty, prime ministerial summit meeting of Mr. Vajpayee and Mr. Sharif in Lahore in late February 1999.

NOTES

[1] The Sangh Combine is the name given to the collective comprised of the Rashtriya Swayamsevak Sangh or RSS (National Volunteer Corps), the Vishwa Hindu Parishad or VHP (World Hindu Council), the Bajrang Dal (Lord Hanuman's troopers), and the Bharatiya Janata Party or BJP (People's Party of India). The RSS, founded in 1925, is the "father" of this collective and its dominant and guiding force. It is a cadre force run on internally undemocratic lines, with top-down selection of its key full-time officials, and committed to an anti-Muslim ideology of Hindu nationalism and right-wing authoritarianism. It has definite fascist characteristics in its ideology and organizational structure. Its key founding figures were open admirers of Hitler and the way he sought to make Germany strong. The RSS has decisive control and influence over the BJP, although the RSS claims to be only a cultural organization. It is in no way democratically accountable to the people of India nor even to the ordinary member of the BJP.

In the early '60s, the RSS set up the VHP to serve as an explicitly religious-cultural front. It also participates in communal and political activities of various sorts and operates worldwide among the Hindu diaspora. The Bajrang Dal are a modern day equivalent of lumpen storm troopers, resorting to physical violence to intimidate the opponents of the Sangh Combine. The RSS also engages (more subtly) in physical violence and, when necessary, promotes communal riots. It also involves itself in positive rehabilitation work and gains support in that way. The BJP is the parliamentary and electoral wing of the Sangh Combine. It has achieved phenomenal success in the last fifteen years. From having only two members in 1984 in the Lok Sabha, or national-level Peoples Assembly, the Lower House of the national legislature, which comprises of 543 MPs, the BJP has, in a little more than a decade, become the single largest party, with more than 180 MPs today.

[2] Immediately after the May tests, top Indian officials in their public statements literally goaded Pakistan into testing. Prime Minister Vajpayee made no distinction between nuclear and non-nuclear conflicts, implying that nuclear weapons would be used by India for "defensive" purposes, even in conflicts of a conventional kind. Home Minister L. K. Advani talked of changes in "geo-political circumstances" and "hot pursuit." The ex-Parliamentary Affairs Minister M. L. Khurana challenged

Pakistan to a fourth war between the two countries, "any time, any place." At the time, all three leaders belonged to the BJP. Whatever chances Pakistan had of avoiding a similar response were almost certainly destroyed by such provocation.

3 Vajpayee referred to China as "an overt nuclear weapon state on our borders, a state which committed armed aggression against India in 1962." He accused China of having "materially helped" Pakistan, a "bitter neighbor," at the hands of which "we have suffered three aggressions," "to become a covert nuclear weapons state." Letter sent on May 11, and published first in *The New York Times*, quoted as "Text of Vajpayee's Letter to Clinton," in *The Hindu*, (Delhi) 14 May 1998.

4 7,000 technicians and 20,000 assistants worked on the program, "Petrochemical Project Three," at a cost of $10 billion. Iraq had built up to 10,000 centrifuges for uranium enrichment, with components and designs secured mainly from German companies. Uranium came from Portugal and Nigeria. Iraq retains the theoretical capacity to produce nuclear weapons. See K. R. Timmerman, "The Poison Gas Connection: Western Suppliers of Unconventional Weapons and Technologies to Iraq and Libya," Simon Wiesenthal Center, Los Angeles, 1990; "Ideale Verstecke," *Der Spiegel* 7/1998; "Palaste um Fadenkrenz," *Der Spiegel* 6/1998.

5 *Hindu rashtra* means "Hindu nation." Less than an hour after Prime Minister Vajpayee's public announcement of a test in the afternoon of Monday, May 11, the principal English language mouthpiece of the RSS, *The Organiser*, hit the stands with an issue devoted to the commemoration of Pokharan I. The issue carried stories with captions like "Time To Tame Pakistan" as well as information that could only have been obtained privately from official sources. The timing and content of the issue was no coincidence, but just one of many instances of the RSS's close connection to the government: the Cabinet list of appointees of this ruling coalition government were first vetted by the RSS top leadership, just as the draft of the founding document of the government coalition, the "National Agenda for Governance," was first shown for corrections to the RSS, before being shown to the other parties in the ruling coalition. The RSS, incidentally, claims to be a non-political, purely cultural, organization!

6 On December 6, 1992, the Sangh Combine calculatedly destroyed the Babri Mosque in the North Indian town of Ayodhya. It did this despite all earlier assurances that it would not violate Supreme Court orders in this regard. It deceitfully claimed that the destruction was a spontaneous expression of uncontrollable, mass Hindu anger. For years before this culminating act, the Sangh had systematically carried out a nation-wide, hate-filled, anti-Muslim campaign, claiming that a temple commemorating the birth of the mythical God-king Rama had been constructed at this site in Ayodhya before allegedly being destroyed and replaced by a mosque in the sixteenth century, on the orders of the first Mughal Emperor, Babar. Not only did this campaign represent the atavistic politics of a cultivated historical grievance and revenge, but no proper archaeological or historical evidence to convincingly substantiate this claim has ever been given; nor does there seem to be any.

Now, a makeshift temple, erected after the mosque was destroyed, stands on the site, awaiting fulfillment of the Sangh's promise to construct (once current legal disputes are over) a magnificent Ram temple. Incidentally, preparations for the construction of such a Ram temple began in 1990, two years before the "unplanned," "unforeseen" act of destruction.

7 *Hindutva* or "Hinduness" is the name given to the most pernicious form of

Hindu nationalism that is the general ideology of the Sangh Combine. The Hindu nationalist ideologue, Veer Savarkar, first systematically articulated the philosophy in the '20s, and M.S. Golwalkar, the second supremo of the RSS, followed with further "refinements."

8 BJP ideologues have always looked upon Israel and Zionism with a considerable measure of sympathy. The BJP strongly endorsed the formal diplomatic recognition of Israel carried out by a previous Congress government. But while the BJP is all for closer ties with Israel, it recognizes that Israel is a regional power, which can only play a minor supportive role to the US in confronting the supposed global challenge of "Islamic civilization." In the larger civilizational scheme of things, Judaism counts for little, and a Hindu-Christian "civilizational alliance" of a kind attractive to Western right-wingers will more or less automatically bring along Israel in its tow. The internationally publicized assaults on the Christian minority that the BJP and its Sangh partners carried out during 1998 and 1999, however, have damaged the prospects that some such alliance might emerge in the future.

9 Vajpayee said, "I have argued for the restructuring of Indo-US relations not just because this will help India—but also because this will help the US itself… Indo-US ties based on equality and mutuality of interest is going to be the mainstay of tomorrow's stable, democratic world order." Excerpt from the text of the speech distributed to the media at the Prime Minister's Office, 28 September 28 1998: 8.

10 The Indo-Sri Lanka Accord effectively endorsed the right of India to be the principal arbiter in Sri Lanka's internal civil war between the Sinhalese dominated central government and the Sri Lankan Tamils of the northern Jaffna region. From being the protector of the Tamils, India effectively became their "hunter," exactly the claim correctly made by then Sri Lankan Premier Premadasa, in justification of the accord. That this accord was accepted by other countries, such as the US, only further enhanced the sense of self-importance of the Indian elite, which overwhelmingly supported the accord and the Indian intervention as the expression of the country's new-found stature as the globally acknowledged regional hegemon. The accord collapsed when India could not fulfill its end of the bargain. Colombo had given India this in return for its sending an expeditionary force to hunt down and crush the Sri Lankan Tamil insurgency. This the cynically named Indian Peacekeeping Force (IPKF) was not able to do. As its presence in Sri Lanka became an ever greater political liability to the incumbent government in Colombo, the latter broke off the Agreement.

11 See A. Vanaik, *India in a Changing World* (New Delhi: Orient Longman, 1995): 83–88, 123.

12 The former chairman of India's Atomic Energy Regulatory Board (AERB), Mr. A. Gopalakrishnan, not only provided a list of safety and construction failures, but also pointed out the absurdity of a situation where the body (the AERB) empowered to monitor the functioning and performance of the Department of Atomic Energy (DAE) is not itself autonomous from the DAE, but comes under its authority. For his pains, Mr. Gopalakrishnan was publicly vilified and his tenure as chairman not renewed. The performance of India's civilian nuclear program remains a sacred cow rarely criticized in public, and certainly never by the members of the "strategic community."

13 In August 1947, when India was partitioned, Maharaj Hari Singh, the Hindu ruler of the Muslim majority province of Kashmir, had yet to decide whether to accede to India or Pakistan. Two months later, troops from Pakistan suddenly

attacked Kashmir. Hari Singh then desperately sought Indian help to expel these assailants. New Delhi promised support only if Hari Singh formally agreed to accede to the Indian Union, which is what he hurriedly agreed to do. This accession is the legal basis for India's claim that the whole of Kashmir belongs to it. Indian troops moved in and halted the Pakistani advance, and under UN auspices a ceasefire line was agreed to in 1948 to bring the war to an end. To this day, Kashmir has been territorially divided in terms of possession according to that Line of Control established in 1948. India holds the Kashmir valley and the regions of Jammu and Ladakh. Pakistan holds the regions of Gilgit, Baltistan, and Muzzaferabad, which together make up what it calls Azad, or "free" Kashmir.

In 1954, Prime Minister Jawaharlal Nehru agreed to the idea of a UN organized plebiscite to ascertain the wishes of the Kashmiri people after Pakistan withdrew its troops. At the time he made the offer, Nehru had every reason to believe that such a plebiscite choice would favor India. Later on, this changed, and Nehru withdrew the offer. Nonetheless, that offer became something of a diplomatic millstone around India's neck. Pakistan made as much as it could out of it, but the offer was also contingent on Pakistani troop withdrawal from the regions occupied in 1948, something that no Pakistan government has ever been willing to countenance. Moreover, the offer was restricted to a choice between India and Pakistan and precluded the third alternative of Kashmiri independence, in part or whole.

After the 1971 war, when India decisively defeated Pakistan, then Prime Minister Indira Gandhi offered to make the existing ceasefire line of control a permanent border. Pakistan did not accept this. That is to say, on the Kashmir issue, India is the status quo power content with the existing division. Only the BJP among the main Indian political parties entertains aims of getting the whole of Kashmir for India. It is Pakistan that is most committed to changing the status quo, and as the weaker power, is constantly seeking to internationalize the Kashmir issue.

[14] Private conversation with Dr. Zia Mian, a Pakistani nuclear physicist and longtime disarmament campaigner currently teaching and researching at Princeton University. He is preparing a major study of Pakistan's post-independence nuclear preparations and policies.

[15] The most detailed study of Pakistan's preparations for making the bomb remains the book by S.R. Weisman and H. Krosney, *The Islamic Bomb* (New York: Times Books, 1981). See also, L.S. Spector, *The Undeclared Bomb* (Cambridge, MA: Ballinger Publishing Co., 1988).

[16] Given the secrecy surrounding the Pakistani and Indian nuclear establishments, estimates of current stockpiles and possible numbers of bombs that could be assembled have to be guesses. A SIPRI study, "World Inventory of Plutonium and Highly Enriched Uranium 1992," gave plausible estimates for what might be the numbers available to India at the end of 1995—about sixty bombs. For Pakistan, the figure was about ten bombs. Given the problems that both countries have had with their reactors, it would not be surprising if, at the end of 1998, both countries had stockpiles not markedly higher than these 1995 estimates. Thus India may now possess materials to assemble between sixty and eighty bombs, and Pakistan ten to fifteen bombs.

[17] It is in bomb designing that Chinese help was probably most significant. Here too, it is not in the field of theoretical physics or calculations, but in regard to arriving at appropriate engineering calculations that the Chinese may have passed on useful information. In many ways, this parallels the help that some US experts

gave to the French in regard to engineering problems the latter had over their hydrogen bomb. (Private conversations with Dr. Mian and Dr. Pervez Hoodbhoy. Dr. Hoodbhoy is professor of nuclear physics at Qaid-e-Azam University in Islamabad and a well-known disarmament campaigner.)

18 Indeed, it is reluctant to concede that the one significant nuclear-related confidence-building measure (CBM), on non-attack of each other's nuclear facilities negotiated between India and Pakistan, will have any validity in a weaponized environment. Pakistan Foreign Secretary Shamshad Ahmad said as much at a breakfast meeting at the Asia Society in New York on July 7, 1998. Cited by W.P.S. Sidhu, Brian Cloughley, et al., *Nuclear Risk-Reduction Measures in Southern Asia*, Report No. 26. November 1998. Washington, DC: The Henry L. Stimson Center: 41.

Chapter 6

Indefensible Arms: The Ethics of War and Nuclear Weapons

Nuclear weapons are quite unlike any other armaments. Their uniqueness lies in their truly awesome power of destruction—on a scale unimaginable until rather recently in human history. Nuclear weapons alone have the potential to destroy all life on earth. No other class of armaments can possibly cause that kind of havoc, through an unstoppable chain of destructive events that include the release of vast amounts of energy through heat blasts, x rays and a range of radioactive poisons, some of which remain lethal for millions of years. There is not, and cannot be, any defense against nuclear weapons, whether military, civilian, or medical. The totality of destruction and the unending lethality contained in nuclear weapons gives them a singularly horrible quality, which is incomparable with any other instrument of war. They are unique even within the category of "weapons of mass destruction."

Thus even the horrific fire-bombing of Dresden between 1942 and 1945 (which killed 100,000) or the massive US incendiary raid on Tokyo in March 1945 (which set off a firestorm that also claimed 100,000 lives) pale beside Hiroshima, where a new kind of war took place. In place of the 350 warplanes that bombed Tokyo, there was only one—the B-29 bomber *Enola Gay*. And in place of thousands of bombs and other kinds of munitions, there was just one bomb. What began at 8:15 A.M. on August 6, 1945, was a vast indefinite butchery, horrible in its indiscriminate character. Hiroshima revealed the reality of the ultimate weapon and a new kind of war, where there might be no survivors. Even today, half a century later, victims of the 1945 bombing continue to perish in Hiroshima and Nagasaki.

Ten years after the Cold War's end, the world still has enough firepower in its 30,000-plus nuclear weapons arsenal to cause a million Hiroshimas, indeed wipe out the human race altogether. At least half of these weapons are in a state of alert or are deployed so as to be ready to be launched in a matter of minutes or hours. It is this sheer awesomeness, this vast, virtually infinite, limitless, destructive power of nuclear weapons that has radically altered the condition of human existence, indeed its very possibility, as never before. At no time in the past has the world experienced such an obsession with a particular type of weaponry. Nor has another class of armaments so fundamentally transformed, distorted, and in other ways affected, the way millions of human beings look at security and defense, experience mortal fear and vulnerability, or feel anxiety and uncertainty of the most profound kind.

115

Nuclear weapons have the potential to terminate human culture, end history, murder the human imagination as we know it.

Nuclear weapons come with a highly evolved sophisticated military infrastructure—command, control, communications and intelligence (C³I) systems, as well as delivery vehicles, production units and storage facilities. Equally important to their existence are elaborate strategic doctrines and political premises: "massive retaliation," "mutually assured destruction," "minimum deterrence," "limited nuclear war." Equally vital is what has been called "nuclearism," or the "psychological, political, and military dependence on nuclear weapons, the embrace of the weapons as a solution to a wide variety of human dilemmas, most ironically that of 'security.'"[1]

Nuclearism is based upon a series of illusions. One illusion holds that security can be derived from insecurity, itself rooted in the capacity of adversaries to inflict limitless violence upon each other. Another is that responsible leadership structures exist at the military and political level that can prudently and effectively "manage" nuclear weapons, so that the citizenry can be reliably protected against the enemy's nuclear weapons. One of the biggest illusions is that nuclear deterrence can, and will always, work dependably, enhancing mutual confidence and security.

Nuclear weapons posit, as Robert Jay Lifton puts it, a strain or break in the "great chain of being," a "potentially terminal revolution," leading to a "radical futurelessness." They are not just weapons. They are something much greater. Secretary of War Henry L. Stimson, who oversaw the Manhattan Project during its critical phase, expressed this acutely when he said in May of 1945 that "this project should not be considered simply in terms of military weapons, but as a new relationship of man to the universe." Similarly, when Harry S. Truman said, "This is the greatest thing in the world," referring to the first atomic bomb, he was not merely describing the awesome power of this new weapon; he was also acknowledging and articulating the unique mystique that is associated with it, and its transformative potential well beyond its military use.

The epochal fear, deep anxiety about futurelessness, and the all-consuming feeling of helplessness that millions of men and women have experienced in respect of nuclear weapons and nuclear war—at one time, more than half the American people thought that a nuclear war was imminent—are only one aspect of the moral, political, and psychological problems that these weapons pose. The central issue is the morality or immorality of the use or threat of their use. This has been the subject of deep and serious discussion and of philosophical, legal, and strategic arguments for a long time—indeed, even before the Manhattan project was launched, and ever since the possibility of developing nuclear fission-based weapons began to unfold in the 1930s. Physicists such as Albert Einstein and Niels Bohr were among the first to question the ethics of developing nuclear weapons.

Just and Unjust Wars

Are nuclear weapons legitimate weapons of war? And are they compatible with the notion of just war? This notion has two components going back to St. Augustine and the ethics of the use of violence: *jus ad bellum* (justice through war, or the justness of war itself) and *jus in bello* (justice in war, or in the conduct of war).[2] For our purposes, it should be evident that the second is more important than the first. The first aspect is relatively simple to deal with, only because nuclear weapons are quintessentially offensive weapons calculated to wreak devastation on an indiscriminate scale. They can have no function in a war waged in self-defense, or to vacate an aggression.

The use of nuclear weapons is simply inconceivable in, say, a war of national liberation, or one waged to defend values of decency, or of democracy and worthy political systems or cultures. Wars are just only insofar as they are waged in self-defense or in pursuit of causes that are noble, such as the opposition to injustice and tyranny. Wars involve the deliberate use of lethal violence, which can be justified only because we recognize "*two* orders of fact, each of them compelling, each of them terrible."[3]

Wars are indeed "destructive to the peace of the world." But they may nevertheless be necessary and just under certain circumstances. John Locke argued by analogy against the categorical-pacifist view:

> They may as well say, upon the same ground, that honest men may not oppose robbers or pirates, because this may occasion disorder or bloodshed...
> If any mischief come in such cases, it is not to be charged upon him who defends his own right.

It is quite impossible to countenance the possibility that a nuclear war could meet any elementary criterion underlying the notion of *jus ad bellum*. How can epochal, apocalyptic forms of mass destruction and insensate violence possibly promote a cause that is noble? The nature of any struggle against tyranny and injustice, however grave, is undermined by the greater tyranny of nuclear destruction. Indeed, even the creation of the gigantic military apparatus necessary to wage nuclear war disregards values such as sobriety, caution, and democracy and replaces them with an obsession with paranoid and jingoistic notions of national security.

At the most, a rather wishful case could be made in favor of the *threat* of use of nuclear weapons—the idea that through active preparation and readiness to use such weapons, one might be effectively and reliably able to deter an adversary from using his own nuclear armaments or other weapons of mass destruction (WMDs). But this really pertains to the issue of nuclear deterrence, its morality and its strategic value, not to the morality of the actual use of such weapons. Nuclear deterrence will be discussed separately.

There are several criteria of *jus in bello*, which have evolved over past centuries through debates in ethics. Some of these have been incorporated into jurisprudence and bodies of international law and international humanitarian law. War and methods of warfare cannot be divorced from rational strategic considerations. The use of force must be *proportionate* to the threat that it is meant to contain. Excessive force or violence is not permissible. Non-combatants must not be targeted. The use of cruel or inhuman methods with pitiless disregard for basic human values is forbidden. For instance, you cannot mass-poison civilians or starve prisoners of war. Prisoners of war have rights, as do combatants, including guerrillas. Wars must be fought well and scrupulously. Certain methods of warfare are totally prohibited no matter how admirable and desirable the end they might achieve. There are rules about sieges and blockades, and about reprisals and retribution.

A multiplicity of rules have evolved over the past centuries, and especially since the eighteenth century, that determine the conduct of warfare. Of these, two principal types are of critical and special importance in regard to nuclear weapons. The first concerns the category of agents or persons against whom violence can be directed. These define *who* can be legitimate targets of attack, or can be killed in war. The second relates to the *manner of exercise* of force: with what methods such combatants may be legitimately attacked or killed.

The first type of rule makes a strict distinction between combatants and non-combatants, and essentially upholds the principle of immunity for the latter. Non-combatants cannot be the principal target of attack. The use of more or less random violence against whole populations is impermissible. Basically, you cannot wage war against those who are not themselves making war.

In war, there is a broad distinction between soldiers, on the one hand, and "innocent" civilians on the other. The notion of "innocence" here is a special one. It has nothing to do with personal intention, choice or culpability. For instance, a reluctant conscript is a legitimate target by virtue of being a soldier, whereas an ordinary civilian, however enthusiastic about the war effort, is not. (Political and administrative decision-makers are of course another category.) In general, soldiers, as soldiers, constitute a threat. Warriors and soldiers are thus legitimately subject to violence.

Over the past decades, the category of combatants has been extended to include those who work in munitions factories, but only insofar as their role as workers and their actual location in such factories goes. Those processing soldiers' food rations are not combatants; however, a distinction is made between those contributing to the role of soldiers directly as combatants, and those enabling them to survive as human beings, independently of their military role.

Again, different categories of personnel have their own rights. For instance, a soldier who surrenders to the enemy is considered to have been granted "benevolent quarantine." Prisoners of war, thus, have a right to try to escape—they cannot be prosecuted for that. If however, in the process, they kill a guard, that is no longer considered an act of war. It is treated as murder: for by surrendering, the soldier had allegedly committed himself to stop fighting (albeit under duress). Such rules have evolved over many years as part of a minimal consensus that humanity has reached.

Indiscriminate Destruction

Nuclear weapons fail each of these criteria. They kill massively and indiscriminately, without distinguishing between combatant soldiers and non-combatant civilians. Indeed, they are quintessentially indiscriminate and acquire their particularly horrifying character precisely because they do kill massively and indiscriminately. The manner in which nuclear weapons kill and maim is horrendously cruel, incinerating life-forms in large swathes of land at dizzying temperatures, flattening structures through ultra-powerful blast- and shock-waves, setting off huge firestorms, releasing blinding light, and spewing out enormous quantities of radiation, with a mix of slow- and fast-acting poisons, some of which will remain in significant quantities in the environment for centuries, even millennia. (For instance, the half-life of plutonium-239 is 24,400 years).

Studies of the victims of Hiroshima and Nagasaki validate the proposition that the use of nuclear weapons is fraught with the cruelest possible forms of death and long-lasting injury and health damage that make "life a living hell" for people and where the description about the "living envying the dead" is not hyperbolic. Morally, it is simply impermissible to use weapons that are so destructive. If the world could outlaw chemical and biological weapons, and even agree to an anti-personnel landmine ban, then surely the case for eliminating nuclear weapons, which are considerably more destructive and more indiscriminate in the damage they cause, is even stronger.

The case extends even to nuclear deterrence, the doctrine that holds that an adversary can and should be effectively deterred from attack by virtue of being threatened with the affliction of "unacceptable" damage. Nuclear deterrence not only legitimizes nuclear weapons, but involves a willingness to use them—whether in anticipation, to pre-empt an enemy attack, or in retaliation or reprisal. Without such willingness, indeed a firm commitment, to use them, deterrence loses its sting. It becomes meaningless. Every established nuclear weapons power has well-formulated, elaborate plans for using nuclear weapons. Whatever the difference in the details of their strategic doctrines—whether they profess a policy of No First Use, and of No Use against a non-nuclear adversary, or are wedded to "extended deterrence" and pre-emptive use of nuclear weapons even against non-nuclear states— each of the P-5 has well-developed plans for the *actual* use of such weapons. These go well beyond mere *intentions*, which are themselves highly objectionable. They involve *actual preparations*: the invention of war-fighting schemes featuring nuclear weapons, and the creation of extremely expensive command, control, communications and intelligence (C³I) infrastructures, which in the US alone have cost $4,072 billion.[4]

It has now been disclosed that even Britain, among the least advanced of the nuclear states, had a full-fledged underground shelter, with a virtual replica of Whitehall, and various ministry buildings, and a "Main Street," and so on. The former USSR's underground cities are as well-known as the US's preparations for nuclear war-fighting in "nuclear environments," which entail "hardening" the war machine and the weapons themselves to withstand extreme conditions, including scorching heat and radiation and the breakdown of normal telecommunications as a result of the electromagnetic pulse released by a nuclear explosion.

Nuclear deterrence is not just an idea or an abstract strategic doctrine. It involves seeking security through the creation of a threat of mass destruction, a threat that must appear credible and realizable. For it to be credible, it must involve the *demonstration* of a military capacity and preparations for a nuclear strike—preparations usually constantly upgraded under a technology-driven regime—as well as the *willingness* to strike. In moral terms, then, your adherence to nuclear deterrence means that you have already crossed the Rubicon, so to speak. You have prepared yourself mentally, potentially, and militarily to wreak mass-destruction upon the enemy. Indeed, you have made the attainment of security and peace *conditional* upon the highest conceivable level of war-preparedness at the maximal level of damage—much like a modern-day Genghis Khan.

Ethically, that makes nuclear deterrence highly questionable—repugnant, abhorrent, and unworthy of respect from a civilized mind. Those who advocate nuclear deterrence seek security through the ability and readiness to inflict unconscionable suffering upon innocent civilians in the "adversary" state, wherever that may be. They legitimize and make the use of weapons respectable and "normal" as a *cornerstone* of military strategy and security policy.

Why Nuclear Deterrence is Abhorrent

Nuclear deterrence marks a moral fire-break. It is akin to endorsing torture. Once you rationalize the use of torture, there is simply no limit that you can rationally place on human rights abuses, on the violation of fundamental entitlements and rights, including the right to life. Similarly, once you embrace nuclear deterrence, you have set your face against all accepted criteria of *jus in bello*. You cannot place any restraint on the *magnitude* of violence that is considered permissible. Not just decimation of the military command apparatus, but wholesale massacres, and barbaric forms of butchery—all get rationalized.

It is wrong to invoke the idea of a "sliding scale" of moral standards in defense of nuclear deterrence. This involves a rejection of the notion of the moral equality of soldiers (combatant equality) and of non-combatant or civilian immunity, in favor of the view that the more just one's cause within the *jus ad bellum* paradigm, the greater right one has to violate the *jus in bello* rules that are part of any reasonable war convention.

Even John Rawls is tempted to advance this line of argument. He says: "Even in a just war, certain forms of violence are strictly inadmissible; and when a country's right to war is questionable and uncertain, the constraints on the means it can use are all the more severe. Acts permissible in a war of legitimate self-defense, when these are necessary, may be flatly excluded in a more doubtful situation."[5] An extreme version of this reasoning is "war is hell"—the Sherman view: the rights of the just are total, they can do anything to win the war so long as it has been waged in a just cause. This means that the only kind of justice that matters is *jus ad bellum*.

In his *Just and Unjust Wars*, Michael Walzer has questioned the sliding scale concept.[6] He argues that there is an alternative to this, besides a position of moral absolutism: "*Fiat justicia ruat coelumn* (do justice even if the heavens fall), is not for most people a plausible moral doctrine." His alternative is summed up in the maxim: "do justice *unless* the heavens are (really) about to fall." This, Walzer says,

> is the utilitarianism of extremity, for it concedes that in certain very special cases, though never as a matter of course even in just wars, the only restraints upon military action are those of usefulness and proportionality. Throughout my discussion of the rules of war, I have been resisting this view and denying its force. I have argued, for example, against the notion that civilians can be locked into a besieged city or reprisals taken against innocent people "in extreme cases." For the idea of extremity has no place in the making of the war convention—or if it is said that combat is always extreme, then the idea is naturalized within the convention.

Walzer holds that

> the sliding scale erodes the convention bit by bit, and so it eases the way for the decision-maker who believes himself "forced" to violate human rights. The argument from extremity permits (or requires) a more sudden breach of the convention, but only after holding out for a long time against the process of erosion. The reasons for holding out have to do with the nature of the rights at issue and the status of the men and women who hold them. These rights, I shall argue, cannot be eroded or undercut: nothing diminishes them; they are still standing at the very moment they are overridden: that is why they have to be *overridden*. Hence breaking the rules is always a hard matter, and the soldier or statesman who does so must be prepared to accept the moral consequences and the burden of guilt that his action entails.[7]

Walzer's position, however, is also less than satisfactory. He says:

> The tension between the rules of war and the theory of aggression, between *jus in bello* and *jus ad bellum*, can be dealt with in four different ways: (1) the war convention is simply set aside (derided as "asinine ethics") under the

pressure of utilitarian argument; (2) the convention yields slowly to the moral urgency of the cause: the rights of the righteous are enhanced, and those of their enemies devalued; (3) the convention holds and rights are strictly respected, whatever the consequences; and (4) the convention is overridden, but only in the face of an imminent catastrophe.

The second and fourth of these are the most interesting and the most important. They explain how it is that morally serious men and women, who have some sense of what rights are, come nevertheless to violate the rules of war, escalate its brutality and extend its tyranny. The fourth seems to me the right argument. It provides the best account of the two kinds of justice and most fully recognizes the force of each.[8]

But it is hard even to conceive of "an imminent catastrophe" that would be so enormous as to justify the use of nuclear weapons, which is liable to kill millions of non-combatant civilians at one go. Indeed, what cause can be so sacred as to *necessitate* the deliberate snuffing out of life on such a scale, while brutalizing our own consciousness on a mass scale so it accepts such unbounded cruelty as "normal," or at least as necessary? In terms of the mere physical effects of nuclear violence, it is hard to distinguish the use of nuclear weapons from an "imminent catastrophe." To most people, such use would *be the catastrophe*.

The moral argument against nuclear deterrence is basically as strong as the argument against the *use* of nuclear weapons and the complete inadmissibility of nuclear war. Whatever is wrong to do is wrong to threaten, especially if threatening involves the intention as well as preparations to use nuclear weapons. Walzer convincingly argues against the Protestant theologian Paul Ramsey that deterrence is "a bad way" to try to prevent nuclear war. Nuclear war "is and will remain morally unacceptable, and there is no case for its rehabilitation. Because it is unacceptable, we must seek out ways to prevent it, and because deterrence is a bad way, we must seek out others."[9]

Bombing Bombay:
More Devastating than Hiroshima?

Any thinking person must realize that old civil defense methods, such as underground shelters and hardened structures, are basically useless in a nuclear attack. They cannot offer any protection against one of the main lethal releases from a nuclear bomb: radioactive fallout. Which is why the slogan of Britain's peace movement, "Protest and Survive," became the title of a famous booklet, mocking the false protection the government's propaganda manual, "Protect and Survive," offered to the populace.

The likely effects of a nuclear weapons explosion over a population center anywhere in the Indian sub-continent would be particularly harrowing. Not only are Indian and Pakistani cities more densely populated; they also have poor civic and medical relief infrastructures. Fire-fighters, emergency aid providers, doctors, nurses and hospitals would be hopelessly ineffective in reaching out to the victims—since, for example, as a proportion of the population, the number of doctors are less than a fourth, and hospitals less than tenth, what they are in developed societies.[1] In relation to the Japanese or European cities bombed during World War II, the sub-continent's cities also have a much higher number of poor-quality buildings and a higher concentration of motor vehicles.

The high levels of road congestion, the prevalence of flimsy structures—one-half to two-thirds of the population lives in shantytowns that cannot possibly withstand hurricane-speed winds, firestorms or blast waves—all would contribute to a sharp increase in the number of casualties and to greater suffering.

Indian and Pakistani scientists and nuclear disarmament campaigners have tried to estimate the likely effects of a single explosion of a Hiroshima-type first-generation bomb, with a yield of fifteen kilotons, over cities such as Bombay, Karachi, Delhi and Lahore—all vulnerable to aircraft or missile attacks. M.V. Ramana, a former MIT physicist, is the author of the most systematic study of this kind.[2]

Ramana's conclusions for the city of Bombay are extremely distressing. He estimates that the "prompt casualties" just from the blast and fire effects of such a bomb would be between *150,000 and 800,000 people*, depending on where the bomb exploded. If a more powerful, 150 kiloton, weapon exploded, the casualties could be even more awesome: *2 to 6 million*. In the case of a weapon exploding at ground level, the areas damaged by fire and blast would be somewhat smaller. But with the terrible fallout, the number of people dying of all causes would probably still be as high as 350,000 to 400,000.

The devastating damage caused by a nuclear explosion falls into three categories: prompt effects, delayed effects and long-term effects. The first includes the initial intense flash of heat and light, release of neutron and gamma radiation, and shock or blast waves.

Winds accompanying the shock wave would reach velocities of more than seventy mph to a distance of two or more miles from the epicenter. The shock wave would destroy everything within a radius of a mile. Up to a little over a mile from the point of explosion, all houses not built with concrete would be destroyed. Many buildings in Bombay, especially older ones, are either badly designed or constructed with poor quality raw materials, such as adulterated cement. Every year several hundred buildings collapse by themselves, especially during the rainy season.

The delayed effects, beginning within minutes of the explosion, include firestorms and radioactive fallout. Firestorms would begin with the coalescing of individual fires started by the initial flash of light and heat. In a Hiroshima-sized explosion over a city like Bombay, the radius of the region under flames would probably be a bit over a mile. Due to its size, the fire zone would act as a huge pump, sucking in air from the surrounding areas and driving heated air upward. This pumping action would create winds with velocities as high as thirty to fifty mph.

The temperature in the fire zone would reach several hundred degrees, making it almost certain that there would be no survivors. Furthermore, fire-fighting would be almost impossible due to the combination of hurricane-force winds, thick smoke, destruction of water mains by the shock wave, and the presence of debris blocking roads.

In industrial cities such as Bombay, Karachi or Calcutta, the damaging health effects would be greatly magnified with the additional release of potent toxins from factories and nuclear installations. For instance, Bombay is home to India's highest concentration of chemical factories (over 2,000 of them) and storage units. The Bhabha Atomic Research Center, with a number of nuclear reactors and chemical plants and other facilities, including reprocessing plants, is located in Bombay. (Karachi has Pakistan's sole functioning nuclear power reactor). And the inhabitants of the many shantytowns use large quantities of plastics and other inflammable materials that produce extremely toxic chemicals upon combustion.

The second delayed effect, radioactive fallout, must not be underestimated. When a nuclear bomb explodes, a large quantity of material is vaporized and forms a cloud of highly radioactive dust that can travel long distances depending on weather conditions, such as wind direction and velocity. Even a wind velocity of fifteen mph is liable to distribute the fallout over an area of up to thirty-six square miles.

Areas that receive high levels of fallout are liable to have a large number of radiation-caused fatalities and sicknesses. But even people living in places receiving moderate fallout will suffer from leukemia and cancers of the thyroid, lung, breast, and bone, as well as non-fatal diseases such as birth defects, cataracts, mental retardation, and keloids.

In Hiroshima and Nagasaki, the mortality rates for all diseases, including leukemia, were 17.6 times higher when compared to an unexposed control group. Increases in cancer rates from an atomic bombing of Bombay would probably be comparable to those among Hiroshima survivors. And to this day, Hiroshima's and Nagasaki's victims, or *hibakusha*, continue to die from illnesses contracted during exposure to the fallout of the 1945 atomic bombing.

NOTES

[1] This does not contend that adequate or effective medical treatment or a cure is possible for the disorders and illnesses caused by a nuclear weapons attack. Usually, none is. But in the Indian sub-continent, even elementary first-aid treatment of severe burns and other serious injuries would be virtually impossible given the appalling state of the healthcare infrastructure and official callousness.

[2] Summary published as M.V. Ramana, "The South Asian Bomb: Effects of a Nuclear Blast Over Bombay," in *Medicine & Global Survival* 5.2 (October 1998): 74–77. The full report, made available to the authors earlier, has just been published by International Physicians for the Prevention of Nuclear War. The discussion here essentially summarizes Ramana's excellent analysis.

The only reliable, and the most reasonable, way to prevent nuclear war would seem to be to abolish nuclear weapons altogether. If there is one cardinal lesson to be drawn from the fifty-year-long history of nuclearism, of the nuclear arms race, and from the persistent reliance on nuclear deterrence for security even after the end of the Cold War, it is this: Abolition is the only way out. There is no substitute for the complete elimination of nuclear weapons. There is no other option.

Is it possible to reconcile a commitment to nuclear disarmament as the ultimate goal, with some kind of conditional acceptance of nuclear deterrence? Two lines of argument have been advanced, besides Ramsey's (which depends heavily on the intention to use nuclear weapons and whose weakness has been adequately demonstrated by Walzer). The first of these is that while the objective of complete elimination of nuclear weapons is the only morally worthy objective possible in the circumstances, a case may nevertheless be made for *interim* reliance on nuclear deterrence, since complete disarmament is unlikely to come about in a short period of time. The fact is, the P-5, in particular the US and Russia, are extremely reluctant to undertake qualitative nuclear disarmament; in the interim, nuclear weapons can serve as useful instruments of national sovereignty, as a "hedge against [the] hegemony" of the Great Powers, as a means of preventing "nuclear blackmail" by them, and so on.[10]

The second argument, that of Pope John Paul II and various Catholic Churches, articulated most explicitly by US Catholic Bishops and members of Pax Christi, USA, held (until recently) that although the use of nuclear weapons is morally unjustifiable, "possession of these weapons as a deterrent against the use of nuclear weapons by others could be morally acceptable, but acceptable only as an interim measure and only if deterrence were combined with clear steps toward progressive disarmament."[11]

The Pax Christi Bishop's Argument

This was the position of the National Conference of Catholic Bishops, as stated in its *Pastoral Letter: The Challenge of Peace: God's Promise and Our Response*. They have now revised their evaluation:

> For the past fifteen years, and particularly in the context of the Cold War, we, the Catholic Bishops of the United States, have reluctantly acknowledged the possibility that nuclear weapons could have some moral legitimacy, but only if the goal was nuclear disarmament. It is our present, prayerful judgment that this legitimacy is now lacking.

The Pax Christi Bishops earlier made their moral acceptance of nuclear deterrence conditional upon

> three criteria: (a) a reliance on deterrent strategies must be an interim policy

only. As we stated then, "We cannot consider it adequate as a long-term basis for peace"; (b) the purpose of maintaining nuclear weapons in the interim was only "to prevent the use of nuclear weapons by others"; and (c) a reliance on deterrence must be used "not as an end in itself but as a step on the way toward a progressive disarmament."[12]

Both lines of argument are flawed, although it must be conceded that the second is less deeply so, which is why the Pax Christi Bishops have moved toward rejecting nuclear deterrence itself as immoral, while adherents of the first have ended up as apologists for nuclear proliferation and for the crossing of the nuclear threshold by India and Pakistan.

The first argument is based on the premise that nuclear weapons are a central determinant of the admittedly skewed world order and unequal distribution of global power, and that the defense of national sovereignty in the face of hegemonic pressures requires the possession of nuclear weapons, especially by third world states. Nuclear deterrence can prevent nuclear "blackmail" of the third world by the hegemonic P-5, especially the three Western NWSs, with their tainted record as bullies who have practiced coercive interventions in so many states of the Global South.

These premises are open to question. Nuclear weapons today are hardly the central determinant of the distribution of power across the globe. The nature of power has itself shifted toward "softer" forms than purely military ones. But even insofar as the military aspect is considered important, nuclear weapons are only one part of that. The great imbalances and divergences between the North and South are social, economic, and environmental; they are about access to resources, unequal trade patterns and flow of capital, etc. Such inequalities cannot possibly be redressed militarily, let alone through the possession of nuclear weapons by the states of the South.

Nor can the possession of nuclear weapons by itself give a state effective power and prestige to influence the course of events. For instance, the possession of nuclear weapons has certainly not prevented Britain's progressive marginalization as a European or world power. Non-nuclear Germany and Japan are more important global players than nuclear France or Britain. "Nuclear blackmail" has never really worked. The nuclear US could not prevent China's entry into the Korean War. The former USSR's nuclear arsenal did not help it avert a humiliating defeat in Afghanistan. Nor did nuclear weapons enable the US to change the military balance of forces in Vietnam. Nuclear weapons, then, are not a valuable or reliable currency of power. Whatever the claim made for what they might do for the already powerful states, they do nothing for the powerless or the not-so-powerful. They have never been instruments that promote or safeguard national sovereignty or defend a state's freedom.

In Pakistan's case, for example, it is hardly likely that nuclearization will enhance its bargaining power vis-à-vis the international financial institutions and banks on whose subventions its tottering economy has become helplessly dependent, especially since May 1998. Ironically, the harder Pakistan tries to acquire a full-fledged nuclear arsenal, and the more it invests in manufacturing warheads and fitting them on to delivery vehicles, the more vulnerable it is likely to become.

The second line of argument, that deterrence can be accepted if it is only an interim measure, is based on a number of ahistorical premises. It is quite clear that deterrence has long been, and remains, a cornerstone of security policy, especially in the US. For all intents and purposes, US reliance on deterrence is "an end in itself" and *certainly* not "a *step* on the way toward progressive disarmament." Deterrence has never had a "progressive" character, not even remotely. Besides, the process of its establishment itself strengthens the military-industrial complex, which has a stake in opposing the very goal of nuclear disarmament.

The Pax Christi bishops are right to note:

> (a) The policy of nuclear deterrence is being institutionalized. It is no longer considered an interim policy, but rather has become the very "long-term basis for peace" that we rejected in 1983. (b) The role of nuclear deterrence has been expanded in the post-Cold War era well beyond the narrow role of deterring the use of nuclear weapons by others. The role to be played now by nuclear weapons includes a whole range of contingencies on a global scale including countering biological and chemical weapons and the protection of vital national interests abroad. (c) Although the United States and the republics that made up the former Soviet Union have in recent years eliminated some of their huge, superfluous stockpiles of nuclear weapons, our country, at least, has no intention, or policy position of eliminating these weapons entirely. Rather, the US intends to retain its nuclear deterrent into the indefinite future...[13]

But they fail to see that it is the logic of deterrence as a security doctrine, not the particular circumstances in which it is practiced, or even its location in the Cold War context, that has driven the US toward institutionalizing its claimed value and expanding the role of deterrence even after the Cold War ended. Once you accept the logic of deterrence, extend it into space and time, and adorn it with different purposes and functions, it is but a small step toward ever-increasing nuclearization. As I.F. Stone remarked, "the finely spun concepts of deterrence give a rational appearance to an irrational process."[14]

The logic concedes in the first place that nuclear weapons are legitimate at least as an effective threat, but since the threat does not become credible unless you are prepared to *use* them, the line between threat and use is thin and easily crossed. There is a gross inconsistency involved in legitimating an illegitimate threat, one that is backed by elaborate preparations for its *translation into practice*, but not actual *use*, which the bishops hold to be totally immoral. The wielders of nuclear weapons and the practitioners of deterrence of course *mean* to use them—reluctantly, in emergencies, under unusual circumstances—but use them nevertheless. Granting moral acceptability to *some function* of nuclear weapons means, at minimum, bestowing legitimacy upon their existence. This, as argued earlier, is akin to accepting that torture is legitimate under certain circumstances and when linked to certain functions or objectives. Once the rules of what is strictly impermissible or inadmissible are thus shifted, there is no telling when and where the "sliding scale" effect will stop. The impermissible becomes acceptable. Wisely, the Pax Christi bishops have drawn back from the brink. But they should, logically, question the morality of the very concept of nuclear deterrence. A commitment to nuclear disarmament is not compatible with adherence to nuclear deterrence.

Even if it is conceded for the sake of argument that there is some "uncertainty" about the moral status of nuclear deterrence, there is no moral uncertainty whatsoever about all the other justifications given for having these weapons—be they claims that they symbolize power or sovereignty, or are useful as tools of "foreign policy support." These other incontestably immoral arguments have been used by all nuclear elites, including those of India and Pakistan.

The Gandhi-Nehru Legacy

Ever since Mahatma Gandhi declared that nuclear weapons "represent the most sinful and diabolical use of science," India's leaders have forcefully characterized (until recently, that is) nuclear deterrence as an "abhorrent" and "morally repugnant" doctrine. Indeed, India's classical position, officially stated by its first prime minister, Jawaharlal Nehru, insisted that not only the use or threat of use of nuclear weapons, but even their manufacture and possession, be "declared a crime against humanity." India's diplomats, spokespersons and ministers until 1998 energetically argued that nuclear deterrence is simply impermissible and morally unacceptable: you cannot achieve security by creating the deepest insecurity, by threatening to kill millions of innocent civilians. As a former Permanent Representative of India to the United Nations said it: "They (the NWSs) are trying to prevent nuclear war by threatening it—a perilous paradox of prophylaxis."[15]

Thus, it was not an aberration that India in 1995 pleaded before the World Court that nuclear weapons are illegal and incompatible with international law and international humanitarian law, and advanced an elaborate set of arguments for outlawing their use, threat of use, manufacture or possession. The written statement of the government of India before the International Court of Justice contends, on the basis of Article 2(4) of the UN Charter, that "any use of nuclear weapons as a measure of use of force to promote national policy objectives would be unlawful" and the "use of nuclear weapons in any armed conflict as a first attack would be unlawful under international law." Further, it argued that the use of nuclear weapons "by way of reprisal or retaliation would violate the principle of proportionality and humanitarian law;" therefore, the "prohibition of the use of a nuclear weapon in an armed conflict is an absolute one, compliance with which is not dependent on corresponding compliance by others;" it is a "requisite in all circumstances."

The Indian official statement reads:

> This brings us to the question as to the legality of the use of nuclear weapons in an armed conflict on the ground that it is open as a measure of last resort under limited conditions as a matter of military necessity. A basic principle of the law of armed conflict and particularly the international humanitarian law, which is contained in Article 22 of the Hague Convention IV (1907) states that "the right of belligerents to adopt means of injuring the enemy is not unlimited." Their right in particular is conditioned by Article 23 of the Hague Regulations, which prohibits the use of poison or poisoned weapons; the 1925 Geneva Protocol, which prohibits projectiles, asphyxiating, poisonous, and other gases, and which incidentally also prohibits the use of weapons that could cause genetic disorders and prolonged illnesses; and by the basic principle enshrined in the 1868 Declaration of St. Petersburg prohibiting any weapon "which uselessly aggravates the sufferings of disabled men or renders their death inevitable."
>
> ...[Therefore] the use of nuclear weapons in response to attack by a conventional weapon would patently violate the principle of proportionality; but also a nuclear response to nuclear attack would violate the principle of discrimination, humanity, environmental security, and probably the principle of neutrality as such an attack would not distinguish between combatants and non-combatants, causing civilian casualties, ravaging the natural environment and contaminating the territory of neighboring and distant neutral countries. Nuclear deterrence had been considered to be abhorrent to human sentiment since it implies that a state, if required to defend its own existence, will act with pitiless disregard for the consequences to its own and adversary's people.[16]

This is not all. India also pleaded:

> Since the production and manufacture of nuclear weapons can only be with the objective of their use, it must follow that if the use of such weapons itself is illegal under international law, then their production and manufacture cannot under any circumstances be considered as permitted. Besides, the manufacture and stockpiling of nuclear weapons would constitute as a threat of their eventual use.

Thus, the statement concluded: "In view of the above, it is submitted that the threat or use of nuclear weapons in any circumstances, whether as a means or method of warfare or otherwise, is illegal or unlawful under international law.[17]

Similarly, it was the long-standing doctrinal continuity in India's radical and categorical rejection of nuclear weapons that led Foreign Secretary Salman Haidar to state at the Conference on Disarmament (CD) in Geneva in March 1996 that India remains committed to the complete elimination of nuclear weapons and wants to locate the CTBT "as an instrument of disarmament." He recalled that India put forward

> a formal proposal calling for the establishment of an Ad-hoc Committee on Nuclear Disarmament to commence negotiations on a phased program of nuclear disarmament for the eventual elimination of nuclear weapons... Nuclear disarmament is not the concern of one group of countries alone but is of universal relevance. We realize that nuclear weapons cannot be eliminated overnight. But surely, in today's world, conditions exist to begin negotiations on this primary disarmament objective.[18]

Most important, Haidar said:

> India's objectives are different. We do not believe that the acquisition of nuclear weapons is essential for national security, and we have followed a conscious decision in this regard. We are also convinced that the existence of nuclear weapons diminishes international security. We therefore, seek their complete elimination. These are fundamental precepts that have been an integral basis of India's foreign and national security policy. It shall, therefore, remain our endeavor in the coming months to try to ensure that the disarmament agenda is not lost in a purely non-proliferation agenda.[19]

New Delhi's embrace of this "abhorrent" doctrine barely two years later, without as much as a figleaf of an attempt at a rational explanation of a change of stance, signifies not so much a change in ground realities or the regional situation, as the moral debasement of the Indian elite and a coarsening of the quality of public discourse in the country. The degeneration of the Indian elite is a long, drawn-out process, but it has become particularly stark and obvious over the past two decades. It is itself related to the evolution of domestic politics since the early '80s—a combination of ascendant Hindu-communal ideology, growing alienation of the elite from the people, a militaristic obsession with India becoming a great power, and the spread of profoundly cynical political ideas.

The BJP's lasting gain since the Ayodhya mosque agitation beginning in the mid-'80s has been not so much in its electoral support as its success in influencing substantial sections of India's social and economic elite—typically upper caste and urban—and ideologically penetrating the higher bureaucracy, judiciary and the professions. This ideology is based on a toxic, belligerent, paranoid and sectarian nationalism, which sees Hindus as the classical victims of invasion and conquest, who must now settle scores with the "invaders" (principally Muslims) by "uniting" and "militarizing" themselves and creating an awe-inspiring Hindu state. This framework regards peace, non-violence, and justice as effete, and secular Gandhi as a villain out to emasculate Hindu "manhood"—someone to be eliminated, as he indeed was, by a fanatic inspired by the ideology of the Rashtriya Swayamsevak Sangh (RSS), the BJP's progenitor, ideological mentor, and organizational master.

Toys for the Boys:
How Nuclearism Works against Women

"A nuclear bomb does not discriminate. Nuclearization does."[1] And it discriminates with a vengeance against women and feminist values and principles. India's and Pakistan's nuclearization took place amid yet another explosion—that of aggressive, bellicose, male-supremacist, tub-thumping, jingoistic nationalism, itself closely tied up with religious sectarianism. The images and symbols used to describe the tests, and the terms in which the nuclear triumph of India and Pakistan was announced—"we have a Big Bomb"—were strongly phallic and deeply rooted in the discourse of raw power, aggression, and penetration.

Prime Minister Vajpayee openly declared: "We have a big Bomb," and picking up the same sexual imagery, a cartoon in a leading newspaper depicted Vajpayee propping up his rickety coalition government with a nuclear bomb. "Made with Viagra," the caption read. Pakistan's Prime Minister Sharif was clear that he was "matching" India in the nuclear competition; he had to. The Vishwa Hindu Parishad, a militant super-patriarchal affiliate of the BJP, was even more categorical. It announced that with the nuclear tests, India had finally demonstrated its "manhood." Earlier, for decades, India had been "ruled by a bunch of *hijras* (eunuchs)."[2] (The Shiv Sena, a fascistic ally of the BJP in Maharashtra, echoed the same sentiment.) For the VHP, India had now become all-powerful. It could take on any force on earth. India must now be declared a "Hindu state," through a constitutional amendment.

The connections between nuclearization, aggression, intolerance toward neighbors, male-supremacism, religious chauvinism, and bellicose nationalism were starkly obvious from the very beginning in both India and Pakistan. That itself should cause concern and worry among women everywhere. But there is an even stronger case why women should want to oppose nuclear weapons.

First, nuclearization will impose a *heavy economic burden* upon the already stretched resources of the Indian and Pakistan governments, themselves deeply in debt, with huge fiscal deficits (see Chapter Seven). In the case of India, the costs of creating even a so-called "minimum credible deterrent"—a fifth the size of China's arsenal, or smaller—have been estimated to be the same as the costs of providing free primary education to all children between age six and fourteen now out of school. Nuclear weapons are liable to claim more resources than what India or Pakistan spends on public health.

Given the fact that the "committed" expenditures of the Indian and Pakistani governments—the foreign and domestic debt servicing, the salaries, the conventional military budget, the various subsidies for the well-off—are over eighty percent of their total revenue, the *additional* outlays that nuclear weapons and missiles programs will claim can only come from *deep cuts* in the already meager and shrinking public budgets for health, sanitation, literacy, primary education, nutrition, drinking water supply, shelter, social security, welfare, and other social sector programs that are of particular relevance to women. It is well established that in India and Pakistan, girl children and women have the least access to these services, even though they need them the most. Such cuts spell a further degradation of public services, an increase in the burden of work placed upon women, and further deprivation and desperate need for many.

India and Pakistan have long been notorious for high levels of deprivation among women, a fact reflected in extraordinarily low sex ratios (in the case of India, 927 women for 1000 males), high levels of malnutrition (as a proportion higher than in sub-Saharan Africa), and abysmally low levels of female literacy (38 and 24 percent for India and Pakistan respectively). Their Gender-related Development Indices, computed by the UN Development Program, are among the lowest in the world, ranking number 128 and 131 respectively among 174 countries. Any reduction in state spending on programs meant to redress the situation would be extremely harmful.

Since women carry a disproportionate share of the responsibility for housework, fetching of water (usually from long distances in villages), supervising children's nutrition and education, and caring for the sick, cutbacks in social spending that mean the decline or collapse of services, would affect them particularly grievously. In the event of a nuclear emergency, it is primarily the surviving women who will be called upon to be the prime caregivers and counselors to the victims.

Secondly, nuclearization is liable to perversely influence and change social values, for the ideology of nuclearism not only sidelines moral questions, but genders them. Within its discourse, the policymaking elite is represented as rational, scientific, modern, and of course masculine, while ethical questions, questions about social and environmental costs, are made to seem emotional, effeminate, regressive, and pre-modern. This falsely implies that questions about human life and welfare are somehow neither modern nor masculine, and that men have no capacity for peace and morality. This can have disastrous consequences for both men and women.

Nuclearism trivializes human suffering. It pejoratively sees human caring as a sign of weakness or effeminacy, as a concern simply of the oppressed. It downgrades non-nuclear countries as "backward" and as unequipped to step into the twenty-first century. Nuclearism breeds a politics based on the relegation of the weak to the margins and a neo-Darwinian survival-of-the-fittest mindset.

This is not all. Nuclearization needs secrecy. It demands obedience and conformity. It is repressive and intolerant of dissent. It condemns democratic protest as anti-national. Nuclearization is not a matter of military and technological activities alone. "Nuclearized India and Pakistan will need to construct a cultural and educational environment that promotes a preference for aggression, violence and revenge."[3]

To rationalize these priorities, the proponents of nuclearization will feed people with glorified images of militaristic heroism, brutality, and the relentless pursuit of aggrandizement. At the same time, they will denigrate images of peaceability, tolerance, and universal goodwill. Nuclearism denies the possibility of drawing upon humane values and life-affirming and -sustaining attitudes and methods. All this, combined with the desire to win public approval for nuclear weapons, will entail promoting a mindset that enhances what are conventionally known as masculine values: violence, eagerness to retaliate, and brutality.

The third effect of nuclearization, particularly in India and Pakistan, pertains to a virulent *religion-based nationalism*, which is strongly masculinist and patriarchal in orientation, and legitimizes the subordination of women, reducing them to passive objects without agency. The ideologies of aggression associated with this variety of nationalism are themselves rooted in rationalizing the capacity for insensate violence. Once the idea that massive, limitless, violence against "the enemy" is legitimate and necessary is rendered acceptable and "normal," it can also be used to rationalize everyday violence against women, and more generally, the underprivileged. Violence becomes merely a "part of life"—and with the imprimatur of religion too. For the construction of both Hindu-sectarian nationalism in India and Islamicism in Pakistan is deeply rooted in, and inseparable from, the diminution of women to mere repositories and reproducers of culture, who then embody the Hindu or Islamic "nation."

Religion-based nationalism is deeply authoritarian and militarist. In the India-Pakistan context, it has involved recruitment of women into militant outfits, or their systematic brainwashing. For instance, recruits into the RSS women's fronts are given daily ideological instruction on the evils of Islam and taught to hate all Muslims. They are trained to translate that hatred into martial action. Such outfits not only glorify women as mothers of soldiers, but also attempt "to perfect a formidable machine for producing an ideal-type woman who is herself a fully militarized being. And she is further exhorted, in their training program, to pass all this on to her children."[4]

Such a militaristic culture feeds increased levels of violence against women. Nuclearism allows such violations to be rationalized and "normalized" in the name of "national security" and the "supreme national interest." Women, then, have a special stake in opposing nuclearization. Feminist groups recognize this. In both India and Pakistan, they have been at the forefront of the struggle for nuclear disarmament.

NOTES

[1] Kumkum Sangari, Neeraj Malik, Sheba Chhachhi and Tanika Sarkar in "Why Women Must Reject the Bomb," *Out of Nuclear Darkness: The Indian Case for Disarmament* (New Delhi: Movement in India for Nuclear Disarmament (MIND), 1998). This box draws heavily upon this lucid essay, and upon the work of other South Asian feminists.

[2] Ashok Singhal, president of the VHP, quoted at Patna, India, in "Test an assertion of Hindu pride: Singhal," *The Pioneer* (New Delhi) 24 May 1998.

[3] Sangari: 53.

[4] Sangari: 54.

Militarist Nationalism in India

With the collapse of the Nehruvian paradigm, consisting of democracy, secularism, non-alignment and "socialism," the top ten to fifteen percent of Indians, the upper-crust of society, have set their face against the rest, especially the poor. Culturally, economically, and politically, they are closer to Northern elites and their own kin in North America and Europe. Strongly influenced by social-Darwinist ideas, they see the poor as a drag on "their" India. They want a shortcut to high global stature. What better route than the military one? Greatness here is defined purely in terms of power untempered by civilized conduct or compassion.

The growing importance of militaristic nationalism in politics is reflected in the duality of India's public discourse. At the grassroots, there is the moral, liberating discourse of rights, justice, self-assertion by the hitherto disenfranchised and underprivileged. But, as if in direct opposition to this, the elite wield a discourse of power and privilege that assumes society to be in a sort of primitive, quasi-Hobbesian state, irredeemably immoral. Within this framework, the real becomes the rational. There is a separation between science and ethics, between technology and social responsibility. Developing instruments of mass destruction is seen as an "achievement" enabling Indians to show the world that they are as *good* as anyone else.

In some ways, the elite's degeneration precedes the rise of virulent Hindu nationalism, and is traceable to the growing crisis of legitimacy of the Indian state since the '70s. Nuclear nationalism has been an undercurrent in the Indian policy debate since the '60s, especially after India's humiliation in the China War of 1962. Thus, there was at best relatively feeble resistance to the change in the official nuclear policy from "No Bombs Ever" to "No Bombs Now" in the late '60s, and later to a position of ambiguity (itself shifting and unstable) during the '70s, especially after India's demonstration of nuclear weapons capability at Pokharan in May 1974.

Far too many Indians belonging to the opinion-making and -shaping category slid into the comfortable cocoon of ambiguity and nuclear deception. For instance, in 1974, hardly any scientists or even peace-minded Gandhians questioned the dubious official claim that India's first test was in fact a "peaceful nuclear explosion," and even fewer challenged the additional, even more ludicrous and crude claim, that what took place at Pokharan was not an explosion at all, but an "implosion"—referring to the *technique* of suddenly bringing together two or more sub-critical pieces of machined plutonium to form a critical mass that rapidly undergoes nuclear fission and explodes or disassembles. A large number among elite groups polled soon thereafter thought that the test explosion—based on a well-established body of physics, much of it available in the public domain—was a "major scientific achievement" and a "breakthrough" for a third world country. They felt it was also an assertion of national sovereignty and independent decision-making in security-related matters.[20]

In reality, what took place at Pokharan in May 1974 was not a "peaceful nuclear explosion," but the test explosion, it was subsequently revealed, of a bomb. Former Atomic Energy Commission (AEC) chairman, the top physicist responsible for the test, Raja Ramanna, disclosed as much, on October 9, 1997.[21] Theoretically, "peaceful" explosive devices are possible, but the term refers to the *intention* behind their use—perhaps to create huge reservoirs or stimulate oil recovery—not to the physical principles involved. These are identical with the principles used in the test of a bomb.

India's insistence that the explosions were "peaceful" had less to do with intentions or actual plans to put that technology to civilian use, than with demonstrating formal compliance with an agreement signed with Canada in 1956 for assistance to build the CIRUS reactor, which committed India to "ensure that the reactor and any products resulting from its use will be employed for peaceful purposes only." (A similar agreement was signed with the US, which provided twenty-one tons of heavy water for CIRUS). The fact is, after the active pursuit and the demonstration of a nuclear weapons capability in 1974, India consciously adopted nuclear ambiguity as a policy. Though the country stopped short of actual weapons development, nevertheless a big psychological and moral barrier had been crossed.

It is hard to answer if New Delhi would have gone on soon toward full weaponization, preceded by some more tests, had there been less of an outcry around the world over Pokharan I, and had the political costs of conducting the test not turned out to be higher than anticipated. Perhaps without the sharp decline in India's international moral stature, the antagonism from the West and from a close ally, the USSR, or the withdrawal of the Canadian and American civilian nuclear technology assistance on which the DAE was dependent to run its rickety power program, India's transition to Pokharan II would have been a little faster.

Indian nuclear ambiguity, as it evolved, meant different things to different people. To those on the extreme right, it was only a temporary pause (far too prolonged for some) on the road to full nuclearization. For some, it was an assertion of sovereignty, no more, not to be pursued by any further action: it was only a way of warning the world, especially the P-5, that one should not be too complacent about the effectiveness of the global non-proliferation regime and the NPT, or about the lack of progress toward global nuclear disarmament. For some others, India's ambiguity reflected nothing more than its policymakers' indecision at the threshold. But the option to cross the threshold was open and could be implemented under certain circumstances.

For yet others, the "option" needed to be expanded through technological upgrading, and ambiguity was eminently amenable to that interpretation. And for a good chunk of people on the left, ambiguity was expedient. Acquiescing in it permitted a passive response to official policy and activity. It was a good catch-all, combining protest against the existing unequal global nuclear order, with some preparation to create a "defensive" nuclear shield (just in case), and a symbol of sovereignty, not to be "surrendered" under coercion or pressure of the hegemonic powers. Why should India give up or foreclose the option unless the P-5 did as well?

Few Indians, barring a tiny fringe of nuclear disarmament activists, called for closing, circumscribing or limiting the option—even by making it conditional upon the pursuit of pro-active disarmament diplomacy, let alone unilaterally. Such initiatives in favor of nuclear restraint and disarmament as were taken by the Indian government through the late '70s and '80s (especially the Five Continent Initiative, the Rajiv Gandhi Plan of 1988, and the Delhi Declaration Gandhi signed with Mikhail Gorbachev) came "from above," not as a result of advocacy and lobbying from outside the government.

What the broadly "consensual" position on the issue—keep the option open, but don't exercise it—accepted, at least implicitly, if not explicitly, was India's "right" to have and develop its nuclear weapons capability, and create and refine the nuclear weapons option, although it drew the line at exercising it. This meant investing nuclear armaments with the respectable role as repositories of national sovereignty, however separated such sovereignty might be from the people and from democratic accountability. And it also meant implicitly granting the Indian government the "right" to acquire at least *the ability to commit mass-scale murder*—merely, or at least largely, because other states possess such instruments of mass destruction and are reluctant to give them up. Or to put it another way: if possessing nuclear weapons is threatening mass murder, then having a weapons capability is to insist on having the "right" to threaten mass murder even if there is no insistence that this "right" should be exercised. Not only is possessing such weapons immoral; so too is claiming the right to do so!

The assertion of India's "right" to a weapons capability sat extremely uncomfortably with India's own stance that the use, threat of use, manufacture, or possession of nuclear weapons were all "crimes against humanity." Thus, Indian nuclear ambiguity was morally premised upon highly dubious foundations: revanchism, and matching vice with vice, following the endless logic of retribution. It was sustained by a false sense of national pride, and a vacuous third worldism—vacuous because it was elitist and desperately dependent on approbation for India as a major world power from the First World. As a BJP spokesperson said in 1993—and this is by no means a rare sentiment: "We don't want to be blackmailed or treated as oriental blackies."[22] Ergo, we *need* a nuclear weapons capability, if not these horror weapons themselves.

Even someone like Amartya Sen, a moral philosopher, chose not to comment on the anomalies, antinomies, and paradoxes of Indian nuclear ambiguity until after May 1998. In a December 1998 interview, while criticizing the tests as a "big moral mistake," he said: "We are thinking of a world in which nuclear weapons are unlikely to be used, so that the moral quality of it is partly a matter of our self-discipline. And the discipline of having the ability to blast nuclear bombs and not doing so has a certain moral quality to it. So this old position India had, whereby it acknowledged that it could make the bomb but nevertheless did not want to pursue a nuclear program, could be described as having an ethical characteristic, which is now completely lost."[23]

As a factual description, this is not inaccurate. India's stature in the world has indeed declined after May 1998. But what is surprising about this statement, coming as it does from a thinker and moral philosopher as distinguished as Sen, is the lack of questioning what India's "ability to blast nuclear bombs" really means. For that "ability" is not a mere technical attribute, itself socially neutral, and morally value-free. Along with it comes an inevitable descent into the abyss of nuclear-deterrence thinking, and the preparedness to visit mass-destruction upon the people of a supposedly adversary state. Surely, the *virtue* of "discipline"—stopping short of manufacturing the bomb—is much smaller than the *vice* of launching such preparations, and building the physical and technological foundations for acquiring nuclear weapons.

The Anomalies of Ambiguity

Many supporters of Indian nuclear ambiguity emphasized only one of the two propositions underlying the dual-faced policy. Ambiguity, on the one hand, meant the acquisition (and perhaps further development and upgrading) of a nuclear weapons capability. On the other, it also meant *not* exercising the option by making the weapons *because* such weapons are evil and must not be made, let alone used. Indian ambiguists tended to stress the first proposition, often within a framework of militant nationalism. They routinely interrogated the government in power about whether it had "surrendered" or "capitulated" to the American pressure to "cap, roll back and eventually eliminate" India's capability. They rarely urged nuclear restraint, or asked for a solemn pledge that India would never cross the threshold. Thus in 1994, when a newspaper disclosed that an Indian delegation was about to start the fourth round of bilateral talks on the nuclear issue with the Americans in London, there was an uproar in Parliament. Deeply embarrassed, the government all but cancelled the talks. The diplomatic exchange in London was reduced to token formal statements and re-statements of known positions.

Even when the hawkish turn on the debate over the Comprehensive Test Ban Treaty became glaringly obvious in 1996, few ambiguists ever stated the second proposition (that India should *not* exercise the nuclear option), let alone articulated the strong moral and political arguments underlying that stance. It was convenient simply to assume that India would not cross the threshold. (Many in the elite said the government of the day would not "have the guts" to do so.)

Since the logic of stopping at the threshold was never stated, a moral vacuum developed, grew, and was quickly filled by assertive hawks, both within and outside the government. For these hawks, "defying" the unequal global nuclear order by blocking the CTBT, refusing all proposals, including eminently persuasive and reasonable ones, in favor of nuclear restraint, and pushing for an Indian nuclear deterrent against imagined potential threats, became a talisman of national sovereignty and independent policymaking. The BJP, with its own toxic, aggressive nationalism, and its long-standing obsessive fascination with nuclear weapons, seized on this, much to the hawks' delight.

Apologists for India's nuclear weapons, and for the violent shift in New Delhi's stated nuclear doctrine that took place in May 1998, have advanced a range of *ex post* rationalizations on the government's behalf. Most of them are as hollow, unconvincing and mutually contradictory as the different arguments emanating from officialdom: that nuclearization was the "logical" response to the Chinese/Pakistani threat (or a combined one from both Beijing and Islamabad), or that it was India's protest against the unequal global nuclear order and the reluctance of the P-5 to give up their dependence on nuclear weapons. And so forth. The only difference was that the non-official apologists went to absurd lengths to invent fanciful reasons: Pakistan was about to test, so India had to do it first; the tests were only a means of reshaping the global nuclear order; India's nuclearization was the consequence of the end of the Cold War and the loss of a reliable ally in the shape of the USSR, etc. (So much for non-alignment and the pursuit of an *independent* foreign and security policy!)

Some of the hawkish arguments are morally perverse and distinguished by a peculiar depravity: they cite Gandhi in justification for the utterly cynical and wholly immoral decision to cross the threshold. K. Subrahmanyam, one of India's most committed nuclear hawks—he has called for the bomb periodically since the early '60s—provides a prime example of such perversity. Subrahmanyam is mentioned here not because of the logic of his pathetic argument, but because he is Convenor of the Advisory Board of India's newly constituted National Security Council, and a prolific writer long in the service of nuclear weapons. He tries to extend the Gandhian notion of non-violence and non-violent resistance, not just to conventional military conflict—which it would be hard to do—but to nuclear weapons! He actually claims that it is possible to derive a justification for India's bombs from Gandhian premises about the justness of the struggle against the "unjust hegemonic and racist [nuclear] status quo." Because nuclear weapons are used "as a currency of power, nuclear proliferation has become an instrumentality (sic) of hegemony and the present nuclear security paradigm and nuclear apartheid are patently unjust."[24]

Subrahmanyam even invents the wholly ludicrous notion of "non-violent nuclear resistance"—a chilling oxymoron, if there ever was one. The idea of "turning the other cheek," of *satyagraha*, of winning the opponent over by demonstrating exceptional moral courage and determination, is here transformed into nuclear muscle-flexing, tit-for-tat retribution, a demonstration of the arrogance of the militantly strong, but morally weak and cowardly. While the key element in Gandhi's "non-violent resistance" lies in the refusal of the oppressed to use the weapons of the oppressor, and instead forge an altogether new instrument of resistance, Subrahmanyam's scheme rests on *imitating* the perpetrators of "nuclear apartheid" by acting identically and with slavish loyalty to their doctrines and nuclear theology.

That is bad enough. Worse, Subrahmanyam wholly ignores the blatant contradiction involved in speaking of non-violence and nuclear weapons—the ultimate instruments of violence and annihilation—in the same breath. This marriage between the two opposites is facilitated by so slight and flimsy a factor—"a hedge against hegemony" of the P-5, and the "imposition" upon India of the CTBT—that it barely deserves mention. But then, Subrahmanyam, like most hawkish devotees of nuclearism, is unburdened by logical consistency: he blithely uses expressions such as Gandhi's successful use of "non-violence *in its offensive mode* to compel the British to quit India." Positions like these would be worth arguing against if they were based at least on an attempt to explain what is meant by "non-violence in its offensive mode" through historical illustrations or even by analogy, if not rational analysis and argument. Alas, they involve nothing more than pure assertion, the stringing together of words, mere phrases meant to rationalize the rise of nuclear belligerence in India.

Subrahmanyam's procedure is typical of the insecure, middle-class Indian mind, which longs for recognition as something more than a bunch of "oriental blackies." He selectively cites certain passages from Gandhi, in particular from a short monograph by Dieter Rothermund, a German scholar, to "show" that Gandhi "refrained from severe criticism of the US using nuclear weapons since he feared that the power of the bomb could be used to dominate the world and impose a mandate on developing countries. He correctly anticipated that big powers could join together to dominate the world—which is today seen in the legitimization of nuclear weapons and imposition of the non-proliferation treaty. Rothermund infers that Gandhiji came out strongly against nuclear weapons only when it became clear that India would become independent."[25]

The first half of this argument is based on a *non sequitur*. Why should Gandhi not have criticized the US action in Hiroshima especially if he feared that the bomb would be used in pursuit of world domination? He would have done so *a fortiori*. As for the second statement, even if it is assumed that Gandhi saw nuclear weapons as instruments of hegemony, it hardly follows that he would make his own pronouncements on the bomb conditional upon India's progress toward independence. By July 1945, it had become abundantly clear that Indian independence was only a matter of time. Therefore it is hard to see the link between Independence and Gandhi's view of nuclear weapons.

It seems much less plausible that Gandhi would have even countenanced the thought that resistance to injustice, however grave, is justified in all forms, however violent, unethical and destructive such resistance might be. If modern India had one stickler for the justice of *means* as well as *ends*, it was Gandhi. Subrahmanyam's forays into morally defending the morally indefensible, and doing so through such a distorted use of Gandhi, only reveal his own utter moral cynicism, and his casual contempt for the seriousness of the moral questions raised by nuclearism.

Serious scholars of Gandhi who, unlike Subrahmanyam, have read the Mahatma, have an altogether different perception. Gandhi was so stunned by the bombing of Hiroshima and Nagasaki that he did not comment on the event for two weeks. He recognized that nuclear weapons had transformed not just the nature of war, but of peace too. Whenever he spoke on the issue—and he spoke a great deal—he was clear, categorical, and unambiguous about the uniquely evil nature of nuclear weapons. He was emphatic about atomic bombs "deadening the finest feelings that have sustained mankind for centuries" and even described the Allies' victory over the Axis powers as "empty" on account of the use of nuclear weapons in August 1945.

Y.P. Anand, director of the National Gandhi Museum in Delhi, has compiled twenty-eight references in Gandhi's writings and speeches pertaining to nuclear weapons.[26] A summary of his views reads: Truth and non-violence are more powerful than the atom bomb. The atom bomb is the weapon of ultimate brute force and destruction. Development of the atom bomb represents the most sinful and diabolical use of science. The atom bomb "mentality" is immoral, unethical, addictive; only evil can come of it. The atom bomb only aggravates violence and never protects anyone against it. It symbolizes the futility of violence. Non-violence is the only antidote against the atom bomb and the only way to redirect hatred and resolve conflict. It is the duty of large nations, and all other nations, in the interest of world peace, to give up the atom bomb. Gandhi made perhaps his most extensive and articulate statement on the issue in Poona in July 1946, on the eve of the first anniversary of the bombing of Hiroshima. This should set at rest all doubts about Gandhi's alleged moral "ambivalence" regarding nuclear weapons.[27]

Gandhi's Second Assassination

The wisdom and humanist passion of the Mahatma on this issue contrasts rather sharply with the cynicism, witlessness, illogic, moral chicanery, and intellectual dishonesty of the bomb's apologists. As an anti-bomb critic has said: "They assassinated Gandhi twice, the first time in January 1948, and for the second time in May 1998." It was not quite an accident that the assassins belonged to the same current: extremist, bellicose, anti-secular Hindu nationalism. It is over Gandhi's dead body—and the body of all the moral ideas he stood for—that the Indian nuclear deterrent was built.

Perhaps the single most disturbing fact that emerged after the Indian tests was the moral insensitivity of India's policymakers. In no country that had previously gone nuclear was the crossing of the threshold made into such an issue of national pride. Although, shamefully, the nuclear bombing of Hiroshima and Nagasaki is to this day supported by a majority of US citizens, the bombs were viewed with a sense of relief, not pride. They were widely (though incorrectly) seen as helping to bring the Second World War to a rapid end. The Russian and Chinese bombs were seen internally as necessary responses to the US and there was, of course, the officially organized drumming up of patriotic sentiment typical of the authoritarian undemocratic regimes that existed at the time the first bombs were developed and exploded in these two countries. In Britain, the public response was far more muted. Indeed, alone of all the NWSs, a major anti-nuclear mass movement and sentiment emerged in Britain in the '50s. In France, a significant "patriotic" sentiment did emerge around nuclear weapons, but there was no euphoria.

In none of the first five NWSs was there anything to parallel or approximate the kind of nationalist euphoria and near-hysterical response that was characteristic of significant sections of upper-caste, upper-class Indian urbanites. The kind of celebratory scenes that were portrayed in the international media gave a misleading impression about the size and depth of popular support to the Indian tests. But although small, the celebrations were real and disturbing in themselves. If similar behavior was to be found in Pakistan after their government tested, it is more understandable, as Pakistanis were celebrating the popular belief that they could now "match" rival India. It is the insecurity, immaturity, and moral insensitivity of the pro-nuclear Indian elite that is most striking. Nobody in Pakistan talked of building a mosque in commemoration of the "grand act." But Hindu nationalist organizations like the VHP actually declared their determination to build just such a temple to worship Shakti, the goddess of power, in commemoration of the Pokharan II blasts.

At one level, it is not difficult to understand (though without condoning) this new elite sense of pride. After all, what else has the Indian elite accomplished over the last twenty years that could be a source of national pride? Poverty, illiteracy, and institutionalized injustices of all kinds continue to haunt Indian society. But to take pride in the possession of what even Indian hawks once used to admit was a "necessary evil" testifies to the existence of a profound moral sclerosis. However necessary one might consider an evil, the fact that it is an evil should preclude celebration or pride in its arrival. But it did not. Equally disturbing was the fact that not a single strategic expert, politician, or media-person among all those who supported the tests criticized the praise (official and non-official) that was showered upon Indian science and scientists following the tests. This was truly extraordinary.

Not *one* prominent supporter of the bomb found the intelligence or integrity to say what could easily have been said: That even as he or she supported the tests and India's newly declared status as a nuclear weapons power, he or she lamented the fact that Indian science had to be *misused* and that the skills of "our wonderful pool of scientists" had to be *abused* to produce these evil weapons (when we would have preferred to use their skills for so much more worthwhile ends). But India felt compelled for security reasons to follow the path of other NWSs, which had similarly abused science and the skills of their own scientific community.

To have said as much, even while supporting Indian nuclearization, would have least shown a recognition of the proper relationship between science and ethics. That no prominent pro-bomb person stated this obvious truth was a striking testimony to the collective absence of a reasonable level of moral sobriety, balance, and sensitivity.[28]

Influential sections of the Indian and Pakistani media selectively played up the "popularity" of the bomb. Based on no more than a few casual phone calls, one of them reported that ninety-one percent of Indians support India's nuclear weapons. The DAE and DRDO scientists and engineers responsible for Pokharan II instantly became heroes. The facts that they disguised their identities, misled their families about their whereabouts, and wore military fatigues, were celebrated as great "achievements." Awards and prizes were showered upon them, as they openly advocated the creation of a "military-industrial complex" and "defense-based development."

Celebrating Mass Destruction

Though this explosion of national chauvinism and celebration of the militarization of science was unprecedented, its foundations had been laid earlier. Raja Ramanna, who headed the "research" team responsible for the first Pokharan test, was similarly lionized in 1974. And Abdul Kalam, who was in large measure responsible for the success of India's Integrated Guided Missile Development Program, which produced the *Prithvi* and *Agni* missiles, was awarded India's highest official honor, the Bharat Ratna, in 1992. This put him in the same league as India's Nobel Prize winners such as Amartya Sen (Economics, 1998) and C.V. Raman (Physics, 1930). The bestowing of such exceptional honor and status emboldened many practitioners of defense-related science and technology to become more assertive and demand more funding for their projects. The militarization of India's science is a distressing trend. Space, nuclear energy, and the DRDO account for two-thirds of all public spending on research and development.

Even the president of India, K.R. Narayanan, a man of the "old Nehruvian school," and justly and widely respected as a person of political integrity and decency, joined in this shameful burst of chauvinistic euphoria without recognizing the deep contradictions involved. As a former diplomat, Narayanan has, not surprisingly, always had a weak spot for nuclear deterrence-based thinking. He earlier supported ambiguity and, in May 1998, the tests. He asserted this position again in the course of a TV interview with the editor of *Frontline*, on the eve of the August 15, 1998 Independence Day celebrations, and there is no indication that it is not his personal opinion.

It would be easy, but false, to claim that those who support deterrence and nuclearism in some fashion are less moral than those who oppose nuclearism. In fact, what is siginificant is not that indecent and immoral people uphold nuclearism while moral people (who can also have terribly immoral positions and attitudes on a host of other issues) do not, but that acceptance of the discourse of nuclearism morally desensitizes and benumbs otherwise humane and decent people. Each human being has a moral personality, even the hardcore realist who believes that international politics is an amoral affair. (Incidentally, this is also a moral position or claim!) Supporting the immoral always diminishes us in some way, small or large; it deforms our moral personalities. The most common reaction of those who so diminish their moral stature is to deny the diminution altogether or at least to minimize its import.

Indian supporters of the bomb failed to stress the proper relationship between science and ethics not because they recognized that it was wrong to so praise science and scientists, and yet they went ahead, but because it did not occur to them that by showering praise upon the bomb and its makers, they committed a serious moral lapse. They lost, or hid from themselves, the moral sensitivity and balance on the nuclear issue that should have been retained at least in some small measure.

This raises a central point about the nature of the discourse of evil. Primo Levi, one of the wisest witnesses to the Holocaust, himself a survivor of Hitler's concentration camps, explained the way ordinary Germans, at least in their overwhelming number, knowing the horrific manner in which Jews were being treated, nonetheless did not allow this to affect them seriously. Levi talked of the "banality of evil." Of how the sheer frequency, regularity and repetition of evil violence, as well as the persistent and routine rationalization and justification of its sources, mechanisms and effects in "normal" political and intellectual discourse—that is to say, the processes by which such violence is made banal—serves to utterly dilute, and even disguise, the evil in question. Language, the medium of so much of human thought, is itself manipulated to fulfill this function. It is used to make the human seem inhuman and to humanize the inhuman. In wartime, the "enemy" is called dehumanizing names—"Gooks" and "Charlies" in Vietnam—to help make their "elimination" more morally palatable. The same phenomenon exists in the everyday language of racism and sexism.

The language and discourse of nuclearism is not only inescapably masculinist, aggressive, and morally callous. It is also euphemistic, deceptive, and misleading. The nuclearist discourse shows both these dehumanizing and falsely humanizing dimensions. Hence all the talk of "collateral damage," "acceptable levels of damage," "atomic diplomacy," etc. US scientists called the first explosive device (July 1945) the "Gadget," and the first bombs dropped on Japan were named "Little Boy" and "Fat Man." The Soviets called their first bomb "The Article." Britain called its first nuclear explosion "Hurricane;" France, the "Blue Mouse;" and China, its first weapon "Device 596." India code-named the successful conduct of the 1974 explosion "The

Smiling Buddha." The 1998 tests were called simply "Shakti," or power.

The general discourse of nuclearism does more than make the morally unthinkable thinkable. It helps routinize and make banal the evil nature of nuclear weapons and nuclear deterrence. When we support or oppose the possession or use or threat or capability of having nuclear weapons (just as when we support or oppose slavery and its justifications), we are, each one of us, making a moral statement that helps shape our own personalities and lives. This affects in howsoever small a way other lives and structures around us.

But opposing nuclear weapons is not merely a personal matter. Certain universal evils must be recognized as such. They debase all of humanity—those that seek to benefit from them as well as those who are its purported or actual victims. Such is the case with evils like apartheid, colonialism, and nuclearism, all of which involve insensate violence. They are often justified in the name of "national security," "the national interest," "national greatness," etc. We cannot create a permanent nuclear-free world unless we value our common humanity and sustain a shared anger for such universal evils as nuclearism. Only on the basis of this shared but controlled anger and passion, whose wellsprings are our individual moral capacities, can we hope to build a wider consciousness across national boundaries. That alone can help bring about the goal of complete and global nuclear disarmament.

To forget the horror and shame of what happened at Hiroshima and Nagasaki, and to fail to draw moral as well as political lessons from it, is to debase and degrade our common and universal humanity.

NOTES

[1] Robert Jay Lifton & Richard Falk, *Indefensible Weapons* (New York: Basic Books, 1982) ix.

[2] This discussion owes a great deal to the moral argument developed by Michael Walzer in his very useful *Just and Unjust Wars* (New York: Basic Books, 1977).

[3] Ted Honderich, *Violence for Equality* (Harmondsworth: Penguin Books, 1980) 35.

[4] See Stephen I. Schwartz, ed., *Atomic Audit: The Costs and Consequences of U.S. Nuclear Weapons Since 1940* (New York: The Brookings Institution, 1998).

[5] Rawls, *A Theory of Justice*, quoted in Walzer: 229.

[6] Walzer: 228-232.

[7] Walzer: 231.

[8] Walzer: 283.

[9] Walzer: 283.

[10] See, for example, K. Subrahmanyam, "Hedging Against Hegemony: Gandhi's Logic in the Nuclear Age," in *The Times of India* (New Delhi) 16 June 1998.

[11] Excerpted in "The Morality of Nuclear Deterrence: An Evaluation by Pax Christi Bishops in the U.S.," *INESAP Bulletin* 16 (Darmstadt) November 1998: 53-54. Flawed as it is, this is one of the few serious arguments about the morality of nuclear weapons to emerge from any religious tradition. Most theological schools have not confronted the moral issue of nuclear weapons at all.

12 "The Morality" 53.

13 "The Morality" 53.

14 Cited in Rikhi Jaipal, *Nuclear Arms and the Human Race* (New Delhi: Allied Publishers, 1986): 61.

15 Jaipal: 61.

16 Government of India, *Status of Nuclear Weapons in International Law: Request for Advisory Opinion of the International Court of Justice* (New Delhi: Ministry of External Affairs, 1995): 3.

17 Government: 7.

18 Salman Haider, Foreign Secretary of India, Statement at the Plenary Meeting of the Conference on Disarmament, Geneva, 21 March 1996: 2.

19 Haider: 3.

20 Aqueil Ahmed and Falguni Sen, "Scientists & Science Policy Formulation: Indian Scientists' View of the Indian Nuclear Explosion," *Journal of Scientific & Industrial Research* 35 (August 1976): 497-501.

21 Ramanna confirmed that the Pokharan-I device "was a bomb. I can tell you now," cited in A.G. Noorani, "Many Question, Few Answers," *Frontline* (Chennai) 20 November 1998: 79.

22 Cited in George Perkovich, "Nuclear Proliferation," *Foreign Policy* Fall 1998: 15. Statements of this sort, often even stronger in tone, are commonly heard in elite circles in India and Pakistan.

23 Quoted in interview with *Frontline* (Chennai) 15 January 1999: 50.

24 Subrahmanyam.

25 Subrahmanyam.

26 Y.P. Anand, *What Mahatma Gandhi Said about the Atom Bomb* (New Delhi: National Gandhi Museum, 1998): 6.

27 Cited in "The Atom Bomb & Ahimsa" in Kai Bird and Lawrence Lifschultz (eds), *Hiroshima's Shadow* (Story Creek, CT: The Pamphleteer's Press, 1998) 258-259.

28 Even the two early public statements that were signed by scientists (the first had 74 signatures, the second had over 200) opposed to the tests and released to the national media, missed this crucial point. While these statements correctly pointed out that the supposed technological achievement was nothing of the sort (first generation bomb-making is a dated, fairly low-level technology), they did not point out the vital and obvious relationship between science and ethics, and therefore the obscenity of showering praise on Indian science or scientists. Just as disappointing was the fact that although the two mainstream left parties, the CPI and the CPM, opposed the tests, they nevertheless felt the need to endorse Indian science and the scientists for their technological achievement.

Chapter 7

An Unaffordable Arsenal: The Cost of a "Credible Minimum Deterrent"

Apart from the intrinsic indefensibility and immorality of nuclear weapons as instruments of war, they pose yet another serious ethical problem: the wholesale distortion of social, economic, and political priorities in the states that acquire, deploy, and stockpile these weapons. All five countries that went overtly nuclear between 1945 and 1964 spent enormous sums of money on the production, deployment, targeting, defense, supervision, and control of their nuclear weapons and delivery systems, as well as on building the infrastructure that would generate the fissile material, warheads, aircraft, missiles, and command and control systems necessary for their nuclear programs. These expenditures acquired truly awesome proportions during the late '60s, and then again during the Second Cold War, inaugurated by President Ronald Reagan in the '80s. Ironically, although expenditures on nuclear weapons acquisition, maintenance, upgrading, and modernization have (expectedly) fallen from the peaks of the '80s, they still remain extremely high in absolute terms even a decade *after* the end of the Cold War.

Nuclear arsenals have tended to defy all rational calculation of security risks and ways of meeting them. At the heart of their persistence is systemic hostility or enmity between powerful states, and competitive confrontation between them, driven by technology, mercantile interests, powerful bureaucracies, and mighty military apparatuses. E.P. Thompson described the process of sustaining this enmity and confrontation: "the armourers excite the other's armourers, the hawks feed the hawks, the ideologists rant at each other like rival auctioneers, and the missiles copulate with each other, and breed on each other's foul bodies the next generation of missiles."

The distortions of nuclearism's obsessive reliance on these weapons of mass annihilation are not confined to the economic sphere alone. They extend to the environment, public health, and to political processes, through the subversion of democratic principles and institutions. The production and stockpiling of nuclear weapons over the past five decades has posed serious security risks to all of humanity. More, it has meant unleashing "a kind of secret low-intensity radioactive warfare... against unsuspecting populations," as Bernard Lown, co-founder and emeritus co-chair of International Physicians for the Prevention of Nuclear War, has put it.

Nuclear programs everywhere involve secrecy and deception and the centralization of enormous power and authority (including managerial, investigative, quasi-judicial, and quasi-executive powers) in small elite groups and institutions. These atomic energy commissions, military top brass, weapons laboratories, and operators of facilities related to the entire "nuclear fuel cycle," meet with very little—or no—public scrutiny. This violates the democratic principle of transparency and the public's right to know by whom, why, and what decisions are made on its behalf. Besides, as we have discussed, nuclear weapons programs have been associated with chauvinism, militarism, extreme intolerance, and jingoism. And nuclearism is inseparable from male-supremacist sexism.

Nuclear weapons production has had a terrible impact on the health of occupational workers in nuclear facilities, people living near nuclear industry installations and test sites, and unsuspecting victims of experimentation on human beings with radioactive materials. Nuclear weapons production has also seriously affected the environment through the deliberate dumping of highly radioactive wastes, accidental releases of harmful nuclear materials and toxic chemicals, contamination of water bodies, acquifers, vegetation, and animal life in different parts of the world—well outside the boundaries of the nuclear weapons states.

In the US alone, a Department of Energy study estimates the cost of cleaning up the mess left by nuclear weapons production to be $260 billion. This figure is roughly four-fifths of the entire annual gross national product of India, home to nearly a billion people.

The consequential immorality of nuclear weapons appears particularly stark in India and Pakistan, because they are two of the world's poorest countries, whose rulers have comprehensively failed to provide even a modicum of real security to the vast majority of their peoples. And yet, policymakers in the sub-continent, as well as many opinion-shapers, have indulged in the delusion that nuclear weapons are relatively inexpensive, and in any case, will not be a heavy burden on their economies. Bomb lobbies in India and Pakistan have consciously downplayed the costs of nuclear weapons programs and the inevitable diversion of scarce resources away from the need-based priorities of development. These programs could prove economically ruinous to both economies.

Nuclear weapons programs have already proved to be extremely expensive in the P-5 states, where they tended to add between twenty to fifty percent to the existing military budget. Secrecy about the exact size of nuclear weapons arsenals and missile programs, as well as scarcity of facts about the sharing of military infrastructures between nuclear and conventional armaments, makes it difficult to put a precise figure on each item of expenditure in all the five nuclear weapons programs. A landmark study, *Atomic Audit*, by the Brookings Institution provides, though, some excellent, detailed, estimates of expenditures by the US, and some hard numbers about the other NWSs, especially Britain and France.[1]

Blowing Up $5,500 Billion

Atomic Audit estimates that between 1940 and 1996, the US spent (in 1996 values) $5,500 billion on its nuclear weapons program. If the (future) costs of dismantling nuclear bombs and environmental remediation are added, the program's bill jumps to $5,821 billion. The per capita expenditure in the US until 1996 works out to $21,646. This is more than *four times* the world's average per capita annual income in 1998. To visualize what this astronomical sum means: it would take 184,579 years to count to this amount if $1 was counted off every second. Or, if bricks were made of dollar bills (about 200 bills make one inch), the $5,821 billion stack of bricks would stretch all the way to the moon and nearly back.

Some of the stunning conclusions of the Brookings study are:

* The US spent "only" $409 billion to build bombs—or 7 percent of the cost of the nuclear weapons program.

* As much as $3,241 billion was spent on the delivery systems (55.7 percent of the program cost).

* A hefty $831.1 billion was claimed by the command, control, communications and intelligence (C^3I) infrastructure (14.3 percent of the total cost).

* An absurdly high $937.2 billion was spent on "defending the bomb," by means such as creating vast physical structures, including 1,500 underground shelters.

This $5,500 billion expenditure accounted for 29 percent of America's total military budget. In other words, the Bomb represented an addition of 40.8 percent *over and above* conventional military spending. The cost of the nuclear program exceeded the total expenditure by the US government on all other categories of spending, barring "non-nuclear national defense" and Social Security. It also exceeded spending on six important sectors put together, including health, education, the environment, space research, and law enforcement. The cost of the lost opportunities is truly staggering. Had the US spent even half of the average $98 billion that it committed to the bomb each year between 1940 and 1996, it would have wiped out every trace of poverty and deprivation in its highly polarized and unequal society.

At the other end of the P-5 spectrum, China, the weakest nuclear power of the five, has already spent over $100 billion on its modest arsenal. In the decade that preceded the 1964 test, China's spending on its nuclear weapons *preparations* alone was the equivalent of $28 billion (at 1996 prices). In France, expenditure on nuclear weapons ran at between 0.4 and 1.2 percent of GDP between 1964 and 1992. At its height, weaponization in a single year (1967) alone claimed $1.9 billion (in 1987 dollars) or today's equivalent of $2.6 billion. Britain's program has only been poorly audited, but according to the Campaign for Nuclear Disarmament (CND), Britain would have to spend something of the order of £1.5 billion ($2.5 billion) a year to operate its small, now pruned, "Trident" nuclear deterrent, which is composed of only four submarines.

What would an Indian nuclear weapons program cost? Even assuming that India is to build only a "minimum deterrent"—that is, not a full-fledged nuclear arsenal that is geared to win in an actual war-fighting situation, or one that remotely aspires to match China in its firepower—the costs will be formidable, if not ruinous, even with a great deal of technological leapfrogging and saving on many items. At the very least, in the absence of a nuclear arms race, the costs would work out to about $10 billion spread over five to seven years. This would mean raising India's already high military spending by *twenty to fifty percent a year*, depending on how fast a so-called "minimum deterrent" is put in place. These estimates are for a bare-bones, no-frills nuclear weapons programs—"a poor man's deterrent," with relatively low reliability, very little back-up, and deep uncertainty about survivability.

Although $10 billion appears puny in absolute terms, it corresponds to about three percent of India's GDP—the equivalent of what the whole country annually spends on such a basic need as primary education. As it happens, the sum also corresponds to what it would cost to provide universal access to primary education to all children between six and fourteen years of age. No wonder, after the May 1998 tests, India's education ministry quietly decided to slow down the program to universalize primary education, even as the government raised the military spending allocation by fourteen percent.

Estimates for an Indian Nuclear Program

The $10 billion figure is reached on the basis of a number of extremely conservative assumptions made by nuclear hawks and government agencies that have a stake in "sweetening" the nuclear bitter pill by underestimating the real costs of a so-called "credible minimum deterrent." Although the Indian government has refused to spell out the size of such a force, various military sources, most notably the late General Krishnaswamy Sundarji, a former army chief, took this to mean roughly 150 nuclear fission bombs, with a yield of 15-20 kiloton equivalent of TNT, similar to the ones dropped on Hiroshima and Nagasaki.

This assumes that India would need to develop the ability to destroy five cities in Pakistan and ten population centers in China, with three bombs each, and a small second strike capability. The number of warheads/bombs assumed here corresponds to "the former AEC official Sethna's own figure of 150 bombs for a credible deterrent" mentioned in a recently declassified 1966 US State Department telegram to the US embassy in New Delhi.

This is a truly modest nuclear strike force by P-5 standards. It represents just about one-third to one-fifth of the number of warheads in China's nuclear arsenal. The costs of each of these no-frills bombs are assumed to be just $1 million each, although the Brookings study puts the range at $1 to 2 million. Similarly, the costs of production of plutonium (of which roughly 1,760 pounds more will be needed in addition to existing holdings) are assumed to be very low: Rs 700 crores (or $170 million) for a dedicated reactor (capital cost).

The "minimum deterrent" is also assumed to have triadic delivery systems: aircraft, ground-based missiles, and submarine-launched missiles. This means refitting a squadron of twenty-four aircraft to carry nuclear bombs, procuring three to five nuclear-powered submarines, 50-60 *Prithvi* missiles, 50-60 *Agni* and extended-range *Agni* missiles (still in the preliminary stage of development), and 15-20 *Sagarikas*, a 300 km cruise missile under development for launching from the sea.

There are no reliable estimates for an Indian command, control, communications and intelligence (C^{3}I) infrastructure, which is the next most expensive component of a nuclear weapons program. Typically, it alone accounts for the equivalent of a fifth to a seventh of what the rest of the nuclear program costs. Even assuming that the fairly arbitrary and probably low estimate made by a nuclear weapons advocate, Brigadier Vijai Nair in 1992, is correct, a C^{3}I system will cost the equivalent of $1 billion.

This does seem to be a gross underestimate. A 1985 exercise undertaken by a group set up by the Indian defense ministry, comprised of senior military personnel and nuclear establishment heads, projected the cost of a nuclear program with a few hundred missiles and warheads (but apparently without a significant C^{3}I system) and came up with an estimate of Rs 7,000 crores ($1.7 billion). In 1998 rupees, this would amount to Rs 20,000 crores, or $5 billion, today. Assuming that a C^{3}I system, with a relatively large import component—much larger than in the case of missiles or warheads—will cost about the same, the cost of the nuclear weapons program as a whole would work out to $10 billion.

Even on the lowest possible estimates for the C^{3}I system and for a defense system for the nuclear arsenal (with phased array radar and anti-missile and -aircraft batteries), research and development, etc, the figure for a "credible deterrent" works out to Rs 40,000 to Rs 50,000 crores ($10 to 12 billion). The following table lists some of the costs, as compiled by Ram Manohar Reddy, an economist and journalist.

Table 1: Investment Costs of Nuclear Weaponization

	Rs. (in millions)
One reactor to produce plutonium:	7,000
One missile production facility:	5,000
Cost of a 150-bomb arsenal:	6,000
Cost of missiles:	40,250
55 *Prithvis*:	3,850
30 *Agnis*:	15,000
25 *Agni-IIs*:	15,000
16 *Sagarikas*:	6,400
Cost of fitting one IAF squadron:	600
Cost of 3 n-submarines:	120,000
Cost of C³I:	35,250+
Cost of two satellites:	20,000
Cost of radar, missiles, etc:	50,000
to protect airbases/launch sites	
Total:	**280,000**

Source: *Ram Manohar Reddy*, The Hindu. *2 September 1998.*

On an annualized basis, this would be the equivalent of 0.5 to 1 percent of India's GDP—or a rise of 25 to 40 percent over India's current military spending.

All this assumes, quite unrealistically, that there will be no nuclear arms racing, and that the additional costs of operating and maintaining the nuclear arsenal will be more or less negligible, because they will be accommodated within the existing military budget with minor systems modifications. But whether there is an arms race or not cannot be determined by India alone—that would depend on India's adversaries too. If China revives its *Dong Feng-25* development program and actively targets Indian cities, New Delhi would come under enormous pressure to speed up and raise the level of nuclear deployment. The history of the Nuclear Age is nothing if not the story of competitive rivalries, with one adversary raising the level of preparation and threat, "provoking" the other to do the same—a vicious spiral leading to ever-increasing accumulation of weapons.

If India gets sucked into this spiral, as its "Draft Nuclear Doctrine" suggests, it could end up spending, like the former USSR did, more than 1.5 percent of its GDP on nuclear weapons alone. This could be ruinous. India cannot possibly match China in the size or firepower of its nuclear arsenal in the immediate future: China has a thirty-year lead as a nuclear and missile power, and an economy that is three times bigger in absolute size.

As the full costs of deployment unfold, the Indian government, with its meager resources, will be tempted to cut corners on the accuracy, safety, reliability and eventually, the size of its nuclear program, especially of the costly C³I system. This will degrade the strength of the Indian deterrent and especially its second-strike capability. This could become a case of "ramshackle deterrence"—which makes the country vulnerable to a nuclear strike without being able effectively to deter an adversary power. Deployment could thus be a Faustian bargain in every sense of the term, even from a conventional military point of view.

High Opportunity Costs

The Indian government, with a fiscal deficit of the order of six percent of the GDP and a falling ratio of total taxes to GDP, can ill-afford any increase in military spending. Already, the national government's spending on the military is more than double its expenditure on health, education, and other social sectors put together. Indeed, as Amartya Sen has argued, there is a strong case for *reducing* India's existing military expenditures.

The opportunity costs of a nuclear weapons program must not be underrated. The cost of each nuclear bomb corresponds to the cost of building 3,200 modest houses under Indian conditions. The expenditure on each *Agni* missile can finance the running of 13,000 primary health centers, all of which are in state of advanced decay. There is a straight trade-off between a "minimal nuclear deterrent," on the one hand, and universalization of primary education or an improved public health program, on the other.

The costs of a program of manufacturing and deploying nuclear weapons and missiles would prove even more onerous in Pakistan, which has had persistent budget deficits of six to nine percent over the past decade. Pakistan currently spends about five percent of its GDP on the military, more than it does on all development programs *put together*. According to Zia Mian, "In fact, 1990 was the last year when military spending equaled the allocation for the annual development program. Since then, development spending has fallen as compared to military spending."[2] Pakistan's foreign debt today is $32 billion, about the same size as its GDP, and its annual debt-servicing burden runs at $5 billion.

India and Pakistan rank among the lowest of the 174 countries listed by the UN Development Program's Human Development Index: Pakistan's rank in the human development index fell from 120 in 1992 to 138 in 1998, while India's rank fell from 134 in 1995 to 139 in 1998. This is not a function of poverty alone, but involves horrendous neglect and callousness toward basic human needs, as well as distorted public spending priorities. Nuclearization will further distort these priorities, reducing the people's real security.

Table 2: Human Development Indicators for India and Pakistan

	India	Pakistan
Life expectancy in years	61.6	62.8
Infant mortality rate, per 1,000 births	73	95
Child (under 5 years old) mortality, per 1,000 births	111	136
Malnourished children, %	53	38
Without access to safe water, %	19	26
Without access to sanitation, %	71	53
Literacy rate, %	52	38

Source: Human Development Report, 1998, Oxford University Press, Delhi.

NOTES

[1] Stephen I. Schwartz, ed., *Atomic Audit: The Costs and Consequences of U.S. Nuclear Weapons Since 1940* (Washington DC: Brookings Institution Press, 1998).

[2] Zia Mian, "The South Asian Bomb: The Politics of South Asia's Nuclear Crisis" *Medicine & Global Survival* 5.2 (Cambridge, MA: October 1998): 78.

Chapter 8

The Deterrence Delusion: Why Nuclear Weapons Don't Generate Security

Most pro-nuclearists would not even attempt to justify the possession, deployment or production of nuclear weapons on moral grounds. Instead, they are content to make the supposed efficacy of nuclear deterrence the centerpiece of their intellectual-strategic-political case for why their country, or any country, should produce and possess nuclear weapons. They put forward other arguments as well. One particular favorite is that nuclear weapons are a currency, a symbol of power, and as such are politically and diplomatically useful in the world we live in. But since ensuring "national security" is the principal purpose for having such weapons, the most fundamental and enduring justification remains the stock of arguments centered on deterrence. In fact, the case for nuclear weapons is so strongly pivoted on this issue that it stands or falls with the strengths or weaknesses of these arguments.

Advocates of nuclear disarmament understand this so well that the literature uncovering the weaknesses of nuclear-deterrence thinking and practice is truly enormous; it is the most common terrain of arguments against nuclear weapons. A deeper level of critique is possible, but it rarely enters the discourse, for the simple reason that most people opposed to nuclear weapons nonetheless operate within the same paradigm of thinking about national security matters as do pro-nuclearists. They differ simply in rejecting the view that nuclear weapons enhance security; they dispute the proposition that nuclear deterrence is effective.

While this chapter will explore the familiar arguments for and against deterrence that are so critical to the case against nuclear weapons, it will also, albeit briefly, explore the other, deeper level of criticism.

The Problem of Realism

Votaries of nuclear deterrence think the way they do largely because they think about national security and its relationship to the world order in a certain way. This way of thinking has a name in the academic literature of international relations: political realism.[1] The spread of this kind of thinking is so wide among those who think about international political, strategic, or security issues that only a few among the more academically-inclined even recognize that it is just one paradigm among others. As such, its value should be judged only after comparison with the merits and demerits of other ways of understanding the global system, international relations, collective security, etc. But most adherents to realism simply see it as "universal common sense."

The basic postulates that make up this "vision" are as follows:

The global system is anarchic since the absence of an acknowledged world authority or government means there is no supreme seat of power (the role played by the apparatuses of the state within a country) which can maintain order or arbitrate between conflicting interests, values and aims. Thus the world order is a self-help system in which states are the primary actors. They are also to be considered as unitary and rational actors. In effect, the world system is an inter-state system where each state must pursue its own national interest and security objectives, above all (territorial) survival. In order to successfully do this, a state must accumulate power. Power is so important a means for achieving the goals of security or national interests that it can be seen virtually as an end in itself. However, the distribution of power between different states is extremely uneven and therefore the general shape or contours of the world system is determined by only a few states which are "Great Powers."

Thus the world can be described as unipolar, bipolar, or multipolar depending on the number of Great Powers, where multipolarity should be understood as only meaning more than two or three Great Powers but not that many more. It is essentially the interaction between existing Great Powers that gives the world system its shape. The more stable this interaction the more stable the world system. Thus Great Powers necessarily have "global responsibilities" thrust upon them. Longer-term historical changes in this global system are related to the fall of Great Powers and the rise of new ones. Within this inescapable inter-state system which has endured for centuries, ultimately the most important form of power is military power because war is the last resort attempt at decisive arbitration and is itself a recurring human and political phenomenon from which no state or part of the world system can ever finally escape.

The most important way in which relatively weaker states cope with the others having more power than themselves is through the diplomatic game of seeking and establishing alliances with other states, alliances which themselves will shift as relations of power between different states shift. Thus the key priorities for any country involved in this game of "competitive power politics" or "realpolitik" must be, above all, two things—maintain and enhance strong military power, and play the diplomatic game of shifting alliances as skillfully as possible. Obviously, the central mechanism for maintaining stability, security and maximum influence in this anarchic global system is to secure and maintain the appropriate "balances of power." The balance of power, then, is the organizing principle which should guide the behavior of the "national security establishments" of the main state-actors in this world arena of the competitive power game.[2]

After adding whatever qualifications or nuances one might wish to this set of assumptions, this description constitutes the dominant common sense of the strategic community in all the NWSs. Belief in the efficacy and importance of nuclear deterrence flows almost naturally from such a perspective. In the nuclear age, security must be sought in the achievement of *nuclearized* balances of power through the reliance on "stable deterrence." Insofar as nuclear rivalry between countries introduces elements of great uncertainty and arms escalation, the answer to this problem is not to be found in abandoning the trust placed in deterrence and nuclear weapons but in ensuring that this rivalry takes a controlled, predictable, and stable pattern. Diplomatic activity to organize arms control between nuclear rivals is thus a necessary part of the logic imposed by the existence of more than one nuclear regime. Pro-nuclearists, then, will simultaneously pursue (a) the steady upgrading of weapons production; (b) institutionalized arms control between nuclearly equipped rivals; (c) formal and meaningless assurances of their continuing commitment to the goal of eventual global disarmament.

This is not the place for a comprehensive critique of the realist paradigm.[3] Pointing out some of its basic flaws will suffice for our purposes, and perhaps some who are otherwise opposed to nuclear weapons might be stimulated to question and reject the mindset that constitutes its deepest port of anchorage.

Among the conceptual flaws that lie at the heart of the realist paradigm are its mistaken understandings of state, power, and the global system, even though these three are the central concepts on which it constructs its "world view." Indeed, hardcore realists who come mostly from the six or seven professions that make up the "national security establishment"—soldier, diplomat, politician, bureaucrat, scientocrat (active or retired), policy-oriented academic, and journalist—pride themselves on their hard-headed understanding of "state power." Realism understands the state as a "national territorial totality," a cartographic notion of the space the state occupies. This effectively eliminates the distinction between the state (understood in the more sociological and narrow sense of being a set of distinct apparatuses) and the national society in which it is located.[4]

This paves the way almost automatically for seeing the global system as overwhelmingly a set of inter-state relationships, when it is actually much more than this. What we call the global system is a complex web of intersecting, overlapping and interweaving relations of various kinds involving a vast array of actors. These are not just governments or their representative structures and personnel. They are, or can be, transnational corporations (TNCs), markets, religious organizations, banks, media-barons, criminal mafias, insurgency groups, social collectivities like classes and popular movements, and many more. In different contexts, at different times, different actors are primary. International relations are not just about wars, conflicts and what happens *between* states but also about what happens *within* and *across* states and also between, within and across *societies*. Relations are between government and government, state and state (the state is not identical with the government), government and state, society and society, government and society, state and society. International relations are not just inter-state and inter-national, but also about the internationalization of domestic conflicts and the domestication of international conflicts. The same processes of internationalization and domestication also affect social and economic aspirations, cultures, and ideologies.

As the twentieth century draws to a close, the global system is better envisioned as an incredibly complex multi-level and multi-dimensional terrain, in which, more than ever before in its history, the *capitalist* world economy is the force-field of all politics.[5] What usually emerges on the international political arena is not the fulfillment of Great Power ambitions or even the compromises associated with supposed balances of power, but the *unanticipated consequences* and *unintended outcomes* of a complex array of intersecting forces.

Realism's assumption that the state is a unitary and rational actor is, of course, quite untenable. Such assumptions help, though, to gloss over the actual dangers that exist when a country goes openly nuclear. In fact, the decisions and politics that perpetuate a nuclear regime are not the result of straightforward, cool, rational thinking by a supposedly unitary state actor but are, like all other state decisions, partly hostage to the interplay of the variety of domestic forces. The assumption that state decision-makers act rationally not only ignores the reality of internal tensions of all kinds, but also ignores the fact that irrational decisions become more likely in conditions of strong hostility between countries, and therefore in circumstances where there are possible or serious war threats. The conditions of hostility that supposedly give rise to the need for nuclear deterrence are precisely the conditions in which irrationality is most likely to surface.[6]

The belief that the state, for all the practical purposes related to international relations, can be treated as a unitary and rational actor stems from a failure to give adequate conceptual attention to the fact that the state is not just an actor, but also a place or site. As such, domestic politics *must* always intrude via the state into the terrain of foreign policy and international politics; the state cannot escape being the site of internal contending political and social forces.

For the most part, there is no such thing as "objective national interest." Barring rare exceptions, such as the struggle against colonialism or fascism, the state hardly ever expresses a truly national popular will or interest. Most of the time, what the national interest is said to be depends on who is doing the defining, and how and why they are doing so. Definite social forces, groups or sets of individuals, usually the decision-makers and decision-shapers of the foreign policy or national security "establishment," engage in this exercise.

The Neutrality Myth

Realism rests on the standard liberal myth that the state is "socially neutral" when, of course, it has no such property. All states have a distinct social character, or at the very least powerfully institutionalized social (class) biases. Most state elites/managers have, unsurprisingly, a highly *state-centric, elitist* and *outward-oriented* conception of national security. Thus state security, when it is not treated as simply synonymous with national security, is nonetheless seen as its central element. And preserving state security is seen as something "above" the domestic interplay of politics, demanding that its authority, writ, and prestige remain undiminished, no matter which political force occupies government or oversees state functions. The assumption that national security is largely a matter of foreign policy is unavoidable, given the theoretical conflation of the state with a national society, as embodied in the map notion of the state so basic to political realism. Any allowance for the "internal dimension" of security usually refers to the need to preserve (against threats from "subversive" forces) "law and order" and the "unity and integrity" of the state—that is, to maintain the internal writ and authority of the state and preserve the inviolability of the demarcated boundaries that make up the national territorial totality of the state.

If the notion of national security is to be at all serviceable in a meaningful way, it must express the aspirations and needs of the large majority of a country's population. The second half of the twentieth century has been, with all its ups and downs, the Age of Democratization. More than ever before, state elites have had to pay attention to popular aspirations, if only to legitimize and thus stabilize their own elite position and authority. This public pressure goes well beyond what realists mean when they acknowledge, somewhat patronizingly, that "public opinion" has some noteworthy influence. In fact, precisely because popular legitimization of elite rule has become far more important than ever in human history, understandings of national security have had to change. Such understandings have become less elitist and more *popular*, less state-centered and more *society-centered*, less outward-oriented and more *inward-oriented*.

Everywhere, the newer and more relevant goals of national security are ecologically sustainable economic prosperity for all; social cohesion; establishing, preserving, and strengthening the institutions of political liberty; moving progressively toward ever more egalitarian forms of democratization and popular empowerment; reducing, and where possible, eliminating external threats—the domain of traditional foreign policy and security thinking.

Realism is increasingly an intellectual-political barrier to the proper recognition and appreciation of this broadening and deepening of the notion of national security. To put it more starkly: Realism, more than ever before, is a barrier against the recognition of reality and any effort to shape it more humanely.

Even if it could acknowledge these goals as primary, realism's obsession with a one-sided and inadequate conception of power precludes it from charting a course toward achieving them. Realism's ahistorical and aggregative concept of power—as means or resources abstracted from any particular ends—never situates the issue of power where it must *always* be situated—in specific contexts. Power to do *what?* Ask this question, and the "means of power" so routinely valued by realists can be seen as enormously "powerless." Once we ask the question—to the pursuit of what various ends, economic, political, cultural, and ideological can nuclear weapons be the means?—we can easily see the enormous barrenness and powerlessness of these weapons.

While there are disciplines such as historical sociology and political science that have addressed the issue of power with depth and sophistication, conventional international relations and political realism have not. There are different *kinds* of power—different in their mechanisms, agencies and effects—and the relationship between them is not necessarily cumulative or reinforcing. All that realism, neo-realism and neo-liberalism can offer are superficial distinctions between "hard power" and "soft power," which includes matters of ideology, legitimacy, popular sentiment, and elite or public morale. The very distinction between hard and soft power carries forward the standard realist bias that precludes the possibility of grappling with the true complexity of the notion of power.[7]

Realism's big crime is that it effectively reduces the understanding and pursuit of security to the understandings and activities of a very traditional-conventional form of *statecraft*. Precisely because realism has a flawed conception of the kind of entities states are, it simultaneously overestimates and underestimates what states can do.[8] Realism is essentially a manual comprised of two parts. One part provides the language of apologetics and justification for the arrogances and abuses of power carried out by more powerful countries against others in the global arena in the name of stability, order, security, etc. The second part comprises a series of practical guidelines—the *dos* and *don'ts* of a very conventionally understood form of statecraft. While this is certainly useful to a point, it should never be mistaken as the manual of serious security thinking and practice it claims to be. This realist manual was originally produced, refined, and finalized in the US in the fairly short period beginning just before the Second World War and ending after the Cold War had been more or less institutionalized.[9]

Its apologetic function was obvious. It provided a discourse in which US imperialism could be presented as the expression or manifestation of the compulsions an anarchic and disorderly world system imposed on the more powerful countries, who had to try to provide "world order." Though the US was an imperial power like many before it in history, it was not an imperialist one. Where imperialism implied a conceptual focus on the abusive use of power, imperial (or Great Power) status implied a conceptual focus on the "responsibilities" of power. So certainly the US might sometimes abuse its power, but this was, and is, to be understood as an avoidable failure to behave sufficiently responsibly rather than anything intrinsic to US behavior.

Though this realist manual was originally produced in the US, it has become popular in other countries like India. Though of very limited use to smaller and supposedly weaker countries, it has a stronger justificatory and practical value for countries with ambitions to become "major global actors." It is a minor but amusing point that Indian realists who have often prided themselves on their frequent "anti-Americanness" are simply unaware how fundamentally Americanized in origin and character is their mode of strategic thinking.[10]

Since it is the US that will have to take the lead in nuclear disarmament if the goal of a nuclear-free world is finally to be realized, a special responsibility falls to disarmament activists and advocates in that country. In the broad spectrum of those who call for nuclear disarmament and reject deterrence there are different kinds of realists. There are those who remain ardently committed to the preservation of US power and its search for global hegemony, a quest that realism rationalizes. George (Lee) Butler, former head of the Strategic Air Command (SAC), and former US Secretary of State Robert McNamara belong to just this category of realists, however "liberally" they might word or understand their own patriotic aspirations. After full careers dedicated to the pursuit of Great Power status, they suffered what might be called the "retirement syndrome," which afflicts some former nuclearists. They have recognized that not only are nuclear weapons potentially catastrophic and immoral, but that they are utterly irrelevant and inconsequential for the pursuit of US global hegemony. Indeed, Butler has explicitly argued that one major reason why he wants a nuclear-free world is that in such a world the US's comparative power advantages over other rivals, actual and potential, would actually become greater than it is now! Such a cynical justification for the abolition of nuclear weapons can be expected to raise many hackles among the nuclear hawks of other countries, and to make some of them more reluctant to abandon nuclear weapons, even if the US were eventually to do so.

Advocates of nuclear disarmament who do not share such views of a Butler or a McNamara have to present a deeper critique of that mindset. This cannot be done without questioning realist common sense. A constant balancing act is therefore required in the effort to generate the widest possible anti-nuclear sentiment and movement. The very fact that the Butlers and the McNamaras belong to the circle of insiders who have disproportionate influence on official nuclear policies means their voices against nuclearism are valuable and welcome. The *dominant* thrust in any mass anti-nuclear movement must be anti-nuclearism and anti-deterrence, not anti-realism. But because the struggle against nuclear weapons also requires us to struggle against more than just nuclear weapons, i.e. against an unjust world order and those who wish to preserve it as such, there is always a necessary and important place for a critique of the deeper sources of nuclearism, oppression, and unjustified militarism.

The Fallacies of Nuclear Deterrence

The advent of nuclear weapons poses a terrible dilemma for humanity. Is security—real and enduring—possible in the nuclear age? On one side are those who say we have no choice but to "live with nuclear weapons" and that it is possible to do so with confidence. Just as we have lived with other kinds of weapons and continue to strive more or less successfully for security, especially national security, we can do the same with nuclear weapons. On the other side are those who insist there can never be enduring or adequate security except by "living without nuclear weapons" and that therefore there is no choice but to bring about complete, universal, and permanent nuclear disarmament. What has been done by humans, can be undone; indeed, *must* be undone. Moreover, we must do this as rapidly as possible. The longer nuclear weapons exist, the greater the chances of their being used, and the greater the possibility of a nuclear holocaust.

To understand why genuine, authentic security is possible only in a world without nuclear weapons, it is essential to grasp the fundamental difference between conventional and nuclear weapons. Conventional weapons, if peace breaks down, can be used to protect oneself or one's country. But nuclear weapons can never actually be used to directly protect a country or achieve security. One can only hope that possessing nuclear weapons will frighten a rival into not using its own nuclear arsenal. Such is the hope of deterrence thinking.

A state of deterrence is simply a "state of mind," a psychological condition. That is all it is. To believe that deterrence will always work, is to believe in a myth. It is to believe that the people you want deterred, the "enemy" nuclear elite—the people in and out of government who shape or make the decisions regarding nuclear weapons-related activity (including the pressing of the nuclear button)—will always behave as your own national nuclear elite will want them to behave. It is to ignore that the opposing elite is subject to a whole host of military, economic, social, political, and cultural factors, as well as a variety of external and internal tensions and confusions whose effects are never under the control of the supposed deterrer.

Nuclear weapons may deter because of their frightening character. But they can *never* deter *certainly, confidently*, and *enduringly*. Those who believe we must always live with nuclear weapons (perhaps because we can never again become technologically innocent of how to make them) are even prepared to claim that nuclear weapons can deter *permanently*. Deterrence advocates make any or all of these claims. To deter is not the same as deterrence, which is a *conceptualization*, a rationalization or theorization about what nuclear weapons are supposed to be capable of achieving. Nuclear weapons did not create the reality of deterrence; instead, deterrence was invented to cope with the reality of nuclear weapons. The spread of nuclear weapons does not lead to the spread of deterrence-based security, but only to the spread of rationalizations and claims that security has increased. Deterrence doctrines legitimize the existence of nuclear weapons as well as desensitize the public to the reality and dangers of nuclear competition. Deterrence makes nuclear weapons both perdition and salvation, peril and hope. The peril is real; the hope, an illusion.

To rely on deterrence of any sort is to seek peace or stability by generating fear and hostility in the opponent. This heightens mutual tensions. It is not an attempt to bring about greater peace through cooperation or reduction of mutual threats or hostilities but through the very opposite route. That is why efforts at deterring so often break down. The contradiction inherent in deterrence—of tying war avoidance to war preparation, of seeking security through promoting hostility—is not necessarily fatal in the case of conventional weapons and warfare. One can sometimes use conventional weapons to protect oneself and one's country. But security can never be generated if nuclear deterrence breaks down and a nuclear attack or exchange takes place. If the country that suffers a first nuclear strike decides to launch a retaliatory nuclear attack on the aggressor country, this would only be an act of revenge, not of security. It could even push the initiator to launch further attacks.

Whatever security value nuclear weapons may be said to possess resides only in the threat of their use, not in their actual use. But the contradiction inherent in deterrence always raises the prospect of a breakdown and of actual use of nuclear weapons. To rely on nuclear deterrence is thus to place a burden of expectations and hope on nuclear weapons and their possession that is never similarly placed on conventional weapons. It is to believe that nuclear deterrence will always hold for as long as one wants it to, although one can *never control fully* the conditions in which deterrence is supposed to successfully operate. That is why to subscribe to nuclear deterrence as a doctrine or belief system and to pin one's hopes for security on it, is nothing but an *irrational act of faith*.

Pro-nuclearists come in two stripes. There are the crude deterrence thinkers and the sophisticated deterrence thinkers. The first lot simply adhere to nuclear deterrence as a security doctrine without any self-troubled awareness of its inherent illogicality and incoherence. The second group has a clear awareness of the fallacy contained within the effort to rest security on nuclear deterrence. But in spite of this they believe that nuclear deterrence does work, at least reliably enough to make pursuit of security through its operation strategically sensible and desirable. Thus these sophisticated "deterrence worshippers" try impossibly to square the circle. "No, nuclear deterrence deep down doesn't work and we must not rely on it and indeed we must work to achieve global disarmament as quickly as possible. But yes, deterrence does work with enough confidence and for enough time, so we should rely on it. But true, we cannot fully ensure that it will work and not break down, nor can we specify the time frame for when it will work and after which it will not work!"

The Instability of Nuclear Detterence

Unsurprisingly, deterrence enthusiasts, especially the sophisticated variant, are repeatedly seeking to assure the wider public that it is possible to achieve a "stable deterrent posture" vis-à-vis rivals, or in the case of lesser NWSs like India, a "stable minimum deterrent posture." But to believe this, is to fail to understand that once security is sought through the production, possession, and deployment of nuclear weapons, a degenerative dynamic is put into place that makes a mockery of any idea that insecurity will not increase, that there can be a stable deterrent posture or that a country's nuclear weapons system will remain static once some supposed minimum is reached. There are a number of reasons for this. We will list eight.

(1) There is the irrationality that lies at the heart of deterrence and gives rise to what has been called the security-insecurity paradox. Or how the search for security through the generation of hostility is so often counter-productive. Of course, nuclear deterrence has a distinctive and frightening irrationality all its own, which distinguishes it from the lesser problems of non-nuclear deterrence. But in both cases the same principle operates. The existence of a prior hostility, rooted in political differences of a very serious nature, pushes one or both sides to decide military-nuclear deterrence is the way to enhance its own security. But such military-nuclear preparations are themselves the symptoms and expressions of the dismal state of hostility. They should be seen as its insufficiently controlled effects.

Moreover, engaging in such military-nuclear preparations as deterrence requires means threatening the other side with greater insecurity and a greater level of physical and material damage. This can hardly be expected to lessen hostilities, which either remain just as strong or become stronger. When a country goes nuclear, a new kind of tension is created, because the political statement now being made, is that the other side is so serious an enemy as to warrant equipping oneself with the ability to inflict the most horrible kind, and scale, of damage possible. Stable peace and security between erstwhile opponents comes from *removing* the political causes behind the tensions and hostilities, not by sustaining tensions and hostilities—or raising them—through quantitative and qualitative increases in the punishment one can inflict on each other. Deterrence operates at the level of effect, not at the level of cause, and as such cannot be the basis for a genuinely stable peace or security between countries.

(2) Part of the irrationality of nuclear deterrence lies in the very high, almost faultless degree of predictability it demands about an opponent's behavior. This is a demand for repeated, regular, institutionalized, predictability and symmetry in the whole chain of moves and counter-moves by each nuclear "player" in the ensuing politics of nuclearism. But what can assure this in the world in which we live? The answer is obvious—there can be no such assurance.

But as long as one nuclear player or the other seeks to establish the conditions in which it believes that such assured, predictable behavior by the other side will follow, seemingly as a matter of course, then it can easily slide into the pursuit of "compellence." That is to say, the side pursuing such a strategy (which involves certain kinds of nuclear preparations and their associated political implications and signals) believes the other side will be "compelled" to follow a pattern set by, and therefore "controlled" by the first player. Not only is nuclear arms escalation written into this "compellence" script, but nuclear tensions are even more heightened. The "certainties" of compellence are substituted for the "uncertain certainties" of "normal deterrence." The US pursued such a compellence strategy as part of its efforts to "stabilize" and "control" (to its own "advantage," of course) the nuclear arms race of the late '70s and '80s.

Either way, of course, there is no certainty that deterrence will hold, but compellence is a more aggressive form of nuclear behavior in which the search for "political advantage" is more pronounced and systematic and where the likelihood of brinkmanship politics is greater. There is no natural firebreak between the instability of deterrence-based nuclear behavior (which is dangerous enough) and the more dangerous instability of compellence-based nuclear behavior.

(3) Once a country seeks security through nuclear deterrence, to be effective, it must be *credible*. The possibility of its use must be real. An opponent will not be deterred if it believes that the deterrer will never use its nuclear weapons. Thus the *capability* and the *will* of the deterring country must not be doubted. The "enemy" should be certain that its nuclear opponent will use nuclear weapons if pushed to the brink, or at least uncertain whether or not the opponent will use them, but never certain that it will not. This capability and will cannot be shown once and left at that. In the face of all kinds of challenges and uncertainties—technological, military, political, etc.—the capability must be constantly updated and the will must be periodically displayed, regularly "fine-tuned" and available for showing in a variety of circumstances. This creates powerful pressure for the generation and sustenance of both an enduring politics of nuclear-related hostility—including nuclear brandishing and brinkmanship—and of arms-racing between nuclearly-equipped rivals or opponents.

(4) Since deterrence is a concept applied to conflictual situations whose sources of distrust are not nuclear weapons themselves, these weapons leave untouched the basic sources of that hostility. Political instability is built into the rivalry and confrontation. This also reinforces the pressure for arms-racing, which in turn sustains nuclear tensions at higher levels of danger and mutual devastation should there be a nuclear breakdown. What happened in Europe between the US and USSR was a classic example of this. The West argued that NATO's stockpile and willingness to use nuclear weapons deterred the USSR from attacking Western Europe. Between 1945 and 1954 it was a few atomic bombs that were said to have done the deterring. By the '60s, the same result was now supposedly being achieved by the deployment of dozens of ICBMs

and submarine-launched ballistic missiles (SLBMs). In the '70s and '80s, the same goal of deterring the USSR had to be achieved through deployment of thousands of warheads.

The Western perception of a Russian danger to Europe changed in the late '80s and especially after 1990 not because of the success of deterrence, but because of a transformation in the political relationship between East and West. Nuclear deterrence did not reduce mutual distrust and fears. Mutual distrust and fears were reduced first and thus rendered deterrence less relevant. The classic paradox in seeking stable deterrence is this: "the conditions which are thought to make it necessary to apply deterrence guarantee that it will be unstable. The extent to which deterrence is genuinely stable is the extent to which it is unnecessary." Britain and France can have a stable deterrent equation between themselves precisely because it is unnecessary for them to have such an equation!

(5) The first principle of effective nuclear deterrence is the survivability of a retaliatory force, or its measure of invulnerability to a first strike by a nuclearly-armed adversary. This is called establishing a "credible second-strike capacity." Unfortunately, the survivability of one's nuclear weapons system is not a stable affair. It is affected by the size and quality of an enemy's nuclear forces and the size and quality of an initial attack. To counter this, one's own weapons system and its controllers push for "survivability enhancing practices" such as high alert deployment, launch-on-warning, hardened silos, constantly airborne bomb/missile-carrying planes, etc. The extreme version of this thinking is, in short, the "use them or lose them" principle.

As it is, technological advances in either the range and accuracy of delivery systems, in warhead capabilities, in surveillance and detection, targeting, and intelligence gathering, all add their own pressures to both quantitative and qualitative arms-racing. Fear of possible technological advances by one's rival reinforces the tendency to maintain a certain level of redundancy in one's own production levels, as compensation for an unforeseeable, but possible, comparative "disadvantage." The tendency toward redundant levels of production is further reinforced by the fact that within a country's nuclear elite there will never be a consensus or agreement on what constitutes a country's "adequate" or "minimum" deterrent capacity. Thus the safest way out is to go along with the "extreme" nuclearists, because if they are satisfied, then the lesser demands of the "moderate" nuclearists are more than covered in passing, as it were.

Precisely because one's own "minimum" is contingent on the opponent's level of preparations, there is no such thing as a "stable minimum posture." A "minimum" is always a moving, never a fixed, position. This is confirmed by the whole history of the arms race between the US and former USSR, between East and West. It is only after the end of the Cold War and the possible emergence of universal arms restraint measures like the CTBT and FMCT that there may now be upper limits to the quantitative and qualitative nuclear arms race, which might circumscribe nuclear ambitions in countries like India and Pakistan.

But even after acceding to such treaties, there is still enough space in which to carry on a dangerous-enough arms race. Moreover, unless the existing momentum is significantly strengthened, there is always the danger of the collapse of the restraint regime.

(6) For deterrence to hold, one has to be confident that one can inflict what is called "unacceptable damage" on the adversary in a second-strike. So as well as trying to retain an adequate second-strike capacity after a devastating first strike by the opponent, NWSs had to wonder whether or not their adversary would feel that the damage inflicted in such a second strike was indeed unacceptable—and therefore a deterring factor. So it was that a morally debased, but nonetheless very serious, debate emerged: what would constitute "unacceptable damage" for the adversary? Did authoritarian regimes like the USSR and China have higher levels of willingness to suffer than democratic regimes like the US, Britain, and France? Did this then not require asymmetrically higher levels of nuclear arms on one side of the Cold War face-off? Would this not cause problems in mutual perceptions/suspicions about intentions and capabilities, not to mention complicate arms control efforts?

To arrive at some figure of what might constitute "acceptable" or "bearable" damage for the USSR, the nuclear elite of the US noted that the USSR had suffered 20-25 million dead in the Second World War and had three-quarters of its industrial capacity destroyed. This then became a kind of benchmark, so that unacceptable damage to the USSR was calculated as the destruction of at least that much of its industry capacity and perhaps a third of its population. But this was still only conjecture. France and Britain also had to make calculations of what might deter the Soviets from a nuclear attack on it, for there was always the doubt about US willingness to go to nuclear war or even threaten nuclear war for the sake of Britain or France. France's President Charles De Gaulle, as justification for constructing an independent nuclear arsenal, once openly declared that the US would not sacrifice New York for the sake of Paris.

So the "proportional," or the "tear-off-your-arm," theory of deterrence came into being. Maybe Britain and France couldn't really inflict unacceptable damage to the USSR in a second strike, but it was still worthwhile for them to use nuclear weapons as a deterrent, because "tearing-off-an-arm" of the USSR was good enough. But if this was good enough, then wasn't this actually "unacceptable damage"? In which case, what was the point of the US or USSR having so much stronger an arsenal? In reality, the supposedly central question of what constitutes "unacceptable damage" has no real answer. Having first decided that nuclear deterrence works and therefore nuclear weapons must be acquired, the nuclear elites found that they could not really decide how much was enough. No country was certain whether they would retain a credible second-strike capacity if the adversary launched a massive first strike. No country was certain that what it could then inflict would be unacceptable damage to its principal rival(s), and therefore whether it could confidently rely on the nuclear deterrent. So it was safest to keep trying to expand one's destructive capacity.

(7) Once nuclear weapons become tools of foreign policy, restricting the range of goals that these "deterrent producing weapons" should be used for becomes difficult. The realist mindset only encourages such a slide. Once upon a time, pro-nuclearists only justified the possession of nuclear weapons with the claim it would deter a nuclear attack or nuclear blackmail by another country. They did not stay satisfied with merely this goal, and other goals and justifications emerged and were sought to be popularized. Sometimes new concepts of deterrence, such as "extended deterrence," were forged to go with these new goals.

Now nuclear weapons are required not just to deter attack or blackmail, but as a general tool providing "foreign policy support," "damage-limitation capability," "escalation control," "prevention of conventional war," "global prestige," and even "promotion of eventual nuclear disarmament." When such an enormous burden of responsibility and expectations has been placed on nuclear weapons, no wonder that they have been contemptuously referred to by anti-nuclearists as the new God of *realpolitik* and "nuclear strategists" as the new "God-worshippers."

During the Cold War arms race, the sophistry of simulation studies, computer gaming, and systems analysis applied to arms procurement and deployment, did nothing to cover up the basic moral and intellectual vacuity at the heart of it all. The supposed sophistication of nuclear strategic thinking is really the search for a Holy Grail, the indulgence in a "strategic easy fix" whose drugging effect on the mind and heart is sought to be disguised by complicated levels of argument (gaming scenarios) at more abstracted levels.

(8) Every country that believe nuclear deterrence will work, nonetheless has to ask itself an unavoidable question. What if deterrence breaks down? In that case, a nuclear exchange or war has to be brought to an end as quickly as possible. That is to say, the capacity to fight a "limited nuclear war" must be established. But building such a capacity at nuclear warfighting by making a "limited nuclear war" more feasible itself undermines the efficacy of deterrence. This "what if" question haunts and shadows all nuclear strategic thinking. Since it is supposedly a hard-headed lack of sentimentality that led to the advocacy of nuclear weapons production and deployment in the first place, a hard-headed, unsentimental "what if" cannot be ignored or unasked. But it simply has no satisfactory answer. This only highlights the deficiency of another kind of answer to another kind of question. *What are nuclear weapons useful for?* Deterrence is not the answer!

How Reliable? Has Deterrence Really Worked?

What has traditionally been called strategic discourse is always strongly speculative in character; nuclear strategic discourse is even more so. Since there has so far (thankfully) been no nuclear war, one cannot cross-check and decisively adjudicate between arguments about the claimed efficacy or inefficacy of nuclear weapons and deterrence by using any real data. The necessarily speculative nature of deterrence arguments enables both sides in the strategic nuclear debate to hold onto their original positions with a fair degree of complacency.

But this does not mean that both sides have an equally plausible case, or that an overall judgment cannot be made on the basis of a "balance of plausibility." The fact is, there are more and less sensible ways of speculating. What is it that distinguishes undisciplined, fanciful, and irresponsible forms of strategic speculation on nuclear security from more sober, informed, and disciplined forms?

At least two things, which is partly why the anti-nuclear position is much stronger and more sensible. When no accepted external criteria or data exists by which one can adjudicate between arguments and counter-arguments, an even higher premium must be placed on the internal coherence of an argument. Here the pro-nuclearists confront a fatal and inescapable dilemma, for they cannot get away from the ingrained incoherence and irrationality of nuclear deterrence as a security doctrine. They can, of course, claim that logic isn't everything. That their losing the logical argument or case does not mean they have lost the political argument. Politics, they might say, is about power, not logic. But since they themselves argue that it is *politically rational* to have nuclear weapons, the existence of a logical irrationality lodged within their foundational concept of deterrence greatly weakens their claim.

Historical evidence also helps distinguish the plausibility or reasonableness of one case against the other. Here too, the anti-nuclearist position rejecting deterrence has shown itself to be the stronger. But this is not conceded by pro-nuclearists, who cling to the "long peace" argument—a historically counterfactual claim that the existence of nuclear weapons has assured the long post-war peace across the political-ideological divide in Europe since 1945.

Generally three claims are made. First: nuclear deterrence prevented the outbreak of nuclear war between the US and USSR in Europe and elsewhere. Second: nuclear deterrence also prevented the outbreak of conventional war in Europe between East and West. Since such a war, given the awesome power, reach, and ambitions of the two principal protagonists, would have been tantamount to World War Three, nuclear weapons prevented the outbreak of such a world war with or without nuclear exchanges as part of it. Third: the absence of even local or regional wars in Europe can also be attributed to the efficacy of the nuclear stand-off.

There is, of course, no way of decisively refuting these claims. But there are plausible ways of arguing to show that simultaneous events—the existence of nuclear weapons and the absence of World War Three, a nuclear exchange, or a local or regional war—should not be mistaken as necessarily having a relationship of cause and effect. Three basic explanatory perspectives are offered for the long peace. First is that which credits nuclear deterrence. Nuclear weapons were not only necessary, but also sufficient, for bringing about the peace. The second perspective argues that nuclear weapons were among a set of factors that ensured the long peace. That is to say, nuclear weapons were a necessary, but *not* sufficient condition. Lastly, the third perspective argues the long peace was determined by a whole set of non-nuclear factors; nuclear weapons and their deterrence capacity were irrelevant.

The third position is far and away the most plausible. The first two arguments suffer from a grave flaw. Having made the presence of nuclear weapons "necessary" for the avoidance of World War Three, it must follow that in their absence, the long peace breaks down and World War Three takes place. In effect they have made nuclear weapons a crucial hinge in explaining the absence of war. This is a single-factor explanation of why world wars take place, even if the second position would also ascribe similar explanatory and causal status to some other "necessary" factors taken separately and individually. This is an absurdly implausible explanation for why world wars take place. World wars neither "happen" nor are they "avoided" because of the presence or absence of a *single factor* such as nuclear weapons. World wars take place because of a whole *complex* of factors operating in an extremely turbulent wider context. The processes that can lead to a world war depend on a *combination* of structural and contingent factors and causes. But so desperate are the champions of nuclear deterrence to prove its worth that they perforce resort to sloppy and superficial forms of historical explanation and argument.

As for the claim that nuclear weapons prevented local/regional wars in Europe, it was not the presence of nuclear weapons, but the freezing of the political status quo during the Cold War era, that made this possible. This glacis was itself the consequence of all the *multiple* factors and causes that in complex combination were behind the making and sustenance of Cold War structures. This is precisely why when the Cold War glacis melted, bitter conventional warfare broke out in the ex-USSR and ex-Yugoslavia, even though nuclear weapons (albeit a smaller number) remain in Europe. If there has not been any serious threat of internecine warfare in the Western part of Europe, this is attributable not to the presumed potency of nuclear deterrence, but to the dramatic changes in Western Europe after 1945. With the emergence of the European Economic Community (EEC) and then the European Union (EU), this part of the world seems to be moving into a historic post-Clausewitzian era, in which major war becomes a thing of the past.

Pro-nuclearists irresponsibly cite the historical fact of the absence of nuclear war since 1945 as evidence that deterrence works. But when the historical record does not provide latitude for such self-comforting interpretations, they ignore or downplay it. Thus, it is a historical fact that during the Cold War both sides engaged in an arms race that led to the accumulation of enormous overkill arsenals and capacities, enough to destroy the world thirty or forty times over. This was utterly irrational behavior! Is there any *sensible* notion of deterrence or security that can explain such insanity? In the face of this actual historical evidence, which directly challenges the rationality claims of deterrence-related behavior, what do pro-nuclearists have to say? The last thing they admit is that this arms race revealed, in a particularly stark manner, the *degenerative and unstable dynamic* contained in deterrence and its associated preparations and practices.

The Myth of Nuclear Blackmail

There is more historical evidence, and little of it can be said to bolster the case of the pro-nuclearists. There is no plausible evidence to show that even a single case of attempted nuclear blackmail ever succeeded in its aims.[11] So much for the supposed efficacy of nuclear weapons as a foreign policy tool! This testifies, of course, to the remarkably astrategic character of such weapons. But the fact that certain nuclear elites have repeatedly attempted such blackmail and that on various occasions the actual use of nuclear weapons has been seriously contemplated itself greatly weakens the claims made for the effectiveness of deterrence.[12]

From Afghanistan to Vietnam, to Suez, to Algeria, and to the Malvinas, nuclear weapons have not deterred non-nuclear countries from fighting and even succeeding against NWSs. Nor, as the Ussuri River border conflict between China and the USSR showed, did the possession of nuclear weapons prevent conventional military conflict between two nuclearly-equipped rivals. Indian and Pakistani policymakers would do well to take note of this point. There is no historical reason to believe that some level of insurgency and conventional military strife between the two countries will not continue, regardless of the nuclear weapons they possess. Kargil is proof of this.

The irresponsible and manipulative manner in which the Indian nuclear elite treats the fact of historical controls on strategic speculation reflects, of course, a general disease among nuclear elites everywhere. But it is nonetheless worth noting. What after all is the historical record of nuclear threats to India that might justify it going nuclear? Those who seek to construct such a case have to stress the China threat. But herein lies the rub. They cannot take recourse to the *actual* historical record to cite examples of belligerent nuclear behavior by China against India, because there are no such examples. Indeed, China, unlike the US or Russia, has never exercised nuclear blackmail against any country. Indian nuclearists cannot deny this historical fact. They cannot deny the historical fact that India has lived comfortably with the Chinese bomb for thirty-four years. They cannot deny the historical record of the ineffectiveness of all nuclear blackmail attempts, nor the military-political defeats of NWSs by NNWSs.

All they can do to justify Indian acquisition of nuclear weapons is to refer to *abstract possibilities*, such that China might win a future conventional war through deployment of nuclear blackmail, or that it might seek diplomatic leverage against India through its nuclear arsenal. In other words, justification is sought through historically undisciplined speculation about future possibilities that have no foundation in actual patterns of Chinese behavior. Perhaps the most striking example of the contempt that Indian hawks show for historically grounded possibilities and probabilities, is the way they tackle the following question: what about a possible Chinese nuclear attack on India after it has declared itself to be a NWS, but has not yet produced or deployed a credible second-strike capacity against China?

Here, the standard answer is that the historical record indicates that China will not engage in any such attack if India does not provoke it by threatening Tibet, which New Delhi has no intention of ever doing. China is a cautious, pragmatic country and has shown itself to be so in regard to its nuclear behavior. This judgment is quite correct. But the irony of the argument is stark. The actual historical record is cited to explain away the fear that China might launch a pre-emptive nuclear attack, even when India provokes China by going ahead to build a weapons system in part directed against that country. But this same historical record of Chinese nuclear non-belligerence is contemptuously disregarded in order to explain why New Delhi must go nuclear for fear of the abstract possibility that China might in future attack or blackmail it. These jumps between the use of arguments that are historically grounded in some serious way, and those that are not, whenever it suits the bomb lobby, is a standard technique and trope of pro-nuclearists everywhere.

If the history of nuclear brandishing, brinkmanship, and near-use by some NWSs was not warning enough about the danger of nuclear weapons, the long history of accidents related to these weapons should be. Pro-nuclearists have, unsurprisingly, always made light of such matters. Isn't it true that after 1945 there has been no nuclear outbreak whether by design, miscalculation, or accident? Nothing will convince such die-hard believers in the "magic" of deterrence, except when a disaster happens. This is not an unusual reflex. Before the Three Mile Island accident, nuclear power lobbyists and advocates repeatedly assured a wider public that the chances of a reactor catastrophe were negligible and that nuclear power generation had been made safe. Before the 1985 *Challenger* shuttle accident, similar extravagant reassurances were given about space launch safety.

Only after the Three Mile Island, Bhopal, and Chernobyl tragedies did serious study and theorization begin about the dilemmas and dangers involved in these hazardous technologies. Those in control, and supportive, of the development and maintenance of nuclear weapons systems have always had strong reasons to deny that accidents pose a serious problem. But the accumulating evidence of fifty years has badly damaged the credibility of their safety claims. Contemporary "organization theory" argues that organizations (and organizations, not statespeople or states, actually control nuclear weapons systems) function within a severely bounded, limited form of rationality.

According to this theory, organizations have three characteristics.[13] They show "interactive complexity," which means they have many interrelated, but unplanned, interactions not easily comprehensible. This is because the organization's various units operate according to routines and standard procedures and rules, not according to individually reasoned decisions. They have "tight coupling" systems that are highly time-dependent and have invariant production sequences. The system has little slack or flexibility. Add to these two structural properties the third trait, that there will always be conflicting objectives within an organization, and you have a recipe for the "normality of accidents" and the "limits of safety." Indeed, even the ability of organizations to learn from their mistakes is limited.

Whatever one's views about the strengths and weaknesses of such theories, the physical record of accidents is deeply disturbing. Shaun Gregory details 224 accidents of various types concerning nuclear weapons systems. He classifies them in four ways. In Group 1 were accidental, unauthorized, or possible detonations of a weapon. Group 2 covers accidental detonation without war risk, but with radioactive contamination. Group 3 refers to accidents to vehicles carrying nuclear weapons. Group 4 refers to other significant accidents. In Group 1, Gregory says there were at least ten such accidents. This does not include the 1954 event in North Carolina when a nuclear bomb accidentally fell off a plane and five of its six safety mechanisms against detonation failed.[14]

Most such knowledge of accidents comes from declassified information from the US, the most open and democratic of the NWSs in this regard. But Russia has had its share of accidents as well. On the night of September 26, 1983, a Russian army officer and software engineer, Stanislav Petrov, was on duty at a surveillance center near Moscow. "Suddenly the screen in front of me turned bright red… An alarm went off… The computer showed that the Americans had launched a nuclear strike against us." Petrov's orders were to pass the information up the chain of command to the then Secretary General Yuri Andropov. Within minutes a massive counterattack could have been launched. Petrov disobeyed procedure and reported a false alarm. A computer error was later discovered. But Petrov lost his job for disobedience.[15]

On January 25, 1995, a Norwegian scientific rocket to study the Aurora Borealis was mistaken for Trident sea-launched warheads. The mistake lasted eight minutes—only two minutes away from the launch of a nuclear missile. The Russian Ambassador in Oslo had been told of the rocket launch, but this information did not make its way up to the top Soviet leadership. If this has been the record of the nuclear superpowers, what reason is there to believe that the "accident factor" or "miscalculation factor" will not be as serious, if not more so, in countries like India and Pakistan, which are technically less sophisticated and whose organizational structures are, if not less sophisticated, at least as unsophisticated?

Ramshackle Deterrence

Little Reliable in the Disaster-prone Sub-continent.

On January 11, 1999, an Avro transport aircraft belonging to India's Defense Research & Development Organization (DRDO) crashed thirty-seven miles from Chennai, killing all eight men on board. This was a major setback to India's effort at fabricating an Airborne Surveillance Platform (ASP), itself part of the country's program to develop an Airborne Early Warning (AEW) system (or eye-in-the-sky).[1]

The airplane, which crashed during a "radar-checking exercise," was a "technology demonstrator," fitted with a rotodome containing sophisticated radars and other surveillance equipment. It was to act as a major "force multiplier" for the Indian Air Force (IAF), giving its fighter pilots twenty minutes' warning to take off and intercept any intruding enemy aircraft—in place of the present three minutes.

The ASP, to be the centerpiece of the AEW, was developed as an indispensable part of the effort at "credible nuclear weapons delivery" by combat aircraft, and at creating a command and control center that a future nuclear strike force could use. Four of the eight killed were the DRDO's early warning system experts. The crash was a body blow to their project.

The accident, caused by the unhinging and collapse of the rotodome, epitomizes in some ways the disaster-prone character of a good deal of Indian (and Pakistani) military, as well as civilian physical infrastructure and hardware, marked as it is by frequent accidents, component failures, substandard designs, poor maintenance, and unsafe operational practices. This raises disturbing questions about the operation of any kind of mutual deterrence equation, indeed the very viability of an Indian and Pakistani deterrent posture.

The sub-continent is notorious for poor engineering capabilities, even in areas where the science has been mastered. Substandard manufacturing practices, which lead to a high occurrence of defects, are rampant in Indian and Pakistani industries, especially in defense production factories, which are shielded from public scrutiny and safety audits. India and Pakistan have among the lowest indices in physical infrastructure development. There are over one hundred prolonged power failures or brownouts a year in virtually every district of India's capital, one of the world's four most polluted and mismanaged cities.

Throughout India and Pakistan, industry and services are afflicted by mismanagement and poor maintenance practices, leading to mishaps and failures. India's military hardware is not immune to this. For instance, between April 1991 and March 1997, the Indian Air Force (IAF) witnessed 187 accidents and 2,729 "incidents," in which 147 aircraft were destroyed and 63 pilots, most of them young, lost their lives. The IAF lost close to eight squadrons. In financial terms this loss exceeds over Rs. 4,000 crore.[2] This works out to about $1 billion, or a tenth of India's annual military budget, and roughly *four-fifths* of the IAF annual budget. Of the 187 accidents during this period, 130 involved fighter jets, most of them in the MiG series.

Among the most accident-prone planes flown by the IAF is the MiG-21, known as the IAF's "workhorse." "I pray for him every time he takes off," a MiG-21 test pilot's wife is quoted as saying about her husband.[3] Over forty percent of IAF accidents are caused by technical defects which, officials say, are primarily attributable to substandard spares. In the past six years, for instance, seventeen helicopters and seven transport planes were lost in accidents.[4]

Little quality control exists for spare parts in the Indian military. Many are bought from dubious arms dealers and firms that are blacklisted. Newspapers have reported "a major racket" in the purchase of spares, "especially for transport planes and helicopters, compromising flight safety and operational readiness."[5] Often, the armed services are unable to obtain basic design data from the manufacturer and hence cannot do enough modification, repairs, or retrofitting. The services lack a developed system for reporting and analyzing accidents and failures. They do hold courts of inquiry when major accidents occur. But these are usually manned by non-experts.[6]

In the past, a number of shady arms deals were foisted upon the Indian armed forces by corrupt politicians and bureaucrats. For instance, after the purchase of *Vijayanta* tanks in the '60s, they were found to be defective and could not be taken to the battlefront.

During the '80s, the Indian army procured supposedly new and expensive Combat Engineering Tractors, only to discover they were second-hand British army rejects. The notorious Westland helicopters, considered unfit to fly, were similarly imposed upon the IAF as part of a political deal between Margaret Thatcher and Rajiv Gandhi. These had to be junked.[7]

Stories abound in India and Pakistan about military equipment not working, subversion of quality standards, breach of contracts, peddling and abuse of influence, vast magnitudes of bribery, etc. It seems reasonable to assume that in an extremely corrupt society and government, levels of graft would be especially high in those sectors that are largely exempt from the scrutiny of the parliament and the citizenry.

A 1996 directive from Air Headquarters saying that "performance of the squadrons in actual flying aspects would not be assessed" offers an instance of the Indian armed services' violation of their own performance standards. Leading experts commented: "Had a war broken out in 1997, most Indian Air Force aircraft would have taken to the skies without having undergone a prior inspection for war preparedness throughout the previous year."[8]

Besides, there are generic problems arising from a poor culture of safety in India and Pakistan. Both are disaster-prone societies, marked by high rates of accidents and mishaps, sloppy precautionary design and planning, little disaster forecasting, poor emergency procedures, and undeveloped relief-provision infrastructures. Many Indians and Pakistanis routinely die in stampedes, train collisions, road accidents, sinking of ferries, or in construction mishaps.

India and Pakistan are among the world's largest recipients of toxic waste, junked ships (for shipbreaking), and unsafe technologies and products. They have among the lowest standards on food safety, environmental quality, occupational safety, and public health anywhere. The frequency of industrial accidents in India is estimated to be four times higher than in the US. Fatalities in road accidents in India (as a proportion of the number of vehicles on the road) is ten times higher than in the OECD countries, and in Pakistan thirteen times higher.[9]

The important point about a generally poor safety culture is simply that if Indian and Pakistani engineers fail to control and reduce the frequency of mishaps in relatively less complex and loosely "coupled" systems such as road traffic, then they do not inspire much confidence that they will be able to safely handle highly complex, "tightly coupled" systems such as nuclear weapons and C^3I structures.

Both India and Pakistan have witnessed major accidents in military installations and ordnance depots. In April 1988, a huge ammunition depot at Ojhri, near Islamabad, blew up, killing more than a thousand people and injuring many more.

India's nuclear power program, run by the same agency—the DAE (Department of Atomic Energy)—that is responsible for making nuclear bombs, has a remarkably poor safety record. One of its worst accidents involved the 1994 collapse of a safety system, no less—the containment dome of a nuclear reactor under construction. (The dome is supposed to prevent radioactivity releases into the atmosphere in case of a reactor accident).

Poor safety culture is bound to affect the working of all the hardware and software involved in any possible C^3I systems India and Pakistan may build in the future. Their present warning and detection technology is grossly inefficient and unreliable. For instance, in December 1995, a large transport aircraft carrying firearms entered Indian airspace across the western border without authorization or warning. Not only was it not intercepted; it was not even properly detected. There was no coordination between the civilian and military authorities involved. The plane crash-landed at Purulia, in West Bengal, over 600 miles from the western border, before its crew was apprehended.

In late May 1997, an IAF MiG-25 fighter plane was reported to have intruded into Pakistani airspace at an altitude of 65,000 feet and a speed of Mach 2. The Pakistan government believed that the breaking of the sound barrier by the MiG was deliberate: its own air force has no aircraft that can reach such a high cruising altitude.

Indian and Pakistani missiles and warheads also pose their own safety problems. Many of these have not been, and are unlikely to be resolved, given the clandestine nature of nuclear and missile programs, and official anxiety to avoid detection and publicity (especially about technical details). For instance, the *Prithvi* missile and the second stage of the *Agni* missile both use highly corrosive liquid fuel. This is extremely difficult to handle, and highly flammable.

Again, it is far from clear if India conducted, or was in a position to conduct the standard "one-point safety" tests for nuclear warheads. (Pakistan probably lacks the capacity). In the absence of such tests, the likelihood of accidental detonation of a nuclear bomb during fabrication, transportation, installation, or flight must be presumed to be relatively high. If there ever was a case of ramshackle deterrence, of deterrence breaking down under the weight of its own practitioners' incompetence, it is likely to be found in India and Pakistan.

NOTES

[1] See "8 killed as defense plane crashes," *The Hindu* (New Delhi) 12 January 1999. Also "8 die as Avroo aircraft crashes near Chennai: DRDO project suffers major setback," *The Hindustan Times* (New Delhi) 12 January 1999.

[2] Wilson John, "Air Force fighters turn pilot-killers," *The Pioneer* (New Delhi) 10 November 1998.

[3] John.

[4] Wilson John, "Dubious deals imperil IAF fighters," *The Pioneer* (New Delhi) 9 December 1998.

[5] John, " Dubious."

[6] Wilson John, "Kalam file nails engine malaise," *The Pioneer* (New Delhi) 11 November 1998.

[7] Rajesh Ramachandran, "Serve and lobby: how the deals are swung," *The Hindustan Times* (New Delhi) 10 January 1999.

[8] Reported by Dinesh Kumar, "IAF planes skipped war preparedness tests," *The Times of India* (New Delhi) 8 February 1999.

[9] Compiled from *World Road Statistics 1998* (Geneva: International Road Federation, 1998). Also interview with Dinesh Mohan, professor of biomedical engineering at the Indian Institute of Technology, Delhi, 6 February 1999.

The India-Pakistan Face-Off

Apart from technical weaknesses, both the Indian and Pakistani nuclear programs are even less subject to public scrutiny and criticism than those of the US, Russia, Britain and France. In the absence of public monitoring of safety efforts, the chances are greater that bureaucratic and military interests will dominate. In Pakistan, it seems that the weight of the military in nuclear decision-making will be even greater and less constrained by a more safety conscious civilian authority. In fact, many things in Pakistan combine to put a higher premium on the possibility of miscalculation or accident. Pakistan is much more likely to disperse deployment and decentralize control, thus raising the chances of unauthorized use in particular. The unfavorable asymmetry of its weapons system vis-à-vis India's create a greater fear of an Indian first strike. Then there is Pakistan's rejection of the No First Use principle and the relatively greater dominance of the military in politics.

Neither India nor Pakistan have either the geographical distance that the US and Russia have from each other, nor the prolonged period of time they have had to learn from innumerable false warnings. At the beginning of the Cold War, the superpowers had many hours to determine the truth and falsity of warnings. In the '60s, ICBM flight time still allowed for about a half-hour to react to alarms. When, in the '80s, some missiles were deployed off each other's coasts, allowing just ten minutes flight time, both countries had accumulated years of experience in dealing with each other's arsenals and with deficiencies in their own warning systems. They had agreed to dozens of CBMs, crisis-handling protocols and procedures. But from the start, once missiles are deployed, India and Pakistan will have much smaller time margins for correcting errors. India, Pakistan, and China all have contiguous borders. Flight times are short, especially between India and Pakistan. Finally, domestic unrest could produce detonations, accidental or otherwise, in a variety of scenarios, from faction fighting within the military, to civil strife in the country.[16]

If there is one obvious lesson to be learned from the Cold War standoff, it is that the likelihood of use of nuclear weapons is always greatest between adversaries at, or near, war. The Cold War remained a Cold War, and for reasons, some of which have been detailed earlier, which made a direct confrontation unlikely. Even so, there were close calls. It is between rivals where the likelihood of a "hot" war is the greatest, that the chances of use are the greatest. If the country that has nuclear weapons feels its national-territorial survival to be endangered, even by opponents who do not have nuclear weapons, the possibility of use also becomes greater.[17] In any such face-off between nuclear rivals that have a history of hot wars between them, matters become even more fragilely poised when one side perceives itself to be strongly "disadvantaged" in regard to the mutual nuclear and military balance. This is precisely what Pakistan feels with respect to India.

It is an asymmetry that Indian talk of a "minimum deterrent" does nothing to alter. This is a "minimum" that will be calculated and pursued with respect to China—not Pakistan—leaving aside for the moment the fact that India is not able to quantify this minimum. Both Indian strategists and the BJP government ruling at the end of 1999 have stated as much, in reaction to the US government's call that India declare precisely what it means by a minimum. This is not possible to quantify once and for all, for reasons already given—namely, that it is a moving position whose point of temporary rest depends upon China's nuclear capacities at any given time. Of all the NWSs, China is the only one that has not significantly reduced the size of its arsenal over the last decade, and has left open the prospect of quantitative expansion of its arsenal, if it believes that changed circumstances require it.[18]

Such a state of affairs does not bode well for Indian prospects for establishing a "stable minimum" deterrent. Even without a submarine-based nuclear-tipped missile force, India may over the next decade develop missiles with the range to hit some of China's population centers.[19] But this is still well short of having an assured second-strike capability against China. At the same time, any notion of an Indian minimum, even a conservatively estimated one, will still be far in excess of the Pakistan arsenal. A Pakistani capacity to produce a survivable second-strike capacity against a massive Indian first strike is more than fifteen, if not twenty, years away. For all this time, Pakistan will be presented with a "use them or lose them" scenario regarding its own missile strength in the face of India's capacity to "decapitate" Pakistan or launch a massive first strike at its military-nuclear infrastructure. Once the two countries openly deploy their weapons, they enter a zone of considerable nuclear tension and danger.

Moreover, no Chinese leadership can remain sanguine in the face of determined Indian efforts to eventually have a triadic pattern of deployment, even if it falls short of building a credible second-strike capacity. All recent accounts indicate that this is what New Delhi currently has in mind. Once India has missiles that can hit China, the latter has to factor India into its nuclear operational and targeting strategy. At this point, China may explore the issue of a closer nuclear relationship with Pakistan, especially if Pakistan has developed a nuclear capacity that can do great damage to India.

Thus the prediction for the medium- and long-term indicate that severe political tensions will remain in South Asia, and the India-Pakistan face-off will be the dominant and most dangerous form of confrontation. Insofar as Pakistan will seek to deploy missiles and India will attempt a triadic pattern of deployment, the chances of accidental detonations and miscalculated launches will remain high. The India-Pakistan security equation is very volatile and unstable. The only reasonable assurance that a nuclear confrontation will not break out between them can come, not through so-called stable deterrence, whether with or without open deployment, but by stopping the manufacture and induction of nuclear weapons and missiles.[20]

NOTES

[1] There is today a very rich debate between realism and its different kind of critics, from very mild ones like liberal internationalism to more radically critical currents influenced by Marxism, feminism, neo-Weberian historical sociology, post-modernism, world systems theory, and ecology. But even in the US, where this debate exists, realism dominates mainstream thinking. And in India, the debate is virtually non-existent. The overwhelming majority of the members of the "national security establishment" are blissfully unaware of its existence. Liberal internationalism shares so many of realism's basic assumptions that it is not a serious critique of it.

These influences (in an unsystematized form) do exist among some Indian security thinkers because insofar as non-alignment was seen as a moral-political alternative to realist bloc politics and balance-of-power gaming, it encouraged ways of thinking about international relations that share many perspectives with liberal internationalism. But with the end of the Cold War and with the Non-Aligned Movement now in disarray, conventional realism dominates Indian security thinking. The principal contemporary legatee of liberal internationalism in the West is the school of neo-liberalism (not to be confused with the most conservative form of neo-classical economics also going by that label), with its greater emphasis on economic global integration and "complex interdependence" between states.

[2] Conventional realism is descriptive and normative but often bemoans the fact that leaders of states do not behave as they should. Thus, among the ranks of realists it is possible to find those who would happily endorse the practice of nuclear deterrence in an "ideal world" but are fearful of what might happen to nuclear weapons in the real world. Neo-realism, by contrast, claims not to be merely descriptive but to provide a scientific-structural theoretical foundation to realism and its normative injunctions. Neo-realism emphasizes more starkly the supposedly compulsive effects and constraints that the anarchic world system imposes on states and inter-state behavior, regardless of the internal composition of these states— whether they are democratic or dictatorial, capitalist or not.

Neo-realism is thus prepared to arrive at prescriptive conclusions for policy with which conventional realists in the West would not agree. Thus Kenneth N. Waltz, the premier theorist of neo-realism (he prefers to call it structural realism) not only argues that deterrence works and that we should rely on it, but that it works so well that the gradual proliferation of nuclear weapons to other states is better than rapid proliferation, or no proliferation at all. Indian nuclearists thus have every reason to welcome Waltz's views, even if few properly understand his attempts at more rigorously theorizing international relations. See *The Spread of Nuclear Weapons: A Debate* (New York: W.W. Norton & Co., 1995), a polemic between the two authors, Scott D. Sagan and Kenneth N. Waltz. The key texts of neo-realism are Waltz's *Man, State and War* (New York: 1959) and his *Theory of International Politics* (Reading, MA: 1979).

[3] For a representative list of comprehensive critiques of realism/neo-realism from a variety of vantage points, see F. Halliday, *Rethinking International Relations* (London: Macmillan, 1994) and J. Rosenberg, *The Empire of Civil Society: A Critique of the Realist Theory of International Relations* (London: Verso, 1994). The above two are Marxists. From the direction of historical sociology, there is A. Giddens, *The Nation-State and Violence* (Cambridge: Polity Press, 1985) and M. Mann, *The Sources*

of Social Power, Vol. II (Cambridge: Cambridge University Press, 1983). From the direction of feminism, see C. Enloe, *Bananas, Bases and Beaches: Making Feminist Sense of International Relations* (London: Pandora, 1989). From the direction of international political economy, there is S. Strange, *The Retreat of the State: The Diffusion of Power in the World Economy* (Cambridge: Cambridge University Press, 1996). From world systems theory, see I. Wallerstein, *Geopolitics and Geoculture: Essays in a Changing World System* (Cambridge: Cambridge University Press, 1991). From a post-modernist angle, see R.B.J. Walker, *Inside/Outside: International Relations as Political Theory* (Cambridge: Cambridge University Press, 1993).

In contrast to the ferocity of these varied assaults on realism/neo-realism, the contemporary debate between realists/neo-realists and neo-liberalism in US academia is very much like two bald men fighting over a comb!

4 "National Territorial Totality" is the felicitous phrase used by F. Halliday, one of the most measured and insistent critics of realism. (See note 3). Sometimes realists in certain contexts do refer to the state in the narrow, sociological sense and can provide sensible enough studies of specific regions, countries, and wars. But this is in spite of their theoretical weakness, not because of their framework or paradigm of understanding. This central weakness nonetheless exacts its heavy price, disqualifying realism from any serious purchase on human reality in modern times.

5 The period of existence of communism as a serious systemic rival also meant the more or less successful challenge to the imperatives of the world capitalist economic and political system.

6 So self-consciously committed is Waltz to the structural-compulsive character of the global system as he understands it, that he dismisses all fears of nuclear deterrence ever breaking down. Indeed, he says the possibility of the use of nuclear weapons is nearly zero. (See note 2). But this quantified probability assessment of his has no evidential basis whatsoever and simply comes out of his head. To claim that the probability of something happening is very low is different from the more categorical claim that it is nearly zero. Waltz relies heavily on the most extreme form of the long peace argument, in which nuclear weapons are deemed necessary and sufficient. Waltz effectively ignores recent revelations about the history of "near misses" regarding contemplated and accidental use of nuclear weapons.

Insofar as he does have to address the "near zero" possibility of deterrence breakdown, Waltz, with breathtaking self-confidence, reassures all and sundry that "should deterrence fail, a few judiciously delivered warheads are likely to produce sobriety in the leaders of all the countries involved and thus bring about rapid de-escalation." (*The Spread of Nuclear Weapons*: 131). Again, there is no serious evidence (how can there be?) or even argumentative basis for this claim, just the Waltzian assumption of high rationality-guiding behavior among leaders of states, even though the neo-realist rationality that insists a nuclear exchange will not take place has broken down in this scenario! Moral issues concerning nuclear deterrence have no place in neo-realism.

7 No empire in human history collapsed as comprehensively, as rapidly and as bloodlessly as did the USSR. By all conventional indices of "hard power," this is simply inexplicable. The fact is that even the ruling elite, which most benefited from the existing system, had long since lost any ideological commitment to the Soviet system and no longer possessed the will to preserve it. The break-up was precipitated not by some supposedly unbearable outside pressure, nor by powerful rebellion from below, but by unexpected political-moral collapse from above.

One would have thought that the manner in which this extraordinary event unfolded, which flies in the face of all realist common sense about the importance of balance of power, hard power or security understood as territorial survival of a state, might lead to serious self-questioning by realists. Especially since the Soviet collapse followed a decades-long history of numerous political-military defeats of the Great Powers by weaker and smaller ones, from decolonizing wars of liberation, to Vietnam and Afghanistan. By all realist indices of hard power, this too had no business happening. Unfortunately, realists show no sign of engaging in such a rethinking.

[8] If instances of realist overestimation of the power and importance of the state and of what statecraft can accomplish in international affairs are obvious and numerous, a classic example of realist *under*estimation of the importance of the state and what new forms of statecraft appropriate to a changing world order can do, is to be found on the issue of economic globalization. If a more humane life for the mass of citizens in a country is to be secured, then the state must intervene to regulate and shape market forces. Realists, though, simply assume that the world capitalist economy is what it was centuries ago and therefore still follows basically a mercantilist pattern. Or that it must be left alone, in fealty to current neo-liberal economic perspectives on how globalization should proceed. In both cases, the relationship between states and markets, between states and the world economy is seen as unproblematic and requiring the state to do nothing, either because it cannot intervene effectively or because it need not, since the world system has not changed in its fundamentals from what it was a few centuries ago. Capitalism is conceptually irrelevant for realism, so there is no question of seeing its own evolution in the latter half of the twentieth century as having a serious bearing on the study of international relations.

[9] E.H. Carr's *The Twenty Year's Crisis* (New York: Harper Torchbook, 1964), sometimes called the founding text of realism, portrays an understanding of realism very different from later US versions. Carr's work showed an acute awareness of the limitations of realism, the necessity for sensible realist thinking to connect strongly to liberal internationalist and highly ethical thinking. He refused to make realism into an overarching ahistorical model of how the global system is supposed to work. Carr, after all, was himself a great historian as well as a former diplomat.

The English school of realism has always been at somewhat of a tangent to the dominant US tradition. It has increasingly separated itself from the waning need of the British to act as an imperial power, and has generally produced more sensitive and intelligent insights than its Atlantic counterpart into what it calls "international society" (as distinct from what US Realists call the "international system"). See the works of its two most famous representatives, Martin Wight and Hedley Bull. M. Wight and B. Porter, eds., *International Theory: The Three Traditions* (Leicester: Leicester University Press, 1991). H. Bull, *The Anarchical Society: A Study on the Order of World Politics* (London: Macmillan, 1977). This English school continues to flourish in the work of Adam Watson and James Mayall, among others.

[10] For decades, Indian realists supported the Indo-USSR relationship on political-strategic grounds. But they remained effectively immune to the conceptual language of Soviet strategic thought. This Soviet thinking was filtered through an extremely crude and highly distorted version of Marxism, but even so, it promoted the use of a superior conceptual alternative to the notion of balance of power. This was the notion of "correlation of forces." It was superior in the era of systemic rivalry precisely because it was broader, more flexible, not pivoted so centrally on the

military dimension but allowing for the incorporation of other economic, cultural, and political-ideological dimensions. That was why it was possible for Soviet strategic thinkers to talk, not inaccurately, of the "world correlation of forces" vis-à-vis the West and US as moving in its favor during the '50s, '60s and much of the '70s, despite the military balance not being weighted in its favor.

In the '80s, when it became increasingly clear that when judged by the other dimensions incorporated in the notion of correlation of forces—the economic, cultural, political-ideological—it was the West that was running way ahead, Soviet strategists increasingly began to prefer concepts like balance of power and "mutual parity," precisely because these notions were more strongly pivoted on the military, and the USSR could thereby reassure itself that it had not lost ground relative to the US and the West. The Soviets thus used the superior concept of the correlation of forces only manipulatively, to self-serving ends. But the important point here is this: Indian realists, despite the prolonged importance of the Indo-Soviet relationship in the post-war history of India, have rarely been inclined to learn anything from the conceptual baggage of Soviet strategic thought, but have been so "Americanized" in their thinking that they have always preferred to use the inferior concept of balance of power as their primary conceptual tool.

11 See Chapter 2. And M. Kaku and D. Axelrod, To Win a Nuclear War (London: Zed Books, 1987).

12 See note 11. Recent declassified material confirms what a 1994 article claimed. In a July 20, 1961 National Security Council Meeting in Washington, the US military drew up a plan for a nuclear first strike on the USSR that was more than a contingency plan. General Lemnitzer, Chairman of the Joint Chiefs of Staff, proposed such a strike in late 1963 and proposed a justification for such a strike by suggesting that tensions be deliberately heightened in the period preceding the sudden assault. See Heather A. Purcell and James K. Galbraith, "Did the US Military Plan a Nuclear First Strike for 1963?" in The American Prospect 19 (Fall 1994): 92.

13 Charles Perrow, Normal Accidents: Living With High-Risk Technologies (New York: Basic Books, 1984); Scott D. Sagan, The Limits of Safety: Organizations, Accidents and Nuclear Weapons (Princeton: Princeton University Press, 1993).

14 See Bruce G. Blair, The Logic of Accidental Nuclear War (Washington DC: Brookings, 1993); Paul Bracken, Command and Control of Nuclear Forces (New Haven: Yale University Press, 1983); Peter Douglas Feaver, Guarding the Guardians: Civilian Control of Nuclear Weapons in the United States (Ithaca: Cornell University Press, 1992); Scott D. Sagan, The Spread of Nuclear Weapons; Shaun Gregory, The Hidden Cost of Deterrence: Nuclear Weapons Accidents (London: Brassey's, 1990). Gregory's account could not take account of material declassified since publication.

15 A BBC Online television program of 21 October 1998.

16 The most dramatic example of risky behavior in a domestic crisis comes from China. In October 1966, in the middle of the Cultural Revolution, Marshall Nie Rongzhen launched a test missile 500 miles across China to pre-empt radical interference in the nuclear program by behaving radically in a dramatic and public gesture of support to the Mao faction. John W. Lewis and Xue Litai, China Builds the Bomb (Stanford: Stanford University Press, 1988): 202-203. See also The Spread: 80-85.

17 In the Yom Kippur war of October 1973, Israel had started to put nuclear weapons on its fighter-bomber planes. See Seymour M. Hersh, The Samson Option: Israel's Nuclear Arsenal and American Foreign Policy (New York: Random House,

1991): 231. In the Gulf War of 1991, there are reports of Israel placing nuclear-tipped Jericho missiles on high alert readiness. See Samson and Bill Gertz, "Israel Deploys Missiles for a Possible Strike at Iraq," *Washington Times* 28 January 1991.

[18] China is very worried about the watering down of the ABM Treaty by the US and current Japan-US discussions about a joint Theatre Missile Defense (TMD) program. This would adversely affect China's capacity to hit the US mainland by its twelve to twenty land-based long-range ballistic missiles in a second strike. Should the ABM Treaty unravel or be perceived in Chinese eyes to have done so, then Beijing will try to compensate by expanding the numbers of land-based long range missiles it has, as well as developing and expanding their submarine arm. At the moment this is very weak.

[19] India is expanding the range of its intermediate *Agni* missiles. It hopes to push this to 2,500 kilometers (1,550 miles) as well as develop even longer range *Surya* missiles. A technology demonstration will not worry China much. But if, over the next five years or so, India can carry out a series of missile tests over the requisite range, then even though New Delhi will still be far from having an assured second-strike capacity against China, the fact that it has land missiles able to reach some main population centers will alarm China and lead to major changes in its strategic planning.

[20] Accidents and miscalculations are less likely if the NWSs resort to only one form of deployment (sea-based submarine platforms). France and Britain are, in fact, moving toward just such a singular pattern of deployment, because while any hope of building a credible second-strike capacity against a rival that is geographically distant (e.g. China's capacity to deter the US, or India's to deter China) may do without airborne or land-based missiles, a strong submarine arm is essential. India currently has no nuclear-reactor driven submarine and is at least twenty, if not more, years from developing a viable submarine-based missile arm.

Chapter 9

From Abstinence, to Ambiguity, to the Nuclear Blasts

The greatest surprise of the May 1998 tests by India and Pakistan was not so much that they took place within just a few weeks of the new BJP government coming to power in New Delhi, but that there was no tangible "provocation." No single event or even a series of developments can be credibly cited as providing an immediate rationale for the crossing of the nuclear threshold by India and Pakistan. The world had long known that the two South Asian states were, at most, "a screwdriver's turn" away from making nuclear bombs; they might even have had "bombs in the basement" for some time. But it was not known that they were both more or less ready to conduct underground nuclear explosions, which require extensive preparations—the drilling of shafts in the desert (in Rajasthan in India) or the mountain (Chagai hills in Baluchistan in Pakistan), the lowering of explosive assemblies and electric cables, the "hardening" of ground-level bunkers, and perhaps the installing of "containment" systems to shield the explosions' impact. Such preparations can take up to a year, if not longer.

Clearly, scientists and engineers in India's Department of Atomic Energy (DAE) and the Defense Research & Development Organization (DRDO) could carry out the detonation of nuclear explosions at short notice—less than two months after the Vajpayee government was sworn in—only because they had not just the bombs, but a number of auxiliary technologies, as well as the physical infrastructure, more or less in place. Pakistan followed India within a fortnight.

Pakistan: Goaded into Testing

The delay is explained not by a lack of preparation, but by the Sharif government's political hesitation to cross the nuclear threshold in immediate response to India. As we have said, the prime minister showed a distinct reluctance to test: in fact, refraining from nuclear testing would have helped Islamabad seize the moral high ground and overcome some of the stigma deriving from its support to Islamic extremist groups such as the Taliban in Afghanistan and Harkat-ul-Ansar in Kashmir. Besides diplomatic advantage, Pakistan also stood to gain heftily in military and economic terms if it refrained from testing. The US, which sent a delegation to Islamabad in May led by Deputy Secretary of State Strobe

Talbott, offered a $5 billion package in economic and military aid to Sharif in return for showing restraint.

Sharif was clearly tempted by the offer, and by the calculus of costs and benefits of non-testing, for him to withstand heavy pressure he faced in the aftermath of the Indian tests—from his political opponents, as well as large segments of the Pakistani Establishment, including former high functionaries, diplomats and generals, not to speak of radical Islamicists. By the end of the week of May 11, it did seem that Pakistan would refrain from testing its nuclear weapons. Some extreme rightwingers in India took this to mean, quite simply, that Pakistan did not have the bomb: why else would it not test?[1]

That is when India's Home Minister Lal Krishna Advani, known for his hardline views, opened a new front in the on-going India-Pakistan hostilities: Kashmir. On May 18, he warned Pakistan that with the Indian tests, the "geo-strategic" situation had decisively changed. He said that India's "decisive step to become a nuclear weapon state has brought about a qualitatively new stage in Indo-Pak relations, particularly in finding a lasting solution to the Kashmir problem." He asked "Islamabad to realize the change in the geo-strategic situation in the region and the world." He demanded that Pakistan must "join India in the common pursuit of peace and prosperity in the Indian sub-continent," and warned Islamabad: "any other course will be futile and costly for Pakistan."[2]

Pakistan's response was, naturally, one of ultra-nationalist outrage, driven by strong Islamicist pressure. More inflammatory statements by Indian leaders followed. Defense Minister George Fernandes in particular, threatened the "hot pursuit" of Pakistani troops and Pakistan-backed guerrillas. These statements could only interpreted as India's taunting, teasing, needling, and cajoling Pakistan into testing.[3] Sharif could not withstand the pressure any more, especially after the Pakistan army chief, following a visit to Azad Kashmir (the Pakistan-held part of Kashmir), reported that his troops' morale would be compromised if there was no nuclear test.

The relative ease with which India and Pakistan crossed the nuclear Rubicon can only be explained in terms of a prolonged process, stretched over decades, involving technological preparation, creation of a physical infrastructure and acquisition of strategic materials, as well as a hardening of the two rivals' nuclear postures. India's transition from a state that campaigned for nuclear disarmament and practiced nuclear abstinence, to one that suddenly embraced the doctrine of nuclear deterrence and self-avowedly tested these weapons of mass destruction, is naturally the more dramatic of the two stories. This transition was itself punctuated for a quarter-century by the policy of nuclear ambiguity. What enabled this transition to occur? At work here was the unfolding of both technological and political processes.

India was the first third world country to launch a nuclear energy program. Homi J. Bhabha, the program's leader, played a major role in the founding of the Tata Institute of Fundamental Research in 1944 and in the creation of a high-profile scientific establishment committed to research in nuclear physics and related areas. This establishment was to form the core of the Atomic Energy Commission (AEC) set up in 1948. The AEC organized a survey of such natural resources relevant to nuclear energy as uranium, thorium, beryllium and graphite, and established a special unit, the Rare Minerals Division. The Commission also emphasized the development of basic sciences and the training of high-quality research scientists as well as the indigenous production of special instruments and support facilities.

The first Indian nuclear reactor, Apsara, went critical in 1956, with help from Britain, which supplied the enriched uranium fuel. Soon after, a second reactor, code-named CIRUS, after Canadian-Indian-US co-operation, went critical. In 1960, a plutonium reprocessing plant was also established. The spent fuel from CIRUS and the ability to reprocess it, coupled with the expertise and experience Indian scientists had gained in the nuclear field, gave India an independent nuclear weapons option. Since the mid-'60s, India has undertaken the construction of nuclear power stations and large research facilities and the establishment of independent "unsafeguarded" sources of weapons-grade plutonium. The civilian program encompasses the entire nuclear fuel cycle.

Currently, India has an installed capacity to generate 1,840MW of nuclear power, and plans to raise nuclear electricity generation to 20,000MW by the year 2020.[4] The mainstay of the nuclear power program is the Canadian Deuterium-Natural Uranium (CANDU) reactor design, although the country's first nuclear power station, a turnkey project built with US aid, is based on an enriched uranium-light water design. India's CANDU reactor program has not performed well; nor has India been able to innovate and stabilize an improved design. This lack of success and financial stringency recently impelled India to contract the import of two Russian-designed VVER-1000 reactors.

India has sought to develop its nuclear program across a broad technological front, which includes a space exploration program and missiles, in addition to such components as material sciences and other auxiliary technologies. India's progress in the field of delivery systems needs to be especially noted. Its nuclear-capable aircraft include the Canberra, Ajeet, MiG-21, -23, -27, and -29, Jaguar, Mirage and Sukhoi-30, which provide a combat radius of 100 to 900 miles (approximately 160–1450 kilometers). The Jaguar and Mirage, and possibly even the MiG-29, are equipped for in-flight refueling.

India started working on space-launches and rockets in the '60s and by the early '80s had "established the basic technology required for missile systems in solid and liquid propulsion, control and guidance and precision fabrication."[5] In 1983, it launched the Integrated Guided Missile Development Program, which aimed to produce five kinds of missiles.

Nuclear-capable missiles being developed in India include the *Prithvi*, a surface-to-surface missile with a range of 250 to 350 km (155–220 mi.) now being serially produced, and the *Agni*, with a range of 1,500–2,500 km (930–1,550 mi.) and three test flights to its credit. When fully developed, the *Agni* would be capable of bringing the Persian Gulf and many Chinese cities into striking distance. The *Agni* was first successfully tested on May 22, 1989. After the third test, in 1994, all further development was put on hold until May 1998.

A longer-range (2,500–3,000 km/1,550–1,860 mi.) version of the missile, known variously as *Agni-II* or *Agni-plus*, is currently under development. There is also a polar space launch vehicle under development, which would be the equivalent of an intercontinental ballistic missile. The Orissa missile test firing range located in the eastern part of India is clearly for missile-related military purposes.

Pakistan was a comparatively late starter developing nuclear and field missiles; it launched its own nuclear program only in the '60s. The turning point came in the mid-'60s, after India had acquired a plutonium-producing "research reactor" (1960) and built a reprocessing plant (1964). The first record of discussion of a nuclear weapons program in the Pakistan cabinet is traceable to 1963. The issue of feasibility of such a program was actively discussed during the 1965 war with India, especially in light of Homi Bhabha's October 1964 statement, following the first Chinese test, that India too could, if necessary, make a nuclear bomb within eighteen months. In 1966 and 1968, the Cabinet again discussed the issue. In 1968, at the urging of bomb enthusiast and Foreign Minister Zulfikar Ali Bhutto, Pakistan commissioned a feasibility study—or rather two different studies, one by the Pakistan Atomic Energy Commission and the other by defense scientists. But their recommendations contradicted one another and neither fructified.

Pakistan's nuclear program was, of course, greatly influenced by developments in India, including the nuclear policy debate in that country. Following the Sino-Indian border war in 1962, and particularly after the Chinese Lop Nor test of October 1964, the nuclear weapons issue invaded parliamentary and public debate in India. The debate, especially the clamor for an "Indian bomb" by several MPs, appears to have provided an additional stimulus to Pakistani decision-makers to pursue a nuclear weapons capability. It was only after the fall of the Yahya Khan regime in the wake of the creation of Bangladesh in 1971, that the new premier, Zulfikar Ali Bhutto, gave a decisive fillip to the country's nuclear program.

"We'll Eat Grass"

In 1972, Bhutto made his famous "we-will-eat-grass-but-we'll-have-our-bomb" speech, emphasizing in his address to top scientists and engineers at

Multan the critical importance of developing a Pakistani bomb at any cost, to "safeguard the country's security" against India. After Pakistan's dismemberment at India's hands in the Bangladesh War, the rhetoric of militant nuclearism acquired a particularly sharp edge. There is reason to believe this was backed with a financial commitment. Pakistan by then had also approached Canada to build a small natural uranium CANDU reactor at Karachi (Karachi Nuclear Power Plant—KANUPP). KANUPP's function was related more to gaining familiarity and experience with the working of nuclear technology than power generation (of which it has a rather poor record).

In the initial stages, Pakistan explored the plutonium route to nuclear weapons manufacture. This is technologically simpler and far easier to manage, once a nuclear reactor is in place, and access to its spent fuel is secured. Pakistan in the '60s and '70s could not have designed or built such a reactor on its own; nor was it in a position to reprocess spent nuclear fuel so as to extract plutonium from it. Under Bhutto's leadership, Pakistan also began to explore the possibility of enriching uranium by the gas-centrifuge process. It first sought French assistance in building a plutonium reprocessing plant. France agreed. Although the plant was to be subject to international "safeguards," it would have nevertheless enabled Pakistan to absorb the technology and possibly accumulate weapons-grade material on the sly.

By 1976, US concerns over Pakistan's nuclear intentions were translated into successful pressure on the French to stop their technology transfer. With the possibility of open external support for its nuclear program effectively curtailed, Pakistan under both Bhutto and his successor, General Mohammed Zia ul-Haq, embarked on a carefully coordinated clandestine effort to secure the components necessary for building a uranium enrichment plant at Kahuta, as well as New Labs, a small pilot plutonium extraction plant in Rawalpindi. It is the uranium enrichment program that provided the decisive breakthrough for Pakistan in the area of weapons-grade material production.

From the beginning, Pakistan's nuclear program has essentially been a "dedicated" one, that is to say, its *raison d'être* is military. In this respect, the program mirrors Pakistan's reactive foreign policy, which is driven by an obsession with India. The Indian nuclear program, on the other hand, reflects a more complex constellation of pressures and motivations. Conceived originally as a purely civilian effort, India's program nevertheless acquired a "dual" character after the '50s under a scientific leadership that was keen to preserve the weapons option, despite the Nehru-era policy of permanent nuclear abstinence.

The potential for military spin-offs and capabilities from the Indian civilian nuclear program did not emerge suddenly or even after a certain technological level was crossed in the nuclear program. It was the result of a conscious choice by the program's leadership to build into it from the start the possibility of obtaining progressively greater militarily valuable technologies and products, and to make the transition from civilian to military use of nuclear capabilities, if required, as quickly and as smoothly as possible. This built-in dual character was reflected in the importance given to plutonium production (in addition to CIRUS, India built the 100MW (thermal) *Dhruva* reactor) as well as work on materials sciences and on auxiliary technologies.[6] Thus, the Pokharan test of 1974 could be organized within a relatively short period of time after the approval to produce a "nuclear device" was granted, which was sometime between 1969 and 1972.[7]

Most accounts of the relationship between the policy-making apparatus in India and the scientific leadership of the nuclear program suggest that the latter has generally enjoyed a certain degree of autonomy. This was especially true of the early period in the development of the Indian nuclear program under Bhabha. Although Bhabha was formally constrained by the Nehru policy of permanent nuclear abstinence—and was, ironically, a Nehru appointee close to the Prime Minister in science policy and planning—in actual practice, Bhabha appears to have pursued a different course. He organized the Indian nuclear effort to keep the weapons option open indefinitely and, indeed, to sustain and develop it to the point of being able to stockpile unsafeguarded weapon-grade material.

Thus, Bhabha devoted a considerable amount of energy to the construction of CIRUS, the "research reactor" built with Canadian and US assistance, but operated without the constraint of safeguards or sanctions. There is reason to believe that Bhabha strove hard to avoid signing a formal agreement with Canada and the US that would in any way compromise or limit India's complete control over the reactor and its output, including spent fuel. The agreements India signed in the '50s committed it to limit the use of CIRUS and its products to "peaceful purposes," but without safeguards or oversight by an external agency. The spent fuel from the CIRUS reactor was later reprocessed at a plutonium separation plant set up next to the reactor at Trombay (near Bombay) in 1964. Eventually, this became the source of the plutonium used in the Pokharan explosive device.

Thus, Bhabha's 1964 statement that India could manufacture the bomb in eighteen months was not an empty boast. By the late '50s, Bhabha apparently had begun to shift toward the view that the policy of permanent nuclear abstinence was probably not in India's long-term interest. He argued that in a world without disarmament, the only effective means of countering "atomic colonialism" (traceable to the nuclear weapons monopoly of the Great Powers) would be a third world bomb. Whether or not Bhabha fully worked out the implications of this proposition with a comprehensive formulation that was radically opposed to India's official policy is not clear. But it is fairly clear that he followed a direction that diverged significantly from the Nehru government's officially stated policy.

One reason why nuclear scientists have been able to pursue programs that diverge in subtle ways from proclaimed policy is related to the structure of nuclear policy-making and implementation. The agency charged with this task is not, as in most policy matters, the Union Cabinet, but the Atomic Energy Commission (AEC), which was constituted under a special act of Parliament. Typically, the AEC is composed primarily of scientists and dominated by the top leaders of the Department of Atomic Energy (DAE). The AEC's chairman serves as the ex-officio secretary to the India government in the DAE and is rated on a par with the topmost bureaucrat. In practice, the minute details of the nuclear program are probably not even discussed in the AEC, but are left to individual scientists to plan and execute in an environment that is relatively insulated from, and hostile to, public scrutiny. The Atomic Energy Act of 1962 institutionalizes secrecy and centralization of control within the AEC, as few Indian laws do for any institution.

The specialized technical nature of the nuclear scientists' work and role in the nuclear energy establishment is an obstacle to "outsiders," "generalists" and political leaders who are trying to effectively control the nuclear program. This *de facto* autonomy of the scientists results from, and is further enhanced by, the overall prestige and high profile that modern science and its practitioners enjoy in most third world countries, at least among the elite. This is particularly the case with India and Pakistan, where scientific achievements with even explicitly stated military implications or aims attract an exceptional degree of praise from an elite that is sometimes quite unfavorably disposed toward political leaders. Scientists are thus able to claim special status and unique importance for themselves and to demand effective autonomy from political leaders.

As we have said, until the early '60s, India's official position, supported by a general consensus, was a policy of permanent nuclear abstinence. To explain how this policy came about, one must examine the particular inflexions of Indian non-alignment during the Nehru era. Non-alignment must be understood in two separate senses. First, non-alignment represented a particular worldview of the international system of states and the conflicts between them. As such, the perspective manifested strong normative and moralist overtones, which were critical of alliance politics and the search for "balances of power." As the name of the broad movement of non-aligned nations (NAM) suggests, it offered the prospect that the movement would play a positive role (under the leadership of certain countries) out of all proportion to its ability to impose sanctions of any meaningful kind. In the second and more fundamental sense, non-alignment was also a foreign policy framework which, by definition, allowed each nation maximum national autonomy to pursue its interests free from the constraints imposed by bloc membership.

The basic tension between these two senses of non-alignment did not really become apparent until the 1962 Sino-India conflict. Through most of the Nehru era, India adopted a high-profile and diplomatically activist approach in international affairs and in such forums as the United Nations, as shown by India's active role in the disarmament negotiations of the '50s and '60s. This role reinforced the credibility and strength of the Indian government's decision not to go nuclear. But the 1962 war with China marked a decisive watershed, after which India's national interests became more sharply focused and essentially regional.

An involution of preoccupations took place: India became less concerned about having a high international profile in various forums, and more concerned about strengthening the components of its national power. Non-alignment became, more or less, a loose synonym for the traditional *realpolitik* approach of pursuing national interests through the projection and expansion of national power. To this extent, a re-evaluation of the role nuclear weapons could play in the foreign policy of India could be expected. Earlier negative attitudes or outright rejection began to give way to more positive perceptions of the linkages between nuclear weapons, deterrence, and national security ambitions.

Despite early criticism from the West, inspired by the influential US secretary of state, John Foster Dulles, India's non-alignment policy came to be accepted and endorsed by both major blocs; and India, unlike China, never had to face either nuclear-armed superpower, let alone both, as a strategic adversary. China embarked on the nuclear weapons path earlier and with fewer signs of vacillation than India; it was never inclined to remain "only" a threshold nuclear state. Despite tensions linked to the US alliance with, and support for, Pakistan, Indo-US relations during the Cold War displayed a complex and fluctuating character that never hardened into a posture of strategic opposition or open hostility. Even the perception of a Chinese "threat," especially after the border war of 1962, was seen as qualified, of interest mainly along the Himalayan crest. During the '50s and '60s and even immediately after the 1962 conflict, India did not display any apprehension of a Chinese-Pakistan line-up, let alone a US-China-Pakistan "axis." The most important consequence of the 1962 war was its impact on India's self-perception and its stimulation of a new self-awareness concerning the aims and means of achieving national "fulfillment."

Pakistan: Reactive Consistency

Pakistan's nuclear preparations and thinking have been based on fairly clear and straightforward premises that, in some ways, lend to its nuclear policy a level of consistency and coherence that is absent in the Indian case. Pakistan does not have a general or universal (declared) policy that is independent of India. Islamabad's repeated declarations after 1971 that India is clearly the dominant power in the region have not prevented Pakistan from seeking military-political parity with India, whether this search was motivated by prestige, defensive considerations, or ambitions over Kashmir.

Pakistan's nuclear preparations, of course, pre-dated the Pokharan nuclear test, but assumed added urgency in its wake. US pressure in this respect was of little avail until the late '80s, when the stiff Pressler Amendment to the US Trade Act was enacted. Neither Zulfikar Ali Bhutto nor his successor succumbed to US pressure. Pakistan's recalcitrance during the Zia-ul-Haq period (1977–88) came as a particular shock to Washington, which had reason to believe that the military regime's unpopularity and hence its greater reliance on US support would render it more pliable concerning its nuclear program. In reality, Zia ul-Haq's regime was completely successful in its clandestine efforts to secure classified designs of a centrifuge-based uranium enrichment plant and to obtain a number of critical sub-systems, components, and materials.

The key figure in all this was Dr. Abdul Qadir Khan, a German-trained metallurgist who had worked at the centrifuge enrichment plant at Almelo, Netherlands, where he almost certainly obtained access to key designs and to lists of suppliers of crucial components. Pakistan is believed to have begun to produce weapons-grade uranium some time in 1986, and stopped doing so under the threat of US trade sanctions between May 1989 and June 1990. It is believed to have resumed production for some time in 1991, but to have stopped production later that year. This suggests that at the time of the tests, Pakistan had accumulated enough highly enriched uranium for eight to twenty Hiroshima-type first-generation bombs.

Pakistan has a range of nuclear-capable aircraft. It has developed two short-range missiles *Hatf-I* and *II*, with a range of 80 km (50 mi.) and 300 km (186 mi.) respectively, and is believed to have received some Chinese M-11 missiles (or at least their components) in a clandestine transfer. The M-11, with a range of about 300-350 km (186–217 mi.), is a borderline case as far as restrictions under the Missile Technology Control Regime are concerned. In April 1998, Pakistan announced the "successful" test flight of a "medium-range" missile, the *Ghauri*, named after an Afghan invader of India during the Middle Ages. Though there is some confusion over its origin (Chinese or North Korean?) and its capabilities, if Pakistani official claims are correct, then many cities in peninsular India, not just the North, could come within the *Ghauri's* range.

Until the early '90s, Pakistan pursued its own version of a two-track policy. On the one hand, it systematically sought to develop a clandestine nuclear weapons capability. On the other hand, it just as systematically put forward a variety of proposals for regional denuclearization which gave it the moral "high ground" in the war of words against India. The proposals included mutual bilateral inspection of each other's facilities, third party verification, the conclusion of a bilateral treaty renouncing nuclear weapons, mutual and simultaneous signature of the NPT, and the establishment of a South Asian nuclear weapons-free zone (NWFZ).

By the mid-'90s, the terms of Pakistan's engagement with India on matters nuclear had changed. The CTBT had emerged as a major issue.

Here too, Pakistan's attitude was to articulate and follow India, rather than make an independent decision. When it became clear in 1996 that India would not sign the treaty, Pakistan too decided to keep out.

Some Indian analysts have argued that Pakistan's nuclear weapons orientation and ambitions were not and are not fundamentally conditioned by Indian actions, but were and are to a large extent independently motivated. In addition to being implausible and unconvincing, these arguments are also somewhat self-serving, in that they tend to obscure India's responsibility as the key player in the South Asian nuclear arms race.

This is not to say that no independent factors have affected Pakistan's nuclear policies. There is, for example, Pakistan's search for prestige in the Islamic world. But the *decisive* factor was India and its preparations, which explains Pakistan's essentially narrow perspective. Pakistan's deliberations have never been encumbered by moral doubt. On the contrary, they have been based on a *realpolitik* approach to threat perceptions. Thus, no evidence suggests that Pakistan ever seriously considered not moving toward a threshold status, once India had achieved it. Until May 1998, Pakistan clearly wanted not to cross the nuclear threshold. This stemmed from the realization that once a nuclear arms race was launched on the sub-continent, the basic asymmetry in power and resources between the two countries would impose a disproportionately heavier burden on Pakistan, assuming that it could even hope to "keep up."

As we have said, unlike Pakistan's, Indian nuclear policy and preparations have been subject to more complex and divergent pressures. In some respects, the end of the Nehru era marked the end of a clear nuclear policy. Since then, until the mid-'90s, within a broad framework of deep reluctance to close the nuclear option, nuclear policy consisted of a series of tactical, *ad hoc* responses rather than a carefully executed, coherent long-range policy. Every incumbent prime minister added his or her own nuances to declared policy and undeclared activities.

During 1966–68, for instance, there was a short-lived flirtation with the idea of a US or Western nuclear weapon umbrella against China. This was also the period of governmental uncertainty over the NPT, the drafting and preparation of which India had put significant work into. By 1968, however, every hope of quick progress toward disarmament had vanished as the nuclear arms race gained momentum. New Delhi's despair over the whole disarmament effort influenced its decision not to sign the NPT, although the primary consideration was that signing the NPT would have meant closing the nuclear option. Also, there was the fact that China would have nothing to do with the Treaty until much, much later. Nearly twenty years later, under Rajiv Gandhi (1984–89), there were some hesitant, uncertain attempts at pro-disarmament diplomacy, but these soon collapsed. Meanwhile, under Indira Gandhi's post-1971 government, nuclear policy underwent some hardening, symbolized above all by the 1974 Pokharan explosion.

Pokharan I: From Abstinence to Ambiguity

What was the motivation behind India's first test at Pokharan? It is hard to relate it to the existence of any real and present threat or danger. In 1974, less than three years after the dismemberment of Pakistan, India's pre-eminence in the South Asian region was as unchallenged as it was obvious. Although China first tended to side with Pakistan during the Bangladesh conflict, China did not become India's strategic adversary. The USSR had proved a dependable friend of India, and New Delhi had signed a Treaty of Friendship and Cooperation with Moscow in 1971. It is impossible to detect any deterioration in India's external security environment in that period.

The fact is, the motivation behind the first Pokharan nuclear explosion was largely *internal*. Indira Gandhi, who had ridden a wave of popularity in 1971 on left-leaning slogans, suddenly found the sands shifting under her feet a year later. By 1973, India had slipped into the century's highest-ever spiral of inflation, led by food prices. Government after state government led by Gandhi's Indian National Congress found itself confronting a rising tide of popular turmoil and protest at economic policy, corruption, and misgovernance.

The Congress party's already insecure base began to erode at a rapid pace, especially in North India. In Bihar and Gujarat, students and youth, protesting against Congress-style corruption and patronage, had managed to cripple the functioning of the ruling party's governments, forcing one of them to resign. The popular mood against the Congress was most forcefully expressed in the railway workers' strike of May 1974, led, ironically, by none other than George Fernandes, defense minister in the BJP-led coalition government that conducted the 1998 nuclear blasts.

The precise timing of the first Pokharan test was determined by these domestic political considerations, in addition to two other factors. First, the nuclear scientists' lobby exerted considerable pressure on Indira Gandhi to conduct the tests. Its anxiety that they be carried out was largely a function of shoring up and raising its falling profile in the science and technology (S&T) establishment, which was itself a result of the hopelessly sub-standard performance of the nuclear power program and its repeated failure to meet targets and stay within allocated (and often, very generous) budgets. Nuclear explosions, based on well-understood principles of physics available in the public domain, offered the *easy option* of proving that the DAE did have some technical competence, a reassurance that an elite audience, searching through the tattered symbols of national greatness, was happy to find. The second factor at work in the timing was simply that the bomb had matured. As Indira Gandhi told an American researcher: "[The PNE] was simply done when we were ready. We did it to show ourselves we could do it. We couldn't be sure until we had tried it... But it was for peaceful purposes only... We had to do it to demonstrate our independent capability."[8]

To the extent there was an "external" motive at all behind Pokharan I, it was to announce and spread the message of new-found Indian power after the Bangladesh war. This was India's own kind of aggressive "self-assertion," a diffused, unfocused "protest" against its exclusion from the Big League, and its rulers' determination—quite unrelated to domestic popular self-perception—that they would force the world to recognize India's power, despite her poverty, misery, deprivation, and illiteracy. That was India's own manifest destiny. And yet, India's leaders were not confident (or brazen) enough to want to claim that the state had crossed the nuclear threshold and become an NWS on a par with the other five, by virtue of conducting the test. They slyly announced that the test was a "peaceful nuclear explosion."

This ambiguity, and the compulsion to tell a half-truth, was prompted in part by the constraints placed by the agreements India signed with Canada and the United States in 1955 and 1956 to use the products of the CIRUS "research" reactor for "peaceful purposes" only. But the ambiguity of the statements also reflected the ambivalence toward the bomb of many in the Indian Establishment. For one, the Establishment was divided over whether to conduct the test and what its consequence might be. Apparently two members of the small group of key individuals who deliberated on the issue—both highly experienced senior civil servants and advisers to Indira Gandhi—were opposed to the test and its timing.[9]

And, for another, the test was not part of, or related to, a larger strategic game-plan. Nor did it serve a greater diplomatic and political objective. There was no long-term policy calculation involved here. India did not follow up Pokharan I with an immediate program of repeated and systematic further testing. Nor did it even attempt to relate the claim of a "peaceful nuclear explosion" to an actual application, such as the creation of reservoirs or stimulation of oil recovery, which could have conceivably been part of an Indian version of Project Ploughshares (for PNEs) in the US. The adverse international fallout of Pokharan I was only one reason why India ceased nuclear testing for a quarter-century after Pokharan I. The absence of a larger game-plan was the main reason, indeed the overwhelming one.

Pokharan I marked a further degeneration of Indian nuclear policy—from permanent nuclear abstinence under Nehru to "No Bombs Now" under Shastri and Indira Gandhi in 1967 to 1974, and then on to a deliberate policy of nuclear ambiguity.[10] Pokharan I not only represented a loss of nuclear innocence. It involved legitimizing the acquisition of the capability to commit mass-scale murder, a capability not remotely related, even going by official pronouncements, to Indian security and real threats to it. So completely at odds with India's stated nuclear doctrine was the test, that it could only be explained in sober terms as the acquisition of the *capability* alone, or the keeping of the nuclear option, but without its implementation. This took the form of the policy of nuclear ambiguity.

This policy had three fundamental components: (1) maintenance of the dual character of the nuclear program, while simultaneously enhancing civilian and military capabilities and potential on a broad technological front; (2) keeping the weapon option open and sustaining it at progressively higher levels; and (3) deliberately sending out conflicting signals on whether and how India would go nuclear. The first two components gave a degree of stability and continuity to the Indian nuclear weapons program and policy, particularly after May 1974. There were certain perceptible shifts, though. While Prime Minister Morarji Desai, who succeeded Indira Gandhi in 1977, was positively hostile to PNEs, he accepted the broad parameters of the Indian posture of refusing to foreclose the nuclear weapons option. The government of Charan Singh, which followed, emphasized the Pakistani threat as part of a more active defense of keeping the option open.

After her return to power in 1980, Indira Gandhi continued the policy of ambiguity. Under Rajiv Gandhi, the only variations were a change of tone with respect to the third factor and the greater frequency with which India delivered nuclear warnings. In other respects, the approach displayed remarkable stability throughout the years, until the mid-'90s. Indian leaders, but more frequently, hawkish nuclear polemicists, tried to justify the retention of the nuclear weapons option by citing the Chinese "threat" and the expansion of China's nuclear arsenal in the '60s. But the complete absence of any Chinese attempt at nuclear blackmail, the historical experience of living with the Chinese bomb, and a sober appraisal of the supposed seriousness of the Sino-Indian border dispute, all helped to diminish the fear of and pre-occupation with Chinese nuclear might.

In comparison to external threat perceptions, India's self-perceptions about its potential political "destiny" and future regional, Asian, and global roles played a much greater part in nuclear policy-making. The argument for accumulating an adequate nuclear arsenal as a counter-deterrent to China was never immediately pressing. From the early '80s, Pakistan's progress toward a nuclear weapons capability and threshold status were far more important to Indian threat perceptions. The acquisition of nuclear weapons was not an "urgent" response to a disturbing *existing* reality, but rather a longer-term perspective appropriate to the coming of age of an India "on the march."

Why did Pakistan aspire to a nuclear threshold status well before 1998? Pakistan's case was distinct from that of the other threshold powers: Pakistan acquired a threshold status because India had done so. The reverse, however, was not true. The Indian government thus found it difficult to justify the preservation of this status in terms of any immediate or urgent security danger. Instead, it cited dangers more remote and long-term in nature, such as the possibility of superpower blackmail. The impact of the one attempt to define a more concrete security risk—namely, the Pakistani nuclear threat—was blunted not only by the latter's willingness to explore the possibilities of regional denuclearization, but also by New Delhi's failure to counter Pakistan's "peace offensive" effectively. While both India and Pakistan could be said to practice a species of "nuclear ambiguity," the Pakistani posture was much less ambiguous because it had less difficulty in defining its insecurities and fears and therefore in discussing the ways in which nuclearization or denuclearization would be related to these insecurities.

"Recessed Deterrence" or Silent Arms Race?

One unanticipated consequence of India's ambiguous posture was that India was unable to prevent the emergence of a nuclear equation between itself and Pakistan. New Delhi repeatedly expressed its hostility to outsiders making such an equation, which implicitly suggests the notion of parity. Nevertheless, by constantly referring to Pakistani nuclear preparations in justifying its own status as a threshold power, India endorsed the validity of the equation that was often drawn.

Under Rajiv Gandhi, the diplomatic dilemma reflected itself in a striking manner, more so than in the case of any of his predecessors. Gandhi's government "authorized" another sovereign nation—in this case, the US—to exert pressure on Pakistan to prevent it from pursuing its nuclear goals. This became the only active component of India's strategy to counter Pakistani and international pressures to take some action in preventing the outbreak of a regional nuclear arms race. But some elite circles in India viewed this as demeaning, because it tended to highlight Indian impotence. The only exception to this seemed to be the advocacy by some in the Indian government of a pre-emptive aerial attack on the Kahuta enrichment plant in Pakistan. In 1983–84, India considered launching such an attack, both on its own and in collaboration with Israel, to cripple Pakistan's nuclear weapons development at an early stage. There was even public advocacy of this, albeit by a nuclear hawk, and expression of strong opposition.[11] In any case, it was not pursued.

The prolonged silent nuclear competition between India and Pakistan since the late '80s impelled many theorists, especially those belonging to the realist school, to posit the concept of "non-weaponized," "recessed," or "existential" "deterrence"—hypothesized as a relatively stable situation that neither state wishes to disturb, because both feel relatively secure in it. But such "non-weaponized deterrence" was anything but stable; even less did it provide security in any sense of the term. For instance, the India-Pakistan nuclear balance changed significantly after Pakistan reportedly succeeded in 1986 in producing sizable quantities of highly enriched uranium, enough for A.Q. Khan to declare confidently, "you can go tell them—we have it [the Bomb]."[12]

Given the policy of ambiguity, it was hard to tell where the line of demarcation lay between the acquisition of a weapons capability, on the one hand, and actual weapons possession and induction, on the other. Given this fuzziness, suspicion and strategic misperception were bound to flourish, which could quickly erode stability and security.

Indeed, that is precisely what seems to have happened at least twice—in 1987 and 1990, years by which not just India, but even Pakistan, had almost certainly reached the nuclear threshold. In 1986–87, a major military crisis erupted during a routine large-scale exercise by the Indian army called Operation Brasstacks. The exercise was seen as an offensive maneuver by the Pakistani army, which moved its troops to forward positions across the border. An eyeball-to-eyeball confrontation ensued, involving among other things, a Pakistani air exercise code-named Hallmark, which could have led to an exchange of hostilities, with a potential for escalation to the nuclear plane.

It is believed that Pakistan brandished its nuclear sword toward the end of the confrontation. The fact that Brasstacks was planned and led by General Krishnaswamy Sundarji, known for his tough stance against Pakistan and his penchant for high technology devices and nuclear weapons (he was the first Indian army commander to plead openly for nuclear weapons, in a semi-public forum at the College of Combat, Mhow), did not help matters at all. Eventually, the crises led to the formal signature in 1988 of a confidence-building measure, "Agreement on the Non-Attack of Nuclear Facilities between Indian and Pakistan," which had been first verbally broached in 1985.[13]

The second crisis, in spring 1990, was by all accounts even more serious. It had an *explicit nuclear dimension*. It too was triggered by misperceptions about each other's military maneuvers, and escalation of tension along the "hot" Kashmir border following Pakistan's large-scale Zarb-i-Momin military exercise. The timing was crucial because it came on the heels of the eruption of the *azaadi* (freedom) rebellion in the Kashmir Valley. Pakistan reportedly felt threatened that India might be tempted to carry out a surgical strike against Kahuta.

In response, according to one version, Pakistan made a deliberately demonstrative move, lining up a convoy of trucks at the gates of the Kahuta enrichment plant, thus signaling that it would be prepared to use its nuclear capability to pre-empt India. The standoff impelled Robert Gates, then US deputy national security adviser, to embark on a special mission to visit New Delhi and Islamabad and defuse the crisis. He finally succeeded, but barely in time.[14]

For the purposes of understanding the limitations of, and the high risks associated with, "existential deterrence," it is less pertinent to ask if the course of the 1990 crisis has been fully documented, than to consider whether such episodes fall within the realm of possibility. The answer must be "yes." Scenarios of the kind painted for 1990 are wholly plausible. Political and strategic misperception, breakdown of communication at crucial junctures, misreading of the adversary's moves, exchange of belligerent threats and warnings by political leaders, as well as military grandstanding—all are realities in the Indian sub-continent. For instance, General Ayub Khan launched what he thought was a pre-emptive strike in Kashmir in 1965 in the conviction that the Kashmir population would rise in rebellion against India. He was disastrously mistaken.

There is a hot-line between the Director Generals of Military Operations of the two states. But it is not regularly used. And in 1998 alone, there were no fewer than 350 cases of firing across the Kashmir border. India and Pakistan both suffer enormous losses by pursuing their strategically absurd war at Siachen Glacier, where altitudes exceed 19,000 feet. They have repeatedly failed to reach an agreement to defuse and resolve the conflict. Since 1947, India and Pakistan have had three wars against each other, which makes South Asia second only to the Middle East as the world's most war-prone region.

The characterization of the silent nuclear competition between India and Pakistan until 1998 as a situation of "stable non-weaponized deterrence," then, was misleading and wrong. The stand-off had a powerful potential to degrade and degenerate. And degenerate it did. This, of course, did not happen spontaneously or automatically, nor even only because a major political change occurred in India when the nuclearly-obsessed BJP came to power in March 1998, important as that development was. It happened with the strengthening of the forces favoring nuclearism in both India and Pakistan in the course of the extremely important debate on the CTBT while it was being negotiated in Geneva in 1994–1996. It is vital to situate the further degradation of the Indian and Pakistani nuclear policies in the context of both that debate and India's shifting foreign policy perspectives that emerged toward the end of the '80s.

The Turning Point of 1988

With the collapse of the Indo-Sri Lanka Accord in 1988, Indian ambitions to become the *acknowledged* and *permanent* hegemon of South Asia also collapsed. Though in November 1988, New Delhi flew in troops to put down a rebel coup in the Maldives, thereby sustaining its President Gayoom, this flexing of regional muscle could hardly compensate for its debacle in Sri Lanka. Nor could this be said to have retrieved some limited "prestige" for India when in May of the same year India revealed itself impotent in the face of a coup in Fiji, which brought in a government that began to seriously repress Fijians of Indian origin. New Delhi was reduced to making feeble protests and calling on Australia and New Zealand to intervene. By the end of 1988, the Indian national security establishment harbored deep uncertainty about India's stature regionally and globally. Whatever foreign policy framework this establishment had become used to operating within was already tottering when, in the next three years (1989–91), the dramatic collapse of the former USSR turned the post-war world upside down.

In those tumultuous years India's foreign policy framework suffered a double blow, from which it has never recovered. What value did the Non-Aligned Movement (NAM) now possess when one bloc no longer existed?

What value was there in India's pursuing its traditional policy of an economic tilt toward the West and a strategic tilt toward the USSR, when the latter was replaced by a smaller and far weaker Russia, itself abandoning all efforts to promote non-alignment among third world countries, and more determined than ever to forge a strategic partnership with the West, especially the US? What alternative did the Indian state now have but to abandon the "third way" of non-alignment and instead adopt the new form of neo-liberal economic globalization being assiduously peddled through what is called the "Washington Consensus," or the collective ideology of the World Bank, the International Monetary Fund and the US government? (The headquarters of the WB and IMF are in Washington and the single strongest influence on the WB/IMF is clearly exercised by the US.)

Actually, there were alternatives, both economic and political. Economically, India could have turned its gaze eastward, to Japan and the "Asian Tigers," for lessons in managing the globalization process. Politically, it could have continued to pursue a more independent path, despite the new weakness of the NAM. But an elite, whose general mindset had become more right-wing and US-oriented than ever before, and which was more insecure and frustrated than ever before, could hardly have been expected to pursue such alternatives. What emerged as a supposed foreign policy framework was a strange amalgam of shifting components.

There were four main ingredients in the brew. First, a soft *Hindutva* (Hindu sectarian nationalism and communalism) affected elite self-perceptions. This promoted a stronger desire than ever that India become a "glorious" power retrieving its "manhood," which in the eyes of a large section of the elite had been "emasculated" by centuries of Muslim rule and invasions. Such views rested on a communal misrepresentation of India's actual history, but this was largely beside the point. The fact remained that such views were widely spread and more strongly entrenched than ever before. This *Hindutva* also fed and shaped another component—an aggressive and belligerent interpretation of the so-called imperatives of *realpolitik*.

The third component was a newer and stronger adherence to neo-liberal economic thinking on the supposed compulsions of globalization. For the Indian elite, the ideological recoil from the model of bad socialism represented by the USSR and its bloc was so strong that it virtually stampeded to adopt bad capitalism. It was the new Congress government of 1991 that adopted the Washington Consensus and its IMF sponsored program of "Stabilization and Structural Adjustment" to cover a temporary, though serious, balance of payments crisis—what has aptly been called the application of a long-term "solution" to a short-term problem. Throughout the '80s Indian economic policy had moved steadily to the right. But the 1991 reforms were nonetheless a *qualitative* acceleration in that direction. Naturally, such an economic reorientation strongly reinforced the desire, and the search, for a much closer relationship with the West, particularly the US. Finally, the fourth and weakest component in this amalgam was the fast fading legacy of the non-alignment era—the lingering elements of third world solidarity.

Over the '90s, this last component has steadily shrunk in importance and the weights of the other three have shifted relative to each other, depending both on changing external circumstances and changing internal developments, such as different governments in power. But for all the confusions and drift to the right in Indian foreign policy thinking since 1988–89, it was *not* inevitable that India would go openly nuclear. To explain why it eventually did so requires a systematic tracing of the historical process by which this emerged. Most of this has already been done in this and previous chapters. Here, it will suffice to bring the story up-to-date by briefly outlining the external developments that shaped the overall Indian trajectory in the '90s.

In one important sense, the failure of certain expectations to materialize helped pave the way for overt nuclearization. After the collapse of the ex-USSR and the dramatic rightward shift in India's economic policy from mid-1991, the Indian elite generally hoped that the US would now re-evaluate its perspectives toward India and assign it a more important role than ever before in its strategic thinking. More specifically, it was expected that the time was ripe for a "new, strategic relationship" between India and the US. India was, in fact, ready to forge a "junior partnership" with the US.

Efforts to forge a closer relationship came from both sides. The neo-liberal economic reforms were warmly welcomed and endorsed in Western capitals. Indian shifts toward greater accommodation with GATT/WTO and a freer global trade and investment regime were similarly applauded. Military cooperation between the US and India reached levels inconceivable during all the previous decades of bloc rivalry and non-alignment. Not only were exchanges of officers, regular meetings and discussions, sought to be institutionalized, but joint military exercises were discussed and some limited forms of this even took place—a historic first in India-US relations. The 1992 Kicklighter Proposals (named after Lt. Gen. Claude Kicklighter, former Commander of the US Army in the Pacific) embodied this new turn. According to the Kicklighter agenda, there would be (1) annual visits to both countries by chiefs of staff; (2) an Indian/US Army executive steering council; (3) reciprocal visits by other senior commanders; (4) combined training activities and information exchange; (5) regular talks between the two armies at staff level; (6) various other forms of joint participation at different levels of the military hierarchy.

The problem lay not in any clash in principle between the US and India about what the general future thrust and direction of mutual relations should be. It lay in the fact that what India hoped to get out of the US from a "junior partnership" or "new, strategic relationship" was not something that the US felt any serious need or reason to deliver. Before elaborating on this crucial point, we should say that the nuclear issue itself (at least before the CTBT negotiations began to impose its distinctive pressures in 1994) was not the main bone of contention. To be sure, the US did not want India to be a declared nuclear power, even in its role as a junior partner or strategic friend (not yet, or quite, an ally). In this respect, right up to the May 1998 tests, the US has behaved consistently. It has always wanted to ensure that South Asia did not become openly nuclearized. Indeed, it wanted at minimum to "cap" the nuclear capabilities of India (and Pakistan), and at maximum to get them to "roll-back and eventually eliminate" their existing capacities.

The US-India-Pakistan Triangle

This India was never prepared to do (and Pakistan would not if India would not)—though in the early '90s New Delhi showed a new willingness to discuss these matters with the US. Between 1992 and 1994, four rounds of bilateral talks did not ultimately resolve mutual differences. Pakistan, of course, always had a running "dialogue" with the US on nuclear-related matters. Thus, a strange scenario emerged, in which both New Delhi and Islamabad were each prepared to talk to Washington on substantive nuclear issues, but not to each other. Even today US attitudes toward India show some continuity. After the tests and the early US surprise, anger, and irritation, things have settled down. The US is now prepared to accept the *fait accompli* of India's nuclear status (but not to formally or legally endorse it) and still wishes to keep both countries' nuclear capabilities at a level where they represent a danger to each other, but do not complicate the nuclear politics played out on a larger, extra-regional, or global arena. A proliferation of nuclearly-armed states outside the US's orbit greatly disturbs and complicates its nuclear-strategic planning and options. Hence the *variable* nature of US pressure on different actual or threshold nuclear states and their preparations. The US has been consistently hostile to North Korea on this score, oblivious if not supportive of Israel, negligent about India, and fluctuating in its attitude to Pakistan. The US is today still telling India that it wants a "partnership."[15]

Thus, the India-US differences on the nuclear issue were an irritant but not a barrier in their mutual search for a closer, more "strategic" relationship. What was (and is) the principal problem was (and is) the enormous disparity between the power and ambitions of the US and India, and therefore the much greater degree of flexibility and range of options available to the US. Naturally, what each country expected out of a closer, "strategic relationship" was different. India, following from its own economic and political shift toward the West, expected that the US, seeing India's greater strategic value and importance would correspondingly shift from its alignment, certainly with Pakistan, and perhaps to some extent from China. This the US was (and is) not prepared to do. Why should it? Why should it take India *that* seriously, despite all the rhetoric about India being potentially a future great power? After all, India is not a great or major regional or world power yet, and may not even become one!

After the end of the Cold War, South Asia became less strategically important to the US. It was never as strategically important as say, the

Middle East, but even by the US's own previous standards, now that Russia is not the rival it was and cannot attempt to "recruit" states in the South Asian region as part of its own global efforts to resist the US or isolate China, South Asia simply matters less—except for the "negative" importance created by the nuclearization of the regime.

In the flux created by the end of the Cold War, the US also has had to rethink its global strategic perspectives. It would be naïve to imagine that it has done so, and can do so for each and every part of the world. But the five great constants of its general strategic thinking in the post-Cold War era, and which enjoy near-consensus from its domestic national security establishment, are the following: (1) The US must secure and maintain strategic-political-military dominance of the oil-rich Middle East (Central Asian oil reserves are far lower by comparison and the region cannot ever have similar importance). (2) NATO enlargement must take place. (3) There must be consolidation and calculated expansion of the North American Free Trade Agreement (NAFTA). (4) The US must maintain a military capacity to fight "one-and-a-half" wars simultaneously, that is, a war on the global level and another on the regional level. (5) The US must maintain the kind of global "open" economic system whereby the dollar remains the informal world currency (with all the benefits that accrue from this) and financial inflows from all sources (including US-owned multinationals) can come in to ensure that the structurally low-saving US economy can nonetheless be sure of high investment and steady growth.

South Asia is not an area that requires urgent strategic attention from the US. It suffices if the US has a clear idea of what it does *not* want in the region, even if it does not have a clear idea of what it *wants* strategically from the region. And what it does not want is to accept some unequivocal regional hegemon when it does not have to, and when India has still not shown the capacity to actually become such a hegemon. So why on earth should the US sacrifice or weaken its relationship to Pakistan just to please India? Even more ludicrous, why should the US give up its multiple options vis-à-vis China (and toward India) just to embrace the idea that a nuclear India would be an important ally in future US efforts to isolate the supposedly rising power of a twenty-first-century China? Some right-wing Republicans or Democrats in the US may join in with some Indian strategists to engage in such speculation, but that is all it is—speculation about possible future benefits. Such birds in the bush cannot be allowed to override in importance (let alone overturn) the management of the birds-in-the-hand reality of the existing complex pattern of US-China relations.

Pakistan is important to the US both for its connection to Afghanistan and Central Asia, and for its long-standing relationship with Saudi Arabia. The latter link fits in very well with the paramount importance the US attaches to strategic control of the Middle East. Here, it is the informal US-dominated nexus pertaining to its influence and control over three states that is of vital significance—Saudi Arabia, Egypt, and Israel. Moreover,

Pakistan, unlike India, is a more pliable and reliable strategic ally for the future, and has proved to be so in the past. The US has no reason whatsoever to interpret the India-US relationship in the way that India's own strategic community understands or interprets it, or to draw the same corollaries concerning the necessary "rearrangements" or "adjustments" attendant upon consolidating such a strategic link between the two countries. For this reason alone, tensions have continued to persist throughout the '90s, despite the new opportunities and inclinations that have arisen for forging a closer Indo-US relationship. It is hardly surprising then, that a somewhat disappointed India should also currently see greater value than it did a few years ago in strengthening its traditional military-political relationship with a Russia also disappointed in its expectations and hopes regarding its new post-Cold War "partnership" with the US.[16]

Throughout the '90s, frustrations about unfulfilled aspirations and disappointed expectations have all played a role in augmenting the desire for nuclear status as a perceived short-cut to India's achieving regional and global eminence. When the CTBT issue came along in 1995–1996 and put the sharpest possible spotlight on the distinctive incoherences of India's posture of nuclear ambiguity, it did so in a general political context where there was greater likelihood than ever before that the Indian stand on the nuclear question, held for more than two decades, would be shaken and could be shattered. After all, India's posture of ambiguity had not been so much a policy as a non-policy.

India did not become a threshold nuclear state because it first formulated or systematized a policy of ambiguity and then followed it. And for most of the time it was a threshold state, it had no nuclear policy worth the name, except for the bottom-line assurance that it would neither close the option nor exercise it. Some strategists both in India and abroad pursued some feeble attempts to rationalize this posture. Accordingly, concepts like "recessed deterrence" and "non-weaponized deterrence" were coined. But for good reason, they impressed few among the hawks, and none among those already opposed to nuclear deterrence thinking. Despite the deep incoherence of the doctrinal justifications that some attempted to give to the posture of ambiguity, one had reason to be thankful that the more irresponsible and adventurist step of going openly nuclear was eschewed. But a non-policy it was, nevertheless.

The Myth of the "Chinese Threat"

One way of seeing this is simply to note that during all this time there existed *no nuclear equation relevant for serious diplomatic purposes, at least, between India and China.* Between 1974 and 1998, China did not perceive India as a nuclear security problem nor did Beijing see itself as posing such a threat to New Delhi. Therefore, it was impervious (though polite) to any attempt by India to put it in that role. Moreover, whatever pro-nuclear lobbyists outside of the Indian government may have thought or said, India was (until the BJP-led coalition came to power in 1998) reluctant to officially postulate that China constituted a serious security threat because the logic of so postulating would be to highlight the importance of engaging in systematic nuclear diplomacy between the two countries. But this was not possible. There cannot be proper nuclear diplomacy between two parties if either does not see the other as a nuclear threat to itself. India repeatedly refused all diplomatic efforts to improve regional security through progressive disarmament of itself and Pakistan citing its concerns vis-à-vis China. But it was unable to propose disarmament or nuclear arms restraint measures involving China because it did not want to openly acknowledge the great difference in their respective nuclear statuses, and hence, the enormous asymmetry in their bargaining positions.

Nuclear diplomacy is only meaningful when both sides believe they have reason to fear each other and that mutual obligations to carry out arms control or disarmament are feasible and desirable. Nuclear bargaining means each side has a bank of bargaining chips whose "value" is roughly related to the comparative strength of their respective arsenals. In regard to China, India did not in the past (and does not even now) come close to having the *minimum bank of such chips to even qualify for entrance* into the nuclear diplomatic game vis-à-vis China. An India whose own self-image demanded that it be recognized as a rough equal of China, entitled to equivalent treatment by the rest of the world community, found it impossible to acknowledge officially its great nuclear "inferiority" and enter into negotiations with China on such a basis. The end result was that India had no positive or active framework of serious nuclear diplomacy to address its own professed security needs.

There were only two ways for India to resolve this diplomatic impasse. Either it could put the Chinese threat into proper perspective and recognize it for what it always has been—an abstract and remote threat, never exercised in any way—and consider it largely irrelevant, in much the same way it views the abstract nuclear threat of the other four NWSs. India could then move toward mutual nuclear disarmament vis-à-vis Pakistan. Or else, India could go openly nuclear, and over time try to establish a nuclear balance of sorts with China, thereby initiating some kind of "relevant nuclear diplomacy" with China, but with no guarantee that it would succeed in this venture.

After May 1998, it is this last course upon which India tragically and foolishly has decided to embark. One should not underestimate the Indian CTBT debate's effect on this decision, as it left the country with a battered self-image. The entry into force clause, which demanded accession as a precondition for the treaty coming into force, was widely seen as a deliberate affront to the country. That the CTBT was nonetheless taken to the UN General Assembly and passed there, despite the Indian veto preventing its passage in the Conference on Disarmament, only poured more fuel on the burning embers of Indian resentment. Certainly, this resentment at how India was being treated during the CTBT negotiations was essentially a self-concocted one, but the resentment was real enough and unfortunately very widespread among the Indian elite. It was systematically fed by some of the most tendentious and dishonest reporting, editorializing and commentary that has ever appeared on any issue in the India print and electronic media. When, in 1996, Indian efforts to secure one of the temporary berths in the Security Council of the UN were unsuccessful, with an overwhelming majority of non-aligned states supporting Japan's bid instead, the feeling of international isolation and "revealed impotence" was almost palpable.

But the fact that it was an elite nationalism frustrated by its own sense of impotence and not any presumed iniquity of the CTBT that constituted the deeper sources for India going openly nuclear, has been strikingly revealed by the Indian attitude to the CTBT after May 1998. Most of those "strategic experts" who cried foul about the CTBT between 1994 and 1996, claiming that opposition to it was a matter of principle and genuine commitment to nuclear disarmament and not just of "national security," now have no problems whatsoever with accepting it—especially if India can get a good behind-the-scenes deal from the US. If the media overwhelmingly supported Indian opposition to the CTBT earlier, now it mostly supports India joining the Treaty as a nuclear power, with no qualms whatsoever about such a public display of cynicism. Foreign Minister Jaswant Singh even used the analogy that one's view changes when one is a passenger on the train, no longer standing on the platform; so India's view of the CTBT has changed, now that it is itself a nuclear power. India's chief negotiator at the CTBT talks, Arundhati Ghose, declared at the UN General Assembly in 1996 that India refused to sign the CTBT not because it wanted to produce nuclear weapons but because it did not want to. But after the tests, she publicly declared that it should have been obvious when India refused to sign the CTBT that it was going to test. She came out in support of the tests and India's decision to go nuclear, but is now among a small minority of the hawks who still believe that India should not sign and ratify the CTBT.

Most hawks know signing the CTBT is the minimum price India will have to pay for ending its international isolation. India can even hope to get a good deal from the US, not because it has a strong bargaining position but because the US government may find it very difficult, perhaps impossible, to get Senate ratification unless it first ties up an Indian agreement to sign the CTBT, and perhaps not even then. Thus the same India whose spokespeople declared that the country's "security was not negotiable" and even that "India does not have to explain" its actions, has sat down to negotiate with the US on precisely such issues. Whatever the outcome of these ongoing negotiations, whether or not India joins the CTBT regime, one thing should be crystal clear: India's break from its old posture of ambiguity is now final and irreversible. Though the mainstream Indian left, namely the two large communist parties, still cling to the illusion that India can, and should, go back to the posture of ambiguity, this is inconceivable. The true choices are moving forward toward nuclear sanity and disarmament, regional and global, while avoiding further weaponization, induction, and deployment of nuclear weapons; or moving backward toward such induction and deployment, emulating the other NWSs. Pakistan will follow the Indian path.[17]

NOTES

[1] This corresponds to the assessment of a sizable section of top scientists of the DAE, who for years believed and argued that Pakistan, with its "considerably inferior" science and technology base, manpower and its generally backward infrastructure, could not possibly match India in mastering a "difficult" and "advanced" technology such as nuclear energy. Especially notable in this regard are Raja Ramanna, who headed the Bhabha Atomic Research Center of the DAE at the time of the 1974 test, and P.K. Iyengar, who headed its physics group at that time. Both went on to become chairmen of the Atomic Energy Commission. They are on record as saying that Pakistan could only have mastered a technology that was "borrowed" or "stolen," as opposed to one developed "indigenously," as in the mis-stated case of India.

This assessment had less to do with a serious, considered, informed analysis of Pakistan's capabilities than with the combination of hubris, "we-are-superior-to-them" attitudes, and the DAE top brass's reluctance to concede that Pakistan could have mastered a technology—uranium enrichment by the centrifuge method—that India had failed to stabilize, let alone industrialize. Some of these factors and the unsoundness of the assessment involved went beyond narrow S&T circles and into the media. Ramanna himself became a junior minister in a (non-BJP) government and has since been nominated a Member of Parliament.

[2] L.K. Advani, quoted in "Pak told to roll back proxy war," *The Hindu* (New Delhi) 19 May 1998.

[3] Pervez Hoodbhoy, a Pakistani physicist and anti-nuclear campaigner, was among the first to point this out.

[4] For the DAE, such targets have been largely meaningless, and they have always been missed. Thus, according to its 1970 long-term plan, it should have been producing 10,000MW of nuclear electricity by 1980. Its actual performance was 800MW. It subsequently revised its target to forecast that it would reach 10,000MW by the year 2000. The capacity at the turn of the century is likely to be only about a fifth of that figure. Ironically, India's own uranium resources are inadequate to sustain 10,000MW of generating capacity in standard (thermal) nuclear reactors, as distinct from fast-breeders, which have proved extremely problematic and dangerous everywhere, including France. France, once their most ardent advocate, closed down its own much tom-tommed Superphoenix fast breeder reactor in 1998.

The DAE has long been notorious as the worst performing department of the Government of India. Its cost and time overruns are huge—typically, of the order of more than 200 percent—and its safety record is appalling. Two of the world's six most contaminated nuclear reactors are Indian. The DAE has exposed over 350 workers to radiation doses well above the maximum permissible limits that it itself stipulates.

[5] Official brochure of the Missile Technology Center quoted in *Nuclear Risk-Reduction Measures in Southern Asia* (The Henry L. Stimson Center, November 1998): 10.

6 Itty Abraham, *The Making of the Indian Atomic Bomb* (London: Zed Books, and Delhi: Orient Longman, 1998): 120.

7 See Rodney Jones, "India" in *Non-Proliferation: The Why and Wherefore* (London: Taylor & Francis, 1985): 121, note 47. Jones believes "the decision to try to fabricate and test a nuclear explosive device almost certainly was made in late 1969," as a close perusal of two sources will make clear. The two sources in question are N. Seshagiri, *The Bomb: Fallout of India's Nuclear Explosion* (Delhi: Vikas, 1975) and J. Bandopadhya, *The Making of India's Foreign Policy* (Bombay: Allied Publications, 1970)." P.N. Haksar, former principal secretary to Mrs. Gandhi, claimed in private conversation with the authors, that the decision was made in 1972.

8 Jones: 114.

9 R. Rammana, *My Years of Pilgrimage*.

10 It has been urged by some writers, including some who are strongly opposed to nuclear weapons, among them Itty Abraham in his *The Making of the Indian Atomic Bomb*, that there is an essential, immanent continuity in India's nuclear policy and doctrine from 1947 to 1998. Abraham holds that the virtual certainty and inevitability of the May 1998 tests (mediated by specific conjunctures, of course) was written into the way the Indian nuclear program was structured and operated (with its potential for dual-use). More fundamentally, it derived from the science-state dialectic that developed in India in the early years of Independence, with all its links with military uses, its limitless faith in the ideology of developmentalism, gigantic projects, secrecy, and so on.

There are several problems with this line of argument. First, it uncritically accepts the validity of, and works on the terrain of, the most right-wing, conservative and hawkish accounts of the evolution of India's nuclear policy, which too (disingenuously) posit such continuity, cutting across the Nehru period of abstinence, the post-1974 policy of ambiguity, and overt nuclearization in 1998. This elides sharp differences at the *doctrinal* level: viz, India's wholly unprincipled embrace of nuclear deterrence in 1998, a doctrine it had for fifty years described as "abhorrent," "repugnant," illegal and "illegitimate;" or the contrast between the equally long-held position that nuclear weapons are not essential to security, and the 1998 stand that "national security" considerations, even "compulsions," were the motive behind the tests.

Second, it wrongly assumes or asserts strong homogeneity and uniformity in policymaking establishments, where in fact there is plurality and difference. For instance, although the Bhabha model of institution-building in science and technology was important for the DAE, it was *not* the sole model in India's S&T. Nor was there unanimity in the top policy apparatus on conducting the May 1974 test. Abraham is similarly wrong to contend that all of India's major political parties welcomed the 1998 tests. They did not. The left opposed them. By the end of year, democratic popular opinion had shifted strongly against nuclearization.

Third, Abraham's line of argument, following post-modernist discourse, overemphasizes the language of signs and symbols—e.g. fetishes in the form of gigantic nuclear reactors akin to the *lingam*—at the cost of substantive programs and policies in identifying the key to legitimizing the state. It thus fails to understand the sources of the crisis of legitimacy and how it might be overcome. In reality, nuclear power and nuclear weapons have played a rather marginal role in resolving the systemic crisis of the state in India and Pakistan.

And fourth, it is factually wrong in inventing secrecy where it did not exist. In Abraham's book, the most glaring example of this is his description of the Indo-Canadian and Indo-US agreements of the '50s in respect of the CIRUS reactor. The arguments did not have, as he claims, "secret" appendices. Nor was that the reason why the Canadians did not strongly accuse India of having breached the accords. Canada did not protest that there was a legal breach because India contended that May 1974 was a "peaceful" explosion. What was involved, it emerged later, was blatant illegality and cheating, for of course the 1974 explosion was a bomb.

11 Bharat Karnad, distinguished for his extreme views—e.g. that India should build a nuclear force adequate to deter even the US—publicly urged that India should bomb Kahuta, if necessary with Israeli co-operation. See "Thinking the Unthinkable: Knocking Out Kahuta" in *Sunday Observer* (Delhi) 17 January 1988. This was strongly opposed by one of the authors (Praful Bidwai, "Our Own Dr. Strangelove," *Sunday Observer* (Delhi) 24 January 1988.

Karnad was later appointed to the National Security Advisory Board, and is known to have exercised considerable influence in the formulation of India's August 1999 "Draft Nuclear Doctrine."

12 Kuldip Nayyar, *The Observer* (London) 1 March 1987. It has been alleged that Pakistan managed to obtain from China vital nuclear weapons-related data (according to some, the design of a Bomb) some time during the '80s. This seems possible, but has been hard to prove. We will have to wait for some exceptional kind of disclosure before this can be conclusively established.

Had New Delhi proof, or even strong pointers to such technology transfer, it would have certainly used that information to demand that it be prohibited. At any rate, much of the data/design in question has long been widely available in the public domain. Pakistani engineers could have easily accessed it. It is hard to argue that Sino-Pakistani collaboration in this regard, even assuming it has been of a longer-term, and not occasional or sporadic, nature, constituted a "provocation" for India to radically alter its own nuclear stance.

13 The most detailed account of the 1986–7 crisis is to be found in Kanti Bajpai, P.R. Chari, et al., *Brasstacks and Beyond: Perception and Management of Crisis in South Asia* (Delhi: Manohar, 1995). See also Lt. Gen. K.M. Arif, *Working with Zia: Power Politics 1977–88* (Karachi: Oxford University Press, 1995).

14 There has been no official confirmation of the nature, degree of seriousness of, or sequence of events in, the 1990 crisis. The most detailed account is to be found in Devin Hagerty, "Nuclear Deterrence in South Asia: The 1990 Indo-Pakistani Crisis," *International Security* 20.3 (Winter 1995-96) and Michael Krepon and Mishi Faruqee, eds., *Conflict Prevention and Confidence Building Measures in South Asia: The 1990 Crisis*, Occasional Paper No. 17 (Washington, DC: The Henry L. Stimson Center, April 1994). The latter is based on a special discussion that the Henry L. Stimson Center organized among some of the key individuals involved in the episode. But the results were not conclusive.

Since then, Kanti Bajpai and Amitabh Mattoo have written an interesting article ("First Strike," *The Pioneer* (New Delhi) 23 April 1995) quoting an unnamed but "highly placed" and "authoritative" source as confirming that the Indian authorities did consider making a nuclear response to the Pakistani move, and that a major power had indeed intervened to defuse tensions between India and Pakistan.

15 Deputy Secretary of State Strobe Talbott, "Dialogue, Democracy and Nuclear Weapons in South Asia," Stanford University, Palo Alto, CA. Reported in

all the major Indian dailies of 23 January 1999. For the full text of his speech, see, "The Strands of a Spreading Cobweb," *The Asian Age* (New Delhi) 26 January 1999. US Assistant Secretary of State Karl Inderfurth has stated that both countries should not go much above the nuclear threshold; that is, that they "define those requirements in a way that are minimum but meet their needs." See "No make-or-break affair: US," *The Pioneer* (New Delhi) 28 January 1999.

16 India and Russia have agreed to a ten-year "strategic accord," which sounds more grandiose and important than it actually is. But it does mean that Russia continues to be India's most important supplier of military hardware.

17 For the importance of the CTBT and the character of the finalized treaty, see Appendix 1. This is based on the small book produced by the authors, *Testing Times: The Global Stake in a Nuclear Test Ban*, in May 1996 when the negotiations were reaching a final stage, and a more recent survey by the authors "Why India should Sign the CTBT: Returning to Our Own Agenda," *Economic and Political Weekly* 19 September 1998.

For a systematic refutation of the criticisms put forward by the anti-CTBT Indian lobby (some of which are shared by some activists of the international peace movement), see Appendix 2.

Chapter 10

Challenges to the Global Nuclear Order: Whose Crisis? Whose Dilemma?

The crossing of the nuclear threshold by India and Pakistan confronts the world with a peculiar dilemma. On the one hand, the two have become NWSs, or at least states that can go on to build and induct, and possibly deploy, such armaments (unless they voluntarily or through a negotiated arrangement agree not to do so). On the other, the existing, officially agreed, inter-state nuclear order cannot concede that status to them. Under the Nuclear Non-Proliferation Treaty (NPT), only the five countries that tested nuclear weapons prior to January 1, 1967 enjoy that status.

Thus, even those, including the US, who formulated and voted for Security Council Resolution 1172, which effectively calls upon India and Pakistan to roll back their nuclear programs and undertake nuclear disarmament, concede that what was done in May 1998 cannot in practice be "undone." As US Deputy Secretary of State Strobe Talbott put it: "We are confronted with a lamentable, but for the foreseeable future, irreversible fact: India and Pakistan have formally and overtly demonstrated that they have nuclear weapons."[1] Similarly, Assistant Secretary for South Asian Affairs Karl F. Inderfurth told the Foreign Policy Association, Washington, on January 21, 1999: "in many respects, our major challenges in South Asia are not so much about prevention, but management of thresholds that have already been crossed."[2]

At the same time, P-5 officials cannot possibly officially acknowledge India and Pakistan to be NWSs. For not only would that mean jeopardizing the stability of the existing global nuclear order, but it would be tantamount in their view, as US Secretary of State Madeleine Albright put it, to "rewarding" India and Pakistan, despite their having breached the political norm against nuclear testing. Besides, it would risk opening up a number of thorny issues, including, for example, the commitments made in the '60s by Germany and Japan to renounce nuclear weapons and become signatories to the NPT as NNWSs.

In some ways, the nuclearization of India and Pakistan must be seen as the second big question mark over the power arrangements among nation-states that were put together at the conclusion of the Second World War. The distribution of power broadly reflected the outcome of the war and was written into the structure and composition of the UN, in particular, the Security Council. Of course, the first question came up almost ten years earlier, with the fall of the Berlin Wall and the end of the Cold War. But in spite of the disintegration of the USSR and the collapse of state socialism in the East, the architecture of power built five decades earlier more or less absorbed the shocks sent out by the end of bloc rivalry. India's and Pakistan's nuclearization must be seen as carrying further the process of alteration of the post-War distribution of power. In conjunction with proposals to expand the Security Council and reform the working of the United Nations system, it acquires a new significance, even if no radical changes are in the cards.

The Skewed Global Nuclear Order

Internationally, South Asia's nuclearization poses a great challenge to the advocates of nuclear disarmament, the vast majority of the world's peoples and states, the five recognized NWSs, and more generally, to the skewed and unequal global nuclear order itself. For the world's non-proliferation regime, it is the first great breakout in thirty-five years. It is also the first time since China in 1964 that an Asian power went overtly nuclear. The breakout does not, however, mean that the non-proliferation regime has failed or that the global nuclear order has been seriously weakened, or even undermined. In the next chapter, we shall deal with the challenge to the world as a whole, and for the nuclear disarmament and peace movement. We concentrate here on the global order, the responses of the P-5 states, and the dilemmas that India and Pakistan themselves face.

The global nuclear order is oriented toward non-proliferation, not disarmament. It is based on three foundations: the Nuclear Non-Proliferation Treaty (NPT) of 1968; the P-5 states' nuclear oligopoly, their continued reliance on nuclear weapons for security, and their reluctance to move quickly toward the abolition of nuclear weapons; and a number of specific arrangements that restrict the sale of nuclear materials or transfer of nuclear and related technologies, such as the London Suppliers' Group (LSG), the Zangger accords, or the Missile Technology Control Regime.[3]

Agreements to establish nuclear weapons-free zones (NWFZs) or measures of voluntary and unilateral nuclear arms reduction by any of the P-5, or de-mating and de-alerting of nuclear warheads and delivery vehicles, and most important, the emerging Comprehensive Test Ban Treaty (CTBT) regime, are not essential to the present global nuclear order; the NPT is. Positive, transitional, steps like these are fully compatible with, and part of, progress toward complete nuclear disarmament. However partial they might be, they do not freeze existing inequalities as the NPT does, with its placing of different obligations upon two different categories of states, and especially its rendering of any obligations that pertain to real disarmament and elimination of nuclear weapons practically ineffectual. The NPT places no real, operational demands upon the NWSs to demonstrate tangible progress toward the goal of nuclear abolition.

It might be argued that the LSG or Zangger accords, or some variant of these, may also be necessary in any disarmament-oriented global order that is making a transition toward a nuclear weapons-free world. There is indeed a strong case for restricting the supply of nuclear materials or missile and rocket technology—and not just to "rogue" states or those suspected to be interested in or capable of transferring them directly or indirectly to military programs. But there is every reason why such restrictions should be *multilaterally* negotiated as part of a *universal* and non-discriminatory agreement, rather than being imposed by already powerful, developed, if not hegemonic, states who have a strong temptation to define what is permissible for others, but accept no restrictions on their own "right" of access to these materials/technologies. In their present, unequal, asymmetrical form, these agreements merely become an integral part of a skewed global nuclear order.

This non-proliferation oriented global order is founded upon the flawed and unequal bargain that lies at the heart of the NPT—not just objectively, but in the eyes of the vast majority of its signatories too, notwithstanding the partly self-serving Indian objection to the treaty. In the perception of that majority, there is a *political* relationship between the acceptance of nuclear abstinence on the part of the non-NWSs (NNWSs), and the process of nuclear disarmament, or progress toward it on the part of the NWSs. As Mueller, Fischer and Koetter argue:

> If Article VI is removed from the NPT, the remaining obligations of the NWSs (essentially not to transfer nuclear weapons to NNWS) cannot be said to establish an adequate reciprocal commitment for the renunciation of nuclear weapons by their non-nuclear weapon Treaty partners. For reasons of legal logic alone, Article VI has considerable weight in the overall framework of the Treaty.

> This legal argument implies, of course, that the NNWS are surrendering a valuable asset in renouncing nuclear weapons. This point is contestable. First, two-thirds of the parties to the NPT are still far removed from the technical ability to build nuclear weapons, even if they wished to do so. However, more to the point, the vast majority of the NNWSs consider that their security interests are better served by not having nuclear weapons and that an effective worldwide legal barrier to horizontal proliferation is very much to their advantage. That is the chief reason why they acceded to the NPT, and it is this conviction which provides the basis of the 1967 Tlatelolco and 1985 Rarotonga treaties and of freely made renunciations such as that confirmed for all time by Germany in the 1990 Treaty on the Final Settlement with Respect to Germany (the Two-plus-Four Treaty).[4]

And yet, it is fair to conclude that

> whatever may or may not be said about the "bargain" between various articles of the NPT, there is no doubt that the history as well as the politics

of the Treaty have made it abundantly clear that a majority of NNWS parties consider it the duty of the NWS to abide by the letter of Article VI. Few expect them to dispose of nuclear weapons at once. Only a few more would insist on obliging them to a very strict timetable for nuclear disarmament. A vast majority, however, encompassing industrial as well as developing countries, call for tangible steps toward a distant goal of nuclear disarmament. The process may be very protracted, but it must go on.[5]

Regrettably, that process has not taken off. The reductions related to START I and II (of which the second faced prolonged delays in ratification), are separate from and do not express a P-5 commitment to the implementation of their Article VI obligations.[6] Because of this fundamental asymmetry, which persists three decades after the NPT came into force, the non-proliferation-oriented order still remains unequal and unfair, in effect freezing the P-5 states' nuclear oligopoly.

Nevertheless, it would be foolhardy to discount the importance of the non-proliferation regime. This derives not so much from the fact that the NPT "has succeeded beyond the expectations of its founders," in reducing the number of potential proliferants from twenty or thirty to about half a dozen, as from the circumstance that without its basic discipline and constraints, including international safeguards—and despite its flaws—it would be considerably more difficult, if not impossible, to negotiate arms control, arms reduction, and disarmament measures.[7] Freedom to proliferate would have led to multiple and potentially runaway nuclear arms races, undermining efforts at arms control and even peaceful resolutions of disputes.

The non-proliferation regime has a deeply contradictory and dualistic character. The NPT *is* discriminatory. And yet, it cannot simply be thrown to the winds as some influential Indian leaders seem to advocate. The contradiction can be resolved only if the discrimination is reduced through visible progress toward nuclear weapons abolition.

What, then, is the challenge that India's and Pakistan's nuclearization poses to the non-proliferation-oriented global order? Three kinds of danger are readily conceivable. First, the direct one: that other nations will be impelled, prompted, or tempted to go nuclear because they feel threatened or because India or Pakistan are likely to clandestinely transfer nuclear materials or technology to them. Second, the danger that other states, in search of prestige, may want to emulate India and Pakistan, especially because they know that the consequences of so doing, while unpleasant, are far from unbearable. And third, South Asia's nuclearization will weaken the evolving political norm for nuclear restraint and disarmament, and reduce international support for the non-proliferation aspect of the present nuclear regime, without generating pressure on the P-5 themselves to undertake nuclear arms reduction and disarmament.

The first two categories of risk are, thankfully, relatively limited. A nuclear India and a nuclear Pakistan do threaten each other, and India has gotten into a potentially adversarial relationship with China (more later about this). But they do not directly threaten their other neighbors, nor are they likely to spur them to seek to meet any realistic security threats by acquiring nuclear weapons themselves. There is no persuasive evidence that India and Pakistan ever transferred, or are likely to transfer, nuclear materials or technologies to non-nuclear states. On the contrary, there is evidence that when requested to do so, India refused.[9]

After all, India and Pakistan are poor examples to emulate. Nuclearization has not earned them prestige. Rather it has lowered their global stature, decreased their moral authority, led to their political isolation, reduced their bargaining power, and narrowed their diplomatic-political options. The risk that states such as Iran or Libya will be more strongly impelled today than before May 1998 to acquire nuclear weapons is rather minimal. The considerations that determine their nuclear pursuits are largely independent of the actions of India and Pakistan. Besides, the international community has long known that India and Pakistan have been developing nuclear weapons, at least since the '70s. This does put them in a different category, especially after Pokharan in 1974, from Iran, Iraq, Libya, and North Korea, which all have far more limited, or even aborted, nuclear programs. This "prior knowledge" in the South Asian case made, among other factors, for a relatively soft reaction to the tests from the international community. A totally new breakout would probably attract much greater opprobrium, stiffer sanctions, and more strategic hostility.

Where Are the Missiles?

A March 1998 Report of the National Resources Defense Council (NRDC) provides, for the first time, authoritative estimates of the sizes and locations of the nuclear arsenals of the US, Russia, Britain, France, and China. The full report contains detailed descriptions, including maps and tables, of today's arsenals, and describes the events that have led to the consolidation of weapons storage sites. What follows is a summary (also prepared for the most part by the NRDC) of that report.

Taking Stock: Worldwide Nuclear Deployments 1998

Though the Cold War's end has transformed relations with Russia, and disarmament agreements have resulted in significant reductions in nuclear weapons worldwide, the NRDC estimates that some 36,000 nuclear bombs still remain in the arsenals of the five nuclear powers.

In the past decade, large-scale reductions in the size of the nuclear arsenals have resulted in significant shifts in weapons locations, shifts unequaled since the earliest days of nuclear deployments. Until now, however, no authoritative estimates of the sizes, locations, and characteristics of worldwide nuclear arsenals have been available.

In the mid-'80s the five powers possessed nearly 70,000 nuclear weapons, widely dispersed in the Soviet Union, Eastern and Western Europe, and Asia, as well as on and beneath the high seas. Since then, an extensive consolidation has taken place, with a five-fold decrease in the number of storage sites, to less than 150.

The NRDC assesses the nuclear arsenals of the five countries as follows:

The United States: Nearly 12,000 nuclear weapons (deployed or stored) are located in fourteen states. New Mexico, Georgia, Washington, Nevada, and North Dakota are the top five and account for about seventy percent of the total. The other nine are Wyoming, Missouri, Montana, Louisiana, Texas, Nebraska, California, Virginia, and Colorado.

The number of US nuclear weapons in Europe has shrunk dramatically, from over 6,000 of many types in the early '80s to some 150 B61 bombs at ten air bases in seven countries (Belgium, Germany, Greece, Italy, the Netherlands, Turkey, and the United Kingdom) by the end of 1997. The US is the only country with nuclear weapons deployed outside its borders.

Russia: Some 22,500 weapons are deployed or stored at about ninety sites in Russia. In a little-appreciated logistical feat, over the last decade, Soviet, and then Russian, members of the 12th Main

Directorate consolidated a far-flung arsenal of tens of thousands of nuclear weapons at hundreds of locations in Eastern Europe and fourteen republics to under a hundred sites in Russia today.

Great Britain: The British stockpile is about to be composed of a single weapon type—the Trident II missile on Vanguard-class submarines. According to the NRDC Report, the last WE 177 gravity bombs were scheduled for retirement by March 1998, when the Report came out. The Tornado bombers that once carried them will have only conventional missions.

France: The French stockpile totals some 450 warheads of three types at four locations, down from a dozen bases at the beginning of the 90s.

China: The Chinese stockpile is estimated at about 400 located at some 20 sites.

Source: *Natural Resources Defense Council, Washington DC.*

Dangers from Altered Security Equations

The most serious risk in India's and Pakistan's neighborhood lies in the altered security equation between China and India. Immediately after the tests, India repeatedly named China as the source of the gravest threat to its security, even though China had made no belligerent gestures, and despite the two major agreements it signed in 1993 and 1996 on "peace and tranquillity" along the disputed border with India and on a number of troop reduction, risk limitation, and confidence-building measures. China was the last of the P-5 states with which India tried to open some kind of dialogue after the tests, largely unsuccessfully. China conveyed its dismay and resentment at being named a "threat" in no uncertain terms, while "strongly condemning" the tests.[10]

Even in early 1999, the Chinese response to India's offer to discuss the nuclear weapons issue was to demand compliance with Security Council Resolution 1172. This was a much tougher line than that of the US, which had noted significant "progress" in its bilateral talks with India and Pakistan and "appreciated" the gestures toward nuclear restraint made by the two states in late 1998, primarily in the form of a No First Use commitment by India, and Pakistan's declaration that it would meet India half-way in defusing their mutual nuclear rivalry (although it did not offer No First Use).

If and when India fully develops and operationalizes the *Agni* missile, and especially its extended-range version (*Agni-II* or *Agni-plus*), China is likely to feel impelled to factor India seriously into its nuclear-military calculations. But if India slows down the pace of missile development and indicates that it has no plans to deploy intermediate-range missiles at least for an extended period of time, perhaps China will not relaunch its intermediate-range *Dong Feng 25* missile development program, which could target cities in the Indian heartland. After the release of the "Draft Nuclear Doctrine," the likelihood of such relaunching becomes higher.

In other words, the tests by themselves are not certain, even very likely, to alter the Sino-Indian security equation decisively. India would have to do *more*—e.g. proceed with rapid development of the *Agni* and explore the possibility of mating a warhead with it and deploying it—before this happens. But this danger is very real and growing. Going by the poor outcome of the visit of Indian Foreign Secretary Raghunath to Beijing in January 1999, and by the statements of Sha Zukang, head of China's department for arms control and disarmament relations between the two states are not about to improve dramatically.[11]

Although India and China have not yet entered into a relationship of strategic hostility, they now oscillate between strategic indifference and strategic rivalry. This should underscore the importance of restraint on India's part in nuclear and missile development and deployment, as well as the salience of a strategic dialogue and further arms-reduction and confidence-building measures between the two countries. Absent this, the danger could increase significantly.

It is the third category of risk, that of the *weakening of the international moral-political norm* and will for nuclear restraint, that is truly grave, and of both immediate and long-term consequence. This must be seen against the backdrop of the failure of the NPT review process and the utter cynicism with which the P-5 have treated it, resisting and dismissing all entreaties and appeals by the NNWSs to move toward nuclear disarmament. In 1998, just days before India's May 11 tests, the NPT preparatory conference in Geneva ended in bitter disagreement and mutual recrimination, with the P-5 stubbornly refusing even the suggestion that there is a legal obligation on them to undertake nuclear disarmament.

The Stockpile Stewardship program, the US failure to ratify the CTBT, Russia's deployment of the new *Topol*-M missiles, and the double standards employed by the Western nuclear powers, especially the US, in regard to Israel, on the one hand, and India and Pakistan, on the other, are all indices of the persistence of the Great Powers' wholly negative attitudes and double standards, and cast serious doubt upon the possibility and feasibility of a world without nuclear weapons. The sub-critical tests conducted by the US and Russia have further strengthened such doubts.[12] If these doubts grow, if there is no progress toward qualitative nuclear arms reduction and disarmament, and if only minor measures of restraint are successfully negotiated (such as an FMCT that only bans future production of fissile material and excludes existing stocks), the will of the world community to erect barriers to proliferation and to grapple with the means to bring about nuclear disarmament will weaken. That would be a serious, even historic, setback, with real and growing possibilities of breakouts from the non-proliferation regime. A world with more nuclear powers would be even more insecure and unsafe than today.

The overt nuclearization of India and Pakistan confronts the P-5 with a dilemma. It effectively, and in a *de facto* manner, although not *de jure*, ends their oligopoly of possession of nuclear weapons, even if it does not seriously undermine the non-proliferation regime. But where and how do they accommodate India and Pakistan? Clearly, they cannot expect them to join the NPT as non-nuclear weapons-state signatories, when they already have the weapons. Nor can the P-5 officially admit them to the Nuclear Club as its full-fledged members.

The P-5 could, at most, succeed in pressuring India and Pakistan to stay fairly close to the nuclear threshold and to manage their mutual nuclear and conventional rivalry within "acceptable" limits, in non-deployment mode. They would at least have to create a new category—a third class, of low-ranking nuclear states, or Nuclear Possessor States, distinct from NWSs. To both these ends, the P-5 would have to engage the two states in a dialogue and seek some assurances of a stable strategic balance in South Asia and a commitment from both India and Pakistan not to enter into a full-fledged nuclear arms race with each other, nor let the effects of their newly required nuclear status spread beyond the boundaries of the South Asian region. This is precisely what the P-5, with the US in the lead, are now attempting.

The core P-5 agenda, as it is emerging, is threefold. First, it seeks to insure that India and Pakistan do not disturb the global non-proliferation regime (however elevated their rhetoric against its iniquities and however loud their complaints against "nuclear apartheid"). Secondly, their emergence as minor NWSs or Nuclear Possessor States must not radically upset regional and global strategic balances. This means containing the nuclear prowess and reach of India and Pakistan to the South Asian region as much as possible. This will require assurances that they (1) will not rapidly stockpile huge quantities of fissile material or develop and test-fly nuclear-capable missiles, (2) will delay the mating of delivery vehicles and warheads, and (3) desist from openly deploying missiles or positioning them close to each other's borders. The third and equally important part of the P-5 agenda involves a tacit agreement that the NNWSs are not allowed by the P-5 (and now India and Pakistan) to seize effective control of the nuclear disarmament agenda. In other words, India and Pakistan must behave like "responsible," loyal junior partners of the P-5, deserving aspirants to, or associate members of, the Nuclear Club, with the same stake as the P-5 in barring fresh entry and keeping all other aspirants as far from the Clubhouse as possible.

This is not to argue that all of the P-5 have identical agendas or that there are no differences in their approaches to the sub-continent, or individually to India and Pakistan. There are indeed significant divergences. For instance, Russia, France, and Britain all refused to impose economic sanctions upon India. France was the first P-5 state that welcomed the visit of a senior level Indian emissary to meet President Chirac after the May tests. It later started a "strategic dialogue" with India, and India has since indicated, following a visit by Defense Minister Fernandes to Paris in January 1999, that it will make sizable arms purchases from France. (The two have had significant military and nuclear cooperative programs in the past).

Russia went even further. Soon after the tests, it supported India's candidature for permanent membership of the UN Security Council. It then signed wide-ranging security cooperation and arms purchase agreements with India during a visit by Prime Minister Yevgeny Primakov in December 1998. Similarly, China was considerably softer on Pakistan than on India; it only expressed "deep regret" over Pakistan's tests, but "strongly condemned" India's. It was also appreciative of Pakistan's "compulsions" to test after India did. The US tended, despite a growing relationship with India, to sympathize with Pakistan's economic plight in the wake of sanctions, and said so openly.[13]

A Multi-Class Nuclear Club

The US and Russia comprise the first class of the Nuclear Club, by virtue of the size and range of their nuclear arsenals. The second-class members are the UK, France, and China. They have their points of tension vis-a-vis the former. China and France once declared that when the US and Russia reduced their arsenals by fifty percent, they would join the reduction/disarmament process. Once this became possible (after the Cold War) both resiled from their earlier commitments and declared, joined by the UK, that the US and Russia would have to reduce their arsenals by ninety-five percent before they join in. China, in particular, resists the idea of a "no increase" pledge, wary as it is of future US Theater Missile Defense plans.

The third-class members, India and Pakistan, also have their points of tension and difference with the other NWSs, which could well surface in the FMCT negotiations. If these talks proceed too fast—and India, for example, is worried that it won't have accumulated "enough" stock by the time the talks are to conclude—then New Delhi could well try to stall matters. Despite these and other significant differences and tensions *within* the Nuclear Club, what unites its members *against* the NNWSs is much more important than what divides them. This must be kept in mind even as the NNWSs try to work on these differences to better pursue complete nuclear disarmament.

The existing five recognized NWSs do not want India and Pakistan to become examples for others to emulate; they must not be allowed to form independent tactical alliances and blocs of their choosing, which might shake up the global nuclear status quo. But whatever the claims of nuclear hawks and ultra-nationalists in the two countries, or even of some in the international peace and nuclear disarmament movement, India and Pakistan have not ended up defying the global nuclear order. All they seek is a place at its margins, in or close to the Nuclear Club. Their freedom of maneuver remains as limited as ever. Indeed, they have lost some of their leverage. Their nuclearization does not represent the P-5's "comeuppance," but largely conforms to the existing order.

So far as India is concerned, the US and China remain at two different poles. China has refused to engage India in substantive negotiations on the nuclear weapons issue. In fact, in early 1999, the head of China's department for arms control and disarmament, Sha Zukang, not only demanded that India and Pakistan "stop and reverse" their nuclear development programs, but also went so far as to implicitly accuse Washington of violating UN Security Council Resolution 1172, which condemned the tests: "It is a direct violation [of the Resolution] to negotiate, or even discuss, with India on India's so-called minimum nuclear deterrence capability."[14] According to another report from Beijing, China opposes any deal that would allow India to maintain a "minimum nuclear deterrent in return for joining the Comprehensive Test Ban Treaty... China has conveyed its stand on the South Asian nuclear issue to the US in clear-cut terms," according to Chinese officials who recalled the June 27, 1999 joint statement issued after talks between the Chinese and US presidents.[15] Following the release of India's "Draft Nuclear Doctrine," the Chinese position is likely to harden.

Unlike China, the US has held substantive talks with India on nuclear and security issues. By early February 1999, the US had concluded eight rounds of talks each with India and Pakistan. At the same time, the US has followed a strategy of economic sanctions and trade embargoes on Indian military and nuclear-related research laboratories, as well as public enterprises engaged in arms production. In November 1998, it released a list naming 200 institutions in India that were to be subject to such embargoes.

Washington's aims, as stated in a Brookings Institution speech by Talbott, as well as by other US officials, are to get India to agree to some measures of restraint, including (1) signature of the CTBT, (2) non-deployment of missiles and aircraft capable in the immediate future of carrying nuclear bombs/warheads, (3) freezing production of fissile material, and (4) instituting strict controls on the export of nuclear materials or technologies. India has repeatedly indicated that it will sign the CTBT. In September 1998, four months after the tests, Indian military scientists prepared the technical ground for this by declaring that no further tests are necessary to achieve reliable weaponization, so India could go ahead and sign the CTBT without compromising its security. They have since reiterated this position.

Indian officials have also indicated that India has no intention or immediate plans to deploy nuclear weapons openly in war-fighting mode, with full command and control systems in place, but that it would like an acknowledgement of the legitimacy of its "minimum credible nuclear deterrent" as the price for this. This "minimum" deterrent proved a sticking point, at least until the end of the eighth round of talks. But the US has moved toward lifting some sanctions and stopped voting against World Bank and other loans to India. The US tilted toward India during the Kargil crisis. And with the October 1999 coup in Pakistan, Indo-US relations seem set to improve further, with a Clinton visit to India likely in early 2000.

If the present US effort succeeds, a compromise accommodating India (and Pakistan) at the margins of the existing world nuclear order would come into being. But conceding the legitimacy of their "deterrent," is thoroughly undesirable if, as is likely, it freezes and extends the nuclear order as it is, rather than radically reforming, and re-orienting it toward disarmament. An opportunity to make a major thrust forward toward both comprehensive and incremental approaches to nuclear disarmament would be lost. The P-5 would be united in bringing about and ensuring just such a loss, even if their own rationalizations for retaining their NWS status and their arsenals, and their approaches to arms reduction and disarmament, all differ significantly from one another.

A Hardening US Position

The US remains the most reluctant among the P-5 to make any meaningful commitment to nuclear disarmament, except as some kind of remote future goal, although President Clinton recently came close to acknowledging, however obliquely and without any reference to the US's own past policies, that nuclear weapons have little to do with achieving peace and security. Immediately after the first Pakistani tests of May 28, he said: "I cannot believe that we are about to start the 21st century by having the Indian subcontinent repeat the worst mistakes of the 20th century, when we know it is not necessary to peace, to security, to prosperity, to national greatness, or personal fulfillment."[16] Yet Clinton badly failed to persuade the US Congress to ratify the CTBT.

With the end of the Cold War, the fundamental rationale of US nuclear weapons, and of NATO strategic doctrine, simply collapsed. It became manifestly clear that the sheer magnitude and size of the US arsenal could in no way be justified in the absence of the Warsaw Pact. The US then invented other rationales for its nuclear weapons and their continued stewardship—first through ideologists and pamphleteers exploiting prejudices about the "Islamic threat," and peddling such notions of security as based on a "clash of civilizations" and "rogue" states or nuclear terrorists, and later through official policies and programs.

Of these last, the Nuclear Posture Review (NPR) of September 1994, the Presidential Decision Directive-60 (PDD-60) and the Science-Based Stockpile Stewardship Program (SSMP) are the most important. They address both the subjective and objective dimensions of "security" based on nuclearism. Subjectively, the NPR and PDD-60 provide the rationale for *retaining* nuclear weapons, while at the same time trying to make them do more things, even though there will be fewer such weapons around than in the Cold War era. PDD-60 advances the notion of winnable nuclear wars, broadens the list of sites that can be struck in China, and allows use against "rogue states" and attackers using non-nuclear weapons of mass destruction.

The introduction of a "single integrated operational plan" (SIOP) in the flexible Strategic War Planning System (SWPS) of 1992 eliminated the distinction between strategic and tactical nuclear planning. Through what is called "adaptive planning," the nuclear target list can be expanded, even as the number of bombs continues to decline. In short, PDD-60 provides a series of nuclear attack *options*. Since not only a lesser number, but older warheads are being asked to do more, the SSMP must ensure their "reliability." Of course, the SSMP is meant not only to better *preserve* aging nuclear weapons systems, but also to better *prepare* for a future qualitative arms race if a breakout from post-Cold War constraints ever takes place.

The formulations that the NPR and PDD-60 offer are so dubious that it is hard to believe they sound plausible even to believers in America's "manifest destiny" or its self-appointed role as world leader, especially to protect it from mass-destruction catastrophes engineered by fanatics, lunatics, and assorted terrorists. It is not the intrinsic, logical value, or even strategic plausibility, of such reasoning, but the prevalence of terrible intellectual inertia, that prevents any rational thinking on issues of security. That alone explains why the NPR and PDD-60 went through with little criticism or discussion.

This inertia entails a refusal to countenance the possibility that the US could achieve adequate security without its thousands of nuclear warheads, missiles, submarines, and aircraft, or without dismantling powerful weapons laboratories, and without severely pruning its still gargantuan nuclear weapons budget, which runs at $35 billion a year a decade after the end of the Cold War. Similarly, not only must the nuclear weapons labs be kept running; they must be given expensive facilities (some call them "exercise machines") to play with—in the shape of the SSMP and direct-fusion weapons experiments, etc. Indeed, in 1995–96, Clinton had to make a deal over the CTBT by giving in to pressure from the laboratories and from Pentagon lobbies, which meant accepting the SSMP as a *quid pro quo*.

Precisely because the security rationale is so weak for retaining huge stocks of nuclear weapons and continuing further nuclear weapons development, including possibly fourth-generation weapons, South Asia's nuclearization has not provoked the least bit of rethinking or heart-searching in the US administration on its nuclear posture and policies. Subjecting these to scrutiny and discussion would open a Pandora's Box. All that the South Asian breakout has done is to prompt the US to co-opt India and Pakistan into the existing nuclear order, without questioning any of the assumptions or foundations of that order.

In Russia, the rationale for retaining the unwieldy nuclear arsenal, which that impoverished country can ill-afford, has had less to do with real security than with a purely subjective rationale, that of shoring up that state's shrinking stature and declining image. Russia has moved in a retrograde direction since its "independence" from the former Soviet Union—rescinding its No First Use pledge, embarking upon modernization of some of its nuclear warheads and missiles, and demonstrating a far greater reluctance than in the Brezhnev or Gorbachev period (when it was far more positive and flexible than the US) to move toward nuclear arms reduction and disarmament or support initiatives to promote these in multilateral forums.

Russia, by no stretch of the imagination, has any need to conduct any more nuclear tests, in order to develop new weapons or designs, in the interests of greater security. And yet, in 1996, it (along with China) insisted on an entry into force clause being introduced into the CTBT text, which was solely designed to get every other nuclear-capable state on board. The logic was: why should we alone suffer the "disadvantage" of not being able to test? Let others suffer too. This, when even the US, normally ultra-conservative, was fairly relaxed about the issue, at least to start with. Clearly, Russia is also trying to get its nuclear weapons (which are fewer in number) to do more and different things: from using them as bargaining chips to trying (futilely) to recover lost "national honor" through them. The new situation in South Asia has not jolted Russia into reconsidering its nuclear policies, either. On the contrary, the rather fanciful idea that Prime Minister Primakov threw up in December 1998 of a grand strategic triangle or partnership between Russia, China, and India suggests that nostalgia for past glory, rather than hard-nosed strategic calculation, plays a significant role in policy-thinking in Moscow.

As for the second-rank NWSs, France, China and Britain, the first two insist on waiting and watching the Big Two—*they* have to set the pace of reduction and disarmament. France and China could take dramatic initiatives unilaterally to accelerate this momentum, but they won't. Britain does not pursue a fully independent nuclear policy of its own. China or France could take a somewhat autonomous stand and lend some support to the NNWSs' demand for implementing the recommendations of the International Court of Justice in favor of completing negotiations on the abolition of all nuclear weapons at an early date. But controlled as they are by the nuclear mindset, they have not been jolted into action or new thinking even in the post-Cold War period.

Clearly, unless pressure is brought to bear upon these second-rank nuclear states through friendly governments, through citizens' groups and NGOs, and through mass campaigns and peace movements, it will prove impossible to recruit them into a bold new initiative that favors nuclear arms reduction and disarmament. How this might be done is discussed in the next chapter.

The New Nukes' Dilemmas

Finally, what of the dilemmas of the New Nukes, India and Pakistan, themselves? Nuclearization has proved a Faustian bargain for them. Their entire foreign policy agendas have been largely narrowed down to limiting the damage caused by the crossing of the threshold. Their economies have suffered grievously, as has their credibility. To hide its embarrassment, and in a desperate move to regain lost ground, India has embarked on a strategy of making largely token gestures of nuclear restraint, and still reiterating some vague commitment to nuclear weapons abolition.

For instance, in November 1998, it moved a resolution in the UN General Assembly calling for the de-alerting of nuclear weapons and separating warheads from delivery vehicles. After stumbling into nuclear testing, and making a number of incoherent statements about its nuclear policy, by early 1999, India fashioned an attempt at a "reasonable" and "sober" formulation: India does not want to amass and deploy large numbers of nuclear weapons. It only wants to build a "credible minimum deterrent." It unilaterally offers never to be the first to use nuclear weapons against an adversary, and never to use them against a non-nuclear state. And so on.

In reality, these are purely token gestures. De-alerting nuclear weapons is a far cry from disarming them or dismantling them. India may even have been making a virtue out of necessity (its own limited capability for full deployment) by advocating that warheads and delivery vehicles be kept separated. This is at best a risk-reduction or arms control measure, not a disarmament measure. Moreover, one of the important aspects of de-alerting is that this is something that can be done bilaterally, and without international treaties. The US and Russia have been discussing and doing this to an extent.

There have been genuine and reasonable worries that India's attempt to make a general resolution of this at this particular time would jeopardize ongoing efforts such as these by forcing a negative vote and a hardening of positions. At some point, a general de-alerting posture makes eminent sense and must be pursued. But grounds for it have to be carefully prepared. De-deploying nuclear weapons is a desirable *step*, but hardly an *end* in itself, nor a *substitute* for genuine disarmament.

The "credible minimum deterrent" concept is too vague and shifting to mean very much. As discussed earlier, it is no assurance that India will not get sucked into a nuclear arms race of the classical Cold War type, albeit on a smaller scale.

India's No First Use commitment does not mark a radical break from nuclear deterrence-based thinking. It is fully compatible with it. True, a commitment to No First Use, even if unilateral and legally unenforceable, even meaningless, is better than the absence of such a commitment, or a doctrine that advocates pre-emptive use of nuclear weapons even when one is not threatened with nuclear weapons.[17] But a No First Use commitment by India can always be overruled in a situation of conflict or of rapid escalation of hostile exchanges, by the invocation of "military necessity," and the citing of the "supreme national interest" or a "national emergency." For, within the dread logic of nuclear deterrence-based thinking, it can be persuasively argued that the threat of use of nuclear weapons, backed by a stark demonstration of preparations and the will to use them, if not the actual use of them, would ultimately be less "costly" than the consequences of staying stuck to No First Use. This is true a *fortiori* when the adversary (in India's case, Pakistan) has made no such commitment and would perhaps have—or at least so many in the Indian elite believe—no compunctions in using its nuclear bombs first. In a situation of "use them or lose them," military considerations of a fairly crude nature are likely to prevail, rather than cautious, sober, principled thinking based upon a recollection of noble offers made in the past, in different circumstances.

The force-of-circumstances argument apart, Indian and Pakistani strategic moves on the ground are bound to be affected in a major way by military personnel who are trained to think of battles and wars in terms such as "element of surprise," "overwhelming the enemy" and establishing not just decisive "superiority," but real "supremacy" over the adversary at an early stage of a conflict. Such generals, admirals, and air marshals can be expected to be loath to surrender the vital option to use, or at least threaten to use, nuclear weapons first. In the Indian subcontinental context, the prevalent uncertainties about each other's intentions, preparations, and even doctrines, only adds to the strategic uncertainties and tensions involved in conflicts. And war is about establishing or re-establishing certainties, about creating decisive, violent shifts in power balances and strategic equations. Few generals are likely to pass up all the options that are effectively denied them by strict, categorical adherence to a No First Use commitment.

In short, a No First Use declaration by India *in current circumstances* is diversionary and hollow. But a No First Use declaration by the existing NWSs is of real importance, and will be discussed in the next chapter.

Besides, the Indian government faces a credibility problem. It has so brazenly, so violently, so comprehensively, and so irredeemably, breached its own stated and well-established policies on the question of nuclear weapons, especially at the doctrinal level, that its word can no longer be taken seriously. There is a double *credibility gap* in the Indian case. Throughout the '90s, New Delhi has often spoken from the moral high ground, only to do the opposite of what it says—especially on the nuclear issue. It would be extraordinarily naive to think that just because it crossed the nuclear threshold, it has shed its hypocrisy and double standards once and for all. Quite the contrary. The world— and all those Indians who stand for integrity and honesty in the conduct of public affairs—must treat New Delhi as being just as culpable of double standards and hypocrisy as any other state, including the most hegemonistic ones.

Pakistan is less hypocritical, and does not profess the same adherence to universal and noble values as does India. But, as discussed earlier, that does not make it less immoral or politically more respectable either in its pursuit of nuclear weapons or in its courtship of the US, which, Pakistan hopes, will favor it over India as an ally and friend. Pakistan, with its economy crumbling, and its state structures in an advanced stage of decay and disintegration, faces a dilemma: manufacturing and deploying nuclear weapons and missiles is liable to impose an unbearable burden on the government and the people. On the other hand, not "matching" India, almost bomb for bomb, could lead to the discrediting of Pakistan's civilian rulers in the eyes of the extremely powerful military and also make its elected governments more vulnerable to the depredations of fanatical Islamicist forces.

Pakistan, for the moment, is trying to convert its weakness (fear of its collapse as economy or state) into a strength in its bargaining with the US. It has a stake in limiting its nuclear rivalry with India, but the horizons of its ruling elite are limited to the South Asian region. It cannot be expected to take a bold initiative in favor of nuclear disarmament at the global level.

South Asia's nuclearization, then, presents different dilemmas, challenges and problems for the different actors involved. The most important of these are the challenges it presents to the advocates of nuclear disarmament and to the peace movements in different parts of the world.

NOTES

[1] Strobe Talbott, address at Conference on Diplomacy and Preventive Defense, Stanford University, Palo Alto, CA 16 January 1999. *Official Text*, US Information Service, New Delhi, 25 January 1999.

[2] Talbott.

[3] The London Suppliers' Group was established in 1975, following India's first nuclear explosion, by seven industrially developed countries working behind closed doors. It was the result of a US initiative to set up a broad-based group to ensure that sensitive nuclear plants and technologies are not supplied to future tactical proliferators. When the "Guidelines for Nuclear Transfers of 1977" (London Guidelines) were published in 1978, fifteen countries adhered to them. The LSG now has more than thirty members, including European Union states, many members of the former Warsaw Pact, and most members of the Organization for Economic Cooperation and Development (OECD).

The Zangger Committee, named after its first chairman, Professor Claude Zangger of Switzerland, was established to define what was meant in the NPT's Article III not only by "source or special fissionable material" but also by "equipment or material especially designed or prepared for the processing, use or production of special fissionable material," since the parties were required not to export such items to any NNWS "unless the source or special fissionable material" is "subject to safeguards." The committee completed its first "trigger list" in July 1974.

The MTCR is a closed-door group set up in 1987 by different states to restrict transfers or sales of missiles or components of missiles above the range of 300 km. It is essentially a non-proliferation measure.

[4] *Nuclear Non-Proliferation and Global Order* (Oxford: SIPRI/Oxford University Press, 1994) 7.

[5] *Nuclear Non-Proliferation:* 7–8.

[6] Article VI reads: "Each of the Parties to the Treaty undertakes to pursue negotiations in good faith on effective measures relating to cessation of the nuclear arms race at an early date and to nuclear disarmament, and on a treaty on general and complete disarmament under strict and effective international control."

[7] George Perkovich, "Nuclear Proliferation," *Foreign Policy* Fall 1998: 12. Perkovich recalls: "Back in 1963, President John Kennedy had feared that 20 to 30 states would build nuclear weapons by the 1970s."

[8] For instance, India's Foreign Minister Jaswant Singh, when asked, "If countries like Iraq, Iran were to conduct tests, would you deny them their right to test?" replied: "No, this is the principle. Do you deny that nations on this earth have not the right to equal and legitimate security?" Interview with *The Indian Express* 28 January 1999.

[9] For instance, India after the 1974 nuclear test was reportedly approached by countries such as Libya, Iran, and Iraq with requests for assistance in the nuclear field. It iurned down three requests. However, as a minister in the Janata Party government of 1977-8, George Fernandes is believed to have strongly lobbied for transferring nuclear technology to Libya. He was overruled by Prime Minister Morarji Desai.

[10] China's initial reaction to India's tests was the angriest of all the responses of the

P-5 states. In May, it accused India of "undermining the international effort in banning N-tests so as to obtain hegemony in South Asia in defiance of world opinion..." It said the tests reveal "nothing but an outrageous contempt for the common will of the international community for the CTBT... and (would) entail serious consequences to peace and stability." "India turns to an old comrade as China talks tough," *The Indian Express* (New Delhi) 15 May 1998.

Later, in an exclusive interview, on the eve of Clinton's visit to China in June, President Jiang Zemin said: "In November 1996, I paid a successful visit to India... I was accorded a very friendly reception by the government and people of India. That visit has left me with very good memories. I was very surprised that they conducted the nuclear tests. I was even more surprised that they cited China as a reason for their nuclear testing. I really don't know what kind of threat China poses." Cited in *The Hindu* (Delhi) 22 June 1998.

The assessment of Chinese experts, quoted in *Jane's Defense Weekly*, is that India will take at least ten more years to establish an "operational nuclear strike capability," and cannot yet pose a grave or "immediate threat" to Chinese security. This follows a review by China's security planners over whether they should upgrade their rating of the threat from India. Cited in *The Hindustan Times* (New Delhi) 30 December 1998.

[11] For Sha's statements, see "China jolts India with nuclear blast," *The Telegraph*, (Calcutta) 14 January 1999.

[12] By early 1999, the US had conducted six sub-critical tests at the Nevada test site. And in December 1998, the Russians officially admitted to having carried out five such tests at an Arctic testing range, between September 14 and December 13, according to the Interfax agency. Cited in *The Hindu* (Delhi) 25 December 1998.

[13] US Assistant Secretary for South Asian Affairs Karl F. Inderfurth said on January 21, 1999 that "the U.S. supports the International Monetary Fund's approved economic plan for Pakistan because it would assist Pakistan to get through this rough economic time.... We did not want to see economic collapse in Pakistan." Cited in *Backgrounder* (New Delhi: US Information Service, 27 January 1999.

[14] See note 11, above.

[15] "China opposes minimum n-deterrence for India," *The Hindu* (Delhi) 28 January 1999.

[16] Quoted widely, among others by Zia Mian and M.V. Ramana, "Stepping Away from the Nuclear Abyss," *INESAP Bulletin* (Darmstadt) November 1998: 13.

[17] The NATO doctrine of pre-emptive first use of nuclear weapons to eliminate the possibility of an adversary attack with non-nuclear weapons of mass destructions such as chemical or biological weapons, is utterly reprehensible and violates both the laws of warfare and the principle of proportionality in ethics.

Chapter 11

The Struggle for Nuclear Weapons Abolition

Them and Us

They are the upholders of the existing nuclear order. We are the opponents of that order. The term "We" includes all those individuals, groups, movements, and governments that are most seriously, honestly, and unequivocally committed to rapid, global disarmament. This distinction between them and us is vital and must be kept in mind if we are even to understand the tasks that lie ahead of humanity, as well as who it is that must be relied upon to pursue their fulfillment most strongly and energetically. The Pakistani and Indian tests are not a wake-up call for *them*. They are a wake-up call and challenge to *us*. The problems created for the existing nuclear regime are of a much lesser and qualitatively different order than the problems created for us.

For *them*, the problems are of the in-house variety. Transposing and somewhat mutilating James Bond's famous remark, the existing nuclear order has been stirred but not seriously shaken, by the recent Indian and Pakistani actions. For *them*, the central concern remains what it was before—keeping the focus of anti-nuclear activities and negotiations on non-proliferation, rather than rapid and steady disarmament. Contrary to popular belief, this situation can continue for a long time. The existing nuclear order cannot "absorb" ten or twenty new entrants. But it can accommodate the new reality of India and Pakistan (and a few more) becoming *de facto* nuclear states. If a state with apparently strong anti-US sentiments like Iran or Iraq were to acquire such weapons capability or cross the threshold, it would certainly complicate matters. The anti-US "red bombs" of the USSR and China did.

Newer entrants such as these will create a qualitatively higher danger of bombs being used or nuclear hostilities breaking out, either through a pre-emptive US nuclear strike, or a terrible new Middle-East face-off. But these are *fundamental* challenges to us, not to them. The existing NWSs have been prepared to live with the dangers of a nuclear bombing or exchange for decades and will keep on doing so. They will continue to stress the importance of maintaining some kind of non-proliferation regime as their primary goal even if the nuclear club was to be further extended to informally include a total of ten or so countries.

What has been called the non-proliferation regime is *not* about to unravel under the weight of its supposed contradictions. That kind of thinking is an illusion that anti-nuclear disarmament activists would do well to avoid: it is a misplaced conclusion drawn from the existence of nuclear hypocrisy. The offensiveness of this hypocrisy is self-evident. It is also written into the very nature of the unequal nuclear order. But hypocrisy never drives other countries to go nuclear. And existing NWSs are not "penalized" for their hypocrisies by such additions. Hypocrisy provides no comeuppance for NWSs through the route of unwanted but limited proliferation. That is why the NWSs continue in their deceits, with their basic orientations persisting, but joined now by newer, junior hypocrites.

If the hypocrisies of the NWSs are to provide a source of possible comeuppance for them, that can only happen through another route. It is only when the existence of such hypocrisies can be harnessed by the real agents of disarmament to tap the wider public anger against the NWSs that pressure can be imposed on nuclear elites to weaken their ranks and erode their power and influence. The central question for us, then, remains effectively what it has been for the last decade: How do we use the window of opportunity created by the end of the Cold War to shift the fulcrum of existing anti-nuclear negotiations from non-proliferation to disarmament? What are the lessons we must learn from the past, especially from our past of anti-nuclear activity and mobilization? Who are the principal agents of that struggle today? How do we go about defining and pursuing our goals, transitional and final? These are the very difficult and complicated issues that this chapter will address, howsoever inadequately or incompletely.

Lessons from Our Past

Certain evils can disappear for good from human societies, never to reappear. This has happened with colonialism and apartheid. It can happen with nuclearism and nuclear weapons. In each of these cases, successful achievement rests on two points. The mindset that would legitimize such evil practices in the name of national or elite power and influence is thoroughly delegitimized, both morally and politically. An alternative emerges that persuades more and more of those who once defended such practices to abandon them because they no longer make sense. This is usually partly because resistance to, and disapprobation of, those practices has become stronger than ever and therefore the "costs" ever higher. And it is partly because the "value" of giving up colonialism, apartheid, or nuclearism becomes obvious and tangible. That is to say, the struggle against an evil like nuclearism and nuclear weapons, if it is to be sustained through its inevitable downturns, lapses and fatigues, cannot simply be connected to something so intrinsically "negative" as the mere striving for survival or peace. Even when it is the survival of the planet and of the human species that is at stake.

The goal of lasting nuclear peace, that is, permanent freedom from the threat of nuclear war, must have some kind of material, social content and shape if it is to inspire millions and arouse them from their myriad problems of everyday life to practically engage, in howsoever a modest way, in the struggle to bring about global disarmament. The problem has never been achieving popularity for, or acceptance of, the ideal of a nuclear-free world, but of convincing enough people to join in the race against time to bring it about before it is too late for some, or all of us, on this planet. The issue has been how to generate the sense of urgency and collective action that together can forge a tool of protest sufficiently powerful as to make a political difference. And then to keep on pressing for positive changes, thus creating a cumulative dynamic of actual disarmament. That sense of *urgency* and that kind of collective *action* cannot be generated by simply ringing the alarms. No amount of warning about the dangers or possibility of a nuclear war will suffice. We have the means to bring about a global holocaust and a possible end to the human species. But the sheer unspeakable horror and incomprehensibility of such a denouement makes the danger seem remote and abstract. Else, how do we live and get on with our lives? The value of nuclear peace must be made tangible in some way, and to do that it has to be connected to the prospects of achieving concrete and visible forms of *progress*, that is, to the realization of more livable alternatives, all the better and clearly so, for being freed from the evil in question. If colonialism and apartheid can disappear forever because there is both the promise and the evidence that a post-colonial and post-apartheid society is better, then we have to generate that same persuasive promise and evidence for a post-nuclear world.

The force of this logic, if accepted, necessarily takes us in a particular direction. The lowest and widest common denominator of anti-nuclearism has to be the collective moral sentiment against such life-threatening evil. But the vision of a collective and shared humanity that this arouses must also be linked, at least in some informal and indirect sense, to a broader agenda of struggle for collective human progress in the twenty-first century. In this vital sense, it remains as true now as in the past, that to fight successfully for peace we must fight for more than peace. To fight successfully against nuclearism, we must fight against more than nuclearism. To fight successfully for a nuclear-free world, we have to be internationalists. And to continue to deepen and strengthen our internationalism on this front, we will have to be internationalists on many other fronts.

What all this means is that the efforts at, and prospects of, moving progressively nearer to a nuclear-free world are unavoidably connected, *but never in any simple or straightforward way*, to the efforts at, and prospects of, moving toward a better world in general. The rhythms and tempos of struggle are different on different fronts. The extent of retreats and advances will also similarly vary, and the networks of mutual influence are complex. It is certainly possible to make very significant advances on, say, the anti-nuclear front but not in many other areas. But insofar as defeating nuclearism for good means defeating a particular mindset and replacing it with a new, internationalist, and humane one, such a new mindset will shape, and be shaped, by the values, beliefs, and emotions that emerge from other struggles against other injustices and inhumanities.

But the nuclear mindset must also be attacked and delegitimized on its own terrain and terms. The lessons of history on this score are clear. First, there has to be the clearest moral perception that nuclear weapons are the closest thing to an absolute evil. Second, there has to be complete consistency in opposing their possession. The idea that nuclear deterrence in some circumstances is justified should be rejected. This consistency is important not because the principle of consistency is a virtue in itself but because both logic and the historical record endorse such consistency. Third, no virtue or positive attribute or property of any kind should be accorded to the possession of nuclear weapons, nor even to the capability to develop, possess, induct, and deploy them. Fourth, there is no place whatsoever for *any* form of nuclear nationalism.

Many otherwise committed and progressive anti-nuclear disarmament activists and supporters have not fully absorbed all of these four fundamental precepts and in failing to do so, directly or indirectly provide props for this nuclear mindset. This is true of sections of the international left (among others) and is most obviously so of the organized Indian left, their parties, leaders and most of their members. This constitutes a particularly serious dilemma because the two main communist parties of India, the CPI and CPM, are among the strongest such parties anywhere in the world, and no mass anti-nuclear disarmament movement worth the name in South Asia can do without their commitment, support and participation.

Marxists and the Bomb

Of all the various activist currents—socialists, Marxists, liberals, pacifists, ecologists, feminists, etc.—that have gone into the making of the mass anti-nuclear movements and activities over the second half of the twentieth century, many Marxists have been among the most ambivalent in their moral attitudes. This ambivalence comes not just from the "charity" with which they have viewed the red bomb of the USSR or China. It also has its source in a weakness within Marxism itself. Marxist discourse has always been filled with moral passion, rhetoric, and appeal. A practical Marxist commitment has always involved and required moral anger against injustice. Some of its central theoretical concepts such as "exploitation" have an inescapable moral dimension. But Marxism has always had an underdeveloped ethical theory, which has often promoted a certain moral insensitivity, especially to the question of the relationship between means and ends.

In the absence of such sensitivity, a class relativism toward ethical issues has often superseded the commitment to universalist principles of justice regardless of class position.[1] Thus many Marxists have displayed disturbing equanimity, even an unruffled complacency, in the face of Soviet and Chinese possession of the bomb. The "red bomb" is as morally unacceptable as the capitalist bomb, but has not always been seen as such. It is really only in the course of the mass anti-nuclear movements—the CND of the '50s and '60s in Britain, and then the peace movements of the '70s and '80s in Europe and the US—that some Western Marxists confronted head-on the distinctive dilemmas posed for Marxist theory and politics by the nuclear question in general, and the red bomb in particular.[2]

Western Marxists brought into the anti-nuclear peace movement a vital emphasis—seeking to give a positive content to the otherwise "empty" notion of peace. In doing so, they helped raise consciousness of the linkages between nuclear behavior and imperialist attitudes, and of the relationship between peace and socialism. Many Western Marxists also learned from the broader peace movement. They learned to recognize the importance of a moral universalism, the fact that the politics of nuclear disarmament in certain ways transcended class politics, and that it could not simply be reduced to a component of, or "fitted into," the anti-imperialist struggle. These are lessons that have never really touched Indian Marxists or the left parties of India. The Russian bomb was welcomed with no moral or political qualms. Much of the organized left also welcomed the Chinese tests of 1964, and where they didn't, it had to do with nationalist sentiments, not internationalist ones. This left has remained insouciant in its defense of the unmistakably immoral, but long-time, Indian stance of nuclear ambiguity.[3]

NOTES

[1] It is not a coincidence that the landmark advance in ethical political theory came not from the domain of Marxism but from liberal political philosophy—the work of John Rawls. Many Marxists, however, have engaged constructively with Rawls and post-Rawlsian philosophy and political theory to deepen and further develop Marxist ethical thinking. Among noteworthy works in this regard, see M. Cohen, T. Nagel & T. Scanlon, (eds.), *Marx, Justice and History* (Princeton: Princeton University Press, 1980); K. Nielsen & S. C. Patten (eds.), *Marx and Morality*, Vol. III of the *Canadian Journal of Philosophy*, 1981; A. Buchanan, *Marx and Justice* (London, 1982); R. W. Miller, *Analyzing Marx* (Princeton: Princeton University Press, 1984); N. Geras, *Discourses of Extremity* (London: Verso, 1990); A. Gilbert, *Democratic Individuality* (Cambridge: Cambridge University Press, 1990); S. Lukes, *Marxism and Morality* (Oxford: Oxford University Press, 1985); R.G. Peffer, *Marxism, Morality and Social Justice* (Princeton: Princeton University Press, 1990); D. McLellan & S. Sayers (eds.), *Socialism and Morality* (London, 1990).

[2] The "red" bomb has been defended in the name of proletarian internationalism, not just of a general or non-class internationalism. That is to say, the Soviet and Chinese bomb was said to have constituted a powerful defense of the international working class, including those sections of it in the US and other capitalist NWSs. But to argue or believe that the "red" bomb best defends the US working class by first having to threaten its complete extinction, requires mental calisthenics of the highest order.

[3] The booklet, *Against Nuclear Jingoism* (New Delhi: National Book Centre, July 1998) was brought out by India's largest Communist party, the Communist Party of India-Marxist or CPM. It contains the party's official statements and contributions by senior leaders and publicly prominent sympathizers.

In opposing the mindset of deterrence, the Indian left, like much of the international left, has been seriously deficient. It has subscribed to the view that there are circumstances in which the possession of nuclear weapons has played a progressive role. Thus the socialist bomb has been seen as a progressive weapon against the capitalist or imperialist bomb. The adjective has been made more important than the noun in a perverse understanding of the history and politics of nuclearism. This left's claim that deterrence has sometimes worked is simply a self-serving delusion. It is not supported by the historical record.[1] On the contrary, the Soviet bomb (as well as that of the US) spurred China to develop it own bomb and then to justify its possession against the US's capitalist-imperialist bomb and against the Soviet "socialist-imperialist" bomb. Once nuclear weapons emerge and are justified for whatever reason—as an expression of anti-imperialism or whatever—they prove extraordinarily difficult to eliminate, even when the conditions which initially "justified" them disappear. The nuclear genie should never be let out of any "national" bottle.

This second precept is also, obviously, connected to the fourth precept, which rejects nuclear nationalism. There are, (especially) in these days of neo-liberal globalization hype, *progressive* forms of political, economic, and cultural nationalism. Nationalism remains a crucial terrain of struggle; imperialism exists—and therefore the anti-imperialist effort must continue. But this should not be allowed to obscure the fact that there is no progressive form of nuclear nationalism. It is precisely because this is the case that an intransigent internationalism always informs the struggle for disarmament. One of the most obvious expressions of this intrinsic internationalism in a world of nation-states is that the adoption of a *unilateralist* disarmament perspective is *always* and *everywhere* (in any and every NWS) a morally impeccable and politically appropriate principle of struggle.

But politically appropriate is not the same as politically *most* appropriate. There are circumstances in which, in terms of political tactics or strategy, some non-unilateralist perspectives could be wiser. This is most obviously the case in South Asia, where securing a South Asian NWFZ, or mutual bilateral renunciation, would be a more effective mobilizing principle. This is not to dispute either the moral grandeur of Indian and Pakistani unilateralism, nor the political courage and usefulness of such a stand in either country. It is only to make a judgment of relative political efficacy in the struggle for regional disarmament.

But the point that is more germane to the present context of discussion is that neither the possession of nuclear bombs nor of nuclear capability can serve a progressive nationalist purpose or function. The organized Indian left supported ambiguity (and welcomed Pokharan I) precisely because it considered India's nuclear capability to be the expression of a progressive nationalist form of anti-imperialist resistance. It considered India's opposition to the CTBT to be the same. This left, at least in the view of some of its spokespeople, was persuaded to assign deterrent capacities to ambiguity, and even to assign other positive virtues to threshold status, thereby violating the third precept. Thus the left insisted that retaining nuclear capability was vital because it constituted a powerful symbol of national independence and sovereignty in a world where "nuclear hegemony" and "nuclear imperialism" was said to hold sway.

But any claim that a nuclear capability alone can deter NWSs endorses the general principle of seeking security through nuclear deterrence. The only difference is that it gives capability the same security-enhancing deterrence capacity as the actual possession of nuclear weapons. Of course, even by the limited "logic" of deterrence thinking, nuclear ambiguity has a distinctive problem—it is a half-hearted and particularly confused form of deterrence thinking, which impresses neither the opponents nor the proponents of nuclear weapons. Similarly, to believe that nuclear capability is a valued symbol of national sovereignty is an argument that is different only in degree, *not in kind*, from the argument that Indian possession of actual nuclear weapons is a valued symbol of sovereignty and independence. As long as the organized Indian left continues to hold such views, and desires a return to ambiguity, it can hardly be expected to be an intransigent and fully committed protagonist in the struggle to completely and permanently defeat and delegitimize the nuclear mindset.

The Fallacy of "Nuclear Imperialism"

One of the most significant mistakes made by the Indian left and, indeed, by many other disarmament activists, is to confuse intentions with reality. That certain NWSs seek to impose nuclear hegemony or pursue a nuclear imperialism, or try to integrate nuclear weapons into imperialist strategizing is undeniable. But to believe that they have succeeded in doing so is another thing altogether. To argue or claim as much is to believe that nuclear weapons do have real political efficacy; that in fact, an NWS in some way *oppresses* or *exploits* an NNWS *through* its nuclear weapons. Such a view necessarily implies belief in either the efficacy of nuclear deterrence or in the status of nuclear weapons as a "currency of power," providing significant and tangible benefits at the *expense* and *deprivation* of the non-possessor of nuclear weapons. Such beliefs precisely replicate the mindset of nuclearism, except that the advocate of nuclear weapons in the name of anti-imperialism awards a minus rather than a plus sign to such claimed properties!

But the great and distressing irony for the NWSs is that deterrence doesn't work, and that nuclear weapons are not a currency of power that delivers significant tangible benefits over non-nuclear countries. Nuclear hegemony or imperialism does not exist. Mere possession of nuclear weapons, or even their flaunting, does not a nuclear hegemony or imperialism make. It is the astrategic nature of nuclear weapons that is their most striking political characteristic. It is precisely because die-hard, arch

US imperialists like the McNamaras and Butlers recognize this reality that that they advocate total abolition with confidence that it would not politically weaken the US.

For anti-nuclear disarmament activists and supporters, the real problem is not the existence or persistence of nuclear hegemony/imperialism. It is the danger represented by the presence of nuclear weapons and their "control" by morally sclerotic and politically misguided nuclear elites. The refusal or failure to recognize this reality and instead to make nuclear imperialism itself the enemy has led many sections of the left, particularly in India, into dangerous dead-ends. It has made them see devils where there are none, thereby opposing what they should not have opposed, such as the CTBT.[2] It has made them defend the indefensible, such as the red bomb or nuclear ambiguity. These are the lessons that the South Asian left needs to learn, if its efforts are to be harnessed uncompromisingly to the struggle for regional and global disarmament.

For example, what if, as is very possible, India and Pakistan do soon enough deploy their nuclear weapons systems? That would mean that the current position of all those opposed to the May tests (which includes the organized Indian left) of demanding no further weaponization and deployment would have become redundant. At this point the left will have to choose between three fundamental disarmament perspectives. One will be unilateralist. A second will be a regional (South Asian NWFZ) or bilateral perspective demanding mutual Indian and Pakistani renunciation. There will be a third perspective strictly counterposed to the first two— Indian renunciation only as part of a global disarmament process. It will not entirely be a surprise if the left parties in India were to choose the third in order not to strengthen "Western/US nuclear imperialism." This, of course, is exactly the position that the pro-bomb lobby in India would adopt. The only difference is that the left would want to return to ambiguity and claim it as the most viable "fourth position," when it is really the most untenable position of all. The left would thus be incapable of generating strong and growing support from anti-nuclear disarmers, since as a posture it has no moral stature whatsoever, and as a practical perspective is neither feasible nor desirable.

For all practical purposes concerning the continuation of anti-nuclear and disarmament activities, the first three perspectives would dominate discourse and practice. If the Indian left aligned itself with the pro-nuclearists in making steps toward regional disarmament *conditional* on equivalent steps elsewhere, then an unbridgeable strategic chasm would open up between this left and other Indian disarmament activists, and also the overwhelming majority of anti-nuclear activists worldwide. One hopes that this will not happen, but it could.

These are not the only lessons to be learned. There are others, too, that have to be absorbed from our past, particularly those provided by the remarkable legacy of the mass nuclear disarmament movements of Europe, the US, and Japan from the '50s to the '80s. One important lesson (already discussed) is the connection between the struggle for peace and the struggle for achieving other progressive goals. There are two more.

For an anti-nuclear movement of truly mass proportions to emerge, there are certain necessary (but not sufficient) conditions. The danger embodied in the existence of nuclear weapons, or in an arms race, or in nuclear rivalry must be a *felt* danger, not an abstract one. The people of the country in question must feel that they are under siege, as it were. The possibility of a nuclear assault or exchange must be widely believed to be real. Without the existence of a felt danger there is no emotional-political foundation for a mass movement. Thus the end of the Cold War, with its welcome ebbing of popular fear, has also rendered the regeneration of anti-nuclear mass movements in Europe and the US much more unlikely in the near future.

No mass movement is possible without an *agitational focus* against one's own government and state apparatus. A mass movement cannot be sustained on the basis of general or vague appeals to global disarmament. It must have certain specific demands directed against its own government or against a number of governments (including one's own), which are wedded to some common project that the movement opposes. Thus the movements have focused (besides other demands) on the central demand for unilateral disarmament in the UK, for non-nuclearization in Japan (which, because of the unique Japanese experience of Hiroshima and Nagasaki, was not an abstract demand), for a nuclear freeze in the United States, for dismantling Euromissiles. Since we live in a world of nation-states, and this unit constitutes the arena where citizenship rights and electoral choice prevail, it is on this terrain that some sense of popular empowerment and peoples' sovereignty is felt and exercised. It is here, therefore, that the organized struggle for change in nuclear policies must be most strongly situated. This is the true dialectic of the national and international on the nuclear issue— not nuclear nationalism versus nuclear imperialism!

Public Policy and Popular Consciousness

No independent mass movement for peace is possible under strongly authoritarian political systems. A minimal requirement is that some reasonable space and freedom be allowed in civil society for mass protests, at least for those kinds that for the most part threaten specific policies, but not necessarily regime rule as a whole. By such a reckoning, anti-nuclear mass movements were not possible in the USSR, or in China past and present. But it would be possible in Pakistan soon, and of course in democracies, from the US to India. Finally, in the generation and sustenance of a mass peace movement, the widest and strongest unifying factor is always the moral dimension. Political sophistication in arguing the anti-nuclear case and countering nuclear theologies is necessary for the leadership of such movements. But moral outrage is what keeps a mass movement together, despite inevitable differences over the strategies and tactics of building and maintaining a mass movement. A moral universalism, then, always lies at the heart of any anti-nuclear movement and is its single most potent attribute.

How do we measure the success or failure of the great anti-nuclear mass movements of past decades? On the one hand, in terms of sheer numbers, the mobilizations associated with this cause have dwarfed those of any other cause, certainly in the first world. Literally millions were persuaded to march the streets and protest. On a global scale, only the Iranian Revolution of 1977–79, which overthrew the Shah, compares with, or exceeds in scale and frequency, the popular mobilizations of first world anti-nuclear movements. On the other hand, in terms of actual demands fulfilled, the paucity of achievement is most striking. Does this mean the great peace movements must be deemed a comprehensive failure? Only if the narrowest of criteria for evaluating success are used.

The dialectic between changes in popular consciousness and changes in public policy is complex and subtle. Mediations between the two are never straightforward. The filtration process is osmotic and capillary, rather than direct and sharply funneled. Unanticipated side consequences and delayed effects on official policy are often quite important, thereby rendering misleading any judgment of success or failure based on the direct comparison to the explicitly stated demands of the peace movement with their degree, or lack, of fulfillment.

The great peace movements helped change the whole discourse surrounding nuclear weapons, breaking the monopoly on public common sense that pro-nuclearists sought to establish. The movements educated a whole generation of activists, some of whom are today carrying on work that is central to the cause. Many are to be found working within what is now an international network of anti-nuclear NGOs. As such they are among the principal actors today in the disarmament effort. The movements forced senior officials in state apparatuses to be publicly accountable and question more deeply than ever before their own rationalizations for retaining such weapons. So when the Cold War ended and earlier rationales disappeared, there was stronger support among decisionmakers themselves for winding down the nuclear arms race. Among many, a stronger commitment to total disarmament appeared. As the struggle for global disarmament moves into the twenty-first century, there has to be unstinting praise and admiration for the pioneering efforts of those great anti-nuclear mass movements. We stand on their shoulders today, surveying a socio-political terrain very different from their own.

Unless current trends shift dramatically or unexpectedly in Europe, or in the US-Russia-China triangle, we are not going to witness the emergence of mass peace movements in the first world for some time to come. But the conditions for the emergence of mass-scale opposition to nuclear weapons could soon appear in South Asia, if India and Pakistan go ahead to erect, improve, and openly deploy weapons systems against each other. It is then, when the likelihood of nuclear conflict breaking out becomes a widely felt danger, that it may become possible for activist groups in the two countries, operating for now at the level of small-scale propaganda, to make the transition to large-scale agitation.

In the wake of the Indian and Pakistani tests, what has so far emerged is a collection of small, urban-based groups that have engaged themselves in anti-nuclear activity, from symbolic forms of public protest, to organizing demonstrations, to trying to institutionalize the production and dissemination of anti-nuclear perspectives through written materials, audio-visual aids, meetings, etc. The peace and nuclear disarmament movement in India and Pakistan is not yet strong enough to influence or alter nuclear policy directions. If the molecular forms of resistance to nuclearism in Indian and Pakistani civil society grow into wider, stronger, and connected pockets of opposition, then they can coalesce to form a national network of resistance and struggle. They could then become the foundations on which mass agitation in the future can be built. [See "No Peace..." page 90] The South Asian perspective for disarmament, if both India and Pakistan deploy nuclear weapons, is an issue that will be discussed later.

What Is To Be Done?

Who is to control the agenda of disarmament and shift it from its current focus on non-proliferation? How is this to be done? Where are the main sites of this struggle?

While there is always a welcome place for the symbolic politics of public protest and opposition, the principal sites of sustained disarmament activities have shifted in the post-Cold War period from outdoors to indoors; from the streets to institutionalized diplomatic settings of inter-governmental negotiations and discussions. The principal forms of disarmament activities have shifted from pressuring through mass actions to pressuring through informed lobbying; from fervent public denunciations to calculated exposures of the fallacies and weaknesses in the briefs of the NWSs; and through practical and carefully worked out projects for accelerating disarmament.

There are three key actors in today's world of disarmament activities. The first are mass movement structures. Then, the anti-nuclear NGOs, which have various kinds of expertise, especially in the understanding of the intricacies of disarmament negotiations, in the technical skills they bring to the discussion of possible restraint and reduction measures, or in the deftness with which they can communicate with a wider public. Finally, there are certain governments that have become thoroughly fed up with the procrastinations and deceits of the NWSs and their non-nuclear allies, and have taken it upon themselves to play a more aggressive activist role in global nuclear diplomacy.

The mass movement structures are to be found in certain countries, most notably Britain, the US, Germany, and Japan. They have some kind of functioning national network or structure of propaganda, membership lists in the thousands, and capacities to periodically or occasionally play a major role in organizing mass actions. In some cases, they have vital links with major national political parties or mass organizations such as trade unions. Perhaps the more important examples of this are Britain's CND and its links with the Labour Party, and the current Greens-SPD coalition government in Germany. Under the umbrella of the Greens, there exist strong anti-nuclear and environmental groups.

The second set of actors are scattered throughout the first world, but again mainly in the US, Western Europe, and Japan. Not all are single-mindedly focused on the nuclear issue, but pursue multiple agendas. Some possess expertise of such high quality that they are valued sources of informational and analytical inputs for governmental delegations of many NNWSs in the various forums of ongoing disarmament-related negotiations in Geneva and New York.

The third set of agents are a select group of governments strongly committed to disarmament. For the first time, an informal concert of countries has emerged that has broken with the fixed mold set by the Cold War of first, second, and third world blocs. It was the advent of the eight-member New Agenda Coalition that really signaled this important development. Seven of those countries (South Africa, New Zealand, Egypt, Brazil, Mexico, Sweden, and Ireland) plus Canada and Australia and a few others like Costa Rica and Norway are the governments now most determined to take the lead in promoting disarmament.

It is not just a question of those countries working in greater cooperation with each other, but also a matter of closer and better coordination between mass movement structures, activist NGOs, individual disarmament "experts" and these governments. This is the organizational challenge that has to be addressed and conquered. Even as a possibility yet to be concretized, this kind of loose association or informal partnership is something new in the history of disarmament efforts. But if it comes to fruition, the arrangement possesses a real potential for achieving what is needed—the acceleration of the global momentum toward disarmament.

Any serious effort at disarmament must *simultaneously* follow two tracks. It must pursue comprehensive or "absolute" measures of total disarmament, as well as pursuing transitional and incrementalist measures of restraint and reduction. Going along the second track but ignoring the first is to fall into the trap happily laid by the NWSs. It risks making each incremental measure a goal in itself and failing to see it as part of a larger process whose direction must be controlled and momentum accelerated. It is to risk following the tempo and pace laid down by the NWSs, which will not only enormously lengthen the time-frame over which total disarmament is to be reached, but risks forever postponing that goal to an ever more distant and difficult-to-see horizon. The longer we postpone total disarmament, the more we risk nuclear disaster. It is also to risk entrapment in a non-proliferation order, rather than fighting to break that order and shift matters toward disarmament.

But following the first track without also pursuing the second is hopelessly impractical. The momentum toward global disarmament cannot be sustained without partial successes. Convincing the governments and peoples of the NWSs to accept *total* disarmament is itself a process that will require partial successes. It is these advances that help generate the realization that a world completely free of nuclear weapons is not just desirable but *feasible*.

In this search for total global disarmament, the first step must be the institutionalization of some body that is multilateral in character and is collectively acknowledged and authorized to carry out negotiations leading to total disarmament. Bilaterally negotiated arms reductions between Russia and the US, or restraint and reduction measures agreed upon between the NWSs are fine. But they are no substitute for the institutionalization of such a multilateral body. Disarmament is too important an issue to be left to the NWSs alone. It is every country's right and need to participate in the process and to make its voice heard. After all, the issue affects all countries and peoples. Moreover, the NWSs cannot be trusted to carry out total disarmament by themselves.

Three Routes

At present there would seem to be three possible routes to bring into existence a multilateral body suitably empowered to carry out such negotiations. None of these approaches excludes the others. They can all be pursued concurrently and separately. But different disarmament activists and groups have different priorities and hopes in this regard. We will spell out the reasons for our own choice of priorities, without meaning that other activists should forego their own efforts and priorities. The front of disarmament activities is a very broad one. Different people perceive different points of potential and promise, and work where they will to bring about a breakthrough. If one point of weakness where a breakthrough was likely were obvious, then a call for collective concentration could be justified. But there isn't any such obvious point where the limited resources of activist groups and individuals or governments must be concentrated. Disarmament activists are still in the process of creating that most obvious weak point, and thus the present offers no escape from a general and ecumenical approach. Nonetheless, we do hope that others may be persuaded to give our choice of priorities more serious consideration. We consider the first two approaches the most likely to deliver positive results.

The first approach is to try to establish a Nuclear Weapons (Abolition) Convention (NWC) which deals with the process and time-frame of disarmament. Already an international consortium of lawyers, scientists, and disarmament experts led by the Lawyer's Committee on Nuclear Policy (LCNP) has drafted a Model Nuclear Weapons Convention (MNWC), which was circulated by the UN in its six official languages in November 1997.[3] This is not meant to be a final draft. But it stimulated discussions and sought further refinement and clarifications. These can be embodied in future drafts. This model draft represents an invaluable service, for it means that it is no longer necessary to wait for a body to be institutionalized before substantive discussions—about the actual content of a global disarmament treaty, for example—can take place.

Already there has been intense discussion on the political, technical and legal requirements for verifiable and coordinated large-scale nuclear disarmament. The ICJ Advisory Opinion has prompted a UN Resolution (52/38) calling for commencement of such negotiations. Many Western states (including the UK and other allies of the US) and China have responded with cautious and qualified welcome to this call for multilateral negotiations, something that France, the US, and Russia continue to oppose. Perhaps the most important point to emerge from the discussions so far is that the comprehensive approach embodied in the MNWC should be integrated with the incremental approach, possibly through a treaty that takes the form of a "framework agreement" incorporating "general principles" that all can agree upon, a phased pattern of progress not excluding unilateral and bilateral initiatives by the NWSs, but providing for multilateral processes of review and accountability.

The main stumbling block, however, remains. When will a NWC come about or start its work? Does one wait till all the NWSs agree to participate in it, which does not seem at all possible in the foreseeable future? Does one wait till some or at least one of the NWSs join in, which may still mean waiting for an unacceptably long period, if one even thinks it possible that the nuclear club will break ranks on so vital an issue? Do the NNWSs go ahead on their own to set up such an NWC, as a way of setting up public pressure on the NWSs to join in? The last is probably the most promising route. It does not require all or most NNWSs to agree to set up and participate in a NWC. But before such a convention can be organized and expected to sustain itself it will require acceptance from, and involvement by, a *critical mass* of NNWSs, including the most pro-active of them on the disarmament issue.

Negotiations between governments that do not include the NWSs have their obvious limitations. But discussions aimed at refining working drafts, reaching agreements among a growing circle of NNWSs in a formalized set-up like the NWC would amount to institutionalizing the existence of such a multilateral body and legitimizing its role as the desirable locus of future negotiations involving the NWSs. All this would also exercise very powerful public pressure on recalcitrant NWSs, whose international isolation would be more sharply highlighted than ever before. The main task of the three sets of agents currently pursuing global disarmament would be to bring about this critical mass of NNWSs willing and able to set up a functioning NWC.

The second approach that needs to be concurrently explored is the possibility of setting up an Ad Hoc Committee on global disarmament in the CD. To begin with it would almost certainly have to settle for a discussion or "deliberative" mandate with no power to actually negotiate. Even this is difficult, but far from impossible, to bring about. The US remains opposed so far to the formation of such a body and the Russians will follow the US in this matter. But Washington has acknowledged that such a committee with a discussion mandate cannot be accused of usurping the functions it believes should only reside with the NWSs. It is also possible to work on the differences between the NWSs in this regard. China is open to the idea of such an Ad Hoc Committee. The Labour government in the UK has been more positive about this initiative than its Tory predecessor. France has also shown sympathy for the idea.

Much will depend on how the FMCT negotiations proceed. The most pro-active NNWSs are determined that the FMCT be connected to the issue of stockpiles, so that it is a genuine restraint measure on the five NWSs, which have already stopped fissile materials production because they have accumulated enough stockpiles to meet conceivable future needs. These NNWSs are also determined that the FMCT be integrated into the disarmament process and one way of doing this is to barter their support for it in return for the setting up of just such an Ad Hoc committee. It is the actual process of negotiations that will determine the final outcome. But current indications are that the NWSs will have real difficulty in not conceding some kind of linkage between the FMCT and wider disarmament concerns. The NNWSs must hold together a very large part of their own ranks as well as win over allies of the NWSs and even some NWSs. If South Africa and Egypt are leading the charge for the formation of such a Committee, five NATO members—Belgium, Germany, Italy, the Netherlands, and Norway—have now called for the formation of an "Ad Hoc Working Group" to "study ways and means of establishing an exchange of information and views within the Conference on endeavors towards nuclear disarmament."[4]

What approach India and Pakistan will take is as yet uncertain. Traditionally, Pakistan (unlike India and the other NWSs) has wanted the FMCT negotiations to feature the issue of stockpiles, as well as a link to the formation of an Ad Hoc committee. But Pakistan, along with India, now wants to establish its credentials as an NWS by showing its sensitivity to the concerns of the other NWSs, especially the US. At the same time, if either government believes it is in their interest to stall the pace of negotiations, so as to build up its stockpiles to a certain level before a final production cutoff, then either or both might see the virtue in joining more strongly with the demand of NNWSs for such a committee or working group. In any case, by doing so, they would pose as NNWSs with a relatively greater concern and respect for disarmament, thereby winning diplomatic points among the NNWSs.

The third approach attempts to use the provisions of the NPT to generate pressure for beginning a disarmament process. The principal idea here is to take advantage of the fact that only one-third of the membership of the NPT have to agree for an amendment conference to be called. There, substantive amendments to put much stronger teeth into, say Article VI, can be put forward. Of course, they will not be passed because the member NWSs each have veto power on all substantive amendments. But the very procedure of convening an amendment conference, putting forward such proposals and having them rejected by the NWSs would have a valuable effect in putting political pressure on the latter. Moreover, such amendment conferences can be repeatedly called to continue the pattern of public embarrassment and exposure of the NWSs.

This approach is obviously an effort to salvage something of the original spirit and purpose of the NPT and to make it move away from being simply the pillar of the non-proliferation regime that it has long since become. Though the attraction of the proposal is that it should be relatively easy to get a one-third consensus to call such amendment conferences, this has not happened so far, which provides a message of its own. Moreover, the idea that in spite of failures to fulfill the substantive purpose of calling such conferences, member NNWSs would still have the enthusiasm to regularly call such conferences, merely to repeat constantly the exposure process, is unconvincing. The reason for putting forward such a proposal is partly to counter another attitude to the NPT, which is not only wholly dismissive of it, but seeks to fully undermine it.

Some disarmament activists and groups, out of complete frustration with the NPT regime, have called for threatening a mass walk-out by NNWSs from the NPT if the NWSs do not begin a process of genuine disarmament negotiations.[5] This is one step further than we would go, although we share this anger and disillusionment with the NPT. But threatening its total dismantling, and then most likely having to carry out this threat, makes very little sense. The threat is a huge gamble. It is a dramatic one-time gesture that will almost certainly fail, and disbanding the NPT altogether eliminates a forum where some kind of diplomatic-political pressure, no matter how feeble, can repeatedly be exercised against the NWSs because of their commitment (their only such legal commitment anywhere) to obey Article VI. While sharing the frustration of those who rail against the NPT, we would not go so far as calling for its total dismantling, nor for expending efforts to work *through* it, but rather for working around and beside it. Our strategy is to ignore the NPT—rather than seek to break it, or energize it—in our search for avenues of movement toward global disarmament.

Before turning to an exploration of those transitional and incremental measures that must also be pursued, it would be fitting to consider the prospects of any existing NWSs giving up their nuclear weapons, even if the rest of the club does not. One of the tragedies of the nuclear age is that once a country goes nuclear, getting it to fully renounce its weapons is very difficult. The experiences of Belarus, Kazakhstan, and the Ukraine, though welcome, were unusual and are to be largely explained by the exceptional circumstances in which they came into existence simultaneously as modern, independent nation-states, and NWSs. For Britain and France, there is today, even by the benighted standards of conventional nuclear security thinking, no security rationale for remaining NWSs instead of giving up their nuclear arsenals. But France continues to pursue its delusions of national grandeur and European eminence even though non-nuclear Germany is the hub of new Europe. The idea of an independent (from NATO) European nuclear deterrent for which the French *force de frappe* might have been the foundation, has fewer takers than ever before. If either France or Britain were to unilaterally disarm, this would give a tremendous fillip to the cause of global disarmament. In one stroke either or both of these countries would raise their global stature immensely, indeed become the undisputed moral and political leaders in the crusade for global disarmament. But the prospects for this coming about are virtually non-existent.

The real disappointment has been Britain, if only because expectations have been higher. Unlike France, Britain experienced mass anti-nuclear movements of enormous scale and considerable duration. These movements were even strongly connected to one of its two main political parties. Indeed, while in opposition, Labour did once officially adopt unilateral disarmament as party policy. The great failure to cash in on this can be ascribed, not so much to the peace movement or to any of its components, as to the weaknesses and limitations of the Labour party's organizational structure and ideology. Internally, it has always suffered from an undemocratic set-up, in which the conservative sections of the parliamentary wing have had disproportionately larger influence than either ordinary members, grassroots activists, or the trade unions.

The result has been that, time and again, genuinely popular aspirations and pressures which emerged from below have repeatedly been throttled from above. The British experience is a classic example of how extra-nuclear factors can have decisive consequences on the anti-nuclear struggle itself. The "New Labour" of current Prime Minister Tony Blair is a decisive departure even from Old Labour. Blairism is the most conservative form of social democracy found anywhere in Western Europe and is the closest cross-Atlantic cousin to President Clinton's "New Age Republocrats." This makes even more dismal the prospect of Britain being the country most likely to break the disarmament logjam through adoption of a unilateralist posture. Blair's party is different from the Tories on the nuclear question. But all this amounts to is that a Labour government is willing to be more transparent in declaring what it has by way of nuclear preparations, and more flexible than the Tories and the US in responding to the concerns of the NNWSs. But any signs that it will break fundamentally from US tutelage, on nuclear and foreign policy, are quite absent.

Denuclearization of South Asia

What about the prospects for denuclearization of India and Pakistan? As the weakest and newest entrants to the nuclear club, what chances are there that they might be prepared to give up their nuclear status and preparations? Dim as the prospects must seem for the near future, there are possibilities here which do not exist in the other five NWSs, even if in the next few years both countries induct and deploy rudimentary weapons systems against each other. Why? Because Pakistan, of all the NWSs, was the most reluctant to acquire this status, the most worried about the sacrifices involved in maintaining it, and the NWS still most willing to give it up if just one other NWS—India—were to do the same. A unilateralist renunciation by Pakistan is very difficult to envisage. But though the struggle for a South Asian NWFZ has become more difficult than it was before May 1998, this perspective continues to retain a relevance and feasibility that makes its prospects of achievement considerably greater than the full and rapid denuclearization of any other NWS or set of NWSs.

This is for three reasons. First, though the section in the pro-nuclear lobby of Pakistan that sees possession of nuclear weapons as a hedge against its inferiority in conventional military strength has become stronger, the prospect of non-nuclear parity between the two countries, if it again appears feasible, will always be strongly attractive to a larger part of the Pakistani elite. So it could well be that a popular anti-nuclear movement in Pakistan would help generate a similar popular response in India. The greater the number of ordinary Pakistanis who call for an end to the regional nuclear madness, the more likely are ordinary Indians to respond in kind.

Second, for all India's determination to build a credible second-strike capacity against China, not only will this take much longer than currently anticipated, but it may not even properly materialize. For all its ambitions, India's nuclear capabilities may remain effectively confined to the South Asian region. If such a situation were to coincide with growing public unease, then the call for regional disarmament in the shape of a South Asian NWFZ could achieve a stronger and growing resonance. Such an unease can develop both because of the dangers of the regional face-off with Pakistan and because of the sacrifices entailed in preserving the nuclear arsenal, given the demands on resources that other problems and priorities—poverty, illiteracy, maintaining internal stability, etc.—will make.

The third is not so much a reason as a condition of possibility. Post-1998 is not the same as post-1945. There is more international anger and greater public delegitimization of such weapons and of the countries that have them. If there are further incremental advances in the process of restraint and reductions, then both India and Pakistan come under more severe pressure for being the only two NWSs who are seeking to increase the size and sophistication of their arsenals, when on the whole the others are slowing down and moving in the opposite direction. Thus the prospects for the denuclearization of South Asia, say in the form of a South Asian NWFZ, are clearly tied to the prospects for successfully achieving other valued restraint and reduction measures. It is to these that we now turn.

The Importance of NWFZs

NWFZs have symbolic-political importance and practical value. As a symbolic measure, they announce in dramatic fashion the renunciation of nuclear weapons in a certain region. When municipalities and towns announce themselves to be nuclear-free zones, often in NWSs or in allied countries, they symbolize resistance by the people and local authorities to official national policy. NWFZs of this kind become mechanisms for raising consciousness, and can sometimes require direct action to prevent the passage or movement of materials related to weapons systems. When a NWFZ covers a group of countries or a continent they symbolize renunciation by the governments in question.[6] When at least some of the countries are nuclear capable or could become so, the renunciation is even more significant.

As a disarmament measure, membership of a NWFZ is a more comprehensive and less contradictory commitment than membership of the NPT. The latter allows NNWSs to have stationed on their territory the weapons of allied countries, such as the US-controlled NATO missiles on German soil. The NPT allows this "crypto-nuclear status," but NWFZs do not. Furthermore, in the creation and sustenance of NWFZs, there are no contradictions of the kind so prevalent under the NPT regime. The NPT "rewards" NNWS members for their renunciation by facilitating their acquisition of the wherewithal to develop nuclear weapons capability clandestinely, if they so wish.

This is not to say that NWFZs have not had their problems. An NWFZ invokes three principles—non-possession by member states, non-stationing, and non-use or threat of use by outside NWSs. The thorny issue in regard to the principle of non-stationing is the matter of naval or airborne transit, especially the former. Coastal states enjoy full jurisdiction only over internal waters (up to twelve nautical miles), but have no such jurisdiction over exclusive economic zones or in the high seas. Any flag state enjoys the right of "innocent" transit in zonal waters. But the real problem is "hostile" transit or passage that is perceived not to be innocent, despite protestations to the contrary. This problem has not been satisfactorily solved by any NWFZ, and has been left to individual member and coastal states to decide as they wish on the matter of naval or airborne transit by NWSs of their nuclear carrying platforms. The third principle enjoins upon NWSs not to target, use, or threaten to use their weapons against member countries of the zone in question. This matter has usually been handled through the addition of separate protocols to the NWFZ treaty in question.

There have been four NWFZs, three other treaties of equivalent nature, and one near-NWFZ. The 1959 Antarctica Treaty, besides prohibiting placement of nuclear weapons, bans nuclear explosions, and disposal of radioactive waste on the Antarctic, subject to future agreements. Its signatories include all the five NWSs. China and India acceded in 1983. In 1967, the Outer Space Treaty was signed and later came into force. It has been signed by all the five acknowledged NWSs, India, and fifty-eight others. It prohibits the placement of nuclear weapons or other weapons of mass destruction in space or earth orbit.

In 1967, the Treaty of Tlatelolco became the first such treaty to denuclearize an inhabited region of the globe—nearly the whole continent of Latin America. Two former threshold powers, Brazil and Argentina, eventually gave up threshold status and signed and ratified the treaty. Cuba joined in 1995 and now the treaty covers every country in Latin America. The treaty prohibits possession, testing, and stationing of nuclear weapons; all five NWSs have signed the protocols demanding non-use and non-threat of use against member countries. The Treaty does allow "peaceful nuclear explosions." This first NWFZ treaty was a landmark that set the standards for subsequent NWFZ treaties, which learned from, and in some ways improved upon, it.

In 1971, the Seabed Treaty was signed and ratified by the US, UK, and USSR and entered into force the next year. China acceded in 1991, but France so far has not. Sixty-six states have so far ratified it. The Treaty forbids the placement of nuclear weapons and WMDs on seabed and ocean floors beyond the twelve-nautical-mile limit. In 1985, the Treaty of Rarotonga, covering the South Pacific, was signed and entered into force the next year. Protocols I, II and III have been signed by the US, UK, and France. Russia and China have so far acceded to Protocols II and III. The Treaty prohibits all possession, manufacture, stationing of nuclear weapons, all tests including PNEs, and disallows dumping of nuclear waste. The Bangkok Treaty, making Southeast Asia nuclear free, was signed in 1995 and came into force in 1997. Apart from the usual prohibitions (such as those in the Treaty of Rarotonga), the Treaty denies transit in seas adjacent to territorial waters, or all zonal waters. The five NWSs have not yet given their support because they (particularly the US and China) contest its claim that it does not violate the right of transit in exclusive economic zones or on the high seas.

The 1996 Treaty of Pelindaba makes Africa nuclear weapons free. It has forty-nine regional signatures. France has approved all three protocols; the other four NWSs, the first two protocols. The Treaty has not yet been fully ratified or come into force. Apart from the usual prohibitions, it outlaws research into nuclear weapons production and testing. The near-NWFZ is the 1992 declaration by both Koreas to make their peninsula nuclear weapons free. Monitoring mechanisms are not in place, though, and the US maintains its suspicions about secret North Korean bomb preparations.

The Southern hemisphere is, except for transit outside territorial waters (and with permission within such waters) nuclear free. But not a single one of these NWFZs has required a strong sacrifice from the NWSs. France, which tested in Africa and the South Pacific, supported the relevant treaties after it decided to finally renounce explosive testing. The Treaty of Pelindaba avoids the question of Diego Garcia (jurisdiction over which is disputed between Britain and Mauritius) and so the island remains on lease to the US, which uses it as a nuclear storage base. Nonetheless, the emergence of these NWFZs is an important gain because of the precedents they have set, for the impetus given to the creation of further NWFZs, and for the concrete advances they express in the effort to make the world totally nuclear free.

The challenge is also to have NWFZs that would involve the practical dismantling of nuclear weapons actually placed, of nuclear weapons capability, or of some degree of jurisdictional control by any of the NWSs. So while NWFZs covering the Nordic region or one in Central Asia (very much on the cards) or in the Balkans (there are suspicions about missiles in Turkey) are certainly desirable and to be welcomed, a real breakthrough would come with a NWFZ in any of the following areas: South Asia (already discussed), Central Europe, Northeast Asia, or the Middle East.

A Central European NWFZ would substantially counter the negative effects of NATO enlargement. Russia would strongly welcome this, for it would mean the effective denuclearization of Germany. But the first step before such a zone becomes feasible is progress in the effort to get NATO to drop its hallowed first-use of nuclear weapons doctrine. Some NATO members, most importantly Germany, have called for just such a reconsideration. This has badly shaken the US, France, and Britain. But though Germany has said it would abide by a majority NATO decision on this score, the call for re-evaluation has led to the release of intra-NATO pressures that cannot now be easily submerged.

The proposed zone of Northeast Asia would include Japan, the two Koreas, and parts of Russia and China. Even if it excluded those Russian and Chinese areas where its missile bases are located, the very idea poses an unwelcome challenge to these two NWSs regarding the issue of their nuclear territorial sovereignty. When a Central Asian NWFZ emerges, as it most likely will, this will give a boost to the efforts to put a Northeast Asian NWFZ on the agenda. But if Japan, a key player, really wants such a NWFZ, then its government must realize that any hopes of moving ahead on this front will be completely dashed if it goes ahead and participates in the Theater Missile Defense or TMD project that Tokyo and Washington are currently contemplating. Contrary to Chinese hopes that the Russians would hold the line and prevent any watering down in the interpretation of the 1972 ABM Treaty, this has happened. An economically desperate Russia has not mustered sufficient political will to prevent a partial victory of the right wing in the US. The US will now plan a deployable National (Ballistic) Missile Defense (NMD) System in three years. But it will defer the actual decision about whether or not to deploy an NMD system for another three years, to 2003. It may still be that an NMD of the kind that would upset China may not come about, but the chances of this happening have become stronger than at any time in the post-Reagan era. START II ratification by the Russian Duma and the regularization of START III reductions, along with other positive restraint measures can still hope to reverse the negative developments that have taken place on the ABM Treaty front.

In the Middle East, a zone free of all weapons of mass destruction—nuclear, biological, chemical—is an idea whose time has surely come. Israel insists on linking this to its desire for an overall peace settlement: that is, a resolution of the Palestine problem and of the possible challenge that Iran and Iraq might pose. But it is not inconceivable that either way—whether or not the political situation improves—more Israelis might be persuaded that such a zone (stretched to include Iran and Iraq) is very much in their interest. Once again, positive advances in this direction are probably contingent on the degree of progress that is made elsewhere in the general restraint and disarmament process.

CTBT and FMCT

That the CTBT must come into force as soon as possible is obvious common sense. India, Pakistan, and North Korea are the current non-signatories. Of them, India is the main problem. But with the US Senate vote against CTBT ratification, a major problem has arisen among the treaty's original signatories. Even if the CTBT is ratified and comes into force, that will not shift the current order from its non-proliferation mode to a disarmament one. But it will represent a significant step forward. [See Appendix 1]. The next step is to push for the permanent closure of all test sites. France has done this with its Moruora site in the South Pacific. The UK relies on the Nevada test site of the US. Russia now has only the Novaya Zemla site. China has closed the Lop Nor site. Indian and Pakistani test sites must also be included in such a general closure. This would go a long way toward foreclosing sub-critical tests, although some of these can be done in the laboratory. Getting the demand for international monitoring of weapons laboratories accepted is much more difficult, but it is a demand that can be raised more strongly after a successful closure of all test sites.

The FMCT is another matter. Three issues of great pertinence arise here. One, the question of linking it to a wider disarmament process through the call for an Ad Hoc committee. This has already been discussed. The second issue is stockpiles. The old and new NWSs, excepting Pakistan, will not agree to its incorporation in current negotiations. It may well be that a production cut-off will have to be agreed upon first. One way to try to get around divergences in approach among different countries is to go for a "framework agreement" and therefore get general acceptance of a continuing but phased approach. Rather than a treaty solely focused on production cutoffs, which is finalized after agreement, the negotiation process would have to be broader, more complex and prolonged, but in the course of which whatever is collectively agreed upon would still be registered as an advance.

Besides the issue of destroying stockpiles, there is also the matter of commercial production and reprocessing of weapons-usable radioactive materials. In the face of the adamant refusal of the NWSs to take up the problems of military stockpiles and commercial production/accumulation, a possible interim proposal that would nevertheless advance matters positively, is to set up an international and open register of plutonium and enriched uranium. At the very least, such public transparency would pave the way for eventual and collectively-agreed reductions from stockpiles of all NWSs. But the initial demands would be for the NWSs and all nuclear capable states to submit full information about stocks, military and commercial; allow for a process of clarification and confirmation regarding these stocks; and for international inspection and monitoring to ensure that withdrawals can only be for non-military purposes.[7]

A No First Use Pledge

There can be no gainsaying the importance of getting such a pledge from the five NWSs. There is an important distinction to be noted between first use and first strike. First strike refers to an initial strike aimed at destroying all or most of the enemy's nuclear weapons system. It is what is called in the jargon, a counterforce strategy, i.e. aimed at military-industrial-nuclear targets and capacities, not at cities or population centers that are called countervalue targets. First use covers all situations of first use, including the first strike scenario. But the Chinese pledge of No First Use, for example, is qualified by not excluding the option to use its nuclear weapons first on its own territory in response, say, to an external intervention. Chinese nuclear behavior vis-à-vis Taiwan is thereby left unclear.

On the whole, though, a No First Use pledge is more encompassing and therefore more valuable than a No First Strike pledge. As it stands, however, such a pledge is unverifiable and capable of being reversed either informally or formally. There is nothing to stop a country that has given such a pledge from violating it in practice. Russia, which had held this position as its declared policy for over a decade, officially dropped it in 1993. If, in spite of these limitations, such a pledge must be deemed to have great value, it is because of the shift in political-strategic thinking that such a change would represent. Once all NWSs publicly declare a No First Use commitment, then they are at least officially stating that nuclear weapons possession is meant *only* to deter a nuclear attack from another country.

Of course, countries that give such a pledge do not simply think the only value of nuclear weapons is deterrence against a nuclear assault. Nuclear elites invariably invest all sorts of wondrous properties in such weapons to justify their possession. But the fact that they are making such a pledge provides a powerful point of entry for opponents of nuclearism. Two public pronouncements that all such NWSs make can then be conjoined to demand that they live up to the logic of their public commitments. The other pronouncement that all NWSs make is that they do believe *ultimately* in global disarmament. Now if all the NWSs agree to this, and also agree that the only purpose of having such weapons is to deter a nuclear attack (the meaning of a No First Use pledge), then no country has reason to retain them and all should be much more amenable to the idea of progressive disarmament down to zero.[8]

NATO's resistance to the adoption of No First Use makes less sense today than it ever did. Its first use doctrine was articulated with the idea of deterring a massive conventional military attack from the USSR or from Soviet-led Warsaw Pact forces. After the end of the Cold War the Warsaw Pact no longer exists, there is no longer Soviet control over Eastern Europe, and the conventional balance of military power, always misconstrued as favoring the Soviet side, is now so obviously reversed that it cannot even be plausibly misconstrued as being the opposite. Indeed, a major reason Russia has dropped its earlier No First Use pledge is that it is adopting the earlier NATO trip-wire principle, to compensate for its perceived inferiority vis-à-vis NATO's conventional military might. The absurdity of retaining NATO's first use doctrine is so obvious that many NATO members, most importantly Germany, Canada, and Belgium, are calling for a review of this policy stasis. This is only the beginning of rumblings on this count within NATO. There will be more to be heard. A NATO declaration of No First Use will also go a very long way toward getting Russia to make a similar pledge once again.

De-Alerting Nuclear Weapons[9]

Measures of de-alerting have multiple possible effects or functions. They can improve the general political atmosphere by easing nuclear tensions. They can be important practical steps to lessen the likelihood of a nuclear outbreak, whether by accident or miscalculation. In their strongest forms, they shade into becoming concrete disarmament measures. They can also make a pledge of No First Use and the promise of No First Strike contained within it not merely something of political-symbolic value, but a commitment that also becomes verifiable in practical terms. These positive consequences of de-alerting arise out of its two principal technical attributes. De-alerting is about removing warheads from delivery vehicles, as well as disabling but not destroying or dismantling fully the warheads themselves. And it is about extending missile-firing time.

The best way to prevent accidental war and also to ease some of the tensions associated with institutional nuclear rivalries/hostilities is through sequestration; that is, separating warheads from delivery vehicles and storing them at a distant depository. Even better is to tag and disable such warheads and store them in conditions where they can be internationally monitored (e.g. in national depositories) under genuine multilateral authority. Such sequestration is easiest to carry out for airborne bombs, not particularly difficult for land-based missiles, but much more difficult for submarine-launched nuclear-tipped missiles.

The most likely form that first use would take is first strike. Strong and effective sequestration, which is also put under multilateral monitoring, is tantamount to establishing a verifiable No First Strike or Use capacity. Even minor cheating (secretly hiding a few warheads) would not enable an effective first strike. Only massively successful cheating would, but a properly monitored sequestration program effectively eliminates this possibility. Certain kinds of SLBMs that are highly accurate, such as the W-88 SLBMs of the US, can double up as first strike weapons. Once a program of major de-alerting is adopted, then, logically, such accurate SLBMs should be verifiably replaced by much less accurate and lower-yield SLBMs.

A further step in de-alerting is to disable the warheads in a manner that is not irreversible, but whose reversal would take considerable time. One way of doing this is to remove tritium bottles from all boosted fission and thermonuclear bombs. If the tritium is mixed with helium and stored under multilateral/international monitoring conditions, then even more time is bought. Removing the tritium in this way eliminates the booster. This does not prevent the primary explosion, but it does prevent the secondary explosion, thereby greatly reducing the yield and making the warhead far less effective as a first strike weapon.

But quite apart from its weakening of first strike possibilities, such a policy of tritium removal would reduce the explosive power of the world's stock of nuclear weapons from thousands of megatons to about a hundred megatons or less. The consequences of a nuclear attack or exchange would still be horrific, but qualitatively less than what it would otherwise be. Removing tritium also nullifies those parts of the stockpile stewardship program that deal with thermonuclear reactions. Most of the rationale (though not all) of inertial confinement fusion programs would be eliminated. Nuclear warheads after tritium removal can be further disabled by a technical procedure called "pit stuffing." Finally de-alerting, if it takes place before the end of 1999, would reduce the risks of the Year 2000 or Y2K problem affecting computer hardware and software. The Y2K problem cannot really cause an accidental launch, but it can affect computer warning signals and screening so as to suggest an enemy attack or launch, provoking a mistaken response. De-alerting, along the lines suggested, buys much more time for all NWSs concerned.

Missile firing can be handicapped and thus delayed by a variety of methods also. Again, it is easier to do this for land-based or airborne missiles than for SLBMs. The motor ignition switches of missiles can be pinned and these pins would have to be manually removed first. The opening of the silos or of the places where missiles are housed can be made more difficult and awkward in a number of ways, from affixing barriers of various kinds on the roofs, to covering silos with large mounds of earth. Crews preparing SLBMs can be ordered to forego removal of flood plates from launch tubes or to carry out routine inspections. This would delay launches by many hours.

The great advantages of de-alerting measures and procedures, given the strong technical aspects involved, is that some of the measures can be carried out unilaterally while others can be agreed upon bilaterally with or without formalized treaty obligations. Thus, should Pakistan and India, for example, move toward open deployment, some such measures will become of paramount importance. Best of all, of course, are those measures, wider and deeper, that can also be connected to procedures for international/ multilateral monitoring by bodies representing both the NWSs and many NNWSs. Such measures would be a major breakthrough, but prospects of achieving these are still some way down a long road ahead.

Even as anti-nuclear activists press for such deeper and wider multilaterally supervised de-alerting commitments, they must be sensitive to the possibilities for implementing unilateral and bilateral de-alerting measures that currently exist. These must not be jeopardized, but strengthened, even as disarmament activists press for more and better de-alerting measures. Today, only the US and Russia have combat-ready alertness of a large part of their arsenal vis-à-vis each other. But some progress in de-alerting procedures has been made. Those deeper and wider de-alerting measures become semi- or near-disarmament measures in themselves. No struggle to shift the agenda from non-proliferation to disarmament can afford to do anything else but treat the issue of de-alerting with the utmost care and seriousness.

Conclusion

What prevents the outline of transitional measures given above from being little more than a wish list? Only the will and determination of the various agents in the struggle for disarmament, and their reservoirs of public support! In the more than fifty years since the nuclear age began, the critical lesson of history is that it is open-ended. Nothing is certain—failure or success. In that respect, Karl Marx was wrong when he declared that humanity only sets those problems for itself that it can resolve. It *can* fail to resolve the problem of nuclearism in time, although we hope it will not. But Marx also said that even in historical circumstances not of one's choosing, one can still hope to shape the general course and direction of human society and future history in a more progressive and humane manner.

At the start of the third millennium, humanity is confronted with certain problems ever more universal and international in character, problems that cry out for universal commitments and universal struggles and solutions. Nuclearism is one such problem. But there are others and each and all of them have to be tackled. How strong or weak the successes or failures on each front will be we cannot know. Anymore than we can know how these successes and failures will reinforce or counteract each other. But that these efforts will be connected in some way we can take for certain. Economic and social inequalities between and within countries are growing. The obscenity of extreme wealth and extreme poverty not only persists, but the distance between the two is widening. By 2050 the world's population could reach the high figure of 10 billion or thereabouts. The pressures this will impose are not today fully imaginable. While there is some consolation to be had from the fact that liberal democratic forms of political governance have spread to cover more countries and peoples than ever before, the bad news is that democracy, like butter, has thinned as it has spread.

With the rise and spread of right-wing ideologies and right-wing parties and organizations, even in the first world of advanced industrial democracies, it can hardly be disputed that these societies are less humane, less economically and socially caring, less democratic than they were in their Golden Age of the late '40s to the early '70s. An unbridled and rampant form of capitalism is exacting the kind of ravages of our eco-system that, if not checked, promises irreversible damage, even possible disaster, sometime in the twenty-first century.

Indeed, there is something of a race between what might come first—a global ecological crisis of the first magnitude or a nuclear disaster of the same magnitude. One aspect of the ecological dilemma was thought to have been overcome when over half a century ago, the power of the atom was harnessed to provide a near-inexhaustible source of safe, plentiful, and constant energy. That is one illusion that the larger part of the comity of nations seems to have recognized and acknowledged. Today, nuclear energy production is widely discredited. The anti-nuclear movements had a major role in helping to do this. It is no longer possible for any first world country to construct more nuclear power reactors to replace older ones, let alone extend their role in power and electricity generation.

But, like most things, the lessons are unevenly absorbed. Even as there is no longer any major first world market for nuclear reactors (even Russia after Chernobyl cannot dare take the route of building more reactors), the five big potential markets for nuclear reactors and components are all in Asia—China, South Korea, Taiwan, Indonesia, and India. Clearly, the discrediting of the claims of the nuclear energy lobby is something that should have fed more strongly into the discrediting of nuclear weapons and their support lobbies worldwide. Surely a world without nuclear reactors for commercial generation, by running down the "plutonium economy" would make a world free of nuclear weapons easier to attain. So along with all those incremental measures aimed at disarmament should we not also be proposing measures to slow and eventually end commercial nuclear energy production worldwide? Can the nuclear disarmament movement afford to downplay the need for alternative energy sources?

This agenda deserves attention. There is a strong case today for establishing an international energy agency promoting the development of sustainable and eco-friendly energy sources as part of the nuclear disarmament agenda itself. But if a world free of nuclear energy production will greatly help in *sustaining* a world already free of nuclear weapons, the fact remains that in *bringing that world about* the winding down of nuclear energy production plays a lesser role. That is part of the reason why this book has not focused on that issue. The other part is that doing otherwise would have resulted in a work even more unwieldy and scattered in its diverse preoccupations than this one may already have become.

Sometime in the next fifty years and certainly before the twenty-first century ends, the world has to eradicate the evil of nuclearism and achieve total disarmament. If it cannot be done over this time span, then it is virtually inconceivable that it can be done over a longer time span, assuming all the while that someone somewhere still does not pull that nuclear trigger. The danger of a nuclear apocalypse tends to provoke a dismally pessimistic note in ruminations about possible futures. It need not and should not. What has happened over the last fifty years and more provides at least as many sources of hope and optimism as it does of despair and pessimism. In fact, the cause of nuclear disarmament, in comparison with so many other worthy causes, starts with an inestimable advantage. Except for a small handful of nuclear die-hards, the vast, overwhelming majority of humanity genuinely believes that a nuclear free world is desirable, necessary, and feasible. The crucial collective project is to make that pervasive sentiment the political force it can and should be. This is the crucial struggle of our times. If it succeeds there is everything—literally, a whole world—to be gained.

NOTES

1 For example, throughout the '50s the USSR had no nuclear deterrent capacity to speak of vis-à-vis the US. Cuba did not show that the Soviet deterrent worked but that the belief of both sides in the efficacy of deterrence was nearly suicidal. See Chapter 2.

2 See *Against Nuclear Jingoism*, and the article by the CPM's senior leader,

Prakash Karat, "Once Again on CTBT" in the party's English language weekly, *People's Democracy* 10 January 1999. The article is partly directed against the authors' stand on the CTBT and follows their rebuttal of all Indian criticisms of the CTBT including those put forward by the CPM and other sections of the Indian Left. That rebuttal was carried in their article in the *Economic and Political Weekly* of 19 September 1998 entitled "Why India Should Sign the CTBT."

Civil in tone and fraternal in spirit, Karat's article is nonetheless deeply disappointing. Karat avoids engagement with even a single substantive argument or rebuttal we made, preferring simply to assert older claims and to justify this by claiming that we "seem to forget or ignore that we are talking of nuclear weapons in the era of imperialism." The expected then follows—the CTBT is an instrument of imperialism, etc. What is most depressing in all this is not so much what is revealed about the CPM's understanding about the CTBT or Karat's failure to engage in a genuine dialogue or debate, but the party leadership's total lack of awareness that, in the light of all that has happened, it might need to carry out serious soul-searching and self-criticism of its whole approach to the nuclear issue, including its presumed relationship to imperialism.

There is not even a hint of remorse that after May 11, the party's official statements, even as they criticized the tests implicitly applauded the performance of Indian science and scientists for the work that made the tests possible. There is not the slightest recognition that the nature and general thrust of the 1994–96 CTBT debate (which the CPM defended in the name of a "national consensus") helped pave the way for the 1998 tests. There is not the least acknowledgement that ambiguity is an immoral position nor any attempt to explain why the party failed to understand that Indian ambiguity compared to that of all other threshold countries was the most unstable. Nor, of course, is there any hint of self-doubt that the CPM's whole understanding of nuclear imperialism might be deeply flawed or that its historical defense of the red bomb was, and is, untenable—a judgment that many other anti-Stalinist Marxists and Marxist organizations in the West arrived at long ago.

3 The MNWC is available in English on the following websites: www.ngo.org/coraweiss/UNDOC.html and www.ddh.nl/org/ialana. See also J. Rotblat, J. Steinberger, B. Udgaonkar and F. Blackaby (eds.) *A Nuclear-Weapon-Free World: Desirable? Feasible?* (San Francisco: Westview Press, 1993); and Box 7 on pages 55–58 of P. Bidwai and A. Vanaik, *Testing Times: The Global Stake in a Nuclear Test Ban* (Uppsala: Dag Hammarskjold Foundation, 1996) where the five basic attributes of any such draft treaty or convention are highlighted—an international authority with powers to override national sovereignty, societal verification, universality of membership, effective technical monitoring, and power of enforcement.

4 There are three distinct proposals and one variation. (1) South Africa has proposed an Ad Hoc Committee with a discussion mandate (19/1/99). (2) Egypt has called for an Ad Hoc Committee with a negotiating mandate (26/1/99). (3) Belgium has called for an Ad Hoc Working Group (2/2/99). The variation is an attempted precursor to the South African proposal in the shape of a call on the CD's President (rotating every four weeks) to appoint a "special coordinator" to consult on the issue.

5 This is the proposal of the former Director of SIPRI (Stockholm International Peace Research Institute), Frank Blackaby, in "Time For a Peasant's Revolt" in the Nov/Dec 1997 issue of the *Bulletin of the Atomic Scientists*.

6 The UN General Assembly in 1975 defined an NWFZ as follows:

(1) A nuclear weapon-free zone shall, as a general rule, be deemed to

be any zone, recognized as such by the General Assembly of United Nations, which any group of States, in the free exercise of their sovereignty, has established by virtue of a treaty or convention whereby:

(a) The statute of total absence of nuclear weapons to which the zone shall be subject, including the procedure for the delimitation of the zone, is defined:

(b) An international system of verification and control is established to guarantee compliance with the obligations deriving from that statute.

Regarding the obligations of the NWSs:

(1) In every case of a nuclear weapon-free zone that has been recognized as such by the General Assembly, all nuclear weapon States shall undertake or reaffirm, in a solemn international instrument having full legally binding force, such as a treaty, a convention or, a protocol, the following obligations:

(a) To respect in all its parts the statute of total absence of nuclear weapons defined in the treaty or convention, which serves as the constitutive instrument of the zone:

(b) To refrain from contributing in any way to the performance in the territories forming part of the zone of acts which involve a violation of the aforesaid treaty or convention:

(c) To refrain from using or threatening to use nuclear weapons against the States included in the zone.

[7] See Martin Kalinowski, "Fissile Cutoff: Overcoming the Disarmament Deadlock" in *INESAP Bulletin* 13 (July 1997) 7–10.

[8] C. Raja Mohan, Strategic Affairs Editor of the Chennai-based Indian English language daily, *The Hindu*, has supported the No First Use pledge given by India and has also said that India may need to retain nuclear weapons even if all other NWSs including the US were to give them up, so as to counter US dominance in a nuclear free world. The last was stated in a public meeting (among other places) at Jawaharlal Nehru University in Autumn 1998 to which one of the authors (A. Vanaik) was also invited. The breathtaking cynicism displayed here should occasion no surprise. But Raja Mohan is considered to be a "moderate" among Indian pro-nuclearists and is a member of the advisory committee of the National Security Council.

[9] This section draws from a useful article by Arjun Makhijani, "De-Alerting: A First Step" in *Science for Democratic Action* October 1998. Published by Institute of Energy and Environmental Research (IEER) in Tacoma Park, MD.

Appendices

Appendix 1: The CTBT

Its Importance

1. The health and environmental benefits to humanity and the world of a permanent end to all nuclear test explosions are self-evident and significant. The political-psychological impact of not ever again having any such test explosions, or having to worry about them, is truly dramatic and valuable. The existing, but fragile, momentum of global arms restraint and disarmament will be strengthened.

2. When it comes into force, the CTBT will weaken the technological push that has fueled the arms race. It will weaken the malign influence of the weapons laboratories as an autonomous lobby.

3. The CTBT will break the "talk-test-build" format. At least until START I and START II were negotiated, the arms control process followed a typical pattern: negotiating measures to control the competition, while simultaneously intensifying it through active testing and construction of new weapons systems.

4. The CTBT will have a major effect on what has been called the "fear factor." If all NWSs agree to restrict the push for technological advance in nuclear weapons, one major source of fear can disappear. Knowing that nothing new or exotic will suddenly emerge makes it easier to deal sensibly with existing problems.

5. A CTBT would create a new climate for further arms limitation and reduction by opening the door to other logical or natural steps, such as a convention to freeze fissile materials production and reduce stockpiles to zero, an end to the flight-testing of new missile systems, a No First Use treaty for all NWSs, a treaty to end deployment of new weapons systems, de-alerting, etc.

6. The CTBT sets vital precedents for the future of negotiations on other arms restraint, reduction, and disarmament measures.

(i) The CTBT negotiating process, for all its weaknesses, and despite the unavoidable fact that different countries had differing bargaining and leveraging capacities, was nonetheless the most genuinely multilateral and democratic such process of any nuclear-arms-related treaty in history. (ii) It was the first treaty that was finished according to the set deadline and which required the full consensus in the Conference on Disarmament (CD) on all provisions. These were excellent precedents, providing (through the principles of formal equality of veto power and unanimity) at least some kind of check for weaker countries against more powerful ones, and for NNWSs against NWSs. (iii) When it comes into force, the CTBT will for the first time ever have set up a truly international monitoring system, which in certain respects overrides all national authorities. In doing this, it sets a crucial and practical operational precedent for the kind of supra-national structures of authority and supervision that will be required to insure that the world of nation-states not only becomes, but remains, nuclear-free.

The Final Treaty

The final treaty was not passed as it should have been by the Conference on Disarmament (CD) because India vetoed it, ostensibly to change Article XIV of the treaty on entry into force, but actually to weaken the CD, since India was fully aware that its veto would not change the Article in question. An overwhelming majority in the UN General Assembly passed it. The Treaty comprises a Preamble, seventeen Articles, two Annexes and a Protocol. As would be expected from a multilaterally negotiated treaty, the final agreed text represented a compromise in which no country got everything it wanted and all major players had to make concessions of one sort or the other to arrive at the final document. The real character of the final treaty, then, is at variance from the view adopted by Indian critics that it was essentially an artifact of the NWSs (led by the US) to perpetuate their "nuclear hegemony."

Precisely because this was not the case, the Preamble of the finalized treaty has had to be misinterpreted and misrepresented by the US executive so as to make it more amenable to manipulation in line with its present and future interests. In this Preamble the key statements are the following: (a) the "objective" of the treaty is "to contribute effectively to the prevention of the proliferation of nuclear weapons in all its aspects, to the process of nuclear disarmament, and therefore to the enhancement of international peace and security," (b) "that the cessation of all nuclear weapon test explosions and all other nuclear explosions, by constraining the development and qualitative improvement of nuclear weapons and ending the development of advanced new types of nuclear weapons, constitutes an effective measure of nuclear disarmament and non-proliferation in all its aspects."

In his September 23, 1997 message to the US Senate, President Clinton presented an interpretation that tried to obliterate the Preamble's distinction between "development and qualitative improvement of nuclear weapons" and "development of advanced new types," in order to obscure the fact that the CTBT says it will "*end* (emphasis added) the development of advanced new types of nuclear weapons." The current US executive would like the treaty to merely constrain such activities. In short, for US hawks to get their way, they have to try to undermine the CTBT's provisions in letter and/or spirit; they cannot scrupulously obey a treaty supposedly fashioned to promote their interests. Incidentally, even these hawks acknowledge that the CTBT "constrains" the US's qualitative weapons advancement.

Regarding the seventeen Articles, the most important that need to be briefly outlined and explained are Articles I, II, IV, VII, VIII, IX, and XIV.

Article I refers to the scope or basic obligations of all signatory members. Each such signatory must abjure "any nuclear weapon test explosion or any other nuclear explosion" on its territory, no matter how small in yield, and prevent any such occurrence under its jurisdiction. Nor can any state party cause, encourage, or participate in any way in such a test or other nuclear explosion. This is what is meant by the famous "zero yield" formulation that was, after much wrangling, put forward during the negotiations in August 1995 and finally became the basis of the agreement on scope by the five major nuclear weapons powers, which are each at a different level of nuclear technological and scientific capability and potential.

Article II gives the character, functions, and distribution of powers and responsibilities of the different tiers of the organization of the CTBT or CTBTO. The three levels of the organization are the Conference of States Parties, the Executive Council (EC) and the Technical Secretariat, which includes the International Data Centre. While the CTBTO will co-operate with other international organizations, such as the International Atomic Energy Agency (IAEA), it is an independent body. The supreme decision-making body is the Conference of States Parties, in which each member has one vote only. This Conference meets (once the treaty comes into force) regularly (annually if accepted) besides any special sittings that may be requested by the Executive Council, the Conference, or any State Party if supported by a majority of members.

On "matters of substance," decisions "shall be taken as far as possible by consensus." If this is not possible, then it has to be by a two-thirds majority of members present (a majority constituting a quorum). The single most important official position is that of the Director-General of the International Secretariat. This will be decided by the Conference, with each term lasting four years and renewable for one more term only.

Between the Conferences of States Parties, the decisionmaking within the parameters set by the treaty will be by the fifty-one member Executive Council, on which each member has the right to serve in due course and by rotation, taking into account geographically distributed quotas. There are no permanent members of the Executive Council; all members are treated as equal and eligible, regardless of their weapons status. The EC will be accountable to the Conference, and its membership will be selected by the Conference with reference to stipulated geographical and technical criteria laid down in the treaty. The EC is charged with seeing to the "effective implementation of, and compliance with, this Treaty" and with supervising the activities of the Technical Secretariat, as well as with organizing the regular and other meetings of the Conference.

The Technical Secretariat is responsible for carrying out the practical verification of compliance, that is, to ensure that there is no cheating by any member signatory regarding a nuclear explosion, test or otherwise.

The Technical Secretariat supervises and coordinates the International Monitoring System (IMS), which comprises variant forms of monitoring stations and activities as well as operating the International Data Centre, which will process, analyze, and evaluate all relevant data.

Article IV deals with the character of the proposed verification regime which has (a) an International Monitoring System; (b) provisions for consultation with and clarification from requested and requesting states parties; (c) on-site-inspections (OSI); (d) confidence-building measures.

All monitoring facilities of the IMS shall be owned and operated by the states hosting them or otherwise responsible for them, as per the protocol of the treaty. But they will be placed under the authority of the Technical Secretariat and their functioning cannot be impeded by national governments. All data, raw and processed, is available to all states parties.

No state party is "precluded from using information obtained by national technical means of verification" (e.g. satellites) to judge whether a demand, for example, for on-site inspection of a particular country should be made. But this information must be obtained "in a manner consistent with generally recognized principles of international law, including that of respect for the sovereignty of States." This is generally interpreted to mean that information from illegal spying activities is not allowed.

The crucial issue, of course, is the impartiality and rigor of the procedures for sanctioning and then carrying out on-site inspections. Any state party has the right to request (from the Director-General and the EC) an on-site inspection of another member country's facilities in order to determine whether Article I has been violated. But even so, the requesting country must obey established procedural norms regarding the provision of adequate information about the environment of the event triggering the request, the estimated time of the triggering event, and it must provide all data on which the request is based. Before the question of whether or not to sanction such a request arises, there is a stipulated procedure concerning the communication of the request to the said country as well as to all other states parties, the awaiting of the said country's clarifications and communication of that to the requesting country. If the requesting country is still not satisfied and insists on an on-site inspection, then this will be undertaken only if thirty or more of the fifty-one members of the EC agree. It can take up to eight days for this procedure of initial request-clarification-sanction of OSI to be completed.

If an OSI is sanctioned, this must be carried out according to strictly laid down procedures in the treaty. There can be no simultaneous OSIs on a given territory. The inspected state party has the "right to take measures it deems necessary to protect national security interests and to prevent disclosure of confidential information not related to the purpose of inspection." Representatives of the inspected state party will be present throughout the inspection and the inspection team will wherever possible "begin with the least intrusive procedures and then proceed to more intrusive procedures only as it deems necessary to collect sufficient information to clarify the concern about possible non-compliance with this Treaty."

The final report of the inspection team will be transmitted to the requesting state party, the inspected state party, the EC, and to all other state parties. The EC will decide whether there has been non-compliance and whether, even if there is deemed to be compliance, the request for OSI was an abusive request or not. In the case of an abusive request, the EC can require the state party concerned to defray the costs of the preparations of the Technical Secretariat. It can go further and suspend the requesting state party's right to request future OSIs for a period of time determined by the EC. It can further suspend the right of the requesting state party to serve on the EC for a period of time.

Regarding the issue of non-compliance with Article I deemed to have been shown by an OSI, the Conference will decide what to do, taking into consideration the EC recommendations. The rights and privileges of a state party can be restricted or suspended by the decision of the Conference. The Conference can recommend collective measures to the states parties against the non-complying country but these have to be "in conformity with international law."

Article VII concerns amendments to the treaty. This can only be done by an Amendment Conference. Such a Conference can be called if a majority of states parties want it. But no substantive amendment to the Treaty can be carried out unless there is a positive majority vote with "no State Party casting a negative vote." That is to say, each state party has veto power. Everybody doesn't have to say yes; a majority will do. But nobody can say no—not even one country!

According to **Article VIII**, there will be (unless a majority decide otherwise) a review conference ten years after the treaty comes into force. This review will take into account any new scientific and technological developments relevant to the treaty. Every ten years after there can be a review conference, or even at lesser intervals if so decided by the Conference of States Parties.

Article IX concerns duration of, and withdrawal from, the treaty. The treaty is of unlimited duration. As is standard in treaties whose signatories are sovereign national states, each state party has the right to invoke jeopardization of its "supreme interests" in order to withdraw from the treaty.

Article XIV deals with entry into force. Here the key point is that the treaty can only enter into force if it is signed and ratified by the forty-four countries listed in the treaty as countries that are deemed by the IAEA to have nuclear power or research reactors. Specifically, the CTBT cannot enter into force unless two countries, India and Pakistan, which have so far refused to accede to the treaty, sign and ratify it. This is clearly unfair to the two countries concerned and seeks to coerce India and Pakistan into going along with a treaty they have rejected, as is their sovereign right to do so.

But far worse than the unfairness to India and Pakistan (an earlier hold-out, Israel, has now signed the CTBT) is the unfairness of this provision to the treaty itself. Its coming into force should not have been made contingent on the accession to it of countries that did not wish to accede to it. It should have been allowed to come into force excluding India and Pakistan, leaving them to decide whether or not they wish to reconsider their decision at some later date. The sooner a CTBT comes into force covering most of the world, the better.

Regarding the powers of the review conference that is supposed to take place in September 1999, three years after the CTBT was passed in the UN, these are strictly defined. Only ratified member-signatories have voting power, with non-ratifying but signing members enjoying observer status. This Conference cannot impose sanctions on countries that are so far not signatories to the CTBT, such as India and Pakistan. It can only consider what measures "may be undertaken to accelerate the ratification process in order to facilitate the early entry into force of this Treaty." Such measures must be decided by "consensus" and in a manner "consistent with international law." International law, and the Vienna Convention on the Law of Treaties, does not allow for any treaty to endorse collective punishment of any sort on a country that refuses to be party to the treaty in question.

Appendix 2: Indian Criticisms of the CTBT

There have been five main lines of criticism of the CTBT in the Indian debate: (1)The CTBT should be linked to a time-bound schedule for global nuclear disarmament to be acceptable. (2) The CTBT is discriminatory in character. (3) The CTBT is decisively flawed and rendered effectively worthless at least for the US and perhaps France and possibly for Britain, China, and Russia. This is because the CTBT in its present form allows sub-critical testing, does not prevent advances in computer simulation techniques that set up a "virtual testing regime" or "informational test ground," and allows research and development of direct fusion weapons to continue through such institutions as the planned National Ignition Facility in the US and the Laser Megajoule facility in France. (4) The CTBT is another building block, after the NPT, in the perpetuation and strengthening of "nuclear hegemony" practiced by the nuclear haves against the nuclear have-nots, led above all by the US. (5) Specific criticisms of some provisions of the CTBT, most notably Article XIV on entry into force; the supposed pressure likely to be imposed on India by the 1999 review conference; and the "intrusive" dangers of the verification procedures embodied in the treaty. Each of these criticisms will be taken up in turn and refuted.

(1) Time and again, countries opposed to positive nuclear restraint or reduction measures have used a standard argumentative technique. Commitment to a grand goal, e.g. global nuclear disarmament, with which every sane person can agree, is cited precisely to block the process of incremental steps by which we can move toward that goal. India was doing exactly this with its demand for a time-bound schedule.

India has a past record as a country more committed than most to the cause of nuclear disarmament. This, and the fact that for so long it did not go openly nuclear despite having proven its nuclear weapons capability, gave it a certain moral capital that inclined a large number of NNWSs to give India the benefit of the doubt as to its motives in proposing this linkage. But the important point is that the other NNWSs did not join India in making or endorsing this explicit linkage between a time-bound schedule for global disarmament and the CTBT. They did not do so because they valued the CTBT in itself sufficiently and did not wish to jeopardize the very possibility of its coming into existence.

In a sense, there were three basic positions during the CTBT negotiations that can be elaborated in the form of an analogy. If the relationship between a measure like the CTBT and global nuclear disarmament is visualized as a staircase, with the CTBT the first step toward the goal of complete disarmament at the top, then the position of the NWSs, especially of the US, could be characterized as follows: they are prepared in their words to go this first step, but are not prepared to be pressured any further. They will decide whether, when, or how they will take further steps up the staircase. The second position was that of the overwhelming majority of NNWSs. The value of the CTBT in their eyes lies not simply in its specific merit, but also as a measure promoting the momentum toward further disarmament. In short, they hope that once the NWSs are standing on this step, they might be persuaded to give a more serious commitment to moving further up the staircase.

The third position was India's. Not only did India not regard the CTBT as a step (at least for the US and possibly France), but it refused to take this one step itself unless the NWSs gave a categorical commitment, not only to move up the entire staircase, but to provide a definite time schedule for reaching the top. India cannot, of course, give a time-bound schedule for solving the Kashmir problem or its own problems of poverty, communalism, or literacy but it demanded on this difficult issue that the NWSs provide just such a timetable right away!

The absurdity of this position was reinforced by the fact that the Indian government was effectively putting the cart before the horse. Before one can sensibly talk of securing a time-bound schedule for global disarmament one first has to secure and institutionalize a genuine, multilateral body that has a mandate accepted by the NWSs as well as the NNWSs to negotiate such universal disarmament. Getting such a body into existence or effectively preparing the ground for this is going to take many years of arduous diplomacy and struggle on the part of NNWSs, given the current reluctance of the NWSs to countenance such a body. One does not jeopardize the efforts to secure such a crucial breakthrough by insisting that the very birth of such a body be made contingent on the NWSs now agreeing to accept a time-bound schedule for total disarmament. In fact, the two most important efforts to secure such a body are the pursuit of the formation of an Ad Hoc Committee on Global Nuclear Disarmament in the CD, and the setting up of a Nuclear Weapons (Abolition) Convention, or NWC.

Both efforts need to be pursued simultaneously and continuously. The first was exactly what the large majority of NNWSs in the CTBT negotiations were pursuing, hoping that they could get a commitment from the NWSs to such a body having at least a discussion mandate, if not a negotiating one, from the start. Such a commitment could have been embodied in the Preamble of the CTBT. Had India been serious about helping to institutionalize such a body, then it could have employed powerful leverage to get this as the price of its acceptance of the CTBT. This emerged as a real opportunity in the crucial weeks before India's June 1996 rejection of the CTBT. In opposing the CTBT because it would supposedly affect its national security interests, India was never interested in seriously negotiating to bring about a stronger or better CTBT more in line with the aspirations and hopes of the majority of the NNWSs and other anti-nuclearists worldwide.

Regarding the NWC, India pays lip service to it. But insisting that the

NWC's very inception be made dependent on the NWSs accepting a time-bound schedule within it for disarmament is nothing but obviously ill-motivated, hypocritical moral posturing out of synchronization even with those NNWSs most committed to rapid global disarmament, which made no such condition. India's ridiculous demand was based on a "big bang" conception of how global nuclear disarmament should take place. The Indian government has now dropped this demand, but not from any sophisticated or deep-seated new-found commitment to disarmament. Rather, it now wants to pose as a "responsible and moderate" nuclear weapons power.

(2) The second criticism claimed that the CTBT discriminates. It is one thing to consider a treaty flawed: then a debate can follow about how significant the flaws are and whether the treaty is thereby rendered worthless for one or more of its signatories. It is another thing altogether to make the more morally charged accusation that a treaty is discriminatory. Who after all wants to be on the side of discrimination? Such a criticism has a much more general appeal to a public lacking the technical knowledge of nuclear arms development that is necessary to assess how flawed the CTBT is. To call something discriminatory is automatically a politically damaging accusation—which is why the sheer irresponsibility of the charge is so great.

The claim that the CTBT is discriminatory betokens precisely that imprecision of language and thought that often bedevils the proper assessment of an issue. The CTBT imposes the same obligations on all member signatories. In this respect, it is fundamentally and decisively different from the NPT, which has discrimination legally enshrined within it by having differential obligations for different classes of members to the treaty. In the NPT, the two different classes of members are the NWSs and the NNWSs and the treaty refers to them as such, as well as spelling out a range of different obligations and privileges for each. In the CTBT, the very language shows the absence of any such enshrined discrimination. The only term used for all members are "states parties" or "states members." There are no separate obligations nor separated classes of members.

It can of course, be argued or claimed by critics of the CTBT that behind the formal or legal "impartiality" and "non-discrimination" of the treaty in question there exists a prior context of discrimination between the nuclear haves and have-nots that the CTBT does not address adequately. But this is fundamentally and conceptually different from the claim that the CTBT itself is inherently discriminatory. In fact, implicit in this claim is a recognition that the real problem with the CTBT is that it is *not* discriminatory! It does not do what its critics think it should—that is, discriminate positively, in favor of the nuclear have-nots, so as to help rectify the real situation of discrimination that exists regardless of, and prior to, the CTBT.

Perhaps the appropriate analogy here is the famous comment of Anatole France that the law, in its impartial majesty, equally penalizes the rich and the poor for sleeping under a public bridge. Is the CTBT, then, something like this, having strong and genuine restraining effects on the poor NNWSs, on nuclear threshold countries like Israel and India and Pakistan, on possibly some of the NWSs, but none on the richest, most notably the US? In fact, this too, is a misleading analogy. The CTBT powerfully restrains all the NWSs, including France and the US.

(3) This brings us to the third line of criticism about the supposedly fatal technical loopholes that exist in the treaty because it allows sub-criticals, computer simulation, and R&D on direct fusion or fourth-generation nuclear weapons. This is related to, but distinct from, the previous line of criticism. Does the pursuit of such activities violate the letter of the CTBT? It does not. But it certainly violates the general spirit informing the treaty, which intends to move away from efforts to qualitatively enhance nuclear weapons development.

Of course, no treaty can effectively monitor and thereby curb computer simulation. Does the existence of these possibilities for carrying out sub-criticals, computer simulation and direct fusion R&D weaken the CTBT to the point of making its restraining effect on all NWSs including the US, effectively useless? Here, the answer is a categorical and emphatic no.

The refutation of the claim that these activities constitute fatal loopholes in the CTBT relies on both arguments and evidence of a technical nature, as well as on evidence of a non-technical and political nature, which can plausibly convince non-specialists of the treaty's efficacy. We will take the more technical arguments first; separately for sub-criticals, computer simulation, and direct fusion weapons R&D, because of their quite different purposes and aims.

Sub-critical experiments (SCEs) are those that do not lead to a nuclear chain reaction but remain below that critical point. Their nuclear yield is therefore zero. These experiments are designed to study the dynamic properties of aging nuclear materials. They can incorporate what is called hydrodynamic testing, which helps in the study of the other non-nuclear components in weapons assembly. But neither hydrodynamic tests nor other kinds of SCEs are of much use in weapons design beyond the first-generation, knowledge regarding which is already widely available in public literature.

The real danger represented by SCEs is that they can "creep up" to the level of hydronuclear testing (HNEs), which is of significant help in the designing of very small yield weapons. HNEs, because they achieve slight supercriticality, are banned by the CTBT. Preferably, there should be no SCEs either. But if they are carried out, their conduct should be sufficiently transparent so that there is public assurance that they have not been allowed to "creep up" to the level of HNEs. But SCEs in themselves are not a serious problem, let alone a fatal loophole in the CTBT in regard to qualitative nuclear weapons advancement.[1]

What about computer simulation and the possibility of establishing an "informational test site" or "virtual testing" that would effectively do away with the need for explosive testing? Here, the crucial issue is whether or not computer simulation alone can lead to the emergence of a new generation of sufficiently accurate weapons codes, which are crucial to developing a new generation of nuclear weapons or making significant qualitative advances in the existing generation of weapons.

What are weapons codes? Think of weapons codes as something like shelves of many, many books, which provide or attempt to provide a deep and integrated knowledge of an extremely complex and vast array of issues. Nuclear weapons codes establish linkages between the empirical evidence gained from previous explosive tests and laboratory work, the existing (though incomplete) state of knowledge about the basic physical processes involved in a nuclear explosion, and the specific design parameters of the device under consideration. They are, in fact, the principal tool of nuclear weapons designers.

The US, unsurprisingly, is the country that has invested the most in the effort so far to develop an "informational test site" through its Accelerated Strategic Computing Initiative (ASCI) which is being carried out in collaboration with five major US universities. What has now been realized from ongoing efforts is that though computer simulation most certainly helps in the development of such weapons codes it nonetheless suffers from insuperable problems. The issue is not whether a new weapon will work or not but whether it will work in the way its designers want it to: that is, will it properly fulfill the function for which it has been designed?

The limitation of existing knowledge about what takes place in advanced nuclear weapons explosions (especially regarding what are called "secondaries") and the complexity of the way various processes are connected is such that codes generated by computer simulation alone are simply inadequate. These connections are so complex and their basis still so incomprehensible that if weapons codes are made or adjusted to be more accurate in one direction, then for reasons unknown, they become more inaccurate in other directions. The significance of these "fudge factors," as they are called, has been repeatedly affirmed by the comparison of results achieved by computer simulation alone to known parameters of devices already established through previous explosive testing.

The effort to establish "virtual testing" is thus deeply ironic. It has led to the greater recognition of the importance of ultimately resorting to actual proof-testing or explosive testing in order to finally design advanced or new generation weapons.[2] Far from substituting for explosive testing, such simulation efforts create pressure for eventually resiling from the CTBT if the US is going to make serious qualitative advances in nuclear weapons development and weaponization. Thus, the existence of facilities for carrying out SCEs, direct fusion weapons R&D and ASCI keeps the necessary software (the small pool of highly specialized scientists) and much of the hardware in operation so that if in the future the US decides to break out of the CTBT, it can move toward the development and deployment of a new range of weapons in the least possible time. What all this indicates is not the irrelevance of the CTBT but, in fact, its vital importance.

Finally, there is the issue of fourth-generation or direct fusion weapons such as laser beam weapons, etc. The CTBT and the banning of explosive testing does not theoretically present an obstacle to the development of such weapons. So the CTBT does not render their development impossible. But to claim that the CTBT is rendered worthless on this count is absurd. The leap from third-generation to fourth-generation weapons is far greater than from first-generation to third-generation weapons. In fact, nobody can say with any confidence that such a leap will ever be made. The physics is simply unknown.

The US National Ignition Facility seeking to develop the key technology of Inertial Confinement Fusion (and France's Laser Megajoule) is a deeply speculative venture to produce "pie-in-the-sky wonder weapons" whose chances of success are regarded as small. The overwhelming majority of knowledgeable nuclear physicists give these facilities less than a ten percent chance of success. The very small minority who are most committed to these projects are themselves not prepared to give it more than a fifty-fifty chance of success.[3]

With a CTBT in place, today's US cannot go ahead to develop any third generation nuclear weapons such as particle beam weapons, enhanced or reduced radiation weapons or battlefield micro-nukes, electromagnetic pulse bombs, etc. It cannot certify any nuclear weapon. Within the range of second-generation weapons, where the US is currently situated (ahead of any other country in the same range) it can, even with the CTBT in place, develop weapons which represent new applications of existing or known designs such as "deep penetration earth bombs," etc. The closer the designs of newer weapons (but not new-generation weapons) are to known designs, the easier they are to make even if the CTBT prevents certification of all weapons. But the further away the new designs are from existing designs, the more difficult they become to make, and indeed shortly after venturing from existing knowledge, they are effectively impossible to design with the necessary confidence that they will actually work.

But it is not necessary to be a nuclear physicist to realize that the CTBT is a genuine and powerful restraint measure on all the NWSs. The non-technical evidence is there for all to see—except those most determined not to see it. In all the NWSs, powerful lobbies centered around sections of the weapons laboratories, defense forces and ardent arms-racers (usually positioned on the hard right of the political spectrum) have strongly opposed the CTBT precisely because they understand full well its powerful restraining effect. In the US, they have gathered around a section of the Republican right with the result that Senate ratification of the CTBT remains deeply uncertain. Why is the US right so reluctant to support the CTBT if it is a measure that serves US imperialist interests and does not seriously restrain qualitative weapons advancement?

The effective answer of Indian critics of the CTBT, notably the left is, and has to be, the absurd argument that the Democrats and other supporters of the CTBT in the US are just more intelligent and sophisticated imperialists than the right-wing Republicans. Such critics of the CTBT have hardly been swayed by the fact that virtually the whole of the international anti-nuclear movement and the overwhelming bulk of the international left have, with varying degrees of enthusiasm, supported the CTBT—as have many first-class nuclear physicists, including former nuclear weapons designers.

The Indian left should realize that the division between pro- and anti-CTBTers in the US does not correspond to the absurd and artificial division between smart and naive imperialists postulated by them. Rather, it reflects the obvious fact that after the end of the Cold War there is a division between arms-racers in the US on one hand and arms reducers/arms moderators on the other. There is no significant or powerful section of arms-eliminators among the US nuclear elite, although the number of voices demanding complete arms-elimination is growing.[4] But after the end of the Cold War, the category of those who no longer see the purpose of continuing the quantitative and qualitative advancement of nuclear weapons has grown stronger. Most of them want an end to this race and considerable reductions in nuclear weapons, even though they do not countenance complete elimination of the US arsenal, and are far from becoming opponents of US political imperialism.

There is further non-technical evidence. The idea that other NWSs like Russia and China would ever have agreed to a CTBT that was fatally flawed is absurd. In fact, the CTBT only became a possibility when the "zero yield" formulation was agreed upon by the US on August 11, 1995. Before that, the US had been pressing for a very small loophole allowing explosive testing up to a two kilogram yield. The position of the other NWSs, particularly Russia and China, was that if a loophole of any sort was to be allowed, it had to be big enough so that they themselves, at a lower level of weapons technology than the US, would be able to benefit.

Thus the Russians demanded a loophole of ten tons while the Chinese wanted allowance of up to several hundred tons. It should be self-evident to Indian critics of the CTBT that the nuclear and scientific establishments of Russia and China (which can safely be assumed to be far more advanced than that of India) went on board after the zero-yield proposal because they recognized that while anything else would have constituted a debilitating flaw in the CTBT, from which the US alone would significantly benefit, a treaty allowing SCEs, computer simulation, and direct fusion R&D was not similarly flawed.

Unfortunately, as in the case of the Republican right opposing the CTBT in the US, the fact of Russian and Chinese acceptance of this treaty despite these presumed flaws has only led to tortuous Indian efforts at rationalization. Among the more ridiculous of such attempts are claims that the US so badly wanted a CTBT that they were prepared to share knowledge and equipment—that is, give away their technological edge in these areas. Thus, whereas once it was argued that the US so badly wanted this "flawed" treaty because they alone could monopolize the benefits of its failings; later it was argued (often by the same critics) that the US so badly wanted the treaty they were willing to give up their monopoly of benefit from its supposed flaws!

Other equally desperate and far-fetched explanations claimed that the Chinese were primarily bent on sustaining the imbalance in their nuclear relationship with India. So long as this was on the cards, the Chinese were not too bothered about allowing the qualitative nuclear technological imbalance between itself and the US to grow, calculating that they had enough of a minimum deterrent against it.[5]

Some such critics also claim that the Russian and Chinese insistence that the CTBT only enter into force if India, Pakistan, and Israel join it, constituted a second line of defense against the Treaty ever coming into existence, thus preventing the US from monopolizing the benefit of its "biased" operation. This is, of course, an extraordinary argument. For its logic, strictly speaking, must lead to the conclusion that should Indian and Pakistani accession to the CTBT become likely in the future (and thus its entry into force) then the Russians and/or the Chinese will resile from the treaty. In fact, Russian, Chinese, and British insistence on Indian, Pakistani, and Israeli accession to the treaty before it could come into force simply and obviously reflected their concern that the "sacrifice" imposed by the CTBT upon them be shared by the nuclear capable threshold states. Given the strength of the anti-CTBT lobbies within their own countries, this was also a way of stalling the Treaty's operation, though certainly not of guaranteeing that it would never come into operation. For such a period then, the CTBT would constitute a moral-legal norm of restraint and behavior on its signatories, but not a punitive one.

The behavior of the other NWSs, notably Russia and China, indicates by all reasonable and balanced inference, that the CTBT was perceived by them as a genuine restraining measure on all countries, including the US. The whole controversy over the entry into force clause (Article XIV) thoroughly undermines the argument that the CTBT was primarily (or even secondarily) a US-led "trap" aimed at containing the threshold nuclear powers, and especially India, which unlike Pakistan and Israel is not deemed a formal or strategic ally by the US foreign policy establishment.

Indian critics who have claimed as much have never bothered (understandably, since it so seriously weakens their case) to either state or emphasize the following facts. India formally announced its refusal to sign the CTBT in June 1996. A month earlier, when it became increasingly clear that India was going to reject the treaty, the US was the first and only NWS to publicly appeal to India, saying that the US would accept India's rejection of the treaty, if India did not block the passage of the treaty in the CD.[6]

Moreover, the US did not attempt to coerce India by insisting on its signature as a precondition for the treaty to enter into force. In fact, the US initially opposed the stands of Russia, China, and UK in this regard, and even sought to get these countries to withdraw this demand in the interests of enabling the treaty to go through. Strange behavior indeed for a country supposedly aiming to "trap" India through the CTBT! While the US could have handled the UK, the Chinese and especially the Russians were adamant. The US then accepted the Russian and Chinese condition because it was important to get these two countries on board the treaty and because even if this condition was withdrawn, India would still have nothing to do with the CTBT. Incidentally, Russia, China, and UK insisted on this clause only after India made its rejection to the treaty clear in late June 1996.

(4) The fourth line of criticism is that the NPT is the central pillar of the non-proliferation regime sought to be sustained by the NWSs (led by the US) and that the CTBT is another building block in the effort to perpetuate and strengthen this regime. The first part of this claim is fundamentally correct, but the second part is based on a gross misrepresentation. Before investigating the true nature of the relationship between the CTBT and the NPT, it is necessary to say something about the NPT, in particular about the utterly unbalanced and inaccurate manner in which it has been criticized in India.

In the mid-'60s, India played a major role in pushing for the NPT and in seeking to draft it. The final draft represented the consensus view of the US/UK and USSR (China and France only joined the NPT in the early '90s), brought about by their own separate discussions and as such had formulations that were unsatisfactory to a number of NNWSs, including India. But the standard criticism that the NPT was inherently discriminatory was not—to begin with, nor at the time of signing—the real problem for India and other NNWSs. It subsequently became convenient for Indian critics to make this discriminatory character the centerpiece of its case against the NPT, but this represents a misleading simplification.

At the time of drawing up the proposed NPT, there were only two choices. Either the treaty should be completely non-discriminatory with equal obligations for all member signatories—in which case the NWSs would never accept it and would have to be excluded from the treaty. Or, in order to get the NWSs in, the proposed treaty would have to have two classes of member-signatories with the principle of differential obligations enshrined within it. This was because, at least for some period, the NWSs would not renounce their possession of nuclear weapons, though this would be the condition demanded of all other signatories. Sensibly enough, most NNWSs at the time felt there would be no purpose in having a treaty that excluded the NWSs. A basic bargain was thus established when the treaty was finalized in 1968 and came into force in 1970. In return for the NNWSs accepting the enshrinement of the principle of discriminatory obligations in the treaty, the NWSs would commit themselves to move eventually toward complete nuclear disarmament. It is this bargain that is embodied in Article VI of the NPT.

The failure of the NPT since its inception—and the main reason why it has become over time the central pillar of the non-proliferation regime (and thus deserves criticism and condemnation)—is not so much its inherently discriminatory character, but the fact that the NWSs failed to live up to their end of the bargain, with their perfidious disregard for the letter and spirit of Article VI in the NPT. Whatever disarmament has since taken place after the end of the Cold War is certainly not because of the NPT, but despite it.

The subtle but important difference between highlighting the central weakness of the NPT as the perfidious behavior of the NWSs and not the treaty's discriminatory provisions becomes acutely relevant when it comes to assessing why India did not sign the NPT. This was not primarily because it was discriminatory and India was initiating some sort of moral-political crusade against the "pernicious" NPT. While the principle of discrimination between nuclear haves and have-nots was accepted within the treaty, this did not mean that there had to be as much of an imbalance as there was in regard to other differential obligations between the NWSs and NNWSs in regard to technology transfers, IAEA safeguards, etc. But this too was not sufficient explanation for the Indian refusal.

Like a number of potential nuclear powers close to the threshold of achieving weapons capabilities—for example, Brazil and Argentina—India, too, did not want to foreclose this option. After the death of Nehru, with the subtle shift in official thinking, from a posture of "no bombs ever" to "no bombs now," and the emergence of a new kind of official discourse, it was now being simplistically claimed by New Delhi that continuing vertical proliferation would be the direct cause of further horizontal proliferation, instead of acknowledging that the latter had an independent dynamic as well.

The NPT banned even peaceful nuclear explosions, which is how the Indian government described its 1974 Pokhran test. All this weighed heavily in shaping the Indian decision. But the decisive factor in leading to the Indian rejection of the NPT was almost certainly the initial Chinese refusal to sign, even as an NWS. Nonetheless, any balanced assessment of the NPT (rarely present in the Indian debate and certainly never during 1994–1996, the anti-CTBT period) would have to point out that it was also initially directed against Japan, Germany, and Italy, the losers in World War Two, each with the capability to produce nuclear weapons. This was something to be supported, not opposed. Later it became a way for the NWSs to maintain non-proliferation among the NNWSs and to rationalize in the longer term (after its unwarranted and condemnable permanent extension in April 1995) their own possession of nuclear weapons.

It is necessary, however, to note that the NPT still contains the only international legal commitment that has ever been made by the five major NWSs to carry out complete nuclear disarmament. Many anti-nuclear activists, not surprisingly, feel that this provides an important point of legal-moral international leverage, which in the absence of anything else, can be of some use in the struggle for global disarmament. They are thus not prepared to go so far as to call for the treaty's dismantlement or to declare its complete irrelevance or to condemn it totally. This is not our view of the NPT; we reject it on much more comprehensive grounds than most left critics in India.[7] But this position, when coming from anti-nuclearists, should not be seen as simply dishonorable or as "supporting nuclear imperialism" or other such over-simplifications forwarded by Indian critics without a balanced or sophisticated understanding of the NPT and the historico-political context surrounding it.

Let us come now to the question of the real nature of the relationship between the NPT and the CTBT. So strongly committed are NNWSs to the idea of the CTBT that even during the effort to draft the NPT, countries like Mexico, Burma, and Ethiopia wanted a CTBT to be reached in conjunction with the NPT. In fact, for the NNWSs that were considering signing the NPT, a CTBT was seen as the single most important expression of the NWSs' commitment to pursue disarmament as embodied in the terms of the treaty. The three NWSs preparing to be a party to the NPT—the USSR, US and UK—adamantly opposed this.

Subsequently, at every five-year review conference of the NPT (1975, 1980, 1985, 1990) the issue of the CTBT was repeatedly raised by NNWSs and consistently opposed by the NWSs. In fact, in the view of many countries, the NPT would itself only survive in the long run if there were effective international safeguards and a CTBT. Thus there has always been a historical connection between the CTBT and the NPT, but of a kind very different from that which has been made out by Indian opponents of the CTBT. When in 1995 the issue of the NPT's extension came up, it was inevitable that the issue of the CTBT would surface. The NWSs only succeeded in getting what they wanted—the permanent and indefinite extension of the NPT—by resorting to very considerable behind-the-scenes arm-twisting of many NNWSs. This permanent extension was extremely unfortunate because it eliminated that degree of leverage the NNWSs would have continued to possess if they agreed only to the NPT's short-term and conditional extension before reviewing it again in the future.

Although the NWSs got what they wanted, they had to pay a price. That price was an explicit and time-bound commitment for the first time ever to completing a CTBT. In the 1995 review conference, new "Principles and Objectives" were established whereby a CTBT had to be completed before the end of 1996. Far from the CTBT being another building block after the NPT in the NWSs' calculated attempt to promote their nuclear hegemony, it was a concession forced upon them by the NNWSs. The NWSs had to make it; otherwise the NPT's permanent extension and authority would have been gravely undermined.[8] As it was, a number of NNWSs had become deeply critical and frustrated by the NWSs' behavior inside and outside the NPT, with some like Mexico even threatening to withdraw from the NPT.

The Indian government had no reason to explain to its public what actually went on at the 1995 review conference, which was attended by numerous anti-nuclear groups, NGOs, and individuals; the pattern and manner of negotiations were public knowledge. But the refusal of the Indian left to even look seriously at what actually happened in those negotiations, let alone at the general history of the relationship between the NPT and the CTBT, is deeply disturbing.

(5) The fifth line of criticism centers around certain claims regarding the iniquity of Article XIV on entry into force in the CTBT; on the supposedly pressing danger to India of the 1999 review conference, thereby justifying the timing of the Indian nuclear tests; and on the putative dangers of excessive "intrusiveness" embodied in the CTBT's verification regime. The first has already been covered in this text. Regarding the second, there is no way that the review conference, which is confined to seeing how it can accelerate the ratification process so as to bring the treaty into force as early as possible, can penalize India or Pakistan if either refuse to accede to the treaty by then. Not only do substantive decisions have to be taken by consensus, but the decisions must be in accordance with international law. Such law cannot allow for punitive measures against any country not a party to the treaty in question. Regarding the third point, the basic parameters have also been laid out in the discussion on Articles II and IV in the CTBT. The Chemical Weapons Convention (CWC) served as an important precedent for the CTBT in respect to how the principle of balancing between concerns of "national sovereignty" and "effectiveness" of international monitoring could be handled. India endorsed the CWC procedure without serious reservations.

It only needs to be added here that Israel and China are the two most secretive nuclear regimes. Hard negotiating brought about the specific provisions concerning verification procedures and authorization of OSIs. The result was a compromise consensus acceptable to both Israel and China. On this terrain too, the Indian objections have been couched in vague terms, carefully avoiding specifying what provisions are unacceptable and why, let alone why Indian concerns about the dangers of intrusive spying are sharper than Israel's and China's. Incidentally, inspections are confined to the site of the explosion only. Is it not obvious that once again, India is resorting to self-serving deception in order to justify its opposition to the CTBT?

NOTES

[1] An Indian staple is that sub-criticals and computer simulation constitute fatal flaws. The left-wing Indian fortnightly magazine, *Frontline*, has long been carrying on a campaign against the CTBT based on precisely the kind of arguments that have been criticized here as distorted. It has though, to its credit, opposed the recent tests. In its July 17 issue, it carried a rare, technical article about the tests, titled "Matters of Authority" by a "Special Correspondent" of genuine authority and worth. The article also accurately portrayed the essential character of SCEs, reinforcing the argument presented here. Certainly, before this article, *Frontline* had not carried anything of comparable technical authority on CTBT-related matters by any Indian writer.

From time to time, Indian critics have very selectively cited the technical criticisms of sub-criticals and computer simulation by Western experts known for their general anti-nuclear stance, such as C. E. Paine, Ted Taylor and Frank N. von Hippel (a particular favorite), but without ever pointing out that these experts have, with various reservations, supported the CTBT—indeed have been advocates both of the treaty and rapid nuclear disarmament. These activities in the US also come under the umbrella of the government-sponsored Science-based Stockpile Stewardship and Management Program (SBSS&MP), which has been severely and correctly criticized as intending more than it formally says: that is, it seems to be involved in weapons designing, rather than just checking the "safety and reliability" of the existing aging stockpile.

The authoritative and regular reports of the Natural Resources Defense Council (NRDC)—a Washington-based NGO—have been of particular importance in this regard. What has not been pointed out is that the SBSS&MP has been attacked by the NRDC not just for promoting efforts at weapons designing despite the CTBT, but also for being financially wasteful and promising more than it can deliver. For an authoritative account of the post-CTBT sub-criticals carried out by the US in 1997, emphasizing the importance of ensuring transparency, see Suzanne L. Jones and Frank N. von Hippel, "Transparency Measures for Subcritical Experiments under the CTBT" in *Science & Global Security* 6 (1997) 291-310.

[2] See in particular, the *Nuclear Weapons Databook* series brought out by the NRDC, especially *Explosive Alliances: Nuclear Weapons Simulation Research at American Universities* by M.G. McKinzie, T.B. Cochran, C.E. Paine (January 1998); and *End Run: The U.S. Government's Plan for Designing Nuclear Weapons and Simulating Nuclear Explosions under the CTBT* by C.E. Paine and M.G. McKinzie (April 1998).

[3] The SBSS&MP justifies the development of facilities such as the Dual Axis Radiographic Hydrodynamic Test Facility (DARHT) at Los Alamos and the National Ignition Facility (NIF) at Lawrence Livermore. The key area of dispute is over the possible relationship of NIF and Inertial Confinement Fusion (ICF) technique to the development of fourth-generation fusion weapons. The theory behind ICF is that giant lasers yet to be built at NIF will produce concentrated pulses of ultraviolet light to explode a tiny gold capsule called a *hohlraum*, itself comprising a pellet of deuterium and tritium. Just before the hohlraum explodes, it is supposed to emit a powerful beam of x rays that will compress and heat the pellet to more than a 100 million degrees Celsius, causing deuterium and tritium to fuse as in a nuclear bomb, but on a very much smaller scale.

The chances of this ever working are, as pointed out, very slim. But the NIF is obviously one of those "big science toys" that keeps weapons labs and their scientists and administrators active and happy. Promising these facilities was one way of overriding, and buying off, much of the opposition from these quarters to the CTBT and getting them to reluctantly accept the treaty. See J. Bairstow, "Switch Off the National Ignition Facility" in *Laser Focus World* (September 1997).

4 The Nuclear Posture Review (NPR) brought out by the US government in September 1994, and the Presidential Decision Directive (PDD) 60 (the November 1997 outcome of a seven-year review process) are key documents in this regard. Their purposes are to rationalize officially the retention of nuclear weapons for the future, but with a new nuclear strategic doctrine that recognizes the changed post-Cold War context. New enemies have to be found, hence the "rogue states" formula; and a much smaller number of nuclear weapons are being asked to fulfill newer, yet to be fully worked out, strategic tasks. PDD-60 is the first such directive related to nuclear weapons since Reagan's last directive in 1981, and reverses that earlier commitment to fighting "winnable" nuclear wars. The US has now accepted that such weapons are for deterrence only.

The point is not that the US will not continue to pursue nuclear imperialism, but that the US finds it difficult or undesirable to completely buck the post-Cold War reality of a new momentum toward disarmament and restraint (though it can try to dilute or outflank as best as it can). The relationship of these new US planning perspectives to restraint measures like the CTBT must be clearly understood. They are not efforts at reorganizing strategic nuclear perspectives through the CTBT, but despite or apart from the CTBT.

5 This extraordinary claim, along with a series of tendentious, politically mistaken and technically ill-informed attacks on the CTBT, is to be found in S. Varadarajan, "Testing the World Order" in *Seminar* 468 (August 1998). The Chinese have always been concerned about their imbalance with the US. Their strike force—of an estimated mere thirteen to eighteen long-range land-based ballistic missiles capable of hitting the US mainland—has always been theoretically vulnerable to a US first strike, located as they are in only two northeastern bases. So much for their possessing at the moment an "adequate" or "credible" second strike capacity against the US.

The Chinese are currently particularly disturbed by possible developments in regard to the US's Theatre High Altitude Area Defense (THAAD) preparations, which in conjunction with right-wing efforts to undermine the 1972 ABM Treaty might eventually lead to that "pale" or "soft" version of a "Star Wars" system of defensive missile interceptors that in its stronger version was once so seriously pressed for by President Reagan. Should this happen and such a ballistic missile defense system be established, then even if the currently feeble Chinese capacity to hit the US in a second strike was somewhat strengthened, it could well be rendered worthless.

6 India did not have to block the passage of the CTBT in the CD after rejecting it. It claimed it had to do so after the emergence of the new entry into force clause so as to put pressure on changing it. But New Delhi was fully aware that blocking the treaty's passage in the CD would have no effect in this regard. It did so for two reasons—as a symbolic gesture of defiance; but more importantly, to deliberately weaken the stature of the CD in keeping with an evolving diplomacy. To be sure, if the entry into force clause had not been changed as it was, the CTBT text would

probably not have been blocked by India in the CD.

But this still does not excuse what India did. India even went to the shameful extent of vetoing the passage of an otherwise consensus factual report of the CD on its activities over the previous two and a half years. This report would merely have concluded that there was a consensus that there was no consensus! But the report's acceptance and formal passage would have salvaged some credibility for the CD by recognizing and acknowledging its efforts and workings, despite its failure to reach the desired final consensus.

7 The NPT has a built-in contradiction. To soften the stick of renunciation of nuclear weapons by NNWSs, it offers the carrot of technical support on the civilian side of nuclear energy production—thus helping to provide the wherewithal for building nuclear bombs. This contradiction has been taken advantage of by, at least, Iraq and North Korea. Moreover the very fact that the NPT promotes the civilian nuclear energy program can be condemned by those who believe that as an energy and power source this too is unacceptable for the innumerable problems, dilemmas, inefficiencies and dangers it poses.

The Indian left does not oppose the production of nuclear energy for civilian purposes. It should take a second, critical look at the issue. The NPT is also a weaker disarmament measure than NWFZs, because unlike the latter it allows NWSs to station nuclear weapons on the territory of NNWSs.

8 Throughout the 1995–1996 debate on the CTBT it was rare indeed to find an Indian critic of the treaty who was even prepared to acknowledge that the CTBT was a concession forced upon the NWSs to secure the NPT's permanent extension, let alone that without this concession the NPT regime could have unraveled. More recently, this has been more widely acknowledged, but in such a manner as to try and rob the point of its legitimate impact.

In order to somehow preserve the basic thrust of this charge, they now have to carry out a desperate intellectual-political contortion by simultaneously acknowledging that the CTBT was indeed a concession (purely token according to them, but still a concession) to ensure the consolidation, even the continued survival of the NPT, and yet insisting that the CTBT is an integral part of the architecture of "nuclear imperialism" centered on the NPT. But how can the difference not be fundamental between a treaty sought after by the NWSs (most notably the US) because it will enhance the NPT regime and one which is finally conceded in order to preserve this regime? See S. Muralidharan, "Unequal Bargain" in *Frontline* (Chennai) 3 July 1998; and S.M. Menon, "The Nuclear Imperium and its Vassal Kings" in *Economic and Political Weekly* (Mumbai) 1–7 August 1998.

Appendix 3: International Resolutions

India and Pakistan at the Receiving End

A stunned world was quick and forceful in reacting to the Indian, and then the Pakistani, nuclear tests. The element of surprise—and outrage—in the reaction was the greater in the Indian case because there was no visible rationale for New Delhi's decision to cross the threshold. Pakistan was widely seen to be reacting to New Delhi, after being goaded into testing by Indian ministers.

The reactions from the neighborhood and the major powers all noted the adverse impact of India's and Pakistan's nuclearization on regional and global security, on their own international stature, and on their external relations. Perhaps the most important reaction was Resolution 1172 of the United Nations Security Council, reproduced below—the strongest such reprimand received by any South Asian state.

The individual reactions of the five NWSs varied in emphasis. China's was the most strongly worded. The P-5 positions were harmonized in their joint statement issued from Geneva on June 4, 1998, in response to "the grave situation":

> The [P-5] ministers condemned these tests, expressed their deep concern about the danger to peace and stability in the region, and pledged to cooperate closely in urgent efforts to prevent a nuclear and missile race in the subcontinent, to bolster the non-proliferation regime, and to encourage reconciliation and peaceful resolution of differences between India and Pakistan.

The statement called upon India and Pakistan to adhere to the CTBT

> immediately and unconditionally, thereby facilitating its early entry into force," and to participate in FMCT negotiations. It reiterated the P-5 goal to be "adherence by all countries, including India and Pakistan, to the Nuclear Non-Proliferation Treaty (NPT) as it stands, without any modification.

For the short run, the P-5 foreign ministers affirmed

> their readiness to assist India and Pakistan, in a manner acceptable to both sides, in promoting reconciliation and cooperation. The Ministers pledged that they will actively encourage India and Pakistan to find mutually acceptable solutions, through direct dialogue, that address the root causes of the tension, including Kashmir... In that connection, the Ministers urged both parties to avoid threatening military movements, cross-border violations, or other provocative acts.

The P-5 resolution fell short of calling for economic sanctions against India and Pakistan, but confirmed their members' "policies to prevent the export of equipment, materials or technology that could in any way assist programs in India or Pakistan for nuclear weapons or for ballistic missiles..."

The Neighborhood Reacts

Closer to home, Bangladesh had the strongest early reaction. The Sri Lankan foreign minister originally gave verbal support to the Indian tests, but a subsequent statement by the foreign ministry expressed "concern" at the South Asian tests.

All other regional states expressed "regret" or "concern" in varying degrees. At the summit meeting of the South Asian Association for Regional Cooperation (SAARC) in Sri Lanka in July 1998, the tests overshadowed all other issues. But given that its charter prohibits SAARC from raising contentious bilateral issues, the summit referred to the tests as "recent developments," without specifically mentioning the explosions or naming the two states.

Beyond this, the tenor of the statements varied. Shaikh Hasina, Bangladesh prime minister, was the most explicit: "the recent nuclear tests in our region is a development that we all wish could have been avoided." Sri Lankan President Chandrika Kumaratunga said that the atmosphere of confidence in South Asia "could be affected by recent developments." Similarly, Nepal Prime Minister G.P. Koirala said: "recent events have given rise to the fear of an arms race in the region. Statesmanship and vision is required to counter this fear of a setback to the painstakingly created atmosphere of confidence in our region…"

The G-8 Position

The June 12 statement of the foreign ministers of the G-8 (comprising the seven most industrialized Western states, and Russia) was far more explicit. It was issued by a "special meeting" in London to consider the "serious global challenge" posed by the nuclear tests. It condemned

> the nuclear tests carried out by India on 11 and 13 May 1998 and by Pakistan on 28 May and 30 May. These tests have affected both countries' relationships with each of us, worsened rather than improved their security environment, damaged their prospects of achieving their goals of sustainable economic development, and run contrary to global efforts towards nuclear non-proliferation and nuclear disarmament.

The G-8 built on the P-5 statement and Resolution 1172, reminding India and Pakistan that "the negative impact of these tests on the international standing and ambitions of both countries will be serious and lasting. They will also have a serious negative impact on investor confidence."

Noting Indian and Pakistani statements that they "wish to avoid" a nuclear and missile arms race, the statement said India and Pakistan should "stop all further nuclear tests and adhere to the CTBT," "refrain from weaponization or deployment of nuclear weapons and from the testing or deployment of missiles capable of delivering nuclear weapons," "refrain from any further production of fissile material for nuclear weapons," and "confirm their policies not to export equipment, materials and technology that could contribute to weapons of mass destruction or missiles capable of delivering them."

The G-8 asked India and Pakistan to

> undertake to avoid threatening military movements, cross-border violations, including infiltrations or hot pursuit, or other provocative acts and statements; discourage terrorist activity and any support for it; implement fully the confidence- and security-building measures they have already agreed upon and develop further such measures.

They should "resume without delay a direct dialogue that addresses the root causes of the tension, including Kashmir...

The G-8 statement sternly added:

> We believe it is important that India and Pakistan are aware of the strength of the international community's views on their recent tests and on these other subjects. Several among us have, on a unilateral basis, taken specific actions to underscore our strong concerns. All countries should act as they see fit to demonstrate their displeasure and address their concerns to India and Pakistan. We do not wish to punish the peoples of India or Pakistan as a result of actions by their governments, and we will therefore not oppose loans by international financial institutions to the two countries to meet basic human needs. We agree, however, to work for a postponement in consideration of other loans in the World Bank and other international financial institutions to India and Pakistan, and to any other country that will conduct nuclear tests.

ASEAN Regional Forum

Besides the G-8, the Indian and Pakistani tests came in for another multilateral reprimand, from the ASEAN Regional Forum (ARF), a group that includes the US, China, and Japan as well as India. At its meeting in Manila on July 27, 1998, the ARF Chairman stated:

> The ministers recalled that as early as 1995 the ARF put emphasis on the importance of non-proliferation of nuclear weapons in promoting regional peace and security. They also noted that the ARF subsequently welcomed the overwhelming adoption of the CTBT... In this connection, the ministers recalled the United Nations Security Council Resolution 1172.
>
> The ministers, therefore, expressed grave concern over and strongly deplored the recent nuclear tests in South Asia, which exacerbated tension in the region and raised the specter of a nuclear arms race. They called for the total cessation of such testing and urged the countries concerned to sign the Treaty on the Non-Proliferation of Nuclear Weapons and the Comprehensive Nuclear Test Ban Treaty without delay, conditions, or reservations. They asked the countries concerned to refrain from undertaking weaponization or deploying missiles to deliver nuclear

weapons, and to prevent any transfer of nuclear weapon-related materials, technology and equipment to third countries. In the interest of peace and security in the region, the ministers called on the countries concerned to resolve their dispute and security concerns through peaceful dialogue."

India engineered a high-powered lobbying effort prior to the ARF meeting in order to change the original wording from "condemn" to "strongly deplore" and to replace an explicit reference to "the tests by India and Pakistan" to "nuclear tests in South Asia."

The NAM Resolution

A little later, in early September, India and Pakistan received yet another rebuke, from the Non-Aligned Movement (NAM) of which India was a founder, and of which it considered itself a "natural" leader. At the opening ceremony of the NAM summit at Durban, President Nelson Mandela commented on the South Asian nuclear tests, linking them with Kashmir. He said all NAM states "remained concerned over the problem in Jammu and Kashmir" and should be "willing to lend all our strength for the peaceful solution of this problem." India protested loudly, its anger all the greater because of New Delhi's earlier close relationship with Mandela. It claimed that Mandela's deputy offered an apology to India the next day. This claim was denied by South Africa.

In the summit resolution itself, India succeeded in altering the original paragraph (number 109) on disarmament. The original read:

> The recent nuclear tests conducted in the subcontinent of South Asia have inevitably added to the complexities of issues relating to non-proliferation and nuclear disarmament. [The NAM countries] further expressed their deep concern at the re-emergence of the nuclear arms race and called for all states which have the capability to produce nuclear weapons to refrain from weaponizing their capability and to desist from placing them on delivery systems.

> [In the final version, the NAM countries] noted the complexities arising from nuclear tests in South Asia, which underlined the need to work even harder to achieve their disarmament objectives, including the elimination of nuclear weapons. They considered positively the commitment by parties concerned in the region to exercise restraint, which contributes to regional security, to discontinue nuclear tests and not to transfer nuclear weapons-related material, equipment and technology.

But the resolution also further "stressed the significance of universal adherence to the CTBT, including by all nuclear weapon states, and the commencement of negotiations in the Conference on Disarmament on fissile materials..."

Resoultion 1172

Following is the verbatim text of Security Council Resolution 1172, deploring the nuclear tests at its 3890th meeting on June 6, 1998.

The Security Council,

Reaffirming the statements of its President of 14 May 1998 (S/PRST/1998/12) and of 29 May 1998 (S/PRST/1998/17),

Reiterating the statement of its president of 31 January 1992 (S/23500), which stated, inter alia, that the proliferation of all weapons of mass destruction constitutes a threat to international peace and security,

Gravely concerned at the challenge that the nuclear tests conducted by India and then by Pakistan constitute to international efforts aimed at strengthening the global regime of non-proliferation of nuclear weapons, and also gravely concerned at the danger to peace and stability in the region,

Deeply concerned at the risk of a nuclear arms race in South Asia, and determined to prevent such a race,

Reaffirming the crucial importance of the Treaty on the Non-Proliferation of Nuclear Weapons and the Comprehensive Nuclear Test Ban Treaty for global efforts towards nuclear non-proliferation and nuclear disarmament,

Recalling the Principles and Objectives for Nuclear Non-Proliferation and Disarmament adopted by the 1995 Review and Extension Conference of the Parties to the Treaty on the Non-Proliferation of Nuclear Weapons, and the successful outcome of that Conference,

Affirming the need to continue to move with determination towards the full realization and effective implementation of all the provisions of the Treaty on the Non-Proliferation of Nuclear Weapons, and welcoming the determination of the five nuclear-weapon states to fulfill their commitments relating to nuclear disarmament under Article VI of that Treaty,

Mindful of its primary responsibility under the Charter of the United Nations for the maintenance of international peace and security,

1. Condemns the nuclear tests conducted by India on 11 and 13 May 1998 and by Pakistan on 28 May 1998;

2. Endorses the Joint Communique issued by the Foreign Ministers of China, France, the Russian Federation, the United Kingdom of Great Britain and Northern Ireland and the United States of America at their meeting in Geneva on 4 June 1998 (S/1998/473);

3. Demands that India and Pakistan refrain from further nuclear tests and in this context calls upon all states not to carry out any nuclear weapon test explosion or any other nuclear explosion in accordance with the provisions of the Comprehensive Nuclear Test Ban Treaty;

4. Urges India and Pakistan to exercise maximum restraint and to avoid threatening military movements, cross-border violations, or other

provocations in order to prevent an aggravation of the situation;

5. Urges India and Pakistan to resume the dialogue between them on all outstanding issues, particularly on all matters pertaining to peace and security, in order to remove the tensions between them, and encourages them to find mutually acceptable solutions that address the root causes of those tensions, including Kashmir;

6. Welcomes the efforts of the Secretary-General to encourage India and Pakistan to enter into dialogue;

7. Calls upon India and Pakistan immediately to stop their nuclear weapon development programs, to refrain from weaponization or from the deployment of nuclear weapons, to cease development of ballistic missile capable of delivering nuclear weapons, to confirm their policies not to export equipment, materials or technology that could contribute to weapons of mass destruction or missiles capable of delivering them and to undertake appropriate commitments in that regard;

8. Encourages all states to prevent the export of equipment, materials or technology that could in any way assist programs in India or Pakistan for nuclear weapons or for ballistic missiles capable of delivering such weapons, and welcomes national policies adopted and declared in this respect;

9. Expresses its grave concern at the negative effect of the nuclear tests conducted by India and Pakistan on peace and stability in South Asia and beyond;

10. Reaffirms its full commitment to and the crucial importance of the Treaty on the Non-Proliferation of Nuclear Weapons and the Comprehensive Nuclear Test Ban Treaty as the cornerstones of the international regime on the non-proliferation of nuclear weapons and as essential foundations for the pursuit of nuclear disarmament;

11. Expresses its firm conviction that the international regime on the non-proliferation of nuclear weapons should be maintained and consolidated and recalls that in accordance with the Treaty on the Non-Proliferation of Nuclear Weapons India or Pakistan cannot have the status of a nuclear-weapon state;

12. Recognizes that the tests conducted by India and Pakistan constitute a serious threat to global efforts towards nuclear non-proliferation and disarmament;

13. Urges India and Pakistan, and all other states that have not yet done so, to become Parties to the Treaty on the Non-Proliferation of Nuclear Weapons and to the agreed mandate, in negotiations at the Conference on Disarmament in Geneva on a treaty banning the production of fissile material for nuclear weapons or other nuclear explosive devices, with a view to reaching early agreement;

14. Urges India and Pakistan to participate, in a positive spirit and on the basis of the agreed mandate, in negotiations at the Conference on Disarmament in Geneva on a treaty banning the production of fissile material for nuclear weapons or other nuclear explosive devices, with a view to reaching early agreement;

15. Requests the Secretary-General to report urgently to the Council on the steps taken by India and Pakistan to implement the present resolution;

16. Expresses its readiness to consider further how best to ensure the implementation of the present resolution;

17. Decides to remain actively seized of the matter.

Abbreviations

ABM	anti-ballistic missile
ACDA	Arms Control and Disarmament Agency (US)
AEC	Atomic Energy Commission
AERB	Atomic Energy Regulatory Board (India)
AEW	airborne early warning
ANC	African National Congress (of South Africa)
ASCI	Accelerated Strategic Computing Initiative (US)
ASEAN	Association of South East Asian Nations
ASP	airborne surveillance platform
ATV	Advanced Technology Vessel (code-name for India's nuclear submarine project)
BJP	Bharatiya Janata Party
BMD	ballistic missile defense
CANDU	Canadian Deuterium (moderated and cooled) Natural Uranium (reactor)
CBM	confidence building measure
CD	Conference on Disarmament (of the UN in Geneva)
CIRUS	Canada-India Research Reactor, United States (Indian reactor, commissioned 1960; source of plutonium for the 1974 test)
CND	Campaign for Nuclear Disarmament (Britain)
CNN	Cable News Network
CPI	Communist Party of India
CPM	Communist Party of India (Marxist)
CTBT	Comprehensive Test Ban Treaty
CTBTO	Comprehensive Test Ban Treaty Organization (Vienna)
DAE	Department of Atomic Energy
DARHT	Dual Axis Radiographic Hydrodynamic Test Facility (US)
DIA	Defense Intelligence Agency (US)
DRDO	Defense Research and Development Organization (India)
EEC	European Economic Community
EU	European Union
FMCT	Fissile Materials Cutoff Treaty
G-21	Group of 21 (non-aligned states in the CD)
GATT	General Agreement on Tariffs and Trade
GDP	gross domestic product
HNE	hydro-nuclear experiment
IAEA	International Atomic Energy Agency
IAF	Indian Air Force
ICBM	inter-continental ballistic missile
ICF	inertial confinement fusion
IMF	International Monetary Fund
IMS	international monitoring system (under the CTBT)
INESAP	International Network of Engineers and Scientists against Proliferation
INF	Intermediate Nuclear Forces (Treaty)
IPKF	Indian Peace-Keeping Force (in Sri Lanka)
KANUPP	Karachi Nuclear Power Plant (Pakistan)
LCA	Light Combat Aircraft (Indian project)
LCNP	Lawyers' Committee on Nuclear Policy

MAD	mutual assured destruction
MARG	Market Analysis and Research Group (India)
MBT	main battle tank
MIRV	multiple independently-targetable re-entry vehicle
MNWC	Model Nuclear Weapons Convention
MPLA	Portuguese acronym for Popular Movement for the Liberation of Angola
MTCR	Missile Technology Control Regime
NAFTA	North American Free Trade Agreement
NAM	Non-Aligned Movement
NATO	North Atlantic Treaty Organization
NGO	non-governmental organization
NIF	National Ignition Facility (US)
NMD	national missile defense
NNWSs	non-nuclear weapons states
NPT	Nuclear Non-Proliferation Treaty (1970)
NPR	Nuclear Posture Review (US)
NRDC	Natural Resources Defense Council (US NGO)
NWC	Nuclear Weapons (abolition) Convention
NWFZ	nuclear weapons-free zone
NWS	nuclear weapons state (often used here interchangeably with the P-5)
OECD	Organization for Economic Cooperation and Development
OSI	on-site inspection
P-5	the five "recognized" NWSs (US, Russia, UK, France, China)
PCI	Italian acronym for Communist Party of Italy
PML	Pakistan Muslim League
PMO	Prime Minister's Office (India)
PNE	peaceful nuclear explosion
PPP	Pakistan People's Party
PTBT	Partial Test Ban Treaty (1963)
RSS	Rashtriya Swayamsevak Sangh (National Volunteer Corps)
SAC	Strategic Air Command (US)
SALT	Strategic Arms Limitation Treaty (between the US and USSR)
SBSS&MP	Science-based Stockpile Stewardship & Management Program (US)
SCE	sub-critical experiment
SDI	Strategic Defense Initiative (US)
SIOP	Single Integrated Operational Plan (US)
SIPRI	Stockholm International Peace Research Institute
SPD	German acronym for Social Democratic Party
START I–III	Strategic Arms Reduction Treaty I/II/III
SSOD IV	Special Session on Disarmament IV (held by UN General Assembly, 1988)
SSMP	Stockpile Stewardship and Management Programme
SWPS	Strategic War Planning System
THAAD	Theater High Altitude Area Defense (US)
TMD	Theater Missile Defense
TNC	transnational corporation
VHP	Vishwa Hindu Parishad (World Hindu Council)
VVER-1000	a Russian pressurized water nuclear reactor of 1000 MW capacity
WB	World Bank
WMDFZ	weapons of mass-destruction-free zone
WMD	weapons of mass destruction

Select Bibliography

Books, Reports, & Monographs

Abraham, Itty. *The Making of the Indian Atomic Bomb*. London: Zed Books, and Delhi: Orient Longman, 1998.

Acronym Institute. *Acronym Reports* (various). London.

Anand, Y.P. *What Mahatma Gandhi Said About the Atom Bomb*. New Delhi: National Gandhi Museum, 1998.

Anderson, Robert. *Building Scientific Institutions in India: Bhabha and Saha*. Montreal: Center for Developing Area Studies, 1975.

Arif, K.M. *Working with Zia: Power Politics 1977-88*. Karachi: Oxford University Press, 1995.

Arkin, W.M., R. S. Norris, and J. Handler, *Taking Stock: Worldwide Nuclear Deployments, 1998*. New York: Natural Resources Defense Council, March 1998.

Azar, E.E. and C.I. Moon, eds. *National Security in the Third World: The Management of Internal and External Threats*. Aldershot, UK: Edward Elgar, 1988.

Babbage, R. and G. Gordon, eds. *India's Strategic Future: Regional, State or Global Power*. London: Macmillan, 1991.

Bajpai, Kanti, P.R. Chari, et al. *Brasstacks and Beyond: Perception and Management of Crisis in South Asia*. Delhi: Manohar, 1995.

Ball, Desmond, *Can Nuclear War Be Controlled?* (Adelphi Paper 169) London: IISS, 1981.

Bandopadhya, J. *The Making of India's Foreign Policy*. Bombay: Allied Publications, 1970.

Barnet, R.J. and R.A. Falk, eds. *Security in Disarmament*. Princeton: Princeton University Press, 1965.

Bennett, John. *Nuclear Weapons and the Conflict of Conscience*. New York: Charles Scribner's Son, 1962.

Bernal, J.D. *Social Functions of Science*. London, 1939.

Betts, Richard K. *Nuclear Blackmail and Nuclear Balance*. Washington, DC: Brookings, 1987.

Bidwai, Praful and Achin Vanaik: *Testing Times: The Global Stake in a Nuclear Test Ban*. Uppsala: Dag Hammarskjold Foundation, 1996.

Bird, Kai and Lawrence Lifschultz eds. *Hiroshima's Shadow*. Story Creek, CT: The Pamphleteer's Press, 1998.

Blair, Bruce G. *The Logic of Accidental Nuclear War*. Washington DC: Brookings, 1993.

Blight, James G. & David A. Welch. *On the Brink: Americans and Soviets Reexamine the Cuban Missile Crisis*. New York: Hill and Wang, 1989.

Bose D.M., et al. eds. *A Concise History of Science in India*. New Delhi: Indian National Science Academy, 1971.

Bothwell, Robert. Nucleus: *The History of Atomic Energy of Canada Limited.* Toronto: University of Toronto Press, 1988.

Bottome, Edger. *The Balance of Terror.* Boston, MA: Beacon Press, 1971.

Bracken, Paul. *The Command and Control of Nuclear Forces.* New Haven: Yale University Press, 1983.

British American Security Information Council. *Nuclear Futures: The Role of Nuclear Weapons in Security Policy.* London and Washington, DC, 1996.

Brodie, Bernard, ed. *The Absolute Weapon: Atomic Power and World Order.* New York: Harcourt Brace, 1946.

Brodie, Bernard. *Strategy in the Missile Age.* Princeton: Princeton University Press, 1965.

Buchanan, A. *Marx and Justice.* London: 1982. Buchan, A., ed. *A World of Nuclear Powers.* New York: Prentice Hall, 1966.

Bull, Hedley. *The Control of the Arms Race: Disarmament and Arms Control in the Missile Age.* New York: Praeger, 1961.

Bull, Hedley. *The Anarchical Society: A Study on the Order of World Politics.* London: Macmillan, 1977.

Bundy, McGeorge, ed. "The Unimpressive Record of Atomic Diplomacy," *The Nuclear Crisis Reader*, Vantage, pp. 42-54 in Gwyn Prins, New York, 1984.

Bundy, McGeorge. *Danger and Survival: Choices About the Bomb in the First Fifty Years.* New York: Random House, 1988.

Buzan, B. *People, States and Fear: The National Security Problem in International Relations.* Brighton, UK: Wheatsheaf Books, 1983.

Calder, Nigel. *Nuclear Nightmares.* Harmondsworth: Penguin, 1981.

Campbell, David. *Writing Security: United States Foreign Policy and the Politics of Identity.* Minneapolis: University of Minnesota Press, 1992.

Carnegie Task Force on Non-Proliferation and South Asian Security. *Nuclear Weapons and South Asian Security.* Washington, DC: Carnegie Endowment for International Peace, 1988.

Carr, E.H. *The Twenty Year's Crisis.* New York: Harper Torchbook, 1964.

Chant, Christopher. *A Compendium of Armaments and Military Hardware.* New York: Routledge and Kegan Paul, 1987.

Cohen, M., T. Nagel & T. Scanlon, eds. *Marx, Justice and History.* Princeton: Princeton University Press, 1980.

Cohen, Stephen Philip, ed. *Nuclear Proliferation in South Asia Prospects for Arms Control.* Boulder: Westview Press, 1991.

"Common Security," Report of the Palme Commission, 1982; J. Rotblat & V.I. Goldanskii (eds), Global Problems and Common Security: *Annals of Pugwash 1988*, Springer-Verlag, 1989.

Communist Party of India-Marxist. *Against Nuclear Jingoism.* New Delhi: National Book Centre, July 1998.

Compton, Arthur H. *Atomic Quest.* Oxford, New York, 1956.

Cortright, David, and Amitabh Mattoo, eds. *India and the Bomb: Public Opinion and Nuclear Options.* Notre Dame: University of Notre Dame

Press, 1996.

Cousins, Norman. *In Place of Folly*. New York: Washington Square Press, 1962.

Dean, A.H.. *Test Ban and Disarmament*. New York: Harper & Row, 1966.

Deger, S. and R. West, eds. *Defence, Security and Development*. London: Printer, 1987.

Department of Atomic Energy, Government of India. *Annual Reports* (various years).

Department of Atomic Energy, Government of India. *Performance Budget* (various years).

Divine, R.A. *Blowing on the Wind: The Nuclear Test Ban Debate, 1954–1960*. New York: Oxford University Press, 1978.

Elasser, Walter M. *Memoirs of a Physicist in the Atomic Age*. New York: Science History Publications, 1978.

Elliot, David, et. al. *The Politics of Nuclear Power*. London: Pluto Press, 1978.

Ellsberg, Daniel. *The Crude Analysis of Deterrence Choices*. Santa Monica, CA: The Rand Corporation, 1960.

Enloe, C. *Bananas, Bases and Beaches: Making Feminist Sense of International Relations*. London: Pandora, 1989.

Feaver, Peter Douglas. *Guarding the Guardians: Civilian Control of Nuclear Weapons in the United States*. Ithaca: Cornell University Press, 1992.

Fetter, S. *Toward a Comprehensive Test Ban*. Cambridge, MA: Ballinger, 1988.

Fischer, D.A.V. *Stopping the Spread of Nuclear Weapons*. London and New York: Routledge, 1992.

Fursenko, A. and T. Naftali. *One Hell of a Gamble: Krushchev, Castro, and Kennedy 1958–64*. New York: W. W. Norton, 1997.

George, Alexander L. & Richard Smoke. *Deterrence in American Foreign Policy: Theory and Practice*, New York: Columbia University Press, 1974.

George, Susan. *The Debt Boomerang*. London: Pluto, 1992.

Geras, N. *Discourses of Extremity*. London: Verso, 1990.

Giddens, A. *The Nation-State and Violence*. Cambridge: Polity Press, 1985.

Gilbert, A. *Democratic Individuality*. Cambridge: Cambridge University Press, 1990.

Goldblat, J. and Cox, D. *Nuclear Weapon Tests: Prohibition or Limitation?* Oxford: SIPRI Publications, Oxford University Press, 1988.

Goldschmidt, Bertrand. *Atomic Rivals*. New Brunswick, NJ: Rutgers University Press, 1990.

Goldschmidt, Bertrand. *The Atomic Complex*. La Grange Park, IL: American Nuclear Society, 1982.

Gopal, S. *Jawaharlal Nehru: A Biography, Volume 2: 1947–1956*. Delhi: Oxford University Press, 1979.

Government of India. *Status of Nuclear Weapons in International Law: Request for Advisory Opinion of the International Court of Justice*. New Delhi: Ministry of External Affairs, 1995.

Gowing, Margaret. *Independence and Deterrence: Britain and Atomic Energy, 1945–1952*, Vol. 1: Policy Making. 1964. New York: St. Martin's Press, 1974.

Gregory, Shaun. *The Hidden Cost of Deterrence: Nuclear Weapons Accidents.* London: Brassey's, 1990.

Hackett, John. *The Third World War.* London: Sidgwick & Jackson, 1978.

Halliday, Fred. *Rethinking International Relations.* London: Macmillan, 1994.

Halliday, Fred. *The Making of the Second Cold War.* London: Verso, 1983.

Halperin, Morton H. *Nuclear Fallacy: Dispelling the Myth of Nuclear Strategy.* Cambridge, MA: Ballinger, 1987.

Hart, David. *Nuclear Power in India: A Comparative Analysis.* London: George Allen and Unwin, 1983.

Hart, Liddell. *The Evolution of Warfare.* London: Faber & Faber, 1946.

Harvard Nuclear Study Group. *Living With Nuclear Weapons.* Cambridge, Massachusetts: Harvard University Press, 1983.

Healey, Denis. *The Race Against the H-Bomb.* London: Fabian Tract, 1960.

Hersey, John. *Hiroshima. 1946.* New York: Vintage, 1985.

Hersh, Seymour M. *The Samson Option: Israel's Nuclear Arsenal and American Foreign Policy.* New York: Random House, 1991.

Hewlett, R.G. and J.M. Holl. *Atoms for Peace and War, 1953–1961: Eisenhower and the Atomic Energy Commission.* Berkeley: University of California Press, 1989.

Holloway, David. *Stalin and the Bomb: The Soviet Union and Atomic Energy, 1939–1956.* New Haven: Yale University Press, 1994.

Honderich, Ted. *Violence for Equality.* Harmondsworth: Penguin Books, 1980.

International Physicians for the Prevention of Nuclear War. *Radioactive Heaven and Earth.* London: Zed Books, 1991.

Jain, J.P., ed. *Nuclear India*, Vols. 1–2. New Delhi: Radiant Publishers, 1974.

Jaipal, Rikhi. *Nuclear Arms and The Human Race.* New Delhi: Allied Publishers, 1986.

Jervis, Robert. *The Illogic of American Nuclear Strategy.* Ithaca, NY: Cornell University Press, Ithaca, 1984.

Jervis, Robert. *The Meaning of the Nuclear Revolution: Statecraft and the Prospect of Armageddon.* Ithaca, NY: Cornell University Press, 1989.

Jones, Rodney. "India," in *Non-Proliferation: The Why and Wherefore.* London: Taylor & Francis, 1985.

Jungk, Robert. *Brighter than a Thousand Suns.* New York: Harcourt, Brace, Jovanovich, 1956.

Kaku M. & D. Axelrod. *To Win a Nuclear War.* London: Zed Books, 1987.

Kaplan, Fred. *The Wizards of Armageddon.* New York: Simon & Schuster, 1983.

Kapur, Ashok. *India's Nuclear Option: Atomic Diplomacy and Decision-Making.* New York: Praeger, 1976.

Kaushik, B.M. and Mehrotra. *Pakistan's Nuclear Bomb.* New Delhi: Sohan Publishing House, 1980.

Kennan, George. *The Nuclear Delusion.* New York: Pantheon, 1982.

Keohane, R.O., ed. *International Institutions and State Power: Essays in International Relations Theory.* Boulder: Westview Press, 1989.

Klein, Bradley. *Strategic Studies and World Order: The Global Politics of*

Deterrence. Cambridge: Cambridge University Press, 1994.

Kosambi, D.D. *Science and Human Progress: Essays in Honour of Kosambi*. Bombay: Popular Prakashan, 1974.

Krass, Allan. "The Evolution of Military Technology and Deterrence Strategy," *World Armaments & Disarmament: SIPRI Yearbook 1981*. London: Taylor & Francis, 1981.

Krepon, Michael and Mishi Faruqee, eds., *Conflict Prevention and Confidence Building Measures in South Asia: The 1990 Crisis, Occasional Paper No. 17*. Washington, DC: The Henry L. Stimson Center, April 1994.

Kumar, Deepak. *Science and the Raj: 1857–1905*. Delhi: Oxford University Press, 1995.

Lewis, John W. and Xue Litai, *China Builds the Bomb*. Palo Alto: Stanford University Press, 1988.

Lichterman, Andrew and Jacqueline Cabasso. *A Faustian Bargain: Why Stockpile Stewardship is Fundamentally Incompatible with the Process of Nuclear Disarmament*. CA: Western States Legal Foundation, 1998.

Lifton, Robert Jay and Richard Falk. *Indefensible Weapons*. New York: Basic Books, 1982.

Lilienthal, David E. *Atomic Energy: A New Start*. New York: Harper & Row, 1980.

Lukes, S. *Marxism and Morality*. Oxford: Oxford University Press, 1985.

Mandelbaum, Michael. *The Nuclear Revolution*. Cambridge: Cambridge University Press, 1981.

Mann, M. *The Sources of Social Power, Vol. II*. Cambridge: Cambridge University Press, 1983.

Manor, James, ed. *Nehru to the Nineties*. Delhi: Viking, 1994.

Marshall, W., ed. *Nuclear Power Technology, Vol. 1*. Oxford: Clarendon Press, 1983.

Maxwell, Neville. *India's China War*. Harmondsworth: Penguin Books, 1972.

May, E.R. and P.D. Zelikow. *The Kennedy Tapes*. Cambridge, Massachusetts: Belknap Press of Harvard University, 1997.

McKinzie, M.G., T.B. Cochran and C.E. Paine. *Explosive Alliances: Nuclear Weapons Simulation Research at American Universities*. New York: NRDC, January 1998.

McLellan D. & S. Sayers eds. *Socialism and Morality*. London: 1990.

Medvedev, Zhores Aleksandrovich. *Nuclear Disaster in the Urals*. New York: Vintage Books, 1980.

Menon, M.G.K. *Homi Jehangir Bhabha, 1909–1966*. London: Royal Institution of Great Britain, 1967.

Metzger, H. Peter. *The Atomic Establishment*. New York: Simon Schuster, 1972.

Meyer, Stephen M. *The Dynamics of Nuclear Proliferation*. Chicago: University of Chicago Press, 1984.

Miller, R.W. *Analyzing Marx*. Princeton: Princeton University Press, 1984.

Mills, C. Wright. *The Causes of World War III*. New York, 1958.

Ministry of External Affairs. *Disarmament: India's Initiatives*. New Delhi:

Government of India, 1988.

Montgomery, B. *The Ethics of War*. London: Collins, 1968.

Nader, Ralph and John Abbots. *The Menace of Atomic Energy*. New York: Norton, 1977.

Nadis, Steven J. *Nuclear Power: Time for Reassessment*. Cambridge, MA: Union of Concerned Scientists, 1979.

Nair, Vijai K. *Nuclear India*. New Delhi: Lancer International, 1992.

Natural Resources Defense Council. *Nuclear Weapons Databook* (various volumes). New York.

Nehru, Jawaharal. *Selected Works*. Second Series, Vols. 1–2, 4–5. New Delhi: Jawaharlal Nehru Memorial Fund

New Left Review, eds. *Exterminism and the Cold War*. London: Verso, 1982.

Nielsen, K. & S. C. Patten, eds. *Marx and Morality*. Vol. III of the Canadian Journal of Philosophy, 1981.

Nuclear Non-Proliferation and Global Order. Oxford: SIPRI/Oxford University Press, 1994.

Nuclear Risk-Reduction Measures in Southern Asia. The Henry L. Stimson Center, November 1998.

Paine, Christopher E. and Matthew G. McKinzie. *End Run: The U.S. Government's Plan for Designing Nuclear Weapons and Simulating Nuclear Explosions under the Comprehensive Test Ban Treaty*. NY: Natural Resources Defense Council, 1997.

Paine, C.E. and M.G. McKinzie. End Run: The U.S. Government's Plan for Designing Nuclear Weapons and Simulating Nuclear Explosions under the CTBT. New York: NRDC, April 1998.

Patterson, Walter C. *Nuclear Power*. Harmondsworth: Pelican, 1976.

Peffer, R.G. *Marxism, Morality and Social Justice*. Princeton: Princeton University Press, 1990.

Penny, [Lord]. "Homi Jehangir Bhabha, 1909–1966," in *Biographical Memoirs of Fellows of the Royal Society*, Vol 13. London: The Royal Society, 1967.

Perrow, Charles. *Normal Accidents: Living With High-Risk Technologies*. New York: Basic Books, 1984.

Potter, W.C. and H. Jencks, eds. *The International Missile Bazaar: The New Supplier Network*. Boulder: Westview Press, 1994: 201–33.

Potter, W.C., ed. *International Nuclear Trade and Nonproliferation: The Challenge of the Emerging Suppliers*. Lexington, MA: Lexington Books, 1990.

Quester, George. *Deterrence before Hiroshima*. New York: Wiley, 1966.

Rajan M.S. *Non-Alignment: India and the Future*. Mysore: University of Mysore Press, 1970.

Ramanna, Raja. *Years of Pilgrimage*. Delhi: Viking, 1991.

Reid, Escott. *Envoy to Nehru*. Delhi: Oxford University Press, 1981.

Rhodes, Robert. *The Making of the Atomic Bomb*. New York: Simon and Schuster, 1986.

Rosenberg, J. *The Empire of Civil Society: A Critique of the Realist Theory of International Relations*. London: Verso, 1994.

Rotblat, J., J. Steinberger, B. Udgaonkar and F. Blackaby, eds. *A Nuclear-Weapon-Free World: Desirable? Feasible?* San Francisco: Westview Press, 1993.

Rudolph, Lloyd I. and Susanne H. *In Pursuit of Lakshmi: The Political Economy of the Indian State*. Chicago: University of Chicago Press, 1987.

Russell, Bertrand. *Has Man a Future?* London: Unwin, 1961.

Sagan, Scott D. and Kenneth N. Waltz. *The Spread of Nuclear Weapons: A Debate*. New York: W.W. Norton & Co., 1995.

Sagan, Scott D. *The Limits of Safety: Organizations, Accidents and Nuclear Weapons*. Princeton: Princeton University Press, 1993.

Sangari, Kumkum, Neeraj Malik, Sheba Chhachhi and Tanika Sarkar in "Why Women Must Reject the Bomb," *Out of Nuclear Darkness: The Indian Case for Disarmament*. New Delhi: Movement in India for Nuclear Disarmament (MIND), 1998.

Scheer, Robert. *With Enough Shovels*. New York: Random House, 1982.

Schell, Jonathan. *The Fate of the Earth*. New York: Knopf, 1982.

Schell, Jonathan. *The Gift of Time*. New York: Henry Holt and Company, 1998.

Schwartz, Stephen I., ed. *Atomic Audit: The Costs and Consequences of U.S. Nuclear Weapons Since 1940*. New York: The Brookings Institution, 1998.

Scott, R.T. ed. *The Race for Security: Arms and Arms Control in the Reagan Years*. Lexington, MA: Lexington Books, 1987.

Seaborg, G.T. *Kennedy, Khrushchev, and the Test Ban*. Berkeley: University of California Press, 1981.

Sen Gupta, Bhabani. *Nuclear Weapons: Policy Options for India*. New Delhi: Sage Center for Policy Research, 1983.

Seshagiri, N. *The Bomb: Fallout of India's Nuclear Explosion*. Delhi: Vikas, 1975.

Sethna, H.N. *Atomic Energy* (25 Years of Independence: India Series). New Delhi: Publications Division, 1972.

Shaker, M.K. *The Nuclear Non-Proliferation Treaty: Origin and Implementation, 1959–1979*. London: Oceana, 1980.

Sharma, Dhirendra. *India's Nuclear Estate*. Delhi: Lancer, 1983.

Sharma, Dhirendra. *The Indian Atom: Power and Proliferation*. New Delhi: Philosophy and Social Action, 1986.

Sidhu, W.P.S., Brian Cloughley, et al., *Nuclear Risk-Reduction Measures in Southern Asia*, Report No. 26. Washington, DC: The Henry L. Stimson Center: 41, November 1998.

Singh, Sampooran. *India and the Nuclear Bomb*. Delhi: S. Chand and Co., 1971.

Sinha, P.B. and R.R. Subramanian. *Nuclear Pakistan*. New Delhi: Vision Books.

Sivard, Ruth Leger. *World Military and Social Expenditures 1996*. Washington, DC: World Priorities, 1996.

Spector, Leonard S. *The Undeclared Bomb*. Cambridge, MA: Ballinger

Publishing Co., 1988.

Spector, Leonard S. *The New Nuclear Nations*. New York: Vintage Books, 1985.

Sreekantan, B.V., Virendra Singh, and B.M. Udgaonkar, eds. *Homi Jehangir Bhabha: Collected Scientific Papers*. Bombay: Tata Institute of Fundamental Research, 1985.

Stockholm International Peace Research Institute. *SIPRI Yearbook* (various years). New York: Oxford University Press.

Strange, S. *The Retreat of the State: The Diffusion of Power in the World Economy*. Cambridge: Cambridge University Press, 1996.

Stutzle, W. Jasani, B, and R. Cowan, eds. *The ABM Treaty: To Defend or Not To Defend*. Oxford: SIPRI Publications, Oxford University Press, 1987.

Thomas, Raju. *Indian Security Policy*. Princeton: Princeton University Press, 1988.

Thompson, E.P. *Beyond the Cold War*. London: Merlin Press, 1982.

Thompson, E.P. *Protest and Survive*. New York: Monthly Review Press, 1981.

Thompson, G. "Verifying a Halt to the Nuclear Arms Race," in Barnaby, F., ed. *A Handbook of Verification Procedures*. London: Macmillan, 1990.

United Nations. *Comprehensive Study on Nuclear Weapons*, UN General Assembly document A/33/392. New York: UN, 1980.

Vanaik, Achin. *India in a Changing World*. New Delhi: Orient Longman, 1995.

Vanaik, Achin. *The Painful Transition: Bourgeois Democracy in India*. London: Verso, 1990.

Venkataraman, G. *Journey into Light: Life and Science of C.V. Raman*. Delhi: Penguin, 1994.

Venkateshwaran, A.L. *Defence Organisation in India*. New Delhi: Publications Division, Government of India, 1967.

Walker, R.B.J. *Inside/Outside: International Relations as Political Theory*. Cambridge: Cambridge University Press, 1993.

Walker, William and Mans Loennorth. *Nuclear Power Struggles*. London: George Allen & Unwin, 1983.

Wallerstein, I. *Geopolitics and Geoculture: Essays in a Changing World System*. Cambridge: Cambridge University Press, 1991.

Waltz, Kenneth N. *Man, State and War*. New York: 1959.

Waltz, Kenneth N. *The Theory of International Politics*. Reading, MA: Addison Wesley, 1979.

Walzer, Michael. *Just and Unjust Wars*. New York: Basic Books, 1977.

Weart, Spencer R. *Nuclear Fear: A History of Images*. Cambridge, MA: Harvard University Press, 1988.

Weinbaum, M.G., and Chetan Kumar, eds. *South Asia Approaches the Millenium: Reexamining National Security*. Boulder: Westview, 1995.

Weisman, S.R. and H. Krosney. *The Islamic Bomb*. New York: Times Books, 1981.

Wight, Martin and B. Porter, eds. *International Theory: The Three Traditions*. Leicester: Leicester University Press, 1991.

World Council of Churches. *Before It's Too Late*. Geneva: WCC

Publication, 1983.

World Health Organization. *Effects of Nuclear War on Health*, Geneva: W.H.O. Publication, 1984.

World Road Statistics 1998. Geneva: International Road Federation, 1998

York, Herbert K. *Race to Oblivion*. New York: Simon & Schuster, 1970.

Zukerman, Solly. *Scientists and War*. New York: Harper and Row, 1967.

Journal Articles

"China jolts India with nuclear blast." *The Telegraph* (Calcutta) 14 January 1999.

"India turns to an old comrade as China talks tough." *The Indian Express* (New Delhi) 15 May 1998.

"Nuclear Power: Heavy Water Constraint." *Economic and Political Weekly* (Mumbai) 9.37 (September 1974): 1555.

"The Architects of Nuclear India." Special issue of *Nuclear India* 26 (October 1989).

"The Morality of Nuclear Deterrence: An Evaluation by Pax Christi Bishops in the U.S." *INESAP Bulletin* 16 (November 1998).

Ahmed, Aqueil and Falguni Sen. "Scientists & Science Policy Formulation: Indian Scientists' View of the Indian Nuclear Explosion." *Journal of Scientific & Industrial Research* 35 (August 1976): 497-501.

Ajwani, S.H. "Thorium Cycle." *Nuclear India* 4.8 (April 1966).

Albright, David. "The Shots Heard 'Round The World." *Bulletin of the Atomic Scientists* July/August 1998: 21–25.

Anderson, Robert. "Growing Science in India–2: Homi J. Bhabha." *Science Today* (Bombay) Nov. 1976.

Aqueil, Ahmad and Falguni Sen. "Scientists and Science Policy Formulation: Indian Scientists' view of Indian Nuclear Explosion." *Journal of Scientific and Industrial Research* 35 (August 1976). 497–501.

Arnett, Eric. "Big Science, Small Results." *Bulletin of the Atomic Scientists* July/August 1998: 46–47.

Bairstow, J. "Switch Off the National Ignition Facility." *Laser Focus World* September 1997.

Bidwai, P. and A. Vanaik. "Why India Should Sign the CTBT." *Economic and Political Weekly* (Mumbai) 19 September 1998.

Bidwai, Praful. "Lid Off Atomic Energy." *Business India* (Mumbai) 4–17 September 1978.

Blackaby, Frank. "Time For a Peasant's Revolt." *Bulletin of the Atomic Scientists* Nov/Dec 1997.

Gertz, Bill. "Israel Deploys Missiles for a Possible Strike at Iraq." *Washington Times* 28 January 1991.

Gupta, Vipin, and Frank Pabian. "Investigating the Allegations of Indian Nuclear Test Preparations in the Rajasthan Desert." *Science & Global*

Security 6 (1996).

Hagerty, Dennis. "Nuclear Deterrence in South Asia: The 1990 Indo-Pakistani Crisis." *International Security* 20.3 (Winter 1995-96).

Hecht, Gabrielle. "Political Designs: Nuclear Reactors and National Policy in Postwar France." *Technology and Culture* 35.4 (1994).

Hibbs, Mark. "India May Test Again Because H-Bomb Failed, US Believes." *Nucleonics Week* 26 November 1998.

Homer-Dixon, Thomas F., Jeffrey H. Boutwell and George W Rathjens. "Environmental Change and Violent Conflict." *Scientific American* 268.2 (February 1993): 16–23.

Jayaraman, K.S. "The Leak that Leaked to the Press." *Science Today* (Bombay) May 1980: 17.

Jones, Suzanne L. and Frank N. von Hippel, "Transparency Measures for Subcritical Experiments under the CTBT." *Science & Global Security* 6 (1997): 291-310.

Kalinowski, Martin. "Fissile Cutoff: Overcoming the Disarmament Deadlock." *INESAP Bulletin* 13 (July 1997): 7–10.

Karat, Prakash. "Once Again on CTBT." *People's Democracy*, (New Delhi) 10 January 1999.

Kaushik, B.M. "India's Nuclear Dilemma." *Strategic Analysis* 1.8 (November 1977): 1–4.

Makhijani, Arjun. "De-Alerting: A First Step." *Science for Democratic Action.* Tacoma Park, MD: Institute of Energy and Environmental Research (October 1998).

Marwah, Onkar. "India's Nuclear and Space Programme: Intent and Policy." *International Security* 2.2 (Fall 1977): 96–121.

Mian, Zia and M.V. Ramana. "Stepping Away from the Nuclear Abyss." *INESAP Bulletin* 16 November 1998: 13.

Mian, Zia. "Pakistan's Nuclear Descent." *INESAP Bulletin* 16 November 1998: 11.

Mian, Zia. "The South Asian Bomb: The Politics of South Asia's Nuclear Crisis." *Medicine & Global Survival* 5.2 (October 1998).

Misra, Ashutosh. "The Pakistani Ghauri Missile." *INESAP Bulletin* 16 November 1998: 14.

Mueller, John. "The Bomb's Pretense as Peacemaker." *Wall Street Journal* 4 June 1985.

Noorani, A.G. "Many Question, Few Answers." *Frontline* (Chennai) 20 November 1998.

Perkovich, George. "Nuclear Proliferation." *Foreign Policy* Fall 1998.

Purcell, Heather A. and James K. Galbraith. "Did the US Military Plan a Nuclear First Strike for 1963?" *The American Prospect* 19 (Fall 1994): 92.

Ramana, M.V. "The South Asian Bomb: Effects of a Nuclear Blast Over Bombay." *Medicine & Global Survival* 5.2 (October 1998): 74-77.

Rosenberg, David A. "The Origins of Overkill: Nuclear Weapons and American Strategy, 1945–1960." *International Security* 7.4 (Spring

1983): 3–71.

Sagan, Scott. "Why Do States Build Nuclear Weapons: Three Models in Search of a Bomb." *International Security* 21.6 (Winter 1996/97).

Sankaran, M.P. "Brain Drain—Do We Need More Scientists or More Science?" *Science Today* (Bombay) April 1980: 9.

Sethna, H.N. and S.N. Srinivasan. "Operating Experience with the Fuel Reprocessing Plant at Trombay," *Nuclear Engineering* 65.94 (Chemical Engineering Progress Symposium Series, 1967).

Sharma Dhirendra. "India's Nuclear Options." *Indian Express* 14 September 1979.

Sharma, Dhirendra. "Another Three Mile Island on the Ganges?" *The Guardian* (London) 28 January 28, 1981.

Sharma, Dhirendra. "India's Energy: Policy Omissions & Commissions." *Philosophy & Social Action* 7.1 (January–March 1981).

Sharma, Dhirendra. "Tarapur: Victim of Cold War." *The Economic Times* (Bombay, New Delhi, Calcutta) 31 July 1981.

Sharma, R.G., M.S. Maheshwari, and S.C. Lodha. *The Indian Journal of Cancer* 29 (September 1992): 126–35.

Strange, Susan. "The Future of the American 'Empire.'" *Journal of International Affairs* 42.1 (1990): 1–77.

Sundarji, K. (General). "Nuclear Deterrence: Doctrine for India, Part 1 & 2" *Trishul* (Wellington, India: The Defence Services Staff College) 5.2 (December 1992).

Sundarji, K. (General). "Nuclear Weapons in Third World Context." *Combat Papers* (Mhow, India: College of Combat) 2 (August 1981).

Tomer, Ravindra. The Indian Nuclear Programme: Myth and Mirages. *Asian Survey* 20.5 (May 1980): 517–531.

Waltz, Kenneth N. "Nuclear Myths and Political Realities." *American Political Science Review* 84.3 (September 1990): 731–745.

Special Documents, Unpublished Papers, and Miscellaneous Other Sources

Atomic Energy Commission. *Atomic Energy and Space Research: A Profile for the Decade, 1970–1980.* Bombay: 1970.

Bose, D.K. and S. Mohan. "The Cost of Nuclear Power in India." Technical Report No. ERU/3/80. Calcutta: Social Science Division of the Indian Statistical Institute, 1980.

Bose, Deb Kumar. "Economics of Nuclear Power in India." Technical Report No. ERU/8/78. Calcutta: Social Science Division of the Indian Statistical Institute, 1978.

Dayal, M. "Experience from Operating and Fueling a Nuclear Power Plant in an Industrially Developing Country." IAEA—SM-178/103: 85–103. Vienna: IAEA, 1974.

Government of India. "Nuclear Explosions and Their Effects." 1956.

Lake Sosin Snell & Associates poll. "Do you feel safer knowing that the US
and other countries have nuclear weapons, or would you feel safer if you
knew for sure that no country including the US had nuclear weapons?"
Appeared in a leaflet issued by the Global Resource Action Center for
the Environment (GRACE). New York: April 1997.

Masani, Minnoo. "The Challenge of the Chinese Bomb." ICWA lecture. 8
December 1964.

McChee, George. "Top Secret" Note on "Anticipatory Action Pending
Chinese Communist Demonstration of a Nuclear Capability."
Declassified Authority: NND 959001. Washington, DC: National
Security Archive, 17 February 1995.

Morehouse, Ward. "Science in India." Hyderabad: Administrative Staff
College on India, *Occasional Papers*, 1971.

Ramanna, Raja. "Development of Atomic Energy in India: 1947–73."
Nehru Memorial Museum. New Delhi, 29 July 1974.

Ramanna, Raja. "Inevitability of Atomic Energy in India's Power
Programme." 39th J.C. Bose Memorial Lecture. Calcutta, 30 November
1977.

Ramanna, Raja. "On Some New Possibilities of the Peaceful Use of Atomic
Energy." 11th Founder Memorial Lecture. Shri Ram Institute for
Industrial Research. New Delhi, 1975.

Sarabhai, Vikram A, et al. "An agro-industrial complex in the Gangetic
plain." Proceedings of the seminar on Nuclear Power. 17–18 January
1970. B.P. Rastogi, ed. Bombay, Department of Atomic Energy: 1–29.

Sethna, H.N. and M.R. Srinivasan, M.R. "India's Nuclear Power
Programme and Constraints Encountered in its Implementation."
Nuclear Power and Its Fuel Cycle 6. IAEA-CN-36/38. Vienna: IAEA, 1977.

Talbott, Strobe. "Dialogue, Democracy and Nuclear Weapons in
South Asia." Conference on Diplomacy and Preventative Defense.
Stanford University. Palo Alto, CA. 25 January 1999.

Timmerman, K.R. *The Poison Gas Connection: Western Suppliers of
Unconventional Weapons and Technologies to Iraq and Libya*. Simon
Wiesenthal Center, Los Angeles, 1990.

Venkatesh, L. and T.P. Sarma, T.P. "Sitting of Nuclear Power Stations in
India." IAEA-SM-188/25 Vienna, 9-13 December 1974.

Wallace, T. *Seismological Research Letters*. September-October 1998.

Waltz, Kenneth N. "The Spread of Nuclear Weapons: More May Be Better."
Adelphi Paper 171, 1981: 1–32.

Periodicals Used as Reference

Arms Control Today, Washington, DC.
The Asian Age, New Delhi.
The Bulletin of the Atomic Scientists, Chicago.

Disarmament Diplomacy, London.
Down To Earth, New Delhi.
Economic and Political Weekly, Bombay.
The Economic Times, New Delhi.
Frontline, Chennai.
Himal, Kathmandu.
The Hindu, New Delhi.
The Hindustan Times, New Delhi.
India Today, New Delhi.
Indian Express, New Delhi.
INESAP Information Bulletin, Darmstadt.
Jane's Weapons Systems. Jane's Publishing Co., Ltd., London.
Mainstream, New Delhi.
Medicine & Global Security, Cambridge, MA.
The Military Balance. International Institute of Strategic Studies, London.
The Nation, New York.
Nuclear India. Department of Atomic Energy, Bombay.
Outlook, New Delhi.
The Pioneer, New Delhi.
Security Dialogue, Oslo.
Seminar, New Delhi.
The Statesman, New Delhi.
The Sunday Observer, Delhi.
The Telegraph, Calcutta.
The Times of India, New Delhi.

Index